Memorial Book to the Holocaust Victims of the Community of Pshaytsh (Przedecz, Poland)

Translation of
Sefer yizkor le-kedoshei ir Pshaytsh korbanot ha-shoa

Original Book Edited by: Moshe Bilavsky, Reuven Yamnik, and Moshe Mokotov

Originally published in Tel Aviv 1974

JewishGen
מרכז עולמי לגנאלוגיה יהודית
The Global Home for Jewish Genealogy

A Publication of JewishGen, Inc.
Edmond J. Safra Plaza, 36 Battery Place, New York, NY 10280
646.494.5972 | info@JewishGen.org | www.jewishgen.org

JewishGen, Inc.
An affiliate of New York's Museum of Jewish Heritage – A Living Memorial to the Holocaust

MUSEUM OF JEWISH HERITAGE
A LIVING MEMORIAL TO THE HOLOCAUST

Memorial Book to the Holocaust Victims of the Community of Pshaytsh (Przedecz, Poland)
Translation of *Sefer yizkor le-kedoshei ir Pshaytsh korbanot ha-shoa*

Editors of Original Yizkor Book: Moshe Bilavsky, Reuven Yamnik, and Moshe Mokotov
Project Coordinator: Roberta Paula Books
Cover Design: Nina Schwartz, Impulse Graphics
Layout and Name Indexing: Jonathan Wind

Printed in the United States of America by Lightning Source, Inc.

Library of Congress Control Number (LCCN): 2022945028

ISBN: 978-1-954176-57-7 (hard cover: 320 pages, alk. paper)

About JewishGen.org

JewishGen, an affiliate of the Museum of Jewish Heritage - A Living Memorial to the Holocaust, serves as the global home for Jewish genealogy.

Featuring unparalleled access to over 30 million records, it offers unique search tools, along with opportunities for researchers to connect with others who share similar interests. Award winning resources such as the Family Finder, Discussion Groups, and ViewMate, are relied upon by thousands each day.

In addition, JewishGen's extensive informational, educational and historical offerings, such as the Jewish Communities Database, Yizkor Book translations, InfoFiles, Family Tree of the Jewish People, and KehilaLinks, provide critical insights, first-hand accounts, and context about Jewish communal and familial life throughout the world.

Offered as a free resource, JewishGen.org has facilitated thousands of family connections and success stories, and is currently engaged in an extensive expansion effort that will bring many more records, tools, and resources to its collections.

Please visit https://www.jewishgen.org/ to learn more.

Executive Director: Avraham Groll

About the JewishGen Yizkor Book Project

Yizkor Books (Memorial Books) were traditionally written to memorialize the names of departed family and martyrs during holiday services in the synagogue (a practice that still exists in many synagogues today).

Over the centuries, as a result of countless persecutions and horrific atrocities committed against the Jews, Yizkor Books (Sefer Zikaron in Hebrew) were expanded to include more historical information, such as biographical sketches of famous personalities and descriptions of daily town life.

Following the Holocaust, the idea of remembrance and learning took on an urgent and crucial importance. Survivors of the Holocaust sought out other surviving residents of their former towns to memorialize and document the names and way of life of those who were ruthlessly murdered by the Nazis. These remembrances were documented in Yizkor Books, hundreds of which were published in the first decades after the Holocaust.

Most of these books were published privately, or through landsmanshaftn (social organizations comprised of members originating from the same European town or region) that still existed, and were often distributed free of charge. Sadly, the languages used to document these crucial histories and links to our past, Yiddish and Hebrew, are no longer commonly understood by a significant percentage of Jews today. As a result, JewishGen has undertaken the sacred responsibility of translating these books into English so that the culture and way of life of these communities will be preserved and transmitted to future generations.

In 1986, a group of farsighted JewishGenners started a project to pool their efforts together in groups based upon their ancestors from each town and donate money to get the Yizkor books of their ancestral towns translated into English. As the translated material became available, it was made accessible for free at www.JewishGen.org/Yizkor. Hardcover copies can be purchased by visiting https://www.jewishgen.org/Yizkor/ybip.html (see below).

It is our hope that the translation of these books into English (and other languages) will assist the countless Jewish family researchers who are so desperately seeking to forge a connection with their heritage.

Director of JewishGen Yizkor Book Project: Lance Ackerfeld

About JewishGen Press

JewishGen Press (formerly the Yizkor Books-in-Print Project) is the publishing division of JewishGen.org, and provides a venue for the publication of non-fiction books pertaining to Jewish genealogy, history, culture, and heritage.

In addition to the Yizkor Book category, publications in the Other Non-Fiction category include Shoah memoirs and research, genealogical research, collections of genealogical and historical materials, biographies, diaries and letters, studies of Jewish experience and cultural life in the past, academic theses, and other books of interest to the Jewish community.

Please visit https://www.jewishgen.org/Yizkor/ybip.html to learn more.

Director of JewishGen Press: Joel Alpert
Managing Editor - Jessica Feinstein
Publications Manager - Susan Rosin

Notes to the Reader

Page numbers in square brackets refer to the original book page numbers.

The images in the original book were reproduced from photographs from the time of the first edition. These reproductions were already of poor quality, being pre-war and at least 30 or more years old. As a result, the images are the best achievable.

A reader can view the original scans of the book on the websites listed below.

The original book can be seen online at the Yiddish Book Center website:

https://www.yiddishbookcenter.org/collections/yizkor-books/yzk-nybc313945/bilavski-mosheh-sefer-yizkor-li-kedoshe-ir-pashyatsh-korbanot-ha-shoah

OR

at the New York Public Library Digital Collections website:

https://digitalcollections.nypl.org/items/c2824310-53e8-0133-43c5-00505686a51c

To obtain a list of Shoah victims from Pshaytsh (Przedecz, Poland), the reader should access the Yad Vashem web site listed below; one can also search for specific family names using the family name option. These lists are continually updated by Yad Vashem, so it is worthwhile to search these lists periodically.

There is more valuable information (including the Pages of Testimony, etc.) available on this website: https://yvng.yadvashem.org/

A list of all books available from JewishGen Press along with prices is available at: https://www.jewishgen.org/Yizkor/ybip.html

Dedication

This translation is dedicated to the memory of my father, Icek Leyb Buks, son of Shimon Aron Buks and Gitl Hertzberg Buks, and to all my Buks/Hertzberg/Przdecki relatives – those who know the family history and those who have yet to discover it.

Icek Leyb Buks was born in Przedecz in 1915. His family had moved to Przedecz from nearby Babiak in the 1800's. As I later learned, there were Buks and Herzberg and Przdecki relatives scattered through several towns in Central Poland, most notably Przedecz and Klodawa. My grandfather, Shimon Buks, and his brother, Arje Buks, lived and sold live animals and kosher meat at Warszawska Street No. 2, right next door to Dawid Zychliński in No. 4. The property was near the town square and went through to the next block. In 1921, Shimon Buks sailed to America with his wife and five young children, leaving behind his brother's family and numerous relatives and friends.

In America his name became Leonard Israel Books. His father Shimon established a kosher butcher shop in Malden, Massachusetts, where my father helped out. When he married, my father started his own businesses, first a lending library business and, later, Kendall Drug in Cambridge, Massachusetts. He was proud to be an American. He was devoted to his new country. He thought, without hesitation, that America was the best country on the face of the earth. And yet of course his roots were in Poland, and he lived with the knowledge of what had been left behind.

My parents spoke Yiddish with their parents and siblings, and we children listened. It wasn't until my parents died that I took up their first language. Translating the Yiddish portions of this Yizkor book was a labor of love. My siblings and I took advantage of the possibilities of America. I knew I was privileged, but

I barely understood the magnitude of that privilege. When I was a teenager, my father tried to tell me about Poland, about Chełmno and the fate of our relatives, but my mother stopped him, saying that I couldn't possibly understand. She was right of course. How could an American child understand the disrespect and lack of opportunity that they had left behind? It wasn't until my trip to Przedecz in 2019 that my eyes teared up involuntarily when, for the first time, I knew how deeply my entire life had been anchored in the small towns that were the birthplaces of my parents, Pshaytsh (Przedecz) for my father and Kamien Kashirskiy (Ukraine) for my mother. On the airplane to Poland that first time, I leafed through the Yizkor book that had sat for some years unopened on my shelf and was stunned to read the entry for Arje Buks. All my Books relatives were in the United States. No one was left in Europe. I would have known, wouldn't I? But when I read that short paragraph, I understood that Arje was my grandfather's brother. It was still later that I learned about Chełmno. And still later that I learned the Polish expression *Jesteśmy stqd*, we are from here, came to care about Przedecz and some of the kind people I met there, notably my friend Halinka Ziecik. This book is for them too, with wishes for the healing we can all use after the terrible events described in these pages.

Even though I haven't found every mistake, it is time to stop and share this effort with others. Some parts of the translation are awkward, as I opted to stay as close to the rhythm of the Yiddish as possible. The original authors probably made factual mistakes too. If you see errors when you read about your family, no disrespect was intended.

Roberta Paula Books, 2023

Photo Credits

Front Cover:

Left: *Sender Przedecki in 1926.* Courtesy of Judy Muratore.

Center: *Mala Aurbach and her brother Chaim at chess, c.1934.* Courtesy of Gila Brand.

Right: *Moishe Zielinski (Morris Zelinsky), center, with a young relative and two fellow officers in the Russian army, c.1898.* Courtesy of Gary Nelson and Bryan Kesselman.

Bottom: *Przedecz town hall and market square, October 2012.* Courtesy of Nina Camic.

Back Cover:

Top left: *Przedecz town hall and market square, 1939.* Public domain. Courtesy of the Polish National Archives.

Right: *Yehoshua Yamnik as a student, c.1930.* Courtesy of Shmuel Inbar and Barbara Cohen.

Bottom: *Aerial view of Przedecz, posted 2020.* Courtesy of Alexander Liebert-Galeria Wielkopolska, https://www.galeriawielkopolska.info/przedecz.

Geopolitical Information

Przedecz, Poland is located at 52°20' N 18°54' E and 89 miles W of Warsaw

	Town	District	Province	Country
Before WWI (c. 1900):	Przedecz	Włocławek	Warszawa	Russian Empire
Between the wars (c. 1930):	Przedecz	Włocławek	Warszawa	Poland
After WWII (c. 1950):	Przedecz			Poland
Today	Przedecz			Poland

Alternate Names for the Town:

Przedecz [Pol], Pshaytsh [Yid], Pshedech [Rus], Presheysh, Pshaych, Pshayts, Pshech, Pshedesh, Pshedetz, Pshedets [Heb]

Nearby Jewish Communities:

Kłodawa 6 miles S

Chodecz 7 miles NE

Izbica Kujawska 8 miles NW

Dąbrowice 9 miles E

Babiak 10 miles W

Lubień Kujawski 13 miles ENE

Krośniewice 13 miles ESE

Grabów 15 miles SSE

Lubraniec 15 miles N

Koło 16 miles SW

Sompolno 17 miles WNW

Dąbie 18 miles S

Kowal 18 miles NE

Brześć Kujawski 18 miles N

Kutno 21 miles ESE

Osięciny 22 miles NNW

Włocławek 23 miles NNE

Łęczyca 23 miles SE

Piotrków Kujawski 23 miles NW

Russocice 24 miles SW

Ślesin 25 miles W

Radziejów 25 miles NW

Gostynin 26 miles ENE

Uniejów 26 miles S

Skulsk 26 miles WNW

Turek 27 miles SW

Konin 28 miles WSW

Dobrzyń nad Wisłą 28 miles NE

Parzęczew 30 miles SSE

Jewish Population: About 700 (in 1900)

BALTIC SEA

LITHUANIA

RUSSIA

Vilnius ●

POLAND

GERMANY

BELARUS

● Berlin

Poznan ●

Przedecz ●

Warsaw ●

Brest ●

Lodz ●

Lublin ●

● Wroclaw

● Prague

● Krakow

CZECH REPUBLIC

UKRAINE

SLOVAKIA

AUSTRIA

250 miles

250 Km 500 Km

POLAND – CURRENT BORDERS

Map of Poland showing the location of **Przedecz**

Table of Contents

To the Community of Przedecz (Pshedetz)		4
In Eternal Memory		5
Forward [Hebrew]	The Editorial Staff	6
Forward [Yiddish]	The Editorial Staff	8
To the Holy Souls of the Fallen of Przedecz	Moshe Mokotov	11
The Soldier Ze'ev Rusk z"l		13
The Soldier Eliezer Perlmutter z"l		17
For the Three Who Fell	Reuven Yamnik	17
The Soldier Ya'akov Burg z"l	Bella Burg	19
Staff-Sergeant Ram (Rami) Levin z"l		23
To the Holy Souls of Przedecz	Yitzhak Levin	31
Captain Yeshayahu Makovitzki z"l		33
To the Memory of My Blessed Family	Shaul Makovitzky	40
A Picture of the Synagogue (drawn from memory)		42
The Last Dance	Y. L. L. Shlomi	42
Extermination Camp in Chełmno	A Testimony	47
On the Day of Slaughter	Reuven Yamnik	52
Chełmno Cries Out to the Heavens		56
The Murders in Chełmno – 1944–1945		59
The Last Hours	Y. Y. L.	60
The Eradication of Przedecz Jewry	Sela Mandlinger (Goldman)	62
My Memories from the Past	Levy Shveitzer	65
In the Poznan Camps	Levi Shveitzer	71
Events from Pshedets (Przedecz)	Davidovitz Yehoshua	75
The Bread of Our Affliction	Y. L. L. Shlomi	79
Quiet Courage	Y. L. L	83
Lament for a Town that is No More	Pnina Leah (Zemelman)	85
A Collection of Memories	Y. L. L.	87
One Tombstone Remains	Y. L. L.	90
Why? (dedicated to Reb Khaim Tarner)	Y. L. L.	92
Memories of My Father's House	Esther (Zemelman) Burg	95
My Father Mikhl Hersh Naymark	Simkha Naymark	97
Memories	Yosef Bilevsky	99
Memories of My Father's Home	Reuven Yamnick	102
Memorial to My Daughter, Whom I Never Met	Yitzkhak Levin	106
Hinda	Yitzkhak Levin Israel	107
One of Many	Y.L.L Shlomi	109
I Am Not an Exception	Yitzkhak Levin	110
My Family, of Beloved Memory	Moshe Bilevsky	114
Testimony to My Family, Who Were Here, but Have Since Gone	Moshe Mokotov	116
Father's House	Leah Zemelman Pnini	123

My Family of Blessed Memory	Fishel Goldman	126
Rukhele the Dairywoman	Y. L. L.	127
Moishe Yakhimovitch of Blessed Memory		129
Reb Itche Kovalsky "The Shammesh"	Moishe Bilevsky	131
Rabbi Zemelman – The Person and the Personality	A. Talmid	135
The Reciting of the Kaddish	Rabbi Itzhak Yedidia Frankel	142
Testimony of the Writer Hillel Seidman		148
On the Grave of My People		151
Tushya Yakhimovitch Calls for Revenge	Y.L.L Shlomi	153
Memories from the Days of the Holocaust	Reuven Yemenik	156
Shabbat in Town	Moshe Bilevski	159
The Trial on Synagogue Street	Yitzkhak Ben Shalom	161
My Town Przedecz	Manik Reuven	164
The Tombstone	Y.L.L	166
Young Mizrachi and Hashomer Hadati	Moshe Bilevsky	167
The Establishment of Tzirey Mizrachi (The Young Mizrachi)	Moshe Bilevsky	173
Interest Free Loan Society Fund	A. Pshaytcher	175
Society to Care for the Sick – Itche Vayden	Moishe Bilevsky	176
The Ludovy Bank	A. Pshaytsher	178
The Town Pshaytch (Przedecz)	Reuven Yamnik	180
Yizkor		189
The Martyrs of Przedecz		190
A Page in Memory of Our Town's Soldiers Fallen in the Battle against the Nazis		260
Sons of Our City who Perished after the Holocaust		260
Conclusion		266
The Organization of Former Przedecz Residents		267
List of Former Przedecz Residents Living in Israel		270
Former Przedecz Residents Living Outside of Israel		271
The History of Przedecz and its Jews	Prof Aharon Brand-Urban	272
Przedecz – General Historical Review		272
The History of the Jews of Przedecz with Some Data about the Jews of the Area		275
The Rabbis of Pshaytsh:		282
Rabbi Yaakov Ori Shraga Horowitz		282
Rabbi Haim Auerbach, of Blessed Memory and Source of His Wisdom		285
R'Moshe Chaim Blum z"l		289
Rabbi Yehoshua Heschel David Goldshlag		292
Yiddish and Hebrew Reading in Przedecz		293
Bibliography		297
Street Map of the City of Przedecz		299
Name Index		300

.

Memorial Book to the Holocaust Victims of the Community of Pshaytsh (Przedecz, Poland)

52°20' / 18°54'

Translation of:
Sefer yizkor li-kedoshe 'ir Pshaytsh

Edited by: Moshe Bilavsky et al.

Published in Tel Aviv 1974

****

Acknowledgments:

Project Coordinator

Roberta Paula Books

****

This is a translation from: *Sefer yizkor le-kedoshei ir Pshaytsh korbanot ha-shoa*

(Memorial book to the Holocaust Victims of the Community of Pshaytsh)

Editors: Moshe Bilavsky, Reuven Yamnik, and Moshe Mokotov

Tel Aviv, Przedecz Societies in Israel and the Diaspora, 1974 (H, Y, 400 pages).

Note: The original book can be seen online at the New York Public Library site: Przedecz
Page numbers in brackets refer to the corresponding page in the original book.
****

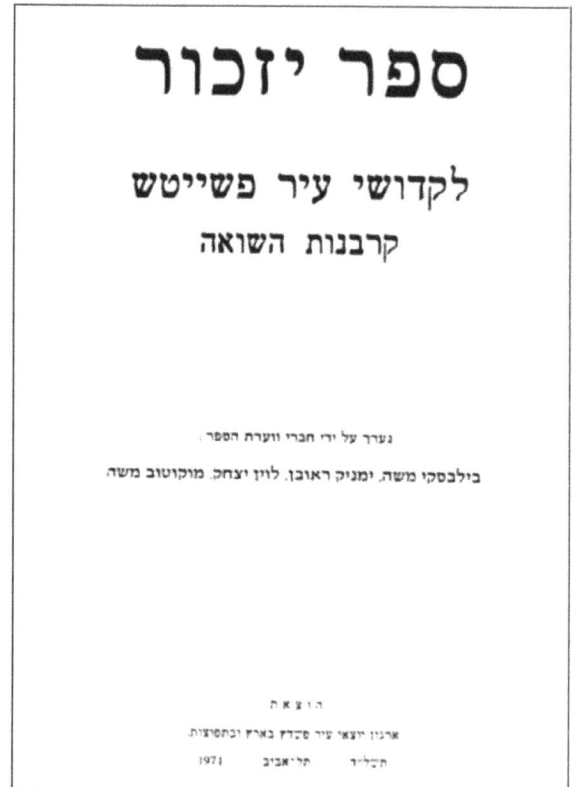

ספר יזכור

לקדושי עיר פשייטש

קרבנות השואה

נערך על ידי חברי וערת הספר :

בילבסקי משה, ימניק ראובן, לוין יצחק, מוקוטוב משה.

ה ו צ א ת

ארגון יוצאי עיר פשדדח בארץ ובתפוצות

תשל"ר   תל־אביב   1971

[BLANK PAGE}

[Page 7]

To the Community of Przedecz (Pshedetz)

Translated by Jerrold Landau

"Would it be that my head were water, and my eyes a source of tears – I would weep day and night over the victims of the daughter of my nation."

(Jeremiah 8:23).[1]

In Eternal Memory
In memory of the souls of our dear ones, the martyrs of our town

Przedecz (Pshedets/Pshaytsh)
(District of Włocławek)

who were murdered at the hands of the Nazis and their helpers, may their names be blotted out,
in Chełmno on 7 Iyar, 5602, May 24, 1942.
and in other places of annihilation. May G-d avenge their blood.
The memorial day was designated as 7 Iyar.
May their souls be bound in the bonds of eternal life.
The survivors of our city in Israel and the Diaspora will perpetuate their holy memory.

Memorial tablet in the Chamber of the Holocaust in Jerusalem

Translator's note: This is an excerpt from the Haftorah of Tisha B'Av morning.

[Page 8]

In Eternal Memory

Translated by Jerrold Landau

May G-d remember the pure martyrs, the Jews of the city of Przedecz (Pshaytsh) who were murdered by the Nazi Germans and their inimical assistants, who were murdered in all sorts of unusual, cruel deaths.

The brave soldiers who fell in the War of Independence for our holy land.

The brave soldiers who fell in defense of the borders of our land during the war of 1948 and in the Yom Kippur War.

The soldiers who fought in the allied armies who fought against the Nazis and fell in the line of duty.

Those who resisted in the death camps, the partisans in the forests, and the ghetto fighters who fell in sanctification of the Divine Name and the nation.

The holy soldiers of our town who fought in the Polish army and in the partisan units against the Nazi troops, and fell in the killing fields.

All of those whose names are not known and are not mentioned in the book.

And those who died, whose graves and gravestones were uprooted and destroyed to the foundation.

May our G-d remember them for good, and may their souls be bound in the bonds of life under the wings of the Divine Presence. May G-d avenge their blood.

The Mourners:

The survivors of the city of Przedecz (Pshedets) in Israel and the Diaspora.

[Page 9]

Forward

by the Editorial Staff

Translated from Hebrew by Harris Werksman (Zvi BenShalom), whose mother, Mindl Buks, was born in Pshaytsh

With fear and trembling due to our sacred mission, we publish this memorial book to preserve the memory of our dear martyrs, the Jews of Pshaytsh who were murdered during the Holocaust in the years 1939–1945 by the Nazis and their helpers, may their names be blotted out.

The terrible Holocaust where six million Jews were killed and obliterated, for the sole reason that they desired to live as Jews, struck us as individuals and as survivors of the city Pshaytsh, and we were left bereft of parents, brothers and sisters, women and children, relatives, friends and acquaintances, and the community of Pshaytsh.

This city is where we were born and lived, breathed its air, and dwelt in the bosom of our families, where we spent our beautiful youthful years among friends, and where each one dreamed and dreamed, each in his own way, of a better and more rosy future.

This city was drained of its Jews.

After the Nazis conquered Poland and entered our city in September of 1939, their first operation was to burn the synagogue. In addition, they blamed the Jews for burning the synagogue, and if this was not enough, the Jews of our city had to pay a fine for burning the synagogue, in gold, silver and jewelry, to the conquering Nazis.

Furthermore, there were selections where a significant portion of the Jews in our city were moved to work and extermination camps where dozens of the people of Pshaytsh were killed by many unusual and cruel deaths that had no parallel in history.

On 7th day of Iyar 5702 – 4.24.1942, the community of Pshaytsh (in Polish, Przedecz and in Hebrew, Pshedets) was destroyed after all the Jews who were left were rounded up in the Christian church, and from there were transferred to the Chełmno extermination camp where they were murdered with poison gas in closed trucks.

We, the survivors of Pshaytsh, some of whom survived all these horrors within the extermination camp Chełmno , a small step away from death, are shaken and shocked, to the depths of our hearts, and we ask: ——

"Why, Oh Why"?

This book is meant as a memorial and yahrzeit candle for the martyred citizens of our city Pshaytsh.

[Page 10]

In this book, we reveal events and deeds in the lives of our dear ones, suffering and joy, laughter and silence, pleasure and sorrow, times of welfare and times of distress, years of persecution and years of tranquility, the suffering and happiness of each family, up to the years of the Holocaust and destruction, and the elimination of our loved ones.

It is clear to us that no book can express the depth of the sadness, the pain, and the grief of a prospering Jewish community, along with its institutions, that was cut down. However, we felt obligated to memorialize the memory of our loved ones in a memorial book that would record the deeds of the citizens of our city, and to engrave in history the eternal condemnation, the deeds, horror, and murder of the despicable Nazi beast, predatory and blood thirsty, the severity of whose crimes where not previously known to mankind, and as we were commanded: —

"Remember what Amalek did to you".

Remember and do not remove the pain from your heart. Remember and don't relinquish from your mouths the eternal curse of the Nazis and their helpers who maliciously destroyed one third of our nation.

This memorial book will immortalize our loved ones, the Jews of Pshaytsh, and shall serve in place of a graveyard. Any time we peruse its pages we shall feel as if we are standing by their graves, because this, too, was not granted them by the murderers. The bones of our loved ones were ground and used to fertilize corn fields surrounding the camps. Holy martyrs, rest within this memorial book. It is your graveyard which we shall always visit. It is your Jewish grave which we take in our hands and let fall the tears mixed with our hearts' blood, and say with sadness and anguish:

Yisgadal v'yiskadash shmai rabbo … ! [the mourner's prayer]

Our Pshaytsh, as we knew her and as she is engraved upon our hearts, shall never be re–established, but her memory shall never be forgotten by the Jewish people.

The images of our relatives, friends and acquaintances will remain engraved upon our hearts forever. We have sworn never to forget them.

This book, which will serve in every house as an eternal candle in memory of our loved ones of blessed memory, is not intended solely to memorialize the souls of our brothers and sisters. Its main aim is so that the young generation which we have raised will study it, will learn about the great suffering and annihilation that the Nazis perpetrated upon the fathers of their fathers, and will learn the lesson of the horrific Holocaust.

In addition to the book serving as a memorial to beloved martyrs and an eternal candle for their souls, this book shall serve as a rebuke and a witness in an indictment that will be served one day on the wicked and malicious world, and against the leaders of the "enlightened" world who watched with indifference the destruction of our people, and stood aside without taking action and without pangs of conscience, thus indirectly contributing to the annihilation of one third of our people.

Let this book be a stratum in the literature of the Holocaust and a source of study for those who will research, in the future, the history of Israel. This, then, is the purpose of this book.

In this book, which is a commemorative monument to the memory of the citizens of our city who were murdered in the Holocaust, we felt the need and the obligation to also mention those citizens of our city who fell in the ranks of the Jewish Brigade that fought within the framework of the British Army that fought against the Nazi beast at the Italian front, and in the war of liberation of our people to establish the State of Israel, and also those who fought in the Polish Army and the divisions of partisans, and who fell on the battlefield.

[Page 11]

Writing and editing this book is a heavy task involving a high degree of responsibility. Together with the disappearance of our loved ones, the sources of information concerning the lives of the Jews hundreds of years ago also disappeared. A portion of the few survivors who escaped the terrible events after going through the seven levels of hell, are satisfied with the silence concerning this subject. They do not wish to re–open their wounds which have yet to be healed. At every stage of our work, difficulties were encountered. Only the commands of our conscience drove us onward, and because of the great efforts expended and the difficult and painstaking work, we succeeded in gathering, sorting, rehabilitating, and putting the finishing touches on the material, inserting layer upon layer to raise up this monument in the form of a memorial book.

In an objective manner, we tried to describe the city with all its institutions, parties, personalities, wheeler–dealers and leaders, events and destruction, and also noteworthy observations regarding its way of life.

Even though we did not economize the time, effort, and work in publishing a perfect job, we know that this book is not complete, and if we missed events, institutions, names, facts, or if we presented incorrect dates or inexact facts, we deeply regret this and beg the forgiveness of all who are related to the matter.

Here it is worth noting that in spite of our remaining few in number after this tremendous destruction, there was a drawing together of the hearts of all the survivors of our city all over the world as we all saw ourselves as one broken family, decimated and orphaned, with one common goal, and that is to raise up this memorial monument (literally grave marker) in the form of this remembrance book to the memories of our loved ones who were murdered in the Holocaust.

We hope and believe that publishing this book will strengthen and bring together all the citizens of our city wherever they may be, and this will give us some small consolation for our martyred loved ones who were murdered in the tremendous destruction during the years of the Holocaust.

Our utmost thanks go to all who enabled us to complete this project. Blessing on all our friends and all of the survivors of Pshaytsh in Israel and the Diaspora who supplied us with material and participated in financing this book, which is an eternal memorial monument to our beloved martyrs of Pshaytsh, may G–d avenge their blood.

[Page 12]

Forward

by the Editorial Staff

Translated from Yiddish by Roberta Paula Books

With solemn trembling and honest emotions, we act to publish this memorial book to preserve for all time the memory of our dear and beloved Pshaytsher Jews (Jews from Przedecz, called Pshaytsh in Yiddish) who were so cruelly murdered in the great Holocaust during the years 1939-1945 by the monstrous Nazis and their collaborators.

This great destruction, in which six million Jews were killed solely for the crime of wanting to live their lives as Jews, happened to us both as individuals and collectively. As individuals we were orphaned, losing our parents, sisters, brothers, wives, and children, and as a group – Pshaytsher (Przedecz) Jewry no longer exists.

This town is where we were born, lived, breathed the air, were surrounded by our families, enjoyed our childhood years among friends and pals, dreamed and struggled, everyone in their own way, for a better future. The town which bubbled with beautiful sophisticated Jewish youth and with loving Jews is now empty and devoid of Jews.

When the Nazis occupied Poland and entered our town in September 1939, their first act was to burn the synagogue, and as if this was not enough for them, they also accused the Jews of Pshaytsh (Przedecz) of having set the fire. To add insult to injury, Pshaytsher Jews also had to pay taxes: -

Money, money and jewelry, required as a fine for burning the synagogue… Afterwards the selections began whereby a large part of our Pshaytsher (Przedecz) Jewry was sent to labor and extermination camps, and there tens of our relatives and friends were exterminated, and on that wretched day of April 24, 1942, the 7th of Iyar 5702, the last Jews of Pshaytsh (Przedecz) were crowded into the Catholic Church and from there they were sent to the extermination camp Chełmno (a village near Koło) where they were gassed and burned.

[Page 13]

And we are the remnants, the small, last living fragments of Pshaytsher (Przedecz) Jewry, most having lived through the holocaust, and endured a terrifying hell in the SS camps, where only a thin thread separated us from those who were killed. We stand here now, shocked and scattered, and asked with pain in our hearts: **why and for what**?

We, the broken and orphaned survivors, have decided to commemorate our beloved Pschaytsher Jews in the form of a memorial book.

This memorial book is a monument and a memorial candle for the martyrs from our city.

In this Yizkor book we bring you history and fact, anguish and joy, prosperity and deprivation, years of suffering and years of happiness, each family in its suffering and fulfilment, up until the years of the Holocaust and the physical destruction and annihilation of our loved ones.

It is true that a book cannot express the deepest grief, anguish and sorrow of a Jewish community which was eradicated in such a terrifying way. However, our obligation is to perpetuate the memory of our dearest and erect a tombstone in the form of a memorial book where the lives of Pshaytsher Jews will be written down, covering all areas, as well as the frightful facts about the Nazi beasts who cannot be compared to anything in human history.

"Remember What Amalek Did to You"

It is our holy obligation to the martyrs to carry the deep grief in our hearts, and it is also our obligation carry on our lips an eternal curse for the Nazis and their collaborators who so savagely murdered one third of our people.

This memorial book which will preserve the memory of our Pshaytsher (Przedecz) relatives and friends and will also serve as substitute for a grave, and every time we take this book into our hands we will feel as if we are standing at their graves as this too was not provided to us by the murderers. The bones of our relatives and dearest ones were ground up and spread as fertilizer on fields, after the pain of their tortured bodies, burned in crematoria.

Here in this book will you have your eternal rest, my beloved friends and relatives. This is your cemetery, where we will come regularly, this is your Jewish grave where we will shed our tears and say

[Page 14]

yisgadol ve yisgadash sh'mei rabo (magnified and sanctified be G-d's great name – the mourner's prayer).

The town of Pshaytsh (Przedecz) as we knew it no longer exists. But it will remain forever in our memory. Also eternally etched in our hearts are the images of our relatives, friends and acquaintances, the appearance of personalities and community workers, elderly Jews, women and children, who were so brutishly wiped out, and our oath not to forget them.

This book, an eternal light to the memory of our relatives and friends of blessed memory, has an obligation to be more than a memorial book; its task is also so that our children and grandchildren learn and teach about this terrifying period.

In addition to serving as a tombstone for our martyrs of blessed memory, and an eternal light for their souls, this book will also be a brick in building the great attested act of accusation against the criminal Nazi government. And also, against the world's welfare providers and humanitarians who stood by calmly and watched the destruction of the Jews, how an entire nation, millions of people, women and small children, were annihilated, and did not react. This book will also be a contribution to Holocaust literature and a source for future researchers who will describe this terrifying period.

This is the goal of this book.

In this book which serves as a tombstone to remember our relatives and friends who were killed in the Nazi Holocaust, we feel it necessary to remember and to mention our friends who fell in battle against the German army on the Italian front in 1944, in the Jewish fighting battalion "Chayil" (Force) and "The Fighting Jewish Division". And also, the freedom fighters in the "War of Independence" in Israel for the establishment of the Jewish state.

We also remember our friends who fell while fighting in the Polish army against the Nazis, as well as those who fell fighting the Nazis in the ranks of various partisan units.

Writing and editing this book is a difficult and responsible work. Together with the disappearance of the Pshaytsh (Przedecz) Jewish community, the sources of information have also disappeared which could have provided us with an exact picture of Jewish life in Pshaytsh tens and hundreds of years ago. Our friends who lived through and survived the Holocaust prefer to remain silent and not reopen the infected

[Page 15]

wounds which are still bleeding. The victims who were killed in the gas chambers and Nazi concentration camps can no longer speak. Only our strong belief that we must fulfill this holy task of immortalizing for all time the memory of our martyrs and of our Pshaytsher (Przedecz) community gave us strength and courage to erect this tombstone.

We tried to present our town with total objectivity, with all its institutions, political parties, personality, descriptions, and religious life: the characteristics of Pshaytsher Jewish life, Jewish professions, joys and suffering and the horrific frightful history of the Holocaust extermination and destruction.

Although we did not skimp or spare any effort, insofar as possible, to publish this book, we know it is far from perfect. Through no fault of our own, we are probably missing documentary material, institutions, and names in the list of those who perished. If anyone feels hurt or insulted, we beg your forgiveness.

It is worthwhile here to mention that, even though few Pshaytsher Jews survived the great Holocaust, when this book was published our townspeople gave with all their hearts. From all around the world they began to contact one another, and suddenly we saw how a broken orphaned family had a common goal, to erect a tombstone for our dear martyrs in the form of a memorial book.

It is to be hoped that publication of this memorial book will embrace and bring even closer together the hearts of Pshaytsher Jews and will provide a bit of comfort for the murdered martyrs of the Jewish catastrophe of our times.

We express our heartfelt thanks to all our friends and townspeople in Israel and abroad who helped assemble material for this memorial book as well as financially helping to create this monument to remember our dear martyrs of blessed memory.

[Page 16] Blank
[Page 17]

To the Holy Souls of the Fallen of Przedecz
Testament to the Fallen

by Moshe Mokotov

Translated from Hebrew by Marshall Grant

From the Jewish Brigade to the Yom Kippur War

The memorial book of the Przedecz community may not be known for its level of "professional literature" – and you should not be surprised. However, the authors of this book's entries have written in the best professional manner the authors can offer, even if they are not professional journalists or writers.

There are other books that surpass this one from the literary perspective, but those have been written by publicists, writers, and other journalists.

Nevertheless, our memorial book is the most updated from all those that have been published in Israel. Those from Przedecz and their descendants have contributed the most meaningful of contributions for the birth of the nation.

Ze'ev (Wolf) Rusk, of blessed memory, from Tel Aviv. He was one of the first volunteers of the *Chil*, the Jewish Brigade in the service of the British military. It was modest and responsible, and operated with complete loyalty, and the brigade fulfilled directives and orders issued by the Jewish leadership and its commanders. He died while attacking Nazi soldiers in the killing fields on the Italian front at the height of the Second World War.

Eliezer Perlmutter, of blessed memory, from Jerusalem. One of the veterans in the defense of Jerusalem, a happy and brave person. He was one of the first Jews to join the English Royal Engineers to fight against General Rommel, one of Hitler's most senior general officers. With honor and wisdom, he protected Jewish soldiers against attacks by non-Jewish soldiers.

May 15, 1948, the State of Israel was founded. Eliezer was amongst those defending Jerusalem. When the War of Independence broke out, the city was disconnected from the coastal cities, food was lacking and the city was under siege. The winding convoy of food and medical supplies slowly made its way through the Jerusalem hills towards the capital. Amongst those protecting these convoys was Eliezer Perlmutter, but this time in the service of the Israel Defense Forces. As the person he was, he was the first to volunteer and among the first to fall!!

Ya'akov (Kobi) Burg, of blessed memory, from Ashkelon. In the 1970s, the War of Attrition raged, a bloody and undeclared war. The prices paid in the war were dear - the lives of our best young soldiers. The blood of our young inundated the hills of Sinai, and our city had suffered our third casualty.

We still remember the beautiful and cordial young man, with a sensitive soul, who took part in the discussions

[Page 18]

for the memorial services held for our community in the Jewish National Fund hall in Tel Aviv. Nothing here is surprising – he was the grandson of Rabbi Zemelman, and the grandson continued the ways of his grandfather, and remained loyal to his beliefs until the end…

Both met a hero's death.

Four years later, the Yom Kippur War. Despite the glamorous victory of our military, we had yet to experience such large disasters.

Some 3,000 of our most loved sons were killed while in service for their country. Again, Przedecz had given its share.

Two young men were taken during the best years of their lives.

Rami Levin, of blessed memory, from Bnei Brak. A third-year student in Tel Aviv University. He had a golden heart who always sought to help others. His young age betrayed his natural wisdom and unique perspective.

It is still a riddle of how this gentle person became a hero, who calmly fought with extraordinary bravely, and charged the enemy with his tank. His friends who were with him in his last moments tell of his actions in battle. It is hard to understand this contradiction, two different worlds. Modesty and heroism. A sensitive soul with an exemplary sense of sacrifice. He fell in battle on October 18, 1973, on the Jewish holiday of *Simkhas Torah*, in the Battle of the Chinese Farm during the efforts to breakthrough towards the western bank of the Suez Canal.

Yeshiahu (Shaika) Mekovitzia, of blessed memory, from Tel Aviv. The second casualty of the Yom Kippur War, one of our city's grandsons.

He stood out early among his friends, still in his early years, and in 1966 participated in a youth delegation from Tel Aviv to France and Italy.

A year later he joined the IDF and became an officer. Several months later he was appointed to be a team commander in the officers' course for supply officers, and several months later was appointed to command this course. Following his discharge from the IDF he studied in the Economics Department in Tel Aviv University, where he earned his degree. Shaika married and exactly one year later arrived to join his military unit even before they were publicly called.

The Yom Kippur War was at its peak, and after 12 consecutive days leading his soldiers, he fell – commanding his platoon.

These are stories of sacrifice that are nothing less than living legends, and their stories have been covered in the most important newspapers around the world. Stalingrad and El Alamein pale compared to the heroism and sacrifice that took place in the Yom Kippur War.

Israeli soldiers, among them the offspring of our city, are now role models in military schools around the world.

The descendants of Przedecz are an integral part of the Yom Kippur War.

May the memory of these young heroes, who in their death gave us life, be blessed through their ultimate sacrifice for their homeland.

[Page 19]

The soldier Ze'ev Rusk z"l

Translated from Hebrew by Marshall Grant

The soldier Ze'ev Rusk, of blessed memory

Son or Moshe Aharon and Rachael

Fell on Nissan 5, 5705, March 19, 1945, in the Italian front while in service of the Jewish Brigade.

Born in Poland in 1941.

Ze'ev Rusk of blessed memory. Fell on the 5th of Nissan, 5705, March 19, 1945, during an offensive launched by the 3rd battalion of the Jewish Brigade. In the Jewish Brigade's first combat experience on the front, the first German POWs were captured.

He was born in 1914 in the city of Kutno in Poland. While still a child, his family moved to Przedecz, where he studied with Rabbi Zemelman and was one his most gifted students. Ever since his youth, he had been active in the Zionist movement and was one of the organizers and activists in the "The Young Mizrahi" (*Tze'erei Mizrachi*) and the "Religious Guard" (*Hashomer Hadati*) movements in our city. He invested much of his time to the Jewish National Fund. His affiliation with the Young Mizrahi movement was given to him from his father, Rabbi Moshe Aharon Rusk, a longtime Mizrahi member and enthusiastic supporter of The Young Mizrahi movement in our city.

He arrived at a training center in one of Poland's cities and made Aliyah in 1934. He was concerned with the future of Jewish settlements and the country and aware of all events that took place there. He was attentive to any request from official institutions, and when his draft orders arrived, he volunteered to the military.

He was quiet and modest, smart, and funny, his jokes always raised the spirits of those around him. He was well liked by his company, he was a friend, loyal and dedicated to those close to him and to those he knew.

May his memory be blessed.

[Page 20]

Ze'ev Rusk, of blessed memory, before his Aliyah.
Among his friends from the Young Mizrahi and Religious Guard movements

Ze'ev Rusk with members of his unit
The picture was taken just several days before the battle in which he met his heroic death.

[Page 21]

In recognition of our friend, Ze'ev Rusk, for his dedicated work for the good of the movement. We are presenting you this Tanach for the eternal memory of your making Aliyah to Israel. "Turn it over, and [again] turn it over, for all is therein".

The Torah and Labor Movement in Przedecz

Zvi [illegible]
Yitzhak Yehuda [illegible]
Moshe [illegible] Tekovsky
[illegible]
Shlomo [illegible]
[illegible] Zvi [illegible]
[stamp: Young Mizrahi Przedecz]

Dedication inscribed in a Tanach given to Ze'ev Rusk
by members of the movement before his Aliyah

[Page 22]

The soldier Eliezer Perlmutter z"l

Translated from Hebrew by Marshall Grant

Eliezer Perlmutter, of blessed memory

Son of Yehuda and Chaya

Fell on April 23, 1948, in the War of Independence while defending Jerusalem.

Born in Poland in 1915

Eliezer Perlmutter, son of Yehuda and Chaya. Born on April 13, 1915, in the village of Przedecz in Poland. He made Aliya in 1934 and worked as a driver and in strip mining in Jerusalem and the surrounding areas. He was a long-time member of the *Hagana*; in 1938 he volunteered to serve in *Notorot* (the Jewish Guard brigade in the British police force) in Jerusalem. From 1940, and until his release in 1946, he served as a driver in the British Air Corps in Egypt, the western desert (was gifted with highly developed orientation skills in the desert terrain), Libya, Tunisia, and Italy. He took his commitments seriously and courageously stood up for his people's honor, even though there were very few Jewish soldiers in his unit. When he once heard British soldiers talking amongst themselves mention degrading things about Jews, he silenced the offending soldier with a winning comment and with his fists. Whenever possible, he would tell the British of his national pride: "We, the Israelis, are envoys of the Jewish Agency, and it was not because we were out of work that we joined the British army, as you want to believe." Due to his unique skills and efficient service, he was "forgiven" for his nationalistic statements.

When the War of Independence broke out, he appeared for service as a driver for an armored vehicle. As a father of four, he was able to exempt himself from serving in dangerous areas, but he never once tried to use this right. He drove an armored vehicle in the Jerusalem-Tel Aviv convoys and inside the city. He was slightly injured when the Jewish Agency building was bombed and his armored vehicle caught fire. After the explosion on Ben Yehuda Street, he worked for 24 hours in rescue missions and removing debris. He would visit his home only on rare occasions and for short periods of time before hurrying back to his service. He fell in *Sha'ar Hagai* while driving an armored vehicle (that was completely burned) in a convoy from Tel Aviv to Jerusalem on April 23, 1948, and was buried in Ma'ale Hahamisha on 9 Cheshvan 5712, November 8, 1951, and reinterred in Har Herzl in Jerusalem. He was survived by his wife, two sons and two daughters.

[Page 23]

For the Three Who Fell

by Reuven Yamnik

Translated from Hebrew by Marshall Grant

For three heroes whose lives too early were taken,
My lament will be loud and heard afar,

The second was Rami, with cordial eyes,
He was generous and hearts around him would naturally

Their only sons lost, parents shaken,
Heroes of the Yom Kippur war.

Day and night I will mourn,
 For those who fell on days so balmy,
 Three heroes, three soldiers, so recently born,
 Ya'akov, Yeshiahu and Rami.

They were three from our town,
 Grandsons of those holy and divine,
 A third of our people destroyed, ashes in the
 ground,
 In foreign lands by the most heinous and vile.

Not in the diaspora our three heroes fell,
 But in their homeland, in battle slain,
 Fighting a vicious enemy from hell,
 Their blood was not shed in vain.

Three charming men so dear,
 Three offspring from a village so small,
 Ya'akov, Yeshiahu and Rami always near,
 The fought till death, gave it their all.

Young, vibrant, and shining bright,
 Smart, alert and refreshing as water from a well,
 An only son, with eyes so bright,
 The War of Attrition, was when Ya'akov fell.

gather,
With an eternal smile always so wise,
A dear and only son to his mother and father.

On Yom Kippur he bid his family adieu,
Kissed goodbye his parents and only sister,
And left to fight a bitter enemy he never knew,
That had invaded our country to raze, ruin and blister.

Sorrow and dread gathered and grew,
Expecting every day, but never receiving word,
Time passed and about Rami no one knew,
On Sukkot he had last written and was last heard.

The home is engulfed with mourning and sorrow,
Tears flow from everyone's eyes,
No word from their missing son, maybe on the morrow,
If he has fallen or is still alive.

Then the news reached home like bitter rattle,
Their dear son had been lost in war,
Near the canal, in a cruel battle,
On *Shimini Atzeret*, he was no more.

The third was Yeshiahu, so dear,
Likable, smart with life's refreshing hue,
Loved, educated and vibrant with no fear,
Dedicated son and husband true.

[Page 24]

Yom Kippur, war, and times of strife,
 The enemy is near.
 Yeshiahu leaves his family and young wife,
 To fight the enemy he most fears.

He had yet to build his home,
 He had yet to start his life,
 He had yet to taste life his own,
 Yet he left for his country for to fight.

Uprooted from his family and wife
 Family sorrow and grief do swell,
 A massive disaster, but in family life –
 Yeshiahu the hero in a campaign fell.

How can a young widow's experience joy,
 Her love suddenly sings no more,
 Yeshiahu fell, but the heart accepts no ploy,
 Of such a young heart that beats no more.

All three left and said goodbye,
Kissed their parents, wives, and sisters and then,
Left to their units to defend and fight,
And their last words were – until we meet again.

Everywhere is sorrow and strife,
The sun has in the afternoon has set,
In their death they gave this country life,
And with their bodies they defended a county secure not yet.

The heart winces at the sight of shrines,
of the best the nation had to offer.
From the Holocaust inferno to surviving embers,
All holy, the best the county had to proffer.

January 9, 1974
Yom Kippur, will be engraved into eternal memory,
as the people of Israel will live forever due to the heroes
who protected it.

[Page 25]

The Soldier Ya'akov Burg z"l

by Bella Burg

Translated from Hebrew by Marshall Grant

The Soldier Ya'akov Burg, of blessed memory

Son of Shimon and Esther

Fell in the War of Attrition on the Southern Front on 22 Nissan, 5730, April 28, 1970; born in Israel.

My Brother Ya'akov Burg

My brother, Ya'akov Burg, the grandson of Rabbi Yosef Alexander Zemelman from Przedecz, fell in the War of Attrition on the banks of the Suez Canal on April 28th, 1970, while in active IDF service.

He was known as Kobi.

He was tall, handsome, and smiled and was so understanding…

I don't know how it's possible to write about him.

If we tell, all we hold in our hearts become words, and that part of my life – deep, deep inside, becomes a written legend.

Should I say he was a hero?

They say that about all the fallen.

Kobi wasn't like this, his body was not made of steel, and his heart was not made of iron.

He was a person, just like all others. He loved sports, but also liked to paint and write poetry. His teachers said he excelled in his studies, and his friends shared that he was a good friend, who was always

[Page 26]

willing to help in lessons or actively participate in holiday activities (as leader of the school's "Youth Parliament", Kobi organized many parties).

When we were young we would fight like all good children did, and he, like everyone else, was also scolded and punished.

I loved my older brother, I loved him and believed in him with all my heart.

I always told him about my problems and difficulties, and I felt that we were good friends.

I always knew that he loved our little country. I always knew he was willing to give it everything he had for it. But I never thought he would really have to give everything he had. A sacrifice for the homeland.

Mother and father were worried about him. They thought something would happen to him. They asked he agree that they intervene to make sure he was positioned away from hostilities, but he would not have any of it. "This is my place, if I won't be posted there, then someone else will have to be."

Even on Pesach, he would not allow his father to ask for his release via the IDF community officer, "Someone else will have to stay here instead of me," he said, and returned to the front.

Kobi had three parents, and to all three he tried to give his love. Among the three he divided his life, and that division remains the same after his death. For the homeland he gave his body, and he left his soul to his mother and father.

He gave his homeland his life, and to his parents he left his letters, thoughts, contemplations, memories, and the pain....

Kobi is not dead. He is still alive. He is deep in our hearts, protected against any more bullets. Safe from enemy fire.

Ya'akov Burg's Bar Mitzvah *Drasha*

Dear parents and honored guests,

I have been alive for 13 years, satisfying years full of unforgettable experiences.

I now stand ready to accept the responsibility of the commandments and I am very excited and I cannot believe that I am now celebrating such a significant event.

Dear parents: I have caused you to worry a lot and you have had to exert many efforts ever since I was born, until today. I thank you for the way you raised me, you honestly taught me so I would be able to be self-sufficient amongst my peers.

It has been many years, and you have borne this large burden with love.

And I – I hope and am confident that I can return the love and dedication you have shown me, should you ever need, my dear parents – I wish you much happiness, satisfaction, and pride.

At this moment I stand before something important and significant, a once-in-a-lifetime event,

[Page 27]

the acceptance of the responsibility of the commandments. I am ready to bear, with pride and honor, all the commandments that have been given to me, and I will not fear nor hesitate before any obstacle that I may face while fulfilling them.

The tasks laying before me for my homeland are many, large and lofty, both in the present and future – for the homeland that has embraced me, given me sunlight, enlightened me with parks, and filled me with courage and the joyfulness of youth into me. I want to be a source of pride, and I will do everything possible for its development and prosperity.

To my grandfather and grandmother, uncle and aunt, who were unable to be with us, this is the day your grandson makes his Aliyah to the Torah; the descendent of those who died as martyrs in the death camps, and of those who fought heroically against the wicked enemy until their last moments.

I inherited a lot from my two dear grandfathers – from my maternal grandfather, the spiritual life, Hebrew literature and poetry, and these continued to be my religious lifestyle and beliefs.

My grandfather who died a hero's death in the Warsaw Ghetto uprising, wanting to return the honor to the people of Israel that had been destroyed, to return the honor to all those who were persecuted and murdered by the Nazis. Although my grandfather was killed and was unable to realize his dream, a dream of redemption and freedom, prosperity and growth and the return of the Jews to the Land of Israel, but his heart still lives and rejoices, and he calls for Jews to come and continue his fight, and I promise that I will continue my dear grandfather's fight and I will realize his most sacred dream.

And from my other grandfather I inherited strength, bravery, and self-respect among my peers and in my environs, and I am proud to have my grandfather's name. May both of my grandfathers be blessed; they accompany and guide me in every step I take.

And for my aunt and uncle who died so I can now safely celebrate, as a Jew, my bar mitzvah.

Thirteen years have passed, and I now stand to receive the commandments. I undertake the most serious commitments, and I must bear them with love and desire as a loyal first son must be to his parents.

And to you, dear guests! I thank you for honoring me with your presence to celebrate this great day with me.

[Page 28]

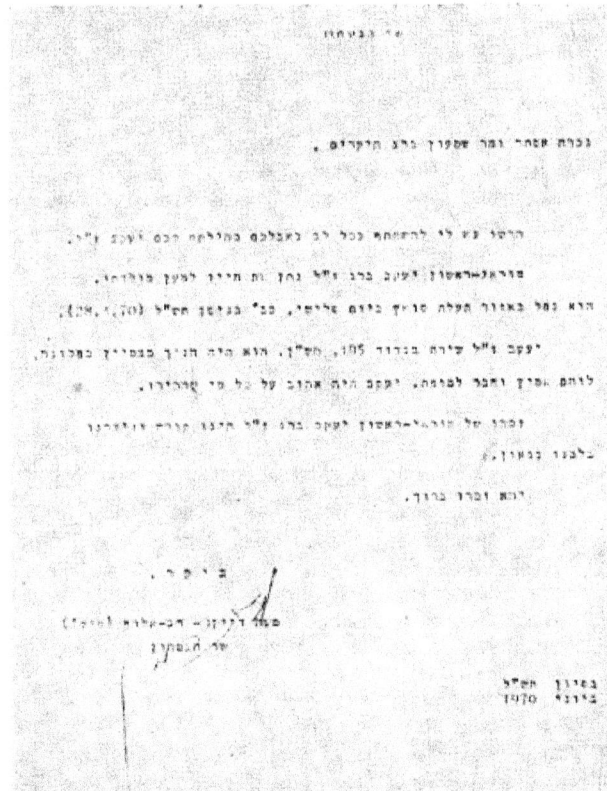

Minister of Defense

Dearest Mrs. Esther and Mr. Shimon Burg,

Allow me to wholeheartedly recognize your sorrow following the loss of Ya'akov, of blessed memory.

First Private Ya'akov Burg, of blessed memory, gave his life for the homeland. He fell near the Suez Canal on 22 Nissan, 5730, April 28, 1970.

Ya'akov served in the 195th battalion. He was awarded "outstanding soldier" in his company, he was a brave soldier and trusted friend – he was greatly loved by all his peers.

The memory of First Private Ya'akov Burg, of blessed memory, is holy and engraved in our hearts forever.

May his memory be blessed,

Sincerely,
[signature]
Moshe Dayan, Lieutenant General (res.)
Minister of Defense

Sivan 5730
June 1970

[Page 29]

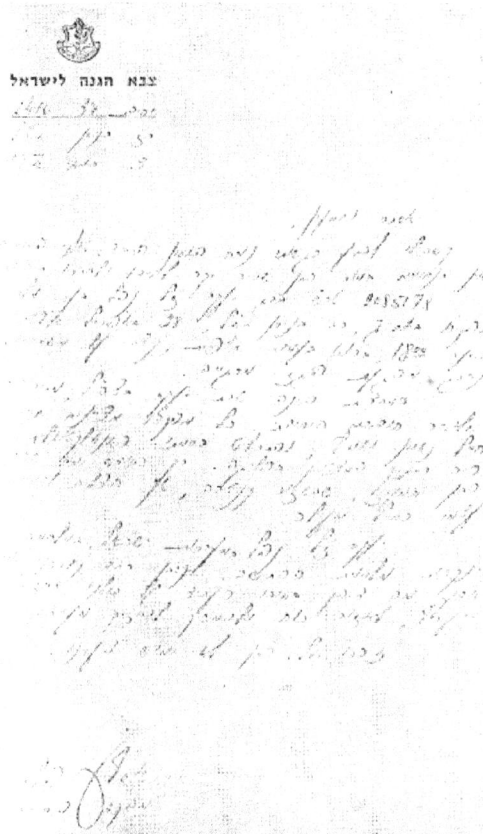

[Page 30]

Staff-Sergeant Ram (Rami) Levin z"l

Translated from Hebrew by Marshall Grant

First Sergeant
Ram (Rami) Levin, of blessed memory

Son or Yitzhak and Dvora

Fell in the Yom Kippur war at the
Chinese Farm on Simkhas Torah -22
Tishrei, 5734.

Born in Poland on 12 Tishrei, 5711 -
October 5, 1950

The unveiling of the memorial plaque in the Holocaust Basement in Jerusalem,
in memory of the holy souls of Przedecz, 1961.
Rami is lighting a candle in their memory.

[Page 31]

Frame of Flowers

Goodbye, dear lady, goodbye and not till we meet again
I met you on an electricity pole, no, no, between the notices.
The frame was quite thick, the letters so black.
In your life, it is only death, just like the other deaths.

I read that you lived for many years
I see that you lived far away. So very far from here.
I heard your husband was well known, not common, but a rabbi or sage
And so many children, I read there are so many.

So why is your frame black and not blue or red
With surrounding flowers, and letters in ink of orange
Isn't death a corridor to the next world, or what?
Maybe a traffic light or crosswalk, towards who, towards what?

Goodbye, dear lady, goodbye and not till we meet again
Is everything over? Here only thoughts remain,
Pardon me for this short poem. It will be thrown away
I don't destroy legends of life or death. A poem written by Rami.

[Page 32]

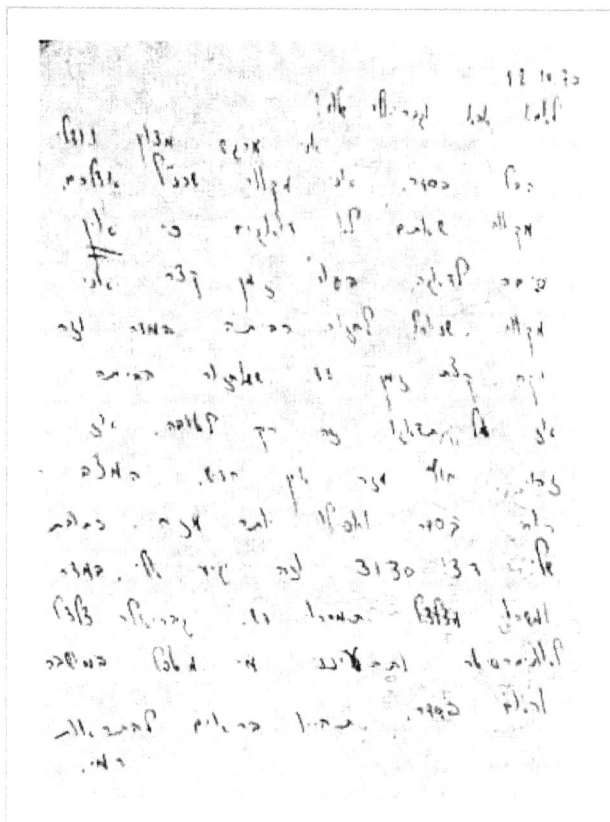

[Page 33]

December 12, 1973

Mother, Father, and Gabriella, shalom!

I feel great and everything is fine with me. I hope you are the same. I hope you aren't worrying because there is no reason for concern. In a short time, I hope we can return home and if it takes some time before I do, don't worry, it's for the best. So that's all, nothing else is new here. Moral is fine, and even better than that. My address is Military Mail 3130, and it will reach me, if anyone calls, give them my regards. Gabriella, call the university find out who is taking care of the farm and if everything is OK. Be healthy, and *lehitra'ot*.

Rami

[Page 34]

[Page 35]

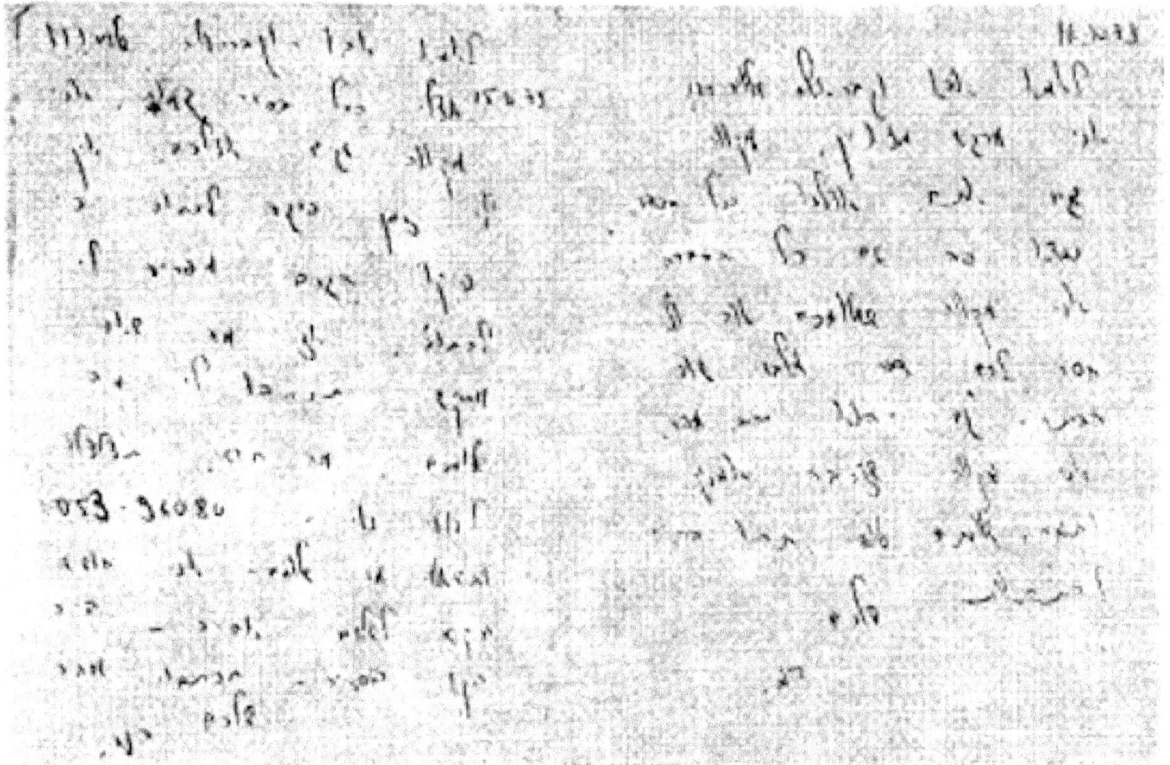

October 16, 1973

Mother, Father, and Gabriella shalom,

I feel excellent, and I hope you do as well. Here everything is fine, I am here with all the guys. I hope you are feeling good and you lack nothing except me being home – and that will happen fast. I hope that Zahava, Amnon and Tamar are well. Be healthy, *lehitra'ot*.

Yours,
Rami

October 15, 1973

Mother, Father, and Gabriella shalom!!

Everything is fine here with me. I hope you are too. I don't have a lot of time now because Pico the thief is bothering me and my writing. So, I am asking you to write me how you are doing, what's new. Call Noa Noy – 053-96080 and ask how they are doing. I am concerned about how her brother is doing. He was on the front line in compulsory service. Write fast.

Yours,
Rami

[Page 36]

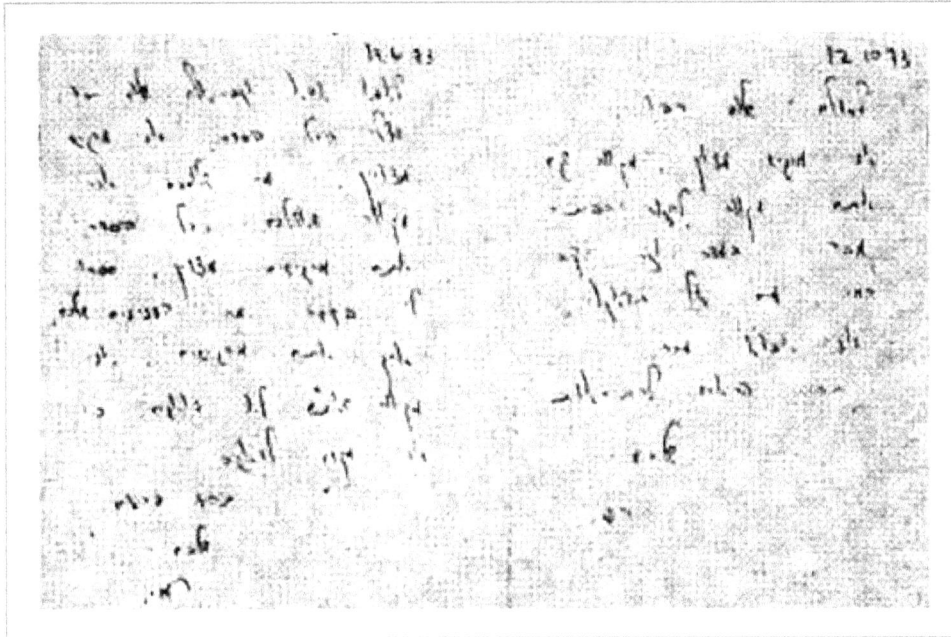

October 12, 1973

To everyone! Shalom!

I am feeling fine, hope you are too. I hope to come home soon and if it takes a few days, don't worry. I will come soon… Be healthy and *lehitra'ot*.

Yours,
Rami

October 15, 1973

Mother, Father, and Gabriella, shalom,

Everything is fine with me. I feel great, how are you? I hope all is well with you and you are feeling good. Tell me please what is going on with you, how are you feeling? I hope you aren't worrying, there is nothing to be worried about.

Yours,
Rami

[Page 37]

צבא הגנה לישראל

Israel Defense Forces
Military Mail Unit 3130
Tevet 5734
January 1974

To the Levin family,

The soldier, Sergeant Rami Levin fell in action during an offensive in the central sector of Sinai on Thursday, 22 Tishrei, 5734, October 18, 1973.

Your son Rami, of blessed memory, served in an armor unit and went into battle as a tank platoon commander. Your son displayed courage and resourcefulness, and was calm under pressure while in combat against enemy tanks and infantry in the area of the *Chinese Farm*.

Your late son filled the role of a platoon commander, even though he was only a sergeant, in exemplary fashion, while leading by example and showing excellent leadership.

The image of Rami will forever be in our memories, his comrades in arms.

In my name, and in the name of all the unit's soldiers, I express my deepest sorrow and we extend our condolences. Soldiers like your son have given us life,

Respectfully yours,
[signature]
Lt. Col. Uziel Ben Itzhak

[Page 38]

January 17, 1974

Shalom Rami,

I never dreamed I would write to you, and surely not when I know you won't receive the letter; but I believe that you knew what I think about you, since besides the loving glance, they were also occasionally voiced. Concerning the irritating day on the "device", when you were the only one who didn't need any urging to go up to the observation and shooting post, and when I was angry at you when you wanted to "booty" from the abandoned Egyptian tank – binoculars that would help you do your job and prevent the enemy from surprising you, only the binoculars, which are now surely in the dunes of the *Chinese Farm*. You probably don't remember that you were mad at me when you removed Ana (the dep. company commander) from the tank, since it took me a few seconds to know, think and understand where to evacuate him.

[Page 39]

You were an excellent soldier; you took the initiative to do things and you did them in the best way possible; and not just in the war. I was so excited when I saw that in the backpack you brought from home was a book about birds in Israel. I hope you were able to look through it during the war and forget about the horrors. We saw a few jackals and foxes later in the field.

I won't tell you about how the war continued, even though this surely would interest you. We don't really believe, but hope with all our heart, that things will be good, there will be peace, and let it be that we can, in the future, travel in the warzone with books about Israel's birds and its plants packed in our backpacks in a real "Jeep", and not in an army pack in the turret's "basket".

Goodbye Rami, and until we meet again, we promise we will meet and see each other often in our memories, with the entire company.

Yours, Ido.

[Page 40]

Words don't do justice for the sorrow and bereavement of mothers who have lost what is dearest to them, and for the sorrow of fathers, who say kaddish for their sons, and no author nor poet is ever able to detail the magnificence of their heroism.

Their memory is etched into my soul until the day I die.

I met Rami, of blessed memory, during his military service. During basic training, in the tank company, in exercises, in the War of Attrition and in reserve service. The grueling exercises were never hard for him, and even when he was exhausted he found the mental strength to smile and make jokes, and to carry everyone around him.

I remember once in the War of Attrition, during one of the nights, his platoon was surprised by an enemy ambush. For a moment, everyone was lost and confused. Rami came to his senses first, opened fire and the enemy attackers retreated. More than anything else, his integrity stood out, along with his willingness to always help and be considerate of others around him. For these reasons, and because of his natural friendly demeanor, he was the center of attention and strengthened and unified the entire company.

His vast experience as a tank commander, along with his previous knowledge, proved themselves during the cruel war, which he was unable to survive.

On October 10, 1973, in a defensive battle along the Suez Canal, Rami, of blessed memory, extracted me from where I lay wounded and helpless in a stricken tank,

I was unable to repay my debt.

Yaakov.

[Page 41]

To the Holy Souls of Przedecz

by Yitzhak Levin

Translated from Hebrew by Marshall Grant

I Believe

Today, the 20th day of Tevet, 5734, January 14, 1974, at 50 minutes past 1 P.M. in the afternoon, will be the 89th day since you, my dear son, gave your life for the country in a cruel and difficult war.

Today is Monday, the falling rain is accompanied by thunder and lightning and stormy winds. We thought of going to visit you, my dear son, to light a candle in your memory and to lay a wreath on your fresh grave. Forgive us, we are no longer young. You gave your life for us, for our safety, and we were afraid to get wet in the rain.

Eighty–nine days since you left your friends, who continue to protect our country. You were laid on the 26th day of Tishrei according to Jewish tradition (*Kever Yisrael*). This was confirmed by the IDF's *Hevrei Kadisha* who handled your burial, and by the municipal liaison officer. I didn't see your body after your painful death, and we also missed your funeral, carried out as an unknown soldier buried according to Jewish law. Until you were identified, and then on the 27th day of Heshvan, more than 30 days had passed from the day you fell until we, the parents, and your sister received the bitter news. I don't know how or why it happened. They promised me your body remained whole and you were traditionally buried and appropriately honored as a soldier who died. Thank G–d for that.

My dear son, what can I tell you? You were six when we arrived in Israel. You loved to sing Hebrew and Israeli songs. Your entire life was one long song. You fell on the day the entire country sang and was happy, on the *Simkhas Torah* holiday. But this year, not one of the Jews in Israel celebrated with song. They mourned the sons who had fallen in heavy combat in a holy war for the survival of the nation.

I believe, and I always will believe, that Jews will continue to celebrate the *Simkhas Torah* holiday with singing and dancing. That is exactly what you fought for, so we could live in our country as a free people, and if there is meaning in your falling, then it is so the people of Israel could live in their own country and build it through song. But our heart, a parents' heart, will always grieve for you, my dear son.

Your life was one large song. You loved to sing while you worked when you studied, always. For those alive and living, for those who fell for their nation, and for those individuals who died a natural death when their time came.

You loved to read history books, you appreciated the heroism of Jewish warriors throughout the years who sacrificed their lives for the integrity and existence of Israel.

At the local school, you planned to be a pilot, and to this end you were an active member of the aviation club. You built models of airplanes and studied their secrets. And in the army, you went to the armor corps. I remember you, Rami, in the Six Day War. You had yet to serve in the IDF, but you were protecting us? Do you remember how you took care of the sick and wounded?

And when you were older, you told us: until now, my dear parents, you have protected me, provided anything that was lacking, and from now on, it is I who must protect and take care of you, and that is what you did. You helped with every household chore. You worked to fund your university studies, and not just

[Page 42]

for yourself. You helped all your friends in their studies. You made sure that they, too, could fund their studies, to the point you never missed any workdays so you could help them. Because you knew the situation their parents were in.

During *shiva* people came, mostly to console us. Among them was Ms. Klein, who said, you don't know me, but it is my obligation to get to know you. I am Rachel's mother. She studied biology together with your son at Tel Aviv University. I am sure you heard her name. And she continued, in a few days, I am entering the hospital for surgery, and I am uncertain what my fate will be. It is my responsibility to tell you that following an operation I had three months ago, you son donated blood for me. He also took care of my daughter and had long conversations with her to divert her attention from her depression due to my condition.

On January 11, 1974, the 16th day of Tevet a man from Haifa named Yaakov Mile came to see us. He was the age of our late son, Rami. In the beginning, he was unable to say anything. After several minutes he collected himself and told us with teary eyes, my military service was spent with Rami, not in the same tank team, but in the same unit. I was discharged from the hospital a few days ago due to an injury suffered in the war. I was released from the army due to my injuries, which have yet to heal. Thanks to your son I am alive and with you today. He was there for us, the members of the unit, like a brother. He was the one who risked his own life to rescue me, wounded, from a burning tank while under enemy fire. And here again, I must emphasize, thanks to your son, Rami, I am alive, and the tears continued to fall from his eyes.

Days go by and people continue to come. Officers and soldiers from the unit in which my son served. Teachers and students from the university where my son studied, acquaintances and friends. We heard only good things about our late son, Rami, and this all appeared to us as in the singing of a wonderful life.

And we want to believe and hope that Jews will forever continue their lives through song, and they will surely sing on *Simkhas Torah*, and the singing of our son's life will never cease. And the voices of many thousands will echo a great song, the song of peace.

The Father of a Soldier

[Page 43]

Captain Yeshayahu Makovitzki z"l

Translated from Hebrew by Marshall Grant

Captain Yeshi'ahu Makovitzky (Shayka), of blessed memory

Son of Shaul and Miriam

Fell in the Yom Kippur War on the southern front, on 23 Tishrei, 5734, October 19, 1973

IDF authorization of rank, September 19, 1968
Awarded the rank of second lieutenant

[Page 44]

Bereavement

Edna Makovitzky

לו פסק הלב הלוכו

לו קשה בשרנו כאבן

לא לכאוב

את השכול

העוקד

ומאכל

בבתרים

אל אלוהי צבאות

הוא הבן

ויחיד

ואותו שאהבנו

איך שלחת ידך אל הנער ?

[Page 45]

Somewhere, date: <u>October 13, 1973</u>

How are you? I am doing very well. Here in Sinai, it is cold at night and hot during the day, and I am starting to get used to it and feel at home. Moral is high, and we all hope the war will end soon. We receive food and equipment in abundance, including soap, toothpaste, postcards, sweets, etc. Tell me what's new with you, what is father's exact job in the *Emergency National Economy*, how he came back from Tivon, how mother feels, and how you are doing in general – what's new in the home front.

Hoping to see you soon,

Yours: Shaika

[Page 46]

שתי הגלויות מהחזית : כתובים ביום נפילתו

The above two postcards were written on the day he was killed

[Page 47]

Certificate of completion of IDF officer's academy

[Page 48]

שר הבטחון

גברת מרים ובני שאול מקוביצקי היקרים ,

הרשו נא לי להשתתף בכל לב באבלכם בהילקח סכם ישעיהו ז"ל.

סרן ישעיהו מקוביצקי ז"ל נתן את חייו למען כולנו. הוא נפל בחזית הדרום בתלחמה יום הכפורים והובא לקבורה ביום כ"ח בתשרי תשל"ד (21.10.73).

ישעיהו ז"ל שירת כקצין קבע בחיל האספקה. הוא היה בוגר קורס קצינים וקורס קציני האספקה. ישעיהו הוגדר כקצין בעל יוזמה, תושיה, אחראי, מסור ואהוד. תחת אש הדריך את חייליו להמשיך במשימה, לאחר נפילתו הועלה לדרגת סרן.

זכרו של סרן ישעיהו מקוביצקי ז"ל הינו קודש ונשמרנו בלבנו בגאון.

יהא זכרו ברוך.

ב י ק י ,

בשם דיין - רב-אלוף (מיל')
שר הבטחון

נשלח תשל"ד
בינואר 1974

Minister of Defense

Dearest Mr. and Mrs. Shaul and Miriam Makovitzky,

Allow me to express my sympathies to you in this difficulty time after the loss of your son Yeshi'ahu, of blessed memory.

Captain Yeshi'ahu Makovitzky, of blessed memory, gave his life for his homeland. He fell on the southern front during the Yom Kippur War and was buried on the 25th of Tishrei, 5734, October 21, 1973.

Yeshi'ahu served as an officer in the standing military in the Supply Corps. He was a graduate of the IDF officers' academy and supply officer's course. Yeshi'ahu was known for taking the initiative, being aware of his surroundings, responsible, dedicated and loved. Under fire he instructed his soldiers how to continue in their mission. He was promoted posthumously to the rank of captain.

The memory of Captain Yeshi'ahu Makovitzky, of blessed memory is holy and engraved with honor in our hearts.

May his memory be blessed.

> Sincerely,
> [signature]
> Moshe Dayan, Major-General (Res.)
> Minister of Defense

Tevet 5734
January 1974

[Page 49]

The Plea of a Bereaved Father
to Our Merciful and Compassionate Father in Heaven

"Out of the depths have I cried unto thee, oh God. God, hear my voice: let thine ears be attentive to the voice of my prayers." Psalms 130

We are Holocaust refugees, we lost everyone dear to us over 25 years ago. We have gathered here, broken in our bodies, but not in our spirit, to build our future here, to make sure a Holocaust will not happen again, to ensure our children will be free in our safe country. We have turned the country that was nothing but wilderness since the destruction of the second temple into a blossoming heaven for our children.

And here we are again facing a Holocaust, and our children, who we thought would grow up safely in our country, had to go to war, a bloody war. Yom Kippur: while the State of Israel fasted and prayed in synagogues, enemy tanks and soldiers from the north and south penetrated the country. War. Thousands of our sons leave synagogues, do not break their fasts, and run to their units to join those defending our homeland. Many continued their prayers on the way to the front, "to recognize the sanctity of the day", and the sanctity of that day was not violated. The opposite is true, sanctity came from our sons joining as soldiers to protect our country, the country you promised us. Thousands fell in this bloody war.

Oh merciful and compassionate father! Until when? Hasn't the land of Israel soaked up enough blood, haven't we sacrificed enough?

More than 25 years ago we stood, remnants from the Holocaust, and prayed and said *Kaddish* to elevate the souls of our parents, brothers and sisters who died in the Holocaust. And now thousands from those same remnants stand in prayer to elevate the souls of the sons who fell in this cruel campaign.

Abraham our forefather, the father of the Jewish nation, was commanded "Take your son, your only son, whom you love, and sacrifice him", and when Abraham carried out the commandment, a redeeming angel appeared and called, "Do not lay a hand on the boy!!" Merciful and compassionate father, thousands of our youth have been sacrificed on the nation's alter in the Yom Kippur War, where is the angel who calls: Do not lay a hand on the young boys!

Were we not faithful in our beliefs to you? For 2000 years, what haven't we suffered, your nation Israel? Decrees, pogroms, inquisitions, and we remained loyal to you. Haven't we sacrificed enough? Haven't thousands of Jews gone to inquisition alters with *Shema Yisrael* on their lips?

Please! Merciful and compassionate father!

From the deepest depth of our hearts, we call you, oh God. God, hear my voice: let thine ears be attentive to the voice of thousands of bereaved fathers. When we stand in prayer and recite *Kaddish* for the elevation of the souls of our sons, accept with compassion and understanding our prayer, the verse that ends the *Kaddish*:

May he who makes peace in his high places grant peace upon us and upon all of Israel…

[Page 50]

To the Memory of My Blessed Family

by Shaul Makovitzky

Translated from Hebrew by Marshall Grant

Much has been written about the Holocaust inflicted on European Jewry by German Nazis, during our life.

I would like to recognize, with utmost respect, the memory of my mother, Evicha, from the Pozner family; my brothers: Eliezer and Shlomo, and my sister Hila, all still so young. And to everyone from the family of my father, of blessed memory, who passed from a terminal sickness two years before the war broke out.

Thirty years have passed since this appalling disaster, and only by chance I am not among them, as my family demanded that I not return as war was about to erupt.

The years have gone by, day by day, full of sorrow and sadness, immersed in bereavement and saturated with longing. It still hangs over me after all these years, and the pain does not cease, and the sorrow does not diminish. And now, a terrible disaster has fallen upon me, and my beloved son, Yeshia'hu, of blessed memory, may god avenge him, fell in the Yom Kippur war when he was only 24 years old.

And thus, I have paid everything dear to me and my only hope has been extinguished.

May his memory be forever remembered.

[Page 51]

Przyjm ode mnie serdeczne pozdro
wienia Hela

[Page 52]

A picture of the synagogue (drawn from memory)

[Page 53]

The Last Dance

by Y. L. L. Shlomi

Translated by Roberta Paula Books

G-d of mine, you who promised Abraham, Isaac, and Jacob to multiply your chosen people as the stars in the heavens, as the grains of sand on the earth, the great one that has created this.

I, your small servant and shepherd of your sheep, do not dare to say your name.

You, omnipotent one, who raised the hand of Abraham, your chosen one, to kill the kidnapper of Lot, his brother's son, and through his mouth said that anyone who raised a hand to a Jew must be killed.

How did such a power come into being that strives to destroy your beloved people, whose priority is to offer him prayers and love songs? G-d of mine, did you really turn your face away from your people and allow them to be eaten alive by these soulless beasts? G-d of mine, strengthen my spirit so it will not fall into doubt. G-d of mine, from the flames of Sodom you saved the pure ones, and here you allow everyone to die? G-d, do you not see that the universal leader of the churches blesses the weapons of this murder machine? Dear G-d! Do not abandon your people...

Rebbe ... Rebbe ... listen to me. Rebbe, listen, it's me, the blond Itche. Rebbe ... huh. He looked at me with tired astonished eyes, as if he was returning from a far, difficult journey.

Do you not see, Itche, everything is breaking and falling apart.

I see, Rebbe. I wanted to, I must speak with you. Should we not be removing the Torah scrolls from the synagogue to save them from the flames that await them?

Think it over for a while.

No! Itche, we are not permitted. The synagogue is locked and sealed. Anyone who enters there will be killed. Now under these conditions, we must think differently. Anyone who wants to defend the totality of the Torah will fall. Now we must protect the honor of the Torah as well as protect human life. If we survive, Itche, we will, with G-d's help, glorify the Torah and give it its proper honor.

And you, Itche? – You!

What about me, Rebbe? I feel I am unable to endure this. Is He that strong?

And now, Rebbe, everyone is against us?

[Page 54]

Listen to me Itche. You good, devoted righteous Itche, listen and let others know, that one must also know how to die, and that very often we must defend the honor of man and our people. And as for the Books of the Torah, it may be preferable that the Torah scrolls go up in flames, because they symbolize our spirituality and our exceptionalism. It is better that they do not become a laughingstock.

Summer that year was dry, without rain. The wheat was beginning to yellow, the trees were bending under the weight of the harvest. Life this year was tiresome and stilted, the unrest paralyzed the spirit. Meanwhile the Days of Awe drew nearer, they were here.

In past years it rained on Sukkot, but not this year, as if nature was serving them. The death machine was working. Jews were burdened with taxes. Meanwhile, Jews were being captured on the spot and put to work. They openly mocked the Jews, forcing them to do excruciating gymnastics. They cut off half of a Jew's beard, making his face appear as a deformed grimace or paralyzed. Robberies, abuses, cruel humiliation.

And the Jews – and the Jews waited, as if frozen. They felt this was the beginning, while understanding that from the point of pain until the end is a long way, a long way filled with chaotic troubles.

They planned to burn down the synagogue without warning, and to heighten the travesty they chose the night of Shmini Atzeret. Even though the Jews comported themselves correctly day and night, this was a terrible blow. Even for those who did not frequently attend synagogue, this was a shocking experience.

The synagogue stood quiet, grey, at the end of the street and looked at the town from its height as though its mandate was unaffected, its door closed until, until ...

You enter the synagogue, taken by the hand by your father, and now a shudder goes through your body physically. G-d's spirit lives here. You look around not knowing where to focus your eyes. Father tells you to pray and a change comes over your body. The systematic swaying and gentle ringing of the crystal chandeliers was as if they were praying with us, and the half round ceiling showed the sky with colorful stars illustrating the symbols of the twelve signs of the zodiac. On the south wall was

[Page 55]

a painting of Rachel's tomb. This was the creation of our genius artist Monish Sayka. On the east wall on both sides of the ark were long narrow windows with colored glass. Over the ark was a window with blue and white panes in the shape of a "Star of David".

The Holy Ark stood silently and housed our holy books, the greatness, the intellect, and the purity of our people. The symbol of "we are your chosen ones".

And when you are called up to read the Torah, you physically feel the connection to the great one-and-only, the highest and oldest and the greatest in the world. You go up on the platform wrapped in a prayer shawl and begin the blessing, and you are so overwhelmed that it never sounds like you would want it to.

Along the length of the west and northern wall, the women's section was built up and covered in artistic carved pillars, where our women would pray on Saturdays and holidays. On those days the prayers took place with a chant that entirely carried you away.

Now the synagogue stands both deaf and orphaned. It is sealed and the great storied key is no longer in the hands of Itche, the beadle (Shames).

A couple of days earlier, a few individuals in grey green uniforms had driven in in a military car carrying some karnisten (קארניסטען) and also some sort of material that had the look of beat-up packages. The town waited.

A cold-bloodedness came over the Jewish population. The days lasted forever, a quiet tempo preparing for suffering. A few held a quiet, far away protest.

It was a clear night. The police forced everyone into their houses. Curtains covered the windows, the street lights were dark, and the streets were dead. One could hear only the rhythmic sound of horseshoes. Something happens around the synagogue; the lights are extinguished in the Jewish homes. With uneasiness and caution, people look out their windows.

By the trees and by the gates around the synagogue, darkness. It is the night of Shmini Atzeres and the synagogue showed some sort of light. At first it seemed like something was probing, seeking, a reddish blue tongue of a flame. It crawled, it climbed, it searched around the podium. It spread out through the pillars of the women's section. Through the windows of the synagogue, you could now see a red bloody flame with smoke, the flames rise and fall, searching and groping, licking the fruit

[Page 56]

near the Holy Ark. The walls become black and the colors explode. The building trembles, bursting into a wild singing and the chandeliers ring out. A pitiless murmur, the flames crackle in a wild dance and search for an exit.

At the same time some people quietly opened the rabbi's door. Old and young came from the furthest corners of town, knowing that this deed threatened their lives. Approximately fifteen men gathered. Among them were Monish Sayka, Yakov Yakubovitz, the son of Krel the tailor, Pinkhas Raukh, Hersh Zingerman, Yakov Burnshteyn, the blond Itche, Itche the beadle and his son-in-law, Yekhezkel Mordkhai Lentshitsky, Abel Kora, and a few other established men. Pleading with outstretched arms, Rebbe, permit us, we want to rescue the Torah scrolls. The Rebbe was deeply moved with their devotion and after a long pause gave them the same answer he had given his assistant Itche a few days earlier. However…

Father, how can you. Why? Even when you disagree with us, don't you feel the pain of your people? Even Hershye Bup is calling you.

It hurts Mordkhai, it really hurts. But I'm not ready to die for material things.

No father, no father, you are not right. Dying as a protest without tangible usefulness is better than dying without a protest, and perhaps we will succeed, I can't agree. I am the unnoticed and often laughed at son of Hershye Bup Frankenshteyn.

From Greenblat's house, a shadow jumped across the street, and with a cat's assuredness crawled through the shadows of the houses at the old marketplace, passed through, jumped the fence of Kubiak's yard and from there ran freely through the gardens. He slid like a lion with great speed. No dog barked. He was already in the garden of Lamen Malkovsky. He then feels the heat from the fire in his face. He jumps around the last part and sneaks over to the window of the synagogue anteroom; with open hands he pushes out a pane. Then rings out a single shot …

The flames spread. They surrounded the Holy Ark like a bouquet of fire. They surrounded the podium and bit of the pillars of the women's section. Elijah the prophet's old chair was also burning. The flames were noisy, squirming and writhing, falling and rising. The Holy Ark shuddered. The women's section was about to

[Page 57]

collapse. The windows formed nightmarish figures out of the flames. With a resounding crash, the Holy Ark fell, the tablets shattered. The parchment of the Torah scrolls screeched and writhed, the letters poured out and vaporized. The women's section collapsed with a loud bang. The gases knocked out the windows and fire flew out of the holes with a wild laughter. The burned-out ceiling no longer protected the roof, the tin sheets rose and fell, the roof breathed.

Dear G-d, why do you punish us? Do not turn your face away from us. Show yourself and save your people.

G-d of mine, protect me from bad thoughts. It cannot be correct when people say religion does not help the weak.

G-d of mine, protect me from doubt. I want to serve you and be your servant until I take my last breath.

Should I throw away my shepherd's stick and spill blood?

Dear G-d, do not allow your sheep to be persecuted. Perhaps if we did not exist, we would be created?

Dear G-d. Permit me to serve you. Listen to my plea.

At the place where the synagogue stood an apartment building is being built
Photographed by Simkha Noymark, 1965

[Page 58]

Tragedy and pain together can break even the strongest.

This is not a punishment; this is general murder. This is not a sentence – I am going. I will die a martyr's death!

With a scream, the tin sheets tear off from the roof and fall to the feet of the patrolling murderers.

Braindl, take a look, whispered the old man Leybke, the water in the lake is red with our blood.

Look children, you too Malke, said Tuvye Burshteyn, they are burning our synagogue. This is the beginning of the end. Our prayers and pleas did not help.

The fire and smoke reach higher, higher and higher. The entire building danced. The last dance. The last Simchas Torah in town. The columns of smoke reach the sky. The flames rise high and spread like a bouquet of red sparks.

They are like laughing stars in the sky, like grains of sand on the ground.

There is no breeze, no rain, and no help from anywhere. Only the old moon looks down with a sad face and is silent.

And the whole world is silent as well -

Extermination Camp in Chełmno

Translated from Hebrew by Marshall Grant

Testimony from Andrzej Miszczak (Polish spelling) from Chełmno , 49 years old, a Catholic Polish farmer, taken on June 14, 1945, in Chełmno by the investigator of the District Court of Łódź, Wladislaw Bednarz.

I am a permanent resident of the village of Chełmno , located in the Koło district. My house stood across from the palace garden (on the side of the Ner River), and when the palace existed you could see its windows through those in my home. I have 55 hectares of land, and I am the manager of a gardening business.

In the middle of November 1941, a group of Gestapo men came to Chełmno , led by Lange. At the same time, the district administrator arrived from Koło (his name, I don't remember). They thoroughly checked the entire palace, including its basements. At the end of the month, they brought building materials and began to build the camp.

The palace grounds were surrounded by a 2.5–meter–high fence made of tight wood slabs; it was only on the side along the river that an area was left with barbed wire. The palace was situated on the hill in a way that prevented a similar wooden fence to be built. Meaning that the hills' slopes were not enough to conceal what was taking place in the palace courtyard.

In addition to the palace, the S.S. Sonderkommando Kulmhof (the name of the Gestapo company that came to build the camp) took control of the pastor's home, the committee building, the hostel and the homes

[Page 59]

Mrs. Mala Brand (Orbach) bows her head
at the Chełmno memorial during her visit to Poland, 1956

of Chełmno 's farmers. The farmers, whose houses were confiscated, were transferred to other villages or they joined other farms. In the beginning, we did not know why the camp was being built.

On December 9, 1941, the first 900 Jews were brought in vehicles from Koło. They were brought in the evening and held overnight in the palace. In the morning, they were led to dark–painted vehicles (which were later named the "Vehicles from Hell") and taken toward the forest near Chełmno . These vehicles would return after about an hour, and they would take additional groups of Jews from the Palace. We noticed piles of clothes beginning to appear in the palace courtyard. That evening a new shipment arrived from Koło, which remained overnight in the palace, and in the morning, it, too, was taken to the forest near Chełmno . This was happened again and again for several days.

Later, there was a change. The Jews would be brought by truck to the palace, taken inside, and later taken outside and led to the Vehicles from Hell. There were rumors about the vehicles being used for gas poisoning. Despite the complete lack of contact between the guards and the local population, people began to hear about what was taking place in the palace. The sources for our information were the Jews working in manual labor, Poles (eight in number) brought from Poznań, from "the 7th Fort" and who also worked as manual laborers, and local women and girls who worked in the grocery warehouse (canteen) and kitchen.

The guards later changed their attitude towards the population, and much could be learned about what was taking place on the grounds of the extermination camp.

[Page 60]

There were three Vehicles from Hell operating in the Chełmno death camp. One was larger than the other two.

I am unable to describe their construction and dimensions because I don't understand automobiles, and no one was ever allowed to come close to these vehicles. I would often later hear the guards say that 150 people could be put in the large vehicle, and between 80–100 in the small ones. In the beginning, they were bringing one thousand people to Chełmno every day, and guards had a saying, "another day – another thousand". Some of the Jews' belongings were taken in the camp, and some were taken in Chełmno . The Jews would undress in the palace and enter the vehicles wearing only their underwear – they were deceived to believe they were being taken to showers. After the "Vehicle from Hell" would leave, their clothes were thrown through the window into the courtyard. A company of Jewish workers would then take them to the large mountain of clothes in the garden.

This pile was 3–4 meters high, and at least 10–15 meters long. The guards would cruelly prod and beat the Jews who were arranging the clothes. Only after the area was cleaned was another group of Jews brought to the palace. I saw the Jews who worked with the removal of the clothes many times. The fact that they were deceiving the Jews when they were telling them they were being taken to showers was shared by the guards themselves. They thought it was a great idea because it saved them the trouble of dealing with the victims. The clothes were taken to Łódź. The drivers were Poles and not allowed on the palace's grounds; when they arrived, they were ordered to wait on the road. German drivers would bring the vehicles into the courtyard where they were loaded and then returned to the road and the private Polish drivers.

The S.S. distributed large amounts of booty to the local Germans. In the spring, a committee arrived at the camp that included a fat civilian (Ed. Comment – possibly Chaim Rumkowski, head of the Judenrat), who the Jews said was the commander of the Łódź ghetto. The committee demanded that the Sonderkommando Kulmhof accept larger shipments of Jews. These shipments reached between 1,000–2,000 people, and they always arrived by vehicle.

When it became hot, the bodies in the mass grave began to decay, "the ground moved", the air was poisoned over a wide area, and the cases of typhoid multiplied. The Germans stopped receiving shipments, and two ovens were quickly built (the chimneys could be seen) and they began to burn the bodies. They dug mass graves and ordered the Jews (from the special enlarged company – "the Forest Company"!) to burn the bodies in the ovens. I heard the ovens were fueled by wood.

After the burning of the bodies (the break lasted about two months), the Germans again began receiving shipments of Jews. I emphasize that I did not only know of the burning of bodies from the Jews who worked there, but also because the ovens expelled smoke and no shipments were brought in.

The Jews began arriving in the summer of 1942. They arrived on a rail line from Powiercie, alighted and were made to march on foot to the mill in Zawadka. They would sleep in the mill and in the morning be led to vehicles that took them to the palace. From this point on, the order of operation was unchanged. I am unable to recall the exact number of shipments that arrived on the rail line; however,

[Page 61]

according to my account, every shipment contained one thousand people. In addition to the regular rail–line shipments, deliveries also arrived in vehicles.

This continued until April 1943.

In April 1943, the Germans began dismantling the camp and concealing any signs of its existence. They took down the fence, removed items, etc. On April 7, 1943, the palace was blown up. Grass seeds were strewn over the graves (they asked me to provide them with the tools to plant the seeds and the Wachtmeister himself borrowed a rake from me. The ovens were dismantled, and the bricks were taken away. On April 11, 1943, the S.S. Sonderkommando Kulmhof left. Only a small company of guards remained that guarded the site of murder. These guards were from the local guard, the commander was from Sompolno.

When the S.S. Sonderkommando Kulmhof left, they took the Poles who carried out manual labor. There were seven names mentioned here, and there was an eighth Pole named Marian, who were mistakenly put in a vehicle and poisoned by gas. This was the beginning of 1942. They buried him separately in the palace garden. These were the Poles who first dug the mass grave in the forest. They were later sent to other jobs, such as repairing the vehicles, carrying belongings, unloading the vehicles. I didn't hear they were checking the bodies; I didn't hear about any Ukrainians.

In addition to the S.S., there were guards and criminal police; there were between 120–150 Germans operating in Chełmno . This number later grew to almost 180, and for the first time Lange was appointed commander (I don't remember his rank or name).

In spring, change came to the camp's headquarters. Hans Bothmann was appointed as the camp's commander, as acting commander in place of Lange. I remember the names of the Germans who worked in "the Camp of Death".

1.   The Wachtmeister (his name I don't remember) managed the economics department. (Ed. Comment: Watchmaster, an NCO rank, possibly Ernst Burmeister)
2.   Lenz (he was called the cruelest of all the German doctors in Chełmno . This sadist had to kill at least one Jew every day).
3.   Burstinger oversaw the jewelry and valuable items.

The members of the S.S. Sonderkommando Kulmhof initially treated the local population harshly. They were forced to work under the threat of beatings, etc. However, relations later improved and became completely civil.

The S.S. first used the telephone belonging to the village's committee. This meant that the village committee's chairman Stanislaw Kaszinski apparently knew too much, so he was imprisoned and executed. Kaszinski sent a letter to diplomatic legal representation in which he described what was taking place. It seems the letter was intercepted, and Kaszinski and his wife were the only residents of the village executed.

I did not hear that the S.S. Sonderkommando Kulmhof took Polish lovers from the local population. Their lovers were Germans from Koło or from nearby villages.

The first Jews brought to the death camp were Jews from surrounding villages, and later from the Łódź ghetto. Jews from all over the world were brought here: from Hungary, Yugoslavia, Czechoslovakia, France, and Greece. After one of these shipments would arrive, the guards would have cigarettes from the country the shipment originated from. In most cases, the Germans would pay

[Page 62]

for food with cigarettes, so we could know where the shipments were coming from. By the way, the guards didn't conceal these facts. I remember they would say that a shipment of "rich Jews from Vienna" and "rich Jews from Hamburg" had arrived. The people in these shipments had more belongings and were dressed better.

The Jews being led to death would sometimes drop notes. I once picked up one of these notes. The first words were "We are Jews from Lviv". The Jews would tear bills of money and bonds and throw them on the road, they didn't know the truth until the last minute, which is why there was no disobedience. There were also shipments of Poles. We knew when shipments of Poles were about to arrive because the shifts during those days were enlarged. This happened often. I think they once brought a group of nuns, once a group of twelve Polish officers, a large group of Polish children, and more. I, myself, never saw these shipments. I was told about them by women who saw them (Helena Kroll and Victoria Kocznica). After the palace was blown up, there were crosses, medallions, etc., found in the rubble.

The Germans would outwardly display the cross on the palace balcony.

In addition to these large shipments, they would also bring busses carrying individuals to the palace. These people would be added to the other shipments.

The Poles were brought until 1942. I remember that "Tony", the driver, once said, "The Polish vehicle is ready". It appears that there was a relatively larger response to the Poles than expected. I also saw gypsies who were brought in automobiles from Koło.

In the middle of 1942 (I am unsure), the committee from Berlin came and three or four Gestapo officers joined it. They were welcomed with respect and shown the entire area. Kazipszinski, a Polish man, told me that while he was putting gas into the vehicle, one of the Gestapo men made fun of him. The next day we found out that they were not Gestapo, they were from "Foreign Espionage". The guards said, "We thought they were one of us, but they certainly were not".

The Germans kept a precise list of those who were murdered in Chełmno. The Jewish communities were required to pay four German marks for every Jew sent to Chełmno. Every driver had a list of Jews he had to bring. In the winter of 1942, Shalk's apartment caught fire. After the flames were extinguished, they ordered me and M. Lodviski to guard the burnt area and make sure the flames did not reappear. That was when I found the bag (Lodviski didn't see this) belonging to the driver who was called "Tony" and who we called Kołonizacja (idiot). The bag contained various documents concerning the transport of Jews. I don't know German, but I understood what was on those lists. I burned the bag because I was scared the Germans would find it in my possession.

In March 1944, the S.S. Sonderkommando Kulmhof again came to Chełmno. They were the same Germans who were here for almost all of 1942, from the spring until the razing of the camp. Many of them did not return. The commander, like before, was Bothmann. Hapla (?) (הפלה) said he was "somewhere in Greece". High wood–slabbed fences were again erected around the entire garden area. Shacks were brought. Two barracks were built in Chełmno (where the clothes were stored) and two were built in Chełmno's forest.

This time, they would bring the Jews directly to Chełmno and hold them during the night in the church. In the morning, they were taken by vehicle to the Chełmno forest, where they were put into one of the barracks that had a sign hung up that said "doctor" and the word "Pub" scrawled on it.

[Page 63]

This is where the Jews would undress. Then they would be put into the killing vehicles while being told they were being led to the third barracks. The doors would be locked, the motor would start and the vehicle would travel towards the ovens. There the bodies would be removed, and the vehicle would return for an additional shipment.

There were always forty Jews working in the forest; they were called the *Waldkommando* (Forest Company). They were the ones who told us about the methods the Germans were most recently using. They would send Jews to me to bring vegetables, so I was in constant contact with them. The Jews lived in a barn, which was also where the workshops of tailors and cobblers were located. The Jewish tailors were confined with handcuffs on the second floor of the barn. Lately there were forty–seven Jews in Chełmno, before there were eighty to ninety. They were then leasing the small mill to grind the bones and also from Locomobile from Powiercie.

Several months later (around July 1944), efforts to raze the camp began. The Jews said that this time 15,000 people were exterminated in Chełmno. It is hard for me to say if this number is correct. Now there were shipments coming from abroad, from across the Czech border, possibly through the Łódź ghetto. This time they treated the Jews humanely so there wouldn't be any resistance. The clothes, which were in better condition, were shipped to Łódź; worn clothes were shredded in a special machine that was brought there for that purpose, and the shreds were shipped to Łódź. The ovens were destroyed and the bricks thrown into the forest; the mill was returned to Powiercie.

In the beginning of 1942–43, the bones were crushed by hand.

The Poles that had worked before in the camp didn't return this time. The guards told me that three of them (names are mentioned here) are no longer alive, and three (here, too, names are mentioned were sent to Oswiecim (Auschwitz).

When the Soviet troops were approaching, the last Jews were to be executed. They were taken out in groups of five. One of them, Mieczyslaw (Mordchai) Zurawski was armed with a knife and broke through the guards and escaped. The guards were unable to find him. The tailors broke the door that led downstairs and when two Germans entered (among them Lenz), the Jews killed them. The Germans pointed their machine guns at the barn door and opened fire while others set it ablaze.

This is the way the last Jews were destroyed. In addition to Zurawski, another Jew survived, Szymon Srebrnik. The Germans shot him in his forehead and left him for dead, but the wound was not critical, and he survived. I am unaware of Srebrnik's address.

I did not see the vehicle found at Ostrovsky's factory, the (הרטנר) from Powiercie would often come to Chełmno, and suitcases full of belongings would be removed. In 1944, a supervisor named Greiser came to supervise Chełmno. I think he also came in 1942. The grounds of the Chełmno death camp were meticulously guarded. The password was changed every day and sent from Poznań.

This hereby ends the protocol, and after reading it, I have come to sign: –

(–) Andrzej Miszczak. (–) Wladyslaw Bednarz, investigative judge.

[Page 64]

On the Day of Slaughter

by Reuven Yamnik

Translated from Hebrew by Jerrold Landau

And it was at the morning watch[1] – a regular, grey morning
Mist covered all existence
Dark and light were still intermixed
And the first sunrays were rising above.

    It was quiet in the ghetto, in the old market.
    Jews were cramped in terrible conditions
    In rooms that were holes, like graves
    With broken roofs and shaky walls.

The tormented Jews were between sleep and wakefulness
After a harsh, tiring day of work
They were lying down, hungry and beaten, powerless
In fear – what will tomorrow bring – who knows?

Jews praying before being taken out to be murdered by the Nazis, may their names be blotted out

[Page 65]

Every slight rustle casts fear into their hearts
Every suspicious motion curdles their blood,
In fear and terror, they hide in their hiding places
They know that their day of disaster is approaching.

The sun rises and casts its rays
A pleasant, spring sun caresses,
"How lovely is the day," says Mother to her children
As she secretly wipes her tears in her apron.

Suddenly, on a bright day, it swoops like lightening
The decree falls upon the Jews
"*Juden Raus*" Get out quickly
"Anyone who hesitates will certainly be shot."

Screams, cries, to the midst of the skies
Terror, fear, running, panic,
Crying children beg for bread and water
The end and destruction of the community approaches.

The youths attempt to save their lives
To flee for their lives from the descent to the grave,
A flight to the fields, through every route and path
They ask their neighbors of yesterday to hide them…

Good neighbor, take a ring – pure gold
It is an heirloom from our ancestors.
Just hide me please in an attic or a pit
For the disaster has approached, the destruction in our homes.

However, the gentile neighbor exults and shouts
Shrugs his shoulders, grits his teeth
"Go away, puny Jew, your end has come…
Indeed, we have awaited this day all our lives."

And in all houses, panicked running
Men, women, youths, and children
Every window is open, every door is broken open
They hasten and run – a large Jewish multitude.

A little girl cries that she cannot run
"Mommy, take me by my hands"

[Page 66]

The mother has another child in her arms
A bundle of food, a bottle of water…

"The father had been sent to the camp some time ago
He has already been incinerated in the fiery furnace

And we, my child are being sent to – where?
Perhaps we will meet Father there…"

    Shots and whips, and Satanic shouts
    Go forth stronger and stronger, deafening the ears.
    Young and old ones, hasten your steps
    For all you puny Jews are still alive.

Frightful scenes, making the hair stand on edge
Weeping and sobbing to the midst of the heavens
Like sheep to the slaughter, old and young are led,
Women, children, and suckling babies.

    Their feet pace through the streets of the city
    The toil of generations remains behind them
    Everyone one has their small bundle in their hands
    The rest they left for pillage by their enemies.

Here are the "enlightened" neighbors and acquaintances
Girded in joy over the loot before their eyes
"The accursed Jews have left."
And now they can live in their houses.

    And through the entire route, a wild crowd
    Laughs, exults, and claps their hands
    "Behold the awaited day has arrived
    And we have been freed from the sneaky Jews."

And now, the entire holy community
Broken, weakened, howling and weeping,
Like sheep to the slaughter, without a leader at the head
Are cruelly pushed into the church building…

    Cramped, crowded, the dead and the living lie
    On the floor of the church, covered with blood
    The screams of the children and infants break through the heavens
    Not arousing mercy, for there is no compassion in judgment.

[Page 67]

    And on the bitter day, 7 Iyar, 5702
    They are all pushed into hellish vehicles
    And are taken to the Chelmno death camp
    Where they all disappear in the crematoria.

    In their final moments, in the throes of death
    Parents, brothers, and sisters embrace
    Shema Yisrael is uttered on their lips
    "Revenge for our blood – remember and do not forget."[2]

Millions were murdered, a nation was annihilated
Thousands of communities, towns, and cities
Including the community of Przedecz, were hauled there
To the gigantic cemetery without graves.

The city (Przedecz) was emptied of all its Jews forever
There is no brother, no sister, no mother, and no father.
We have become orphans, we will weep and recall their memory forever
And recite *Yisgadal Ve Yiskadash Shmei Raba.*[3]

Translator's Footnotes:

1. Exodus 14:24
2. Based on Deuteronomy 24: 17-19
3. The opening words of Kaddish.

Chełmno Cries to the Heavens

Translated from Yiddish by Janie Respitz

A heavy sadness lies in our pained hearts. This sadness is called – Chełmno . This singular word conveys so much cruelty, so much pain and suffering. Innocent blood was spilled, young lives of hundreds of thousands of Jews ripped apart, young and old, women and small children in this isolated place between Koło and Dombia, where the German murderers killed three hundred and fifty thousand Jews.

Here is where hundreds of Pshaytsher Jews (the town's Polish name is Przedecz, its Hebrew name is Pshedetz) were murdered by the Nazi criminals, and their innocent spilled blood cries to the heavens.

Chełmno was the first death camp for Jews in Poland. This is where the murderers tried, for the first time, the new method of mass killing by gas. This was the beginning of a methodical preplanned action to totally wipe out European Jewry. At first the murders were carried out in a very primitive way. They brought a group of "criminals" in trucks

[Page 68]

to the forest. They told them to dig their own graves, lie down facing the ground, and shot them with one shot in the head. Soon the German executioners turned to more "cultured" methods. They transformed the magnificent mansion in Chełmno into a "bathing establishment". Three modern gas trucks were provided to serve the "bathing establishment", beginning this devilish game … then they began to bring transports of Jews from the surrounding area. They brought them to the mansion where a large sign hung with the words "bathing establishment". An S.S. man explained to the newly arrived Jews that before they can go to work, they must bathe. Once the Jews had undressed and stood naked, the S.S. beat them pitilessly and sent them to the other side of the mansion where the gas trucks were waiting. Around 80-100 people were shoved into one truck. Once the doors were hermetically shut you could hear the heartrending screams, which lasted a few minutes. As the motor ran, a large quantity of benzene was produced. The poisonous burning gas entered the floor of the sealed truck through two pipes, poisoning the air which those stuffed in the truck had to breathe. The people started to choke … after a short time all was quiet.

After driving a few kilometers into the forest, they reached the "Death Brigade" whose job was to bury the dead. The trucks were unloaded quickly so as not to waste any time. The dead were laid *en masse* in the graves. This method proved to be impractical since the corpses began to pollute the air. So, in a large clearing, they built two primitive crematoria where they began to systematically burn the corpses. The crematoria were nothing more than long iron rails which served as furnace grates upon which they placed a layer of wood and on the wood a layer of the dead, poured benzene on everything and set it on fire. The bones which did not burn entirely were ground in a special mill. The ground human bones were put in bags and sent to be used to build the walls of guard posts and as fertilizer. The clothing of the deceased was brought to a church in Dombia. The off-loading and sorting were done by Jews, who were brought there every day

[Page 69]

from Chełmno to work. To prevent them from running away, their feet were shackled in chains.

Transports of Jews began to arrive in Chełmno. First from the surrounding area, and then Jews and non-Jews began to arrive from abroad. Due to the influx of transports, they used all the surrounding churches to contain the people until their death.

The 7th of Iyar 5702, April 24th, 1942, was the saddest day for Pshaytsher Jews. On this day, the barbarians sent more than 600 of our closest ones, the last remaining Jews of our town, to Chełmno to be gassed and burned.

When this annihilation action was completed in Chełmno, the German criminals destroyed the mansion so no remnant of their deeds would remain.

They also destroyed the crematoria in the forest.

From all the Jewish transports, forty-five specialists were kept alive to work in the tailor shop. When the Red Army approached Chełmno on the nights of January 16-17, 1945, the Germans confined all the workers to the shop and began, in groups, to shoot them. When one worker tried to stab two of the Gestapo, the Germans poured benzene and set the shop on fire with everyone still inside.

As in all the other death camps, the German barbarians in Chełmno attempted to wash away all traces of their crimes after their great defeat, but they did not succeed.

Besides surviving witnesses, the local Polish population saw and knew a lot, and there were also silent witnesses to the German atrocities.

One of the silent witnesses was the ruined castle the Germans destroyed when the Red Army arrived.

Another witness was the mill which ground the human non-burned bones. It remained standing near where they made bonfires.

The willows near the small river were also silent witnesses of the horrific, bloody murders. The same river where they threw the ashes of burned people.

The fields fertilized with human ashes of our martyrs also stand as silent witnesses.

[Page 70]

Also, the fruit trees soaked with the blood of hundreds of thousands of Jews.

Another silent witness is the empty mansion in the forest where the secret of hundreds of thousands of gassed and buried-alive Jews lies deep. Everything extracted from there was handed over to the bonfires.

Chełmno will remain one of the saddest chapters of Jewish martyrdom.

Chełmno will remain as all the other extermination camps like Majdanek, Treblinka, Sobibor, Auschwitz, an eternal stain of shame on the conscience of the German people.

*Mrs. Khave Musman (Zielinsky) with her husband and
daughter at the memorial monument at Chełmno*

Excerpt from the Book "Destruction and Uprising" From the Jews From Warsaw

Chełmno was a village on the Ner River, approximately twelve kilometers from the city of Koło (Koyl in Yiddish) on the road from Warsaw to Poznań, where it appears the first large extermination camp in Poland was built in 1940, where the Jews from western Polish regions were murdered, and from Kalish and Łódź regions – the region the Germans called Warthegau.

[Page 71]

The extermination system – gas poisoning in large special trucks. The Jews sent there were taken to the nearby forest. According to the numbers of the Central Commission of Investigation of German Crimes, 330 thousand people were killed in Chełmno. Jewish sources say 300 thousand Jews were murdered there.

These overviews of the Chełmno Death Camp were taken from the book "From the Holocaust Era"

The Chełmno Death Camp at the Beginning of its Operation

Translated from Yiddish by Jerrold Landau

At the end of November 1940, the Gestapo came to Chełmno in the Koło District. This place was selected by the Hitlerist executioners as a vale of death. Panic arose amongst the population, as they burnt down the house of the priest, the garage, and many other buildings. The renovation of all sections, as well as the hall of the local palace, was completed on December 9, so that they would be ready to receive people. That day, the first shipment of Jews arrived from the city of Koło, numbering seven hundred individuals. Shipments from Dombia [Dąbie] and other nearby towns were brought to Chełmno during the night. Until the spring, they would bring daily shipments of up to 2,000 individuals. These people were taken to the nearby forest, three kilometers from the palace in Chełmno. The vale of murder was prepared in this kilometer-long area. Trees were cut down in two places, and two fields were created. In one field, pits were dug, six meters wide and sufficiently deep, in which they would place the corpses of the people who were brought there. In the other field, they began to build crematoria, to burn the corpses of the victims. The Germans would trick the people arriving in Chełmno, stating that they would be traveling to work, and that their lives were not in danger. Before they brought the victims to the forest, they would bring them to the palace, where they were ordered to strip. Then they would force the stark-naked people onto vehicles, without sparing beatings from whips. The vehicles were hermetically sealed. Within these vehicles were special mechanisms that caused exhaust gas to enter the vehicle, so that the people in the vehicle would be poisoned even before they arrived in the forest. This mode of operation continued until June 1944, when it was stopped due to the rotting of the corpses that were placed in the pits. In the meantime, crematoria had been built, in which they began to cremate the corpses of the victims.

Later, shipments from other cities in Poland, Romania Czechoslovakia, and other places began to arrive. This continued until December 1943. The clothing of the victims was sent to Germany. The crime was covered up, the place was bombarded, and the vale of murder was covered with grass.

The first commandant of the camp was Lange [1], and then Major Bothmann [2]. His deputy was Oberlieutenant Otto Lange, and then Plata, the commander of the shipments. Burstinger oversaw the receiving of gold and valuables. He was later appointed as director of the cremation materials. Landmeister served as the physician. The overseers of the crematoria were Runge and Klatshmer [3]. Neufela [4] ran the enterprise.

Translator's footnotes:
1. See https://en.wikipedia.org/wiki/Herbert_Lange
2. See https://en.wikipedia.org/wiki/Hans_Bothmann
3. Probably Kretschmer. See https://www.holocaust-lestweforget.com/Chełmno -perpetrators.html
4. Probably Häfele. See https://www.holocaust-lestweforget.com/Chełmno -perpetrators.html

[Page 72]

The Murders in Chełmno – 1944–1945

Translated from Hebrew by Marshall Grant

In March of 1944, the Gestapo came to Chełmno and again began to prepare the camp for groups of workers, such as tailors, cobblers, and more. They later built two structures: one was used to store gold and valuable belongings, and the second was for clothes and various items that were stolen from the people who arrived.

Two huge ovens were built in the forest to burn the bodies along with two additional structures. In one of the buildings the people who arrived were made to undress, and the second was used as a bathhouse and on the third was writing stating the doctor was examining patients inside.

The first shipment of prisoners arrived in Chełmno in the month of June. They were transferred to the local church where they remained until the next day. They were crowded tightly into the church, tired, hungry, and thirsty. They almost suffocated.

The next day, the trucks arrived and they began taking people to the forest, to the shacks, to the doctor; they deceived the people and told them that they were being taken to work. The people were taken into the structure where they were ordered to strip off their clothing. They were told they were being taken to a bathhouse. They were made to write postcards to their families and friends that said:

We have arrived in Munich. The journey passed peacefully. We are very good. Life is very good. We are working at dismantling houses that were bombed.

Others were ordered to write letters with similar content and indicate in the address that they were in Leipzig.

The families that received these postcards were happy and willingly registered for upcoming shipments.

This is the way that almost 15,000 people were poisoned with gas for three consecutive months. There were reports of people being cooked alive in Chełmno. Everything but the skeleton, which was sent to Berlin, was discarded.

The Red Army stopped this. The Nazis began razing all the facilities they had used for the murders. They left 87 Jews for this task.

On the night of January 17, 1945, when the Red Army was approaching Chełmno, the Nazis killed the last of these Jews. The Nazis took them out in groups of five, five of those who lived in the same building. They ordered the Jews to lie down and they were shot in the head. Twenty had been killed when the Jews resisted after understanding what was happening to those who had been taken. The resistance killed two Gestapo soldiers. The resistors were burned alive in the barn. One Jew, Macislav Zurawski, succeeded in escaping the barn and survived. Another Jew, Shimon Srebrnik, 15 years old, lay outside amongst the dead and he too was able to escape. Following the murder, on January 17, 1945, at 10:00 in the morning, the Nazis left Chełmno.

[Page 73]

The Last Hours

by Y. Y. L.

Translated from Yiddish by Roberta Paula Books

Translator's note: Written down by Y. Y. L., as related to him by Sala Goldman Mandlinger. The teenager Sala obtained a written permit enabling her to take a brief leave from her work detail and visit her family. She was allowed to rejoin her work detail, in part because of the written permit and in part, it seems, because one of the German officers in charge was favorably inclined towards her. Thus, her extraordinary eyewitness account.

My uncle came home at five am, drained of color and dispirited, speaking softly: the shtetl is surrounded. We knew what that meant. It was over. What did this mean? This meant that it was finished, that at eight am we must be in the church, there was no way out.

Already several days ago, they had announced that on 24.4.42 all those still clinging to life must assemble in the church under threat of harm. They announced this with the help of Oyfek, as though this world was normalized, like sweeping the streets or raking the grass from between the stones as in Sklodowski's times (i.e., when Jews were serfs to the lords). Even before the designated hour, Jews had begun to gather, as though they would soon be at the end.

You saw walking the remnants of families, as though to their own funeral. Mothers carrying small children in their arms, also small children who held onto their mother's skirt. Old women, old men, sick people who were supported under their arm. Not one complete family; everyone already had someone missing. They had been transported out to work in the labor camp, tortured to death, killed on the spot. They dragged the remnants of the Jewish families. Weary, starving, beaten down, there were only a few young men among them. This time, the Poles did not laugh or rebuke. Included among them were some men who were supposed to have been deported. Although they were identified, going to be turned in, and captured, clandestine individuals very actively helped. We were some sort of wild beast, their latest diversion. We were permitted to rut without penalty, each time. They even gave us a prize for this. And that was even recognized as virility. Next to the corpses hanging on the gallows, the Nazis took photographs and films and sent these souvenirs home to their parents and their loved ones.

And after everyone was already gathered, they still searched their homes. There was no place left to hide. Yes. Two individuals chose not to show up. Shmuel Abe Abramovitch, who had hidden himself at the home of the Christian shoemaker Ostrushke, who that same day turned him into the SA Mann Henkel (a local follower of Hitler, a criminal and robber), who robbed him of everything he had on him and then shot him. (*Translator's note*: SA is an abbreviation for Sturmabteilung, a group created in 1921 by Hitler.) The second was Menachem Rufsky, who hid

[Page 74]

in the Jakubow forest, and there he was murdered by a local follower of Hitler, Fredrich Henebower.

In the church, those who had been assembled were guarded by members of the SS. Each of those gathered had brought something with them. Maybe a small package, a bit of food, a bottle of water, a bit of clothing. Others also brought a bit of jewelry, a watch. People had reasoned and hoped for perhaps a miracle. To purchase a human spark of pity from the executioner. But no such miracle happened. They took all the packages from the people. The old woman Khava Vayden had brought with her a small basket with a bit of food and a bottle of water for her yet older husband Mordchai Ber. It could be that she had also hidden

This photo was in the possession of a German soldier, who
was taken captive by our friend Yitzhok Levine

the 50–year–old wedding band, and her entire wealth, and she simply couldn't let go of it out of her hand, and the SS man fought with the old lady and told her you need nothing, none of you need anything. These are your last hours. The Germans beat them, pushed and beat them: You aren't standing correctly, you aren't sitting correctly. They searched for reasons to justify their cruel habits, their wild instincts.

There were about six hundred Jews for the last walk.

What was collected was a little mountain of packages, and

[Page 75]

the murderous eyes gleefully looked at this pile of packages and beat them with great glee also. They beat them with sticks, with police batons, with whips, with feet, with bare hands, they hit a lot, with joy and laughter, until they were satisfied. But no one cried, no one screamed, not even the children. Not even a groan, not even a Jewish painful groan was heard. Yes, something was heard. A sort of a murmur. Men said their Vidui (confession of sins).

Someone in a corner had dropped something onto the cement floor, and he squashed it, and one of the murderers heard it. He was furious, and he beat this man. Meanwhile, he speculated with great fury. Such a guy you break, but you don't break a watch. And he couldn't calm himself.

And the Jews prayed quietly to G–d. Quietly, without voice. With pale lips. Many had lips that didn't move and very dry eyes raised to the heaven, and they stood like that.

No. No. Dogs did not guard them. Except them, no living creature was guarding them.

Around 12 o'clock, big, heavy trucks, draped with black tarps arrived. With screams and beatings, the remnants of the Pshaytsh (Przedecz) Jews were chased onto the trucks. That is when a wail broke out. A loud, unrestrained cry. This was a frightening cry. I never heard such a cry. Not before and not since. The worst is that no one was in a condition to record this frightening cry.

I don't know what kind of trucks these were. I also don't know how many there were. Maybe they were gas chambers on wheels. I can say no more. They were covered with black tarps.

But from those machines I saw no one come out and never saw them again.

But yes, yes. They were our mothers, our fathers, brothers and sisters. There, had they murdered my heart.

There was my world, my youth, my old age. Everything. Everything.

Written according to the story of Sala (Goldman) Mandlinger

[Page 76]

The Eradication of Przedecz Jewry

by Sela Mandlinger (Goldman)

Translated from Hebrew by Marshall Grant

Ed. Note: Please see also Sela Goldman's testimony about what she saw in those final hours in the Church, as transcribed in Yiddish from her story, and then translated from the Yiddish in the article "The Last Hour", pp. 73–75.

In this letter, I wish to shortly write about what I have experienced under the Nazi regime during the years of the Holocaust and the unfolding of events that took place in my hometown of Przedecz (Pshedetz in Hebrew).

To be objective, I must admit that I did not feel anti–Semitism in our town until the arrival of the German Nazis. This was when the bombings started – until then things had been completely quiet. There was no panic and no one tried to leave the city. Thousands of refugees who had run away from neighboring towns found shelter with us, and each of us felt the obligation to take in one of the refugee families and help them to the best of our abilities. No one knew what awaited us and what tomorrow would bring; the days of hunger, persecution and smuggling had begun. When we heard rumors the Germans were approaching, the refugees who had flooded the town earlier left. They ran without direction – and fell straight into the hands of the Germans. None of us had ever imagined such sadism. We felt on our own bodies. In 1941, the Germans arrested one hundred Jewish girls; they were collected inside the Christian church and from there were sent to forced labor. This group of one hundred girls was divided into three equal groups and each was sent to a different location. I was part of a group of thirty–five girls sent to a farm near the town of Inowroclaw. We worked there from sunrise to sunset, and we received letters and packages from home. We were later sent to the Lojewo (Lavoye in Yiddish) camp where we were given various jobs, all hard for us, but in that camp, we didn't feel persecution or spite because the guards were Polish. Even the camp director was Polish. One day, two girls and I approached the director and requested authorization to visit our homes. It was understood that this would not easily be approved since this placed much responsibility on his shoulders, but he gave his consent based on his human values. We arrived home and found very few young people in the city and the mood was dreadful. Three days later, we left our families with a heavy and painful heart and returned to the camp. Sometime later, several girls were released from the camp due to sores, Esther and Ravitza Frankel, Yatka Goldman and Lavenia Zielienska. They were very happy to be travelling home, and we envied them, but it ended in disaster. One day I received a letter from my mother, sister, and brother, saying that they very much want to see me, and I of course did not hesitate and immediately walked, nervous and crying, to the director. I begged him to allow me to go home. He didn't waver and told me that the situation was very tense and bad for the Jews. He waits every day for the Nazi S.S. to come and check if the camp's prisoners can be accounted for and no one is missing, so of course he can't allow me to travel home. But he could offer a proposal. If I had a sister at home that could come and replace me, then I could travel home. I immediately wrote home with the offer. Several days later, my sister, Ronia, arrived at the camp, and I said goodbye to everyone. Who could tell – maybe this is the last time I would see them? I travelled home. I am unable to describe the happiness at home when they saw me, but I was sorry to see that all the Jews had been forced to live in the old market and the tension was almost physical. Nevertheless, for me, the fact that I was able to reach home brought me great joy and I appreciated my luck. Unfortunately

[Page 77]

this happiness did not continue for long. Five weeks after I had arrived home, one of the camp's Polish guards, who had guarded us at the Loyabu camp, arrived with travel papers for me and the girls who had been previously released from the camp. He tells us they are removing all the Jews from the neighboring towns and transporting them to a death camp, and he has come to take us back to the labor camp. For me, he had individual papers. He came in the evening and told me, Selka, get ready, tomorrow morning we are going. But he didn't want to give me my travel papers, he just told me where he was staying. We left early the next morning.

Mrs. Miriam Sochachevsky, Avraham Goldman, his wife
Traina, their late son, Heniach, and their daughter Ronia, a
resident of the USA

At 4 o'clock in the morning, my uncle Yehial Yosef Goldman comes and tells us: "You know what? The entire town is surrounded by policemen and S.S. soldiers, and they are taking all the Jews to the Catholic church". My mother asked me to run and get my travel papers and return to the camp. I leave the house and tell them I will be back soon with the papers, but when I returned home exhausted, to my dismay, I found no one any longer there. I run to the field, the field where Dacha Zechlinski lived. There was an outhouse there in the field and when I entered, I found that Regina Skovorondkin and Yetka Goldman were already hiding there. We made a plan to escape back to the camp that night, to where I had permission to travel. A short time later, the Christian, Novakovski Fajka arrives, opens the door, and says: "Ahh! It is you, the Jewish girls, stay here, maybe the Lord will save you". But he was a liar and deceitful, and he went and sent the Gestapo, and they took us to the church, where all the other Jews had already been sent. I was reunited with my mother and brother. My mother told me, "Go to the policemen and show them your papers, maybe they will let you go". I didn't want to hear any of this because I was afraid of them. In the church were

[Page 78]

five armed policemen who guarded us, made people run and beat them, and I was scared to approach them. But my mother was adamant and pushed me "Go already!" I eventually accepted her advice because I knew nothing would come of it. Why should they do something like this and release one Jewish girl? This could be a mark against them.

I approached one policeman and showed him my papers and said, I came from a labor camp, and I want to return and work there. He told me to go to another person and he will arrange it. I went to the next policeman, and he told me that he needed to go to the city's governor to confer with him. He left and didn't return for a long time. A policeman and the governor, Milanvach, later arrived and asked: Who is this Goldman girl? I go out and say that it is me, and he says, "You are going back to the camp". I swear that for me this was a disaster, not a stroke of luck – to leave my mother and brother who are surely going to their deaths. But my mother encouraged me and said, "You are still young, maybe you will enjoy your life".

My heart turned to stone. I asked the policemen if I could stay with my mother until the last minute, and they consented. Cars came and everyone was ordered to stand outside the church. I don't have the words to describe this terrible, terrible moment. Blood simply flowed like a river. I will not forget that picture for as long as I live.

After all I had been through, I am the only Jewish girl in the city, of course with travel papers issued by Milanvach, the governor. Everyone in the city asked me, "You aren't scared to come here? They could kill you." The Nazi Haflaks–Deutsch approached me and asked me, "What are you doing here, Ms. Goldman? Come to the police." I show him my papers and explain. He replies, "You really are lucky, so much importance has been given to one Jewish girl! But travel to wherever you want to go." After the devastation I had experienced, and after all the other trying experiences and efforts, I made it back to the camp. I told about everything that had happened there since everyone had someone in the city who had been lost. And that's how we worked in forced labor for days and nights, weeks, months, and years, in different camps, my sister and me. We were liberated from Bergan–Belsen in Germany on April 15, 1945.

[Page 79]

My Memories from the Past

by Levy Shveitzer

Translated from Yiddish by Roberta Paula Books

Across my thoughts swim images that I cannot forget, and they cause me grief. How could the culture have sunk to such a low level?

In the summer of 1939 (a surreally normal life, full of nervous tension), but still the thinking didn't change and the attitude wasn't that of formulating a plan. Every few evenings, after a hot summer day, people would congregate in those homes that had radios to hear the evening news on Polish radio.

Afterward, a discussion would ensue. Most people did not believe there would be a war, and in this fashion August drew nearer. Hitler's Germany made its final preparations to attack Poland. Poland mobilized, and our town of Pshaytsh (Przedecz in Polish) wasn't left out. Besides the many Jewish youth who were doing their regular military service, many more Jews from Pshaytsh (Przedecz) were mobilized. Many of those who were drafted were married, fathers of small children; accompanied by their families, they all went to City Hall, where trucks were waiting to take them away. They said their goodbyes. Many of them were never seen again. This is when the anxious days and nights began, when life was disrupted. In big letters, the headline of the last newspaper to arrive was "Europe Mobilizes". On the morning of September 1st, we heard warnings on Polish radio that they were coming, they were on their way. That was the announcement that German airplanes were bombing Polish cities. Pshaytsh (Przedecz) is situated amongst the cities of Włocławek (Yiddish Vlatslavek), Kutno, and Koło, but it did not have any military or industrial installations. The town was not bombed by the Germans and no military actions took place there. In fact, during the first days of the war, Jews from other towns such as Koło, Kalisz, Turek and others fled to our town to escape the bombing in their town and because they feared the advance of Hitler's followers.

We received these Jews as brothers. Most houses were overly full, including the vestibules. Among those who arrived were many who had spent the First World War living in Pshaytsh (Przedecz) and who spoke about the warm reception in that time too.

But unfortunately, this war had a different character. Hitler's Germany was carrying out a war of annihilation of Jews everywhere.

[Page 80]

The nights were dark. Our electric current came from the electric station in Włocławek (Yiddish Vlatslavek), which was destroyed after a German bombardment.

The situation was worsening by the day. We began to live in fear as we saw the Polish military retreat from the fronts around Pomerania (???) and Poznań, marching by Pshaytsh (Przedecz) in the first days of the war. Many in the retreating Polish military were also antisemitic and wondered why there were so many Jews. They boycotted Jewish businesses and shouted threats, and this while they had to run away since Hitler's army was chasing them. This was difficult for the Jews. On one side, fear of the threats from the fleeing Polish military, which was retreating from the front, and on the other side, fear of the advancing Hitler forces who were approaching our region quickly.

Meanwhile disorder ruled. High–ranking Polish officials, led by the police, left town. Power was temporarily assumed by a Polish militia comprised of former fighters from the First World War who belonged to the ruling party of pre–war Poland. Meanwhile Hitler's armies were advancing. With each day, more cities around Pshaytsh (Przedecz) are captured. Large battles take place in Kutno, Gostynin and Lubicz. The refugees who had come to Pshaytsh (Przedecz) began to leave. Many Jews who returned home found their homes and businesses plundered. In great panic, nearly all Jews returned to their place of residence.

Each day the situation worsened. Włocławek was captured by the German military. They pushed further in the direction of Pshaytsh (Przedecz).

In mid-September 1939, the second day of Rosh Hashanah (Friday, September 15th), in the early hours of the morning, we anticipated that Hitler's men would arrive that day. This brought pain and suffering to the Jews of Pshaytsh (Przedecz). The day was rainy and cried for the fate that awaited the Jews under the barbarian regime. Jews were in the midst of praying when news entered the Houses of Prayer that a German patrol could be seen at the edge of town. Greatly upset by this news, the praying was interrupted and, with half folded prayer shawls in their hands, everyone ran home to his family. Everyone throughout the town now knew the Germans were at the home of Moishe Raukh on Hadetch Street. The German pastor goes to greet them. The Hitlerists [Nazis] order the rabbi of our town, Rabbi Zemelman, to be brought to them immediately, as well as the Christian

[Page 81]

clergyman from town by the name of Geyzler. They are both warned against any resistance from the populace.

When they arrived in town, they began to search the houses for weapons and simultaneously hung a swastika from the top of the roof of City Hall.

From the day the Hitler regime began, the pain and suffering of the Jews increased. They took over the new fire station, situated in the middle of the new market. The situation of the Jews in the region became more difficult. Because of the Hitlerists, they were the first ones appropriated and sent to various tasks. One of the first Jews dragged from his home and forced to work by the Hitlerists was Rabbi Zemelman. Also, other well established, wealthier Jewish elders who lived around the new market were sent to work to humiliate them in front of the non–Jewish population.

This was the goal of the National Socialist German Third Reich.

I cannot skip and want to mention this: when the Hitlerists caught the Rabbi and forced him to carry planks of wood, the Jewish boy Yakov Yakubovitch approached and asked the military men if he could do the work instead of the Rabbi, and asked them to free the Rabbi. They considered this request insolent and beat Yakov Yakubovitch bloody. People lived in great fear. It was a small town. With the help of the Christians, the Germans soon learned everything about the Jews. They knew each day who to drag out of their house to do various jobs on the streets. The Jews were forced to chop wood, clean the streets, and remove, with a spoon, the grass growing around the stones by the new market.

I, too, was forced to work, with many other Jews, mainly older Jews. The Hitlerists did not forget about Rabbi Zemelman. They made him responsible for ensuring that nobody escaped work.

It is hard to describe how this appeared. Everything was done to humiliate us and gain the sympathy of those Christians who hated the Jews. They showed the local Christians they came to carry out a common goal, which was to harass the Jews. They also wanted to divert their hatred toward them for invading Poland.

The capturing of Jews and sending them to work became a daily occurrence. There was hardly a Jewish home which the Hitlerists

[Page 82]

did not find.

There were trained soldiers whose main task was to capture Jews. There was one small elegant soldier that the Jews called "August". He was a constant Jew grabber. When small children saw him, they said: Father, hide. August is coming to snatch you for work.

Every day brought new edicts to the Jews of Pshaytsh (Przedecz). The Germans ordered all stores remain open. They went into every Jewish store and ordered them to hang a sign saying, "Jewish Store", and began to implement the Nuremberg anti – Jewish laws of Streicher, Rosenberg and Goebbels. The unsold goods in the Jewish stores had to be sold without replenishing with fresh goods. At Leyzer Zikhlinsky's, the largest grocery store in town, everything was sold out, even kerosene. A Christian woman reported to the German commandant that they did not want to sell her kerosene. As a result, accompanied by armed soldiers, Zikhlinsky's son Bunim was led through all the streets in town with a big sign on his chest and back which said, in Polish and German, that this Jewish swine refuses to sell to Poles. Soon, there were more and more of this type of denunciations. Nobody knew what awaited him the next day.

Soon after, the pious religious life that Jews had led up to this point was affected. Thus, the first Jews were seized by the Hitlerists and their beards shaved off. Several Jews who had to go out hid their beards. Reb Shmuel Yamnik, the ritual slaughterer, tied his beard with a colorful kerchief as he secretly went to private homes to slaughter the sacrificial chicken (kaporos) on the eve of Yom Kippur. This was all connected to fear and anguish. Jews did not want to give up their religious life. Even though the Germans closed all the prayer houses and collective prayer was absolutely forbidden, this was the first Yom Kippur under Hitler's rule, and the Jews risked their lives to organize prayer in private homes. In the midst of praying, the Germans, probably with the help of the local Christian population, managed to capture a few Jews. Still wearing their prayer shawls, they were brought to the commandant and beaten for their transgressions.

This is how religious life was forcefully repressed. Jews had to change their outward appearance, remove their Jewish traditional clothing which they had been wearing for generations.

It was now the Days of Awe. The Germans understood in detail the Jewish holidays and went to great lengths to instill more suffering and anguish during these times. During the first days of Sukkot, the Germans demanded that

[Page 83]

the Jews of Pshaytsh (Przedecz) pay a high tax of over twenty thousand Polish zlotys. They warned of severe consequences if the Jews did not pay up. Upset by this Hitleristic demand, the Jews tried to find a way to fulfill it. They approached a Polish German resident, the former schoolteacher in the folk school named Lorentz, who also could not tolerate these Hitleristic deeds. Mr. Lorentz went with the Jewish representative to Włocławek, to the regional board. The Hitleristic regional board told Mr. Lorentz not to get involved and not to pay for them. Sorely disappointed and afraid of the threats, the Jews began to collect the money. But the suffering and anguish did not stop. On the second day of Sukkot, on the night of Shmini Atzeret, the Hitlerists perpetrated a huge crime. They set fire to the Pshaytsh (Przedecz) synagogue. It is hard to describe the shock felt by all the Jews in town. The next day, all the Jews in town, young and old, were shrouded in sorrow and there was pain in every Jewish heart. After the holiday, the Rabbi, accompanied by his son, went to the place where the synagogue once stood and the coals were still burning. The synagogue which had taken in several generations of Jewish prayers. The Rabbi eulogized the synagogue. While the community was still mourning the burned synagogue, the military commandant ordered the leaders and other well–known religious Jews to come to him and mockingly said: I have good soldiers who told me that the Jews burned down the synagogue. With these words, he wanted to increase their pain even more. They were forced to sign that Jews were responsible for setting the synagogue on fire … there was not even one calm day or night.

It is now the end of October 1939. It is starting to get cold, the days rainy. On one of these rainy nights, the Hitlerist soldiers were let loose through the entire town, breaking into Jewish homes, and dragging all the Jewish men from their beds, including the old and the weak. They were gathered together by armed soldiers, taken to an uninhabited part of town, where there were stables, where the roads were not paved, only muddy due to the wet rainy weather. This is where the Nazis began their sadistic pranks. Accompanied by beatings and threats of being shot, they forced the Jews to obey their various commands. They were ordered to lie down and roll in the mud, as well as other sadistic exercises. As if this was not enough

[Page 84]

torture, the soldiers brought them to the water pump, where the soldiers poured cold water on them. The Jews arrived home with wet clothes, covered with mud, tortured, and bruised. In the hours of late afternoon on the same day, the Hitlerists brought, on a Polish wagon, two Poles from the hamlet of Brunisawa who, according to them, had been shot. They gathered more Jews and forced them to bring the corpses to the fire hall. With that, the Hitlerist military finished their torture for the day. A few days later, they left town. Military gendarmes replaced them temporarily, until a commissar and an adjutant were sent by the so–called Third Reich. They took over the local authority and, through various means, began to eliminate whatever Jewish life still existed. The gendarmes continued to send Jews to work in Katarzyna village [*Translator's Note*: part of the outskirts of Pshaytsh], where they confiscated property and assumed responsibility for administration. And in this way, Jews were brought there, chained in rows, every day to work. The new commissar ordered that the head of the Jewish community, Dovid Zikhlinsky, come to him and ordered him to be the representative for the Jews. He now had to make the Jews of Pshaytsh (Przedecz) aware of all anti–Jewish commands.

It was now a bit easier, now that the Jews were not being captured for work. The number of Jews sent to work was now carried out by the Jewish representative.

Dovid Zikhlinsky got a few Jews to work with him. They succeeded in normalizing [the system] so that old and weak Jews weren't called up for forced labor. The commissar and his Hitleristic assistant, together with local so called VolksDeutche [*Translator's Note*: people of German extraction but without German citizenship], who supported the Hitleristic party, began systematically to destroy the orderly life of Jews in town. They began to confiscate Jewish homes, giving people just a few hours to leave, requiring that they leave furniture, bedding, and all valuables behind for the Germans. The commissar's first demand was another tax of forty thousand Zlotys, demanded with threats. The Jews could no longer assemble this amount of money. Therefore, the Hitlerists let loose through the town, going from store to store until they took every last bit of merchandise. From that day on, Jewish businesses were liquidated, and the stores were closed for good.

The Hitlerists made laws for the Jews. Every day, anti–Jewish edicts were announced, how they had to wear the yellow patch

[Page 85]

on the shoulder of their clothing. It was also forbidden for Jews to walk on the sidewalks. They had to walk in the middle of the road.

Living under these medieval conditions had a terrible impact on everyone. A portion of Jewish youth, in various ways, began to run away toward the east to the German Russian border in an attempt to enter the Soviet Union. Many would later join the Red Army or the Polish procured army to heroically fight the Nazis.

Unfortunately, many did not make it due to various reasons.

Pshaytsh (Przedecz) and the surrounding area was occupied by the Third Reich. They chased out Jews and Poles from the region to the not occupied part of Poland called the Protectorate which spanned from Lyubitz near Kutno until the Lublin region. They began to hear that the Nazis took all the Jews from the nearby town of Lubien and made the town the first in the area to be clean of Jews. They were all sent to the Lublin region. Hearing this sad news everyone wanted to be together with their families in case this happened to them.

People lived with great anxiety, and no one knew what to do. Time passes and everyone remains together under Hitler's rule. No one can leave, and all Jews faced the same fate. The name of the town was changed to a German name "Moosburg".

The commissar announced the Jews of Pshaytsh (Przedecz) will not be sent away and could remain. But he still demanded the representative send a set number of Jews to work every day. The forced laborers were guarded by local VolksDeutche armed with weapons and sticks. They ran the work site. It happened often that Jews were bloodily beaten.

The Jewish representative and his helpers sent Jews to work on a regular basis. They also organized a system that if was someone's turn to work and he wanted to be freed because he had an opportunity to earn some money, he would pay a sum of money and another who needed a few zlotys went to work in his place.

The Jewish representative was often called to the commandant and fearfully had to report to him and return with bitter news. This is how the Nazis sent the order to liquidate the Jewish cemetery and destroy all the tombstones. Some of these tombstones were

[Page 86]

hundreds of years old and were distributed among the farmers in the surrounding villages. Jews had to witness this. It pained every Jewish heart to see how the Nazis desecrated the Jewish cemetery. The holy place where the bones of relatives and friends rested. The Nazis took local Polish citizens to carry out this desecration, which they did with sadistic joy. Every time they ripped out a tombstone, they shouted insults to those who had found their eternal rest. After they removed all the tombstones, the cemetery was levelled, and the commissar ordered two benches be placed under the two tall trees. He would go there every afternoon with his retinue and look at the nearby river.

They were happy to have liquidated the Jewish cemetery and put a stop to religious life. The House of Study was transformed into a shoe factory for the Germans, the Prayer House where simple, good hearted Jewish artisans prayed, such as shoemakers, tailors, and hat makers, was confiscated and every vestige of open Jewish religious life was burned.

However, the Germans could not take away the inner beliefs of the Jews. Jews risked their lives and gathered in a minyan (quorum) to pray in people's homes. Jewish parents ensured their children would not forget the Hebrew alphabet and should continue to learn what they had previously studied in school.

The Germans also put an end to all communal and cultural activities that had existed until this time. The two libraries were closed. The Sholem Aleichem Library was closed even before the war by the Polish government. The second one, the Public Library was closed by the Germans. Yet many homes had a lot of books which the children used. Books were passed from hand to hand and were read by many, helping to stay connected to a cultural life the Germans tried to destroy.

Jewish soldiers who were taken prisoner by the Germans when they heroically fought in the ranks of the Polish army were freed and began to return to Pshaytsh (Przedecz). They brought with them news of soldiers who fell in battle against the Nazi beasts. Their names were Itche Danielsky, Ezriel Danielsky, Yitzkhak Frankenshteyn, Notte Krel.

We also learned about soldiers who were captured by the Germans and, right after being released, were murdered.

[Page 87]

Their names were: Naftali Volf Kladovsky, his brother Khonen Kladovsky and Mikhl Hersh Goldman.

Exact details about the mass murder of many Jewish prisoners were recounted by Abba Buks. He himself had escaped from a prison camp. He told how the Kladovsky brothers hugged each other while being shot by the barbarians. The stories about the crimes committed frightened and shocked everyone.

Life for the remaining Jews in Pshaytsh (Przedecz) became even more restricted. They were now starting to liquidate the artisan workshops. The Jewish representative was called and was ordered to tell the Jews they were not permitted to work at their trades in their homes. The Germans then went through the town with a local Volksdeutsche resident. He was a tailor who had trained with Jews. They went into every tailor's home and confiscated all sewing machines and other tools of the trade. If they found a piece of fabric, they took it away. The name of this VolksDeutche was Velder. He took some of the sewing machines for himself, and the Jewish tailors had to work for him without compensation.

The commissar walked around town and, with his cane, pointed to all the buildings that should be confiscated, and the work must be done by Jews for very little pay.

To buy a few essentials, Jews had to sell their last few possessions.

Artisans such as tailors and shoemakers sometimes managed to make something for a Christian and would receive some essential goods in return, and hoped to live to see Hitler's end.

By early spring, 1941 there were once again many German soldiers in town. People were saying that many soldiers were heading toward Warsaw. This is eastward toward the Russian German border. The soldiers from our town were also heading east.

On the morning of June 22nd, 1941, we heard that war broke out between Hitler's Germany and the Soviet Union. The situation for the Jews is getting worse. The Germans begin to send Jews from surrounding towns to camps. The local commissar still needed the Jews of Moosburg (the German name for Pshaytsh) to work for him and told the representative he will not allow them to be sent away. However, the Jews knew about German promises, and many awaited the same fate,

[Page 88]

and no one was sure what tomorrow would bring, although most were sitting and waiting with their families.

A few months later this is what happened. On the eve of Yom Kippur, the elder called me and Daniel Ravsky to him. He told us that the next day, which was Yom Kippur, we had to go to a village to work for a German farmer so that all the other Jews could remain in town, fast, and observe Yom Kippur and the holiness of the day will not be disturbed. We appreciated the importance of this deed. We happily carried out our work on Yom Kippur knowing that, thanks to us, the whole Jewish community was free from work on this holy day of Yom Kippur. Only when we returned from our work did we learn what kind of Yom Kippur the Nazis made for the Jews.

A group gathered for prayer at the home of Yakov Volf Klar, which, was near the Study House. With broken hearts and wrapped in prayer shawls, the Jews chanted the prayers. Many tears were shed over the bitter fate awaiting the few remaining Jews. The VolksDeutsche Velder suddenly appeared looking for a Jewish tailor to do some work. He saw the Jews wrapped in their prayer shawls and ran to the commissar to inform him of this great crime that Jews were committing. The Germans came running, and found the Jews in their prayer shawls, and dragged them out to the new market. The Jews were given brooms and forced to sweep the street. Children were not spared, and leading them all was the rabbi, Rabbi Zemelman.

This was how the last Yom Kippur looked for the Jews of Pshaytsh (Przedecz). In 1941, on the first day of Sukkot, two groups of girls, including married women without children, were sent to a camp in Inavratslov. A few days later the Germans demanded the men be sent as well.

The Nazis let loose in town, chasing people out of their homes. I too was caught then and, together with sixty other Jews from Pshaytsh (Przedecz), was sent to camps in Poznań.

[Page 89]

In the Poznań Camps

by Levi Shveitzer, Kiryat Motzkin – Haifa

Translated by Roberta Paula Books

Wednesday the 7th of October 1941, in the middle days of Sukkos, the town had not yet settled down from the heartache inflicted four days earlier when the Hitlerists took all the girls aged fourteen and up, together with childless women, and sent them to camps near Inowrolaw (Inavratslov in Yiddish). Then a new shock. When most of the Jews in town were on the road coming back from forced labor, where they were required to be, the Jewish spokesperson, Dovid Zikhlinsky, arrived and delivered the disturbing news; the German commissar had told him that they required Jews to be sent away to work. Immediately, the gendarmes and Hitlerists, with swastikas on their armbands, fell upon them with batons in their hands. They chased people out of their homes; everyone had to line up in the market near city hall. Just about everyone knew the fate that awaited them. The turmoil was considerable, and, under the watch of the gendarmes and Gestapo, we were driven into the Christian church. The mothers and the wives of the men who were taken tremble and cry. With grieved and broken hearts, they bring a bit of clothing and, to the extent possible, a bit of food, taken from our mouths. Dovid Zikhlinsky finds us in the church, asking who needs a bit of money.

Outside, the peasants were already waiting with horses and wagons, and in the middle of the night they took us away, accompanied by the shouts and cries of our nearest and dearest, which reverberated throughout the town. This is how we parted from our dear and near ones, for good. We travelled by wagon until the station Szatki (Tseti in Yiddish). From there we went by small train to Wloclawek (Vlatslovek in Yiddish), and then to Poznań (Poyzen in Yiddish). Arriving in Poznań, at the train station, there were guards already waiting for us, as well as agents of the Gestapo, who took us to the horrible camp stadium (***Translators note:*** Probably the Edmund Szyc Stadium on Dolna Wilda Street in Poznań). This is where the main supervisors over all the forced labor camps around Poznań were situated. The appearance of the camp left a terrifying impression on all of us; It was surrounded by barbed wire, and gallows stood in the middle of the mustering place. The Gestapo would bring in Jews from other camps to be hanged when their only crime was taking a piece of bread from a Christian or straying too far from their workplace. The camp had already been in existence for half a year when we, the Pshaytsher Jews (Przedecz),

[Page 90]

arrived.

The Germans brought the first Jews here from Łódź and Ozorkow (Ozerkov in Yiddish). Across from the camp was another camp in one building which had been a mustard factory, called "Remo". There were Jews in this building from the neighboring towns to Przedecz – Chodecz (Pshaytsh – Khadetch in Yiddish), Izbica Kujawska (Izbitzia – Koyabsky in Yiddish), Koło, Turek, and many others. These young Jews were brought there by the Hitlerists at the outbreak of the German–Russian war, and we sixty Pshaytsher (Przedecz) Jews were held in the camp stadium. We were assigned one room in a building that had at one time been used for human waste…. Soon after we arrived at the camp, they led us to work every day, very early in the morning, guarded by Polish uniformed watchmen who had a good mastery of the German language and who, before the war, belonged to the anti – Semitic political parties Endeks (the National Democratic party) and "Nara" group. Their leader was the big anti – Semite Shlibitsky, an outspoken antisemite, a distinguished person in pre-war Poland. Our job consisted of digging channel ditches to lay pipes to a depth of more than three meters connected to the military factories. The factories called it the prakhavnye (Yiddish for "the Wonder"). There was also a wagon factory, where many English prisoners of war worked. The work was overseen by a German firm named Tsun . This is when terrifying days began. With this work, overseen by German and Polish "mining masters". They immediately begin to warn us and threaten us: "For not wanting to work well, you know where you belong …" The Poles tell us they brought us here to annihilate us. When we returned to camp after our first day at work, we immediately realized that this was one of the worst and most horrible places to work, and how many Jews were beaten bloody here? Meanwhile, the first letters from home begin to arrive. Our loved ones know where we are. This sweetens our lives a bit. The work is becoming even worse. The German master who the Poles called "Bambrovitz – Bombardier" beat us every day with our work tools, throwing punches wherever they landed. Thus, every day Jews would return to camp from work with bloodied heads. The factory was surrounded by a tall fence, closed with concrete fasteners. Outside Gestapo agents are on watch. The murderers beat us at will. One took me inside the barrack and began to mercilessly beat me with a rubber baton. I ripped open the door and with a loud scream ran out. After this, when they let others in to be beaten, they closed the door tightly…. The English prisoners of war,

[Page 91]

soldiers who worked there, helped us as much as possible. Once, they lured the man called "Bombardier" to them and beat him up. He made a lot of noise and ran over to the German soldiers who were guarding us, only he made no fuss over it. It also happened that a Polish woman cried out asking why are you beating us. Right away, a Gestapo agent came and arrested her. We later learned that she received a six–month sentence. The situation got even worse when they took us to work at the police target range. The Poles called it the "Warsaw Gate". The place was called "Malta" and had once been a coffee factory. Our lives were now completely unprotected. We were beaten freely and unrestrainedly. Our only comfort was returning to camp and finding a letter from a loved one at home. We received letters again with sad news. Jews were being sent to Inowroclaw (in Yiddish, Inovaratslav) to a work camp. Ten days later, another transport of Jews; that is how the Hitlerists emptied our town of Jews, despite the promises from the commissar that Moosburg Jews would remain. The German name for Przedecz was "Moosburg". Our letters are censored, but our fathers, mothers, husbands, and wives know our situation is worsening by the day. Our group of Jews from Pshaytsh (Przedecz) in the Poznań camp stadium remained together. We did not give up hope and belief that their end will come. We find a German language newspaper on the way home, after a day of work which was always accompanied by beatings and abuse. Khaim Aron Aurbakh sits up until late at night and reads everything thoroughly. Very early in the morning, we go to work in chains and pass the news from one to another. We are happy when we hear they have suffered severe losses on the front. But we often receive bad news from home. We begin to hear about mass abuse and deportations in unfamiliar directions. We begin to hear about a camp called Chełmno , about which none of us believe that all the Jews brought there are being killed. The more news we receive, the sadder it is, and weakens our resolve about returning home. The only ones remaining at home are lonely mothers with small children and elderly parents. They are all worried about their fate and ours. Our dear ones sell off whatever they have left in order to buy and send whatever food and clothing they can, to sustain our lives in the camps. Often, our loved ones would stand in line all day at the building of the

[Page 92]

gendarmerie, but at the end of the day were unable to send off a package. This is what my dear mother wrote to me.

The situation in the camp is becoming worse and worse. Our food consists of 200 grams of black bread daily. (perhaps eight slices of bread, or about 500 calories) For lunch, we received a little bit of Kohlrabi with water, cooked without a drop of oil or meat. We were very hungry. We were becoming weaker by the day. People were swollen from hunger. A typhus epidemic broke out. They locked down the camp and no longer took us to work, as they feared contaminating the surrounding population. Every day brought new corpses due to hunger and typhus. Every day, a wagon came to the camp, pulled by two white horses. They called it Pirak's wagon. The wagon would be filled with Jews dead and swollen from hunger. The first to die from Pshaytsh (Przedecz) was Vova Danielsky, the son of Mikhl Danielsky who lived on Khatcher Street. The winter was very difficult. Lots of snow and frost. It was January 1942. Our work for the firm "East German High and Deep Building Company" was done. Sitting in the camp in Building 4, we worried about our future. Two Jewish camp police come running in and take four strong men to do a work. They took the brothers Mendl and Meir Kazimiersky as well as Efraim Engel and Tuvia Goldman. A few hours later, they returned in a Gestapo vehicle, their clothes covered in blood. In a dejected state, they told us how they were taken to Gestapo headquarters, where they saw crates filled with guillotined people. They took the crates out to a crematorium to burn. They quickly realized these were highly educated Poles, whom the Gestapo regularly killed. Right at the camp is the office of the camp leader. New orders are issued from there very often. They tell us to write home and say we can receive two German Marks in each letter. Immediately, each person writes home that they should include two marks in a letter and send it to us. The first comes to us, and every family sends several letters with two marks enclosed. But this does not come to us. The leader of the camp takes it all. This is just to squeeze the last of what our dear ones at home still have. After this, when they sent us back to work, our group from Pshaytsh (Przedecz) was divided up and sent to different camps such as Shteynek, Lenchik, and others. [Translator's Note: I was unable to locate these camps.] Among us there were many brothers who wanted to be together. They rode to the camps together. I remained in the camp stadium. I received letters from home that in the small towns around Pshaytsh (Przedecz) there are fewer and fewer Jews. There are no longer

[Page 93]

any Jews in Kłodawa, Koło, Chodech, Lubien and Izbica, and other towns around Pshaytsh (Przedecz).

It is April 1942. The Jews in Pshaytsh (Przedecz) are living as if on an island. There is no longer any other Jewish life that exists. The letters we receive from home on different levels become very worrisome, the word Chełmno appears in various ways … the last cards we received, that they wrote to me: "it is Passover, we are sitting at our Seder table, and we poured oceans of tears. We are preparing for the battle (khasene – the word also means wedding), the battle (khasene) is nigh". Our pained hearts understood everything. My last letter from home said: "we are off to battle (khasene). We wanted to see you again" … This was my last contact with my home. In the camp, we are determined with every hope to remain living. No one could stop crying, knowing we will no longer have any contact with our loved ones…

War was raging in Poland. The hunger in the camp was great. People were distended from hunger. Every day there were fresh corpses. There are fewer of us from Pshaytsh (Przedecz). People are signing up for transports. In reality, these transports were taking people to their death at Chełmno . Nobody believed the rumors that were being spread that people were being sent east to the inhabited regions of Russia. The Germans told us they were sending people back the Łódź ghetto. Many Jews from Łódź and Ozorkov sign up with the hope of greeting their loved ones in their home …

Every day fewer people were sent to work, due to the numbers sitting in camp with swollen feet and bodies. I can also not neglect mentioning the low–down treacherous treatment by the Jewish camp police, who blew a whistle very early every morning to wake us for work. They poked us with rubber batons, chased us out of the building and didn't pass up the chance to beat our skinny, bony bodies which could no longer feel the beatings. They believed that with such behavior they will be the only ones to survive the Poznań camps. They did not believe or did not want to understand that the Hitlerists used them against their own Jewish brothers. A Jew remains a Jew. The Germans will not take this into account and will kill them after they use them.

We, the remaining Pshaytsher Jews (Przedecz), were assigned to a new work unit. We walked a few kilometers to the so-called workplace, where a wild VolksDeutche (people whose language and culture had German origins, but who did not hold German citizenship)

[Page 94]

Stelmanshtsik, together with his helper, a Polish enemy of the Jews named Shikorsky, would sadistically beat us continuously at work. He would hand out our lunch, which consisted of cabbage cooked in water. While we stood in line waiting for our food, he would pour it into the Cybina River which ran nearby our workplace, or he would pour gasoline into our food … and then portions it out to us to eat. Our work consisted of loading small wagons of sand. If the wagons were not completely filled, we would be penalized and threatened and reported to the Gestapo, deprived of food and so on. When we returned to our camp stadium, we would often receive news; the Gestapo brought Jews from other camps to be hanged. The engineer Noyman is the head of all Jewish forced labor camps around Poznań. He brought the hangman's rope (noose), the gallows is a constant which always stands in the middle of the mustering place. That's where many Jews from other camps are forced to watch the hangings of these victims, this is all brought forth under the watchful eye of the Gestapo armed with machine guns.

After the second year of horrible suffering in Hitler's forced labor camps around Poznań, a large proportion of Jews were killed in various ways. All the work camps in the region were liquidated in September 1943. And we, the few who remained from Pshaytsh (Przedecz) and Jews from other towns, were sent to Auschwitz. In Auschwitz a new hell began. I was separated from my few townspeople and sent to a concentration camp named Swietochlowice (Shventikhlovitz in Yiddish) near Katowice (Katovitz in Yiddish). When I got there, I found Khaim Skubronsky, who arrived there before me. The suffering there was horrific. Every day, the Jewish workers were beaten by the S.S who were helped by the camp Capos. We were bloodily beaten and bitten by their wolf hounds. When we saw these conditions, we realized we could not survive there for long. I decided with two other Jews from the town Ozorkow (Orzukhov in Yiddish) to risk our lives and join another work detail which worked outside the camp. When we returned to the camp in the evening, we were called out during roll call and we were required to report to the head of the camp. When we did not step out of line, the Capos and the S.S. came to us in line and beat us brutally. For a long time, we were unable to return to work.

After two months, we were taken in closed trucks, guarded by S.S. to Birkenau. This was the largest

[Page 95]

extermination camp at Auschwitz. I met with several people from Pshaytsh (Przedecz) who had also overcome much in many different labor camps.

It is hard to describe my encounter with our Pshaytshers. No one knew who among us would live to see the next day.

There was also here a women's camp with few girls from Pshaytsh (Przedecz) who were sent here from the Inowroclaw (Inavaratslav) camps. In January 1944, I went with a group of Jews to work. We walked through the deep snow, which covered the swamps of the death camp Bzezinke (in German, Birkenau). We came to a place where a group of women and girls were standing, deep in snow, bent over from the freezing cold and work. They are taking apart a wooden hut. When I looked at them, I heard someone call my name in a surprised voice. It was Gitl, one of the two Rivnitsky sisters. Immediately, the rest of the girls from Pshaytsh (Przedecz) began spontaneously to scream and call out Levi, Levi. From a distance, they began to ask me about relatives and acquaintances who were sent with me to Poznań. Unfortunately, we could not get closer since the murderers were guarding us.

The majority of them, I did not see again. There in Birkenau, the largest portion of the Pshaytsher youth were brought to death by the Hitlerists. Forever, they remain before my eyes. While there, I also saw Hersh Topolsky. He was killed in a struggle against the Germans when he participated in an uprising against the Sonderkommando, November 6th, 1944.

After three months of surviving various illnesses and selections, I was sent to other camps, Buna, Glaybitz, Flusenburg and Dachau where we were liberated on April 29th, 1945, by the American army. There I met Moshe Ahron Yakubovsky, Fishl Goldman and Ezriel Skabransky. Unfortunately, Ezriel died after we were liberated from Dachau.

I cannot make peace with the fact that all of this happened, and I can still visualize the wretched truth. When the American army sent a transport of Poles back to Poland, I was among them.

I arrived in Pshaytsh (Przedecz) during the middle days of Sukkos. Exactly four years earlier, I was torn away and sent to Poznań with sixty others. Of that group, only three remained living.

It is hard to describe my arrival in town. Beginning on Khatcher Street where we arrived, I walked through the new market, the old market, and other small streets. The houses were still standing and before my eyes I still see the Jews who once lived there and

[Page 96]

who had their businesses there. Like in every other town, everyone knew every name and every nickname which was acquired through the generations. Not one of them is left.

There were now others inhabiting homes that had belonged to Jews, and other salespersons running the stores that had previously belonged to Jews.

Meanwhile, living in Pshaytsh, having returned from the camps, Moishe and Beltsya Yakhimovitch, Yosef Burnshteyn, Mendl Frankenshteyn. Everyone who came back to Pshaytsh (Przedecz) stayed with Moishe and Beltsye Yakhimovitch.

A select few arrived who had survived under various difficult conditions. Some returned from the Soviet Union (Raten Farband) where they served in the Red Army and heroically fought against Hitler's murderers and helped to free Poland, and for that they received distinctions of honor.

However, we were received with menacing looks from the Polish population. They saw in us that we were coming to disturb their quiet life in the stolen homes and businesses that once belonged to the Jews.

Everyone who survived and then returned to Pshaytsh (Przedecz) fulfills his mission of visiting the graves of his parents before leaving Poland.

Holocaust survivors from Pshaytsh (Przedecz) dispersed to all parts of the world, but the majority yearned for Israel and settled here. And there remained with everyone the memory of the Jewish life that had once existed in the town of Pshaytsh (Przedecz).

[Page 97]

Events from Pshedets (Przedecz)

by Davidovitz Yehoshua – Tel–Aviv

Translated from Hebrew by Leon Zamosc
and from Yiddish by Roberta Paula Books

The events in the town of Przedecz during the Shoah.

With reverence and a heavy heart, I sit down to write about the days of destruction and annihilation that befell the Jews of Przedecz when the German Nazis arrived in our town. In doing so, I will contribute to the task of assembling this Book of Remembrance for the martyrs of our town. I will try my best to refresh my memory and put in writing the horrible events of those days and years. (I switch to writing in Yiddish so that I can express myself better).

Pshaytsh (Przedecz) in 1939

The small Jewish town of Pshaytsh (Przedecz in Polish, Pshedets in Hebrew) lived in happiness and suffering. The majority of the Jewish population were craftsmen: tailors, shoemakers, hat makers. They worked hard all week to earn a living, travelling from Sunday to Friday to fairs from one town to another, selling their handcrafted goods. This continued until the outbreak of the Second World War on September 1st, 1939. The Germans entered our town on Rosh Hashanah. By chance, it was raining, and all the Jews were gathered in the prayer houses chanting the prayers of the Days of Awe. When the German military marched in, we Jews ran from the synagogue and the prayer houses and hid wherever we could.

On Hoshana Rabbah, the Germans burned down the synagogue. The next morning, they called the leader of the Jewish community, Dovid Zikhlinsky, to them and demanded a tax and accused the Jews of burning down the synagogue. The amount was large, but the money was collected and given to the Nazis. At the same time, the soldiers seized Rabbi Zemelman, of blessed memory. They forced him to clean the street and carry heavy beams of wood from the Engel brothers' place on Khadetsher Road to the new marketplace. It is unimaginable how the Rabbi managed to do this. They also sheared off his beard. I will never forget that scene. They were not yet bothering the young people. Later, a commissar came and took control of the German military. The fact is, from that moment on, life in Pshaytsh (Przedecz) normalized. Three work units were formed, the young under the direction of Efraim Engel, the middle– aged under the direction of Binyumin Frenkel, and the older people under the direction of Leybush Ash. The Jews' elder was Dovid Zikhlinsky. It is important to establish that – over a brief period of about a year, nothing special

[Page 98]

transpired.

We continued to live in the same place. The Poles claimed that we ruled the town under the leadership of Dovid Zikhlinsky. At this time Rabbi Zemelman, of blessed memory, befriended the commissar, to the extent that he often called on the Rabbi. Fortuitously, I was once present when the two of them were together discussing religious philosophy. The military occupied the house of prayer. They, too, were good to the Rabbi and showed him respect. This world came to an end when an order arrived from the work division to which all the girls had to submit. This was the beginning of 1941. They were all confined in the Catholic Church and at dawn were sent to a work camp in Inowroclaw. This blow was the first tragedy for the Jewish families of our town. Immediately after that came an order for the young men to present themselves, and the same heart wrenching scene was repeated. I will mention that not all the young men obeyed the order, so the gendarmes, together with civilian Germans, went from house to house and searched in every corner, and despite this found only a small number. My brother Avrom Zalman, of blessed memory, and I managed to hide. The transport went to Poznań, and hardly anyone from this transport survived. However, my brother Avrom Zalman of blessed memory and I were on the second transport. They sent us to Inowroclaw (in Yiddish, Inavaratslav). We were there for two years. We were town workers in a variety of jobs. We also worked with the trains. We didn't know hunger and we were not guarded, but this freedom took a victim. The horrible tragedy happened one Sunday when my brother Zalman went to look for our sister Rokhl in Lojewo (in Yiddish, Layove), eight kilometers from our camp, where there were many girls from Pshaytsh. The Gestapo caught them both outside the camp, arrested them and brought them to a disciplinary camp. As described by others, they were horribly tortured and accused of smuggling survival supplies, since my sister gave him a lot of food. And they were killed there by bloody Nazi hands. Yakov Prakhovsky was also killed by the Gestapo. He was caught putting a letter in a mailbox. Zelig Bornshteyn was also killed there. He was caught in town with food. Hersh Zingerman died a natural death, and they buried him in the Polish cemetery. There were also two selections, meaning selecting people to send to Chełmno (an extermination camp). The first taken

[Page 99]

were elderly Pshaytsher Jews that were with us. Unfortunately, I don't remember all their names. I do remember Itche Vaydn, Moishe Ravsky, Shimshon Zikhlinsky the boot stitcher, Moishe Plotsker, Pinkhas Romer, Moishe Raukh, Yisroel Khaim Zielinsky, Avrom Ekert, and Mordkhai Pozner. The second selection took place at the end of 1943. Each of us, without exception, was taken to the Gestapo site, as well as people from other camps, so many Jews gathered there. It is a fact that thirty-five Jews from our camp were sent back, saying that this was thanks to the Inowroclaw city council, because they needed the Jews to work in the city. All the Jews were taken to Chełmno. It was difficult for me to understand why I and a few others were saved, since they took other tall, heathy, strong men to Chełmno, for example the son of Yekhezkel Mordkhai Lentsitsky and others. They probably went according to a list. The number of Pschaytsher Jews that they took was about forty. Unfortunately, I don't remember their names. Around Rosh Hashanah 1943, the Nazis closed all the province camps and sent everyone, without exception, to Auschwitz. Our group from Pshaytsh was kept together as much as possible, since we rode in one railroad car. The trip to Auschwitz took about twenty-four hours in confined train cars without air, without food, without drink. One person could not help the other. Faint, weakened, devastated, and broken, we arrived at the hell called Auschwitz, which I cannot describe. Literally hell in this world. At night it was very dark, their huge wild dogs bit off pieces of flesh of unlucky ones, and the Nazis beat us over the head with their rubber sticks. The yells and shrieks of the tortured and torturers were frighteningly loud. After a selection at the train station, we were put in vehicles, and were sure they were taking us to be incinerated. Hershl Vishnievsky, who was coincidentally sitting by me, began to recall his wife and children, each individually. He recited with tears the Vidui (prayer of confession that Jews say before dying) and the Kriyat Shema (prayer professing faith in monotheism, which Jews recite every morning and evening). With great lament, we arrived at the camp of Auschwitz on a grey morning, went through another selection when we were divided into various labor camps. I was sent to the large factory of A.N Farben in Buna. Very few Pshaytsher Jews were at Buna. Abba Buks soon arrived, also Yakov Fisher who today lives in America, and Mendl Frankenshteyn, who lives in Pshaytsh.

In January 1945, as the Russians were approaching, the Germans liquidated all the camps around Auschwitz. After fifteen hours we arrived in Gleiwitz. This is where I

[Page 100]

found women from Pshaytsh, including the Rabbi's daughter Esther. I'm mentioning her because Esther Zemelman gave me bread which kept me alive. We then wandered, chased by the Germans for about two weeks until we arrived in Buchenwald. We were liberated on the 28 day of Nissan 5705, April 11th, 1945, by the American military. To my great surprise, in Buchenwald I found our childhood friend and pal Ruven Yamnik. I don't remember why we did not stay together, but the main thing is we are now together in Israel, we the survivors, gathered together in Israel, let our children and families find consolation …

My Family and Parental Household

Translated by Jerrold Landau

Finally, a few words about my parental household and my family of blessed memory. As is known, my father, Reb Mordchai Binyumin, was a watchmaker by trade, a trade that he had inherited from his ancestors in Kłodawa. He was a great scholar, and an endless wellspring of words of Torah and *pshetls* [1]. One could sit with him for hours and listen to his Torah statements. He was a constant visitor of Rabbi Zemelman of blessed memory. It was a set custom for all the scholars and important people of the town to join him for the third Sabbath meal [*Shalosh Seudot*], and to participate in all the Torah discussions. He would also study in the *Beis Midrash* every evening. There certainly still are those who remember my grandmother Herisheshitzerun, as she was called in town. Certainly, they still recall that she traveled to the Land of Israel in 1924 to her daughter Sheindel, who was already in the Land along with my uncle Bunim Berkenfeld. However, to my great sorrow, they did not manage to acclimatize to the Land, and they returned to Lubin in Poland, where they had lived before they made *aliya* to the Land of Israel. They had a clothing store.

My father Mordechai Binyumin, Mother Chava, sister Zelda who was married to Mendel Fiszer and had two children, were in Przedecz until the final liquidation. My second sister Rachel was in the Łojewo Camp near Inowrocław, and was killed along with my brother Avraham Zalman, may G-d avenge their blood, when he visited her in the camp. The S.S. men captured them outside the camp and murdered them. My third sister Gitl (Guta) died around 1933 of an illness due to the lack of proper medical care. My youngest brother Yisachar Leibush went to Poznań [2] with the first transport. There was almost no survivor from that camp. Father was a native of Kłodawa. He had two brothers and two sisters. Not one survivor remains of the large family aside from one cousin whose name is also Yehoshua Dawidowicz. My aforementioned cousin made *aliya* to the Land in 1934. Relatives from my mother's side lived in Lubin – a brother and sister, Aunt Sheindel, and David Bunim Berkenfeld. They were in the Land for a certain period, but did not acclimatize at the time, so they returned to Poland, as was mentioned above. Another sister of my mother was Golda, married to Hersh Lipman Perla, who was a scholar. They had five children: two sons, Avraham Zalman and Mordchai, both Yeshiva lads, and three daughters, who studied the knitting trade on machines that were brought to Przedecz. At the end, they sold their house and moved to Łódź after uncle

[Page 101]

Hirsch Lipman suddenly died, around 1935. Around that year, the scholarly man, my teacher and rabbi, Rabbi Avraham Hirsch Skobronski of blessed memory, also died suddenly. His only son was my good friend, Yisrael Leib, who lived with me in the Inowrocław Camp, but was not able to maintain himself. The Germans took him along with his uncle Shimshon Wiclinski, Moshe Rabski, and others, and they never returned…

Zalman Dawidowicz and his friends of blessed memory at the time of the dismantling of the building of the teachers' residence in Przedecz. Among them is Levi Szwajczer, may he live, who lives in Israel.

In 1937, my parents sent me to study in the Yeshiva in Łódź. I studied there for about two years. I went to the fowl market on Wolborska Street next to the Great Synagogue every week to receive letters from home from Moshe Rauch. The wagon driver was Efraim Engel, for there were no buses to Przedecz at that time. Alter Wysniewski, the son of Yosef Wysniewski, lived next to the market. I ate at his place once a week. His brother-in-law Abba Buks worked with him for a certain period. Isser Morgensztern's daughter Tzipora and her husband Reuven Zielinski the son of Elia Zielinski also lived in Łódź. Reb Yitzchak Yosef Orbach, a scholarly man, moved to Łódź where he served as the *shammes* [beadle] in the Gerrer Hassidic house. I traveled home from time to time with the wagon driver Efraim Engel. We left Łódź toward evening, and arrived in Przedecz the following morning. There was a group of Yeshiva students from Przedecz. The brothers Moshe and Shlomo Toronczyk, the sons of Binyumin Toronczyk, studied in Warsaw. Yisrael Leib Skobronski studied in Lubicz, through the efforts of the Hassid of Lubicz, Reb Itche Majdan of blessed memory, a precious Jew, the *gabbai* of the *Beis Midrash*, who occupied himself with charity and benevolence, and about whom it is worthwhile to dedicate an honorable place in the book. He was with me in the labor camp, but not for a long time. They took him after he weakened. Along with him, they also took Moshe Placker the butcher, Moshe Rabski,

[Page 102]

Shimshon Zichlinski, and others. This was about a half a year after we were in Inowrocław. During the latter half of 1938, I returned home from Łódź, and I brought a sock machine with me. I also taught my brother Avraham Zalman. We progressed well, and we bought another machine. We had many plans, but everything was hidden and melted away at the outbreak of the war.

Life was bustling in the city during the years 1938-1939. Almost all the political organizations existed. Brotherhood and unity pervaded among all these organizations. I belonged to the Jabotinsky camp, in Brit Hachashmonaim flank. We received the *Heint*, *Moment*, and other newspapers daily. The aforementioned Chaim Aharon Orbach of blessed memory received *Heint*. We received five copies of *Moment* and distributed them. It should be noted that Rabbi Zemelman of blessed memory was an enthusiastic reader of *Moment*, and he identified with the Jabotinsky movement on many occasions. We would visit him almost every day with the brothers Moshe and Shlomo Toronczyk, and we knew the rabbi from up close. He was a very great man in all realms. This is the way the town was with its Jewish life, each person with his activities, thoughts, and deeds my family among them, until the Nazi destroyed rose and annihilated them all, may G-d avenge their blood.

Recall that which Amalek did unto you from generation to generation forever.

Translator's footnotes:
1. Does not translate that well into English, and may be equivalent in general with *Dvar Torah* [words of Torah – or explanations of Torah]. The nuances are a bit different. See https://jel.jewish-languages.org/words/1543
2. Probably https://en.wikipedia.org/wiki/Fort_VII

The Bread of Our Affliction

A composite of events described to Y. L. L. Shlomi by Tuvshe Yakubovitch, Rushke (Shoshana) Yakhimovitch, and perhaps the daughter of Khaim Kladovsky and others

Translated by Roberta Paula Books

Sit down, please, and recline. After all, today is the first Seder night. There are no feathers in the blankets or pillows; the Germans ripped them all up and threw the feathers to the wind. They searched for gold, silver, and jewelry in the pockets.

Sit, sit, make yourself comfortable and listen, since this is the last Seder in town, and the second under such circumstances. We will not sing here anymore, even though we haven't been singing for a long time.

These are my memories of the last Seder in the town of Pshaytsh (Przedecz in Polish) in 1942, shortly before the poisoning in the gas chambers in Chełmno . We remember little about the Haggadah, about the miracle of leaving Egypt, nor do we mention matzah because we have none, just a poor man's bread, the real "Bread of Affliction", large quantities of maror (in English, bitter herbs) – bitterness; nonetheless, we prepare a Passover Seder.

(Translator's Note: the next few paragraphs were told by Tuvtshe Yakubovitch.)

One hundred girls and one boy, Avromek Zikhlinsky, were in the first transport in 1940, recalled Tuvtshe Yakubovitch. We had been assembled via a list from the Jewish council. They said we were going to pick potatoes and beets in the fields. It was around the time of Sukkos (Translator's note: October). They divided us into three groups once we arrived

[Page 103]

in the region of Poznań. We were sent to three farms which were converted into labor camps: Gnojno, Lojewo (in Yiddish, Layove) and Tuczno. I was with my sister Hella. We brought with us bedding, clothing and underwear. We worked hard from dawn until dusk. The local Volksdeutsche (people whose language and culture had German origins, but who did not hold German citizenship) guarded us and liked to beat and whip us to show their importance and power. The camp had its own kitchen, but at the beginning we received packages and a bit of money from home. Understandably, not all parents could help. We also received help from friends. We were not free to wake up and go to sleep at will, because of lights in the living space, nevertheless the possibility

*Mrs. Kayle Yakubovitch, of blessed memory, and her daughters: Hella and
Tuvtshe, may they live long.
They live in Israel.*

of legitimate cultural activity didn't exist. The exchange of letters with our families was limited. We asked after and thought about them. From time to time, someone would go home for a few days. We had to buy a furlough with money or a gift for the head of the camp, the Volksdeutsche Urbansky, or other services for the Hitleristic low life creatures.

The worst was when they took us from one place to another. We had already settled in a little, placed a bit of straw on the plank beds we slept on, become familiar with the surrounding population through which we were able to offer our belongings

[Page 104]

and goods — so–called — for a bit of food, and then they moved us to a new place. For a long time, we slept in the hall of the theater in Inowroclaw (in Yiddish, Inovrotslav) on bare boards on the stage, and this was in winter, with a frosty wind blowing in from all sides. We all caught cold. Understandably, we sent or wrote letters in Polish or German. We had to write carefully. Writing between the lines, not everything could be inferred.

Before Passover 1942, thanks to some money my sister Hella and I received from home, I received a three–day furlough.

It had been two years since I had seen my parents and brother. My brother Mordkhai was in a prisoner camp as a Polish soldier, which I hadn't yet learned. But I still had my parents and two brothers, Yakov and Notte.

Sitting anxiously impatient on the train, I had to remain inconspicuous, since I did not have permission to ride this means of transportation.

With great fear, I got off the train at the last station in the hamlet of Szatki (Tseti in Yiddish) and walked the last eight kilometers.

I arrived in town on Passover eve, at night (**Translator's note:** Wednesday evening, 1 April 1942), when Jews are required to go to the synagogue, but I met nary a Jew. I was overcome with fear in that horrible stillness.

I could not enter my house. My parents had been moved to the ghetto and had left everything behind. A Christian let me know where to find the Jewish quarter. Pshaytsh (Przedecz) is a small town, and it was not difficult to find the place where those remaining were, in a very crowded, destitute situation.

I found my mother in the house. My father was still at work. The curfew (police hours) hadn't yet come. He worked as a tailor for a VolksDeutche woman living in the former apartment of the Rappaport family. My brothers were already in one of the murderous camps, and in my lifetime, I would never see them again.

Many parents came to me asking about their daughters. I could not offer them anything more than greetings. I could not tell them the whole truth. But in my last visit, our parents had talked only about Chełmno and how the liquidation of the Ghetto was approaching. They knew exactly what was happening there. My father returned late, and after he finished praying, we sat down for a Seder. Many women were in the group. Their husbands were in camps. Among them were widows — although not all – knew about that yet. Some little boy

[Page 105]

asked the questions "Why is this night different". In the middle, he burst into choking tears and cried out Chełmno . The child was perhaps five years old. I don't remember whose child he was. The windows were curtained. Two candles burned on the table. My mother managed a few dry white pletzels (a flatbread similar to focaccia). All of us tried with all our might to hold back our tears, but when my father came to the passage "we shouted unto G–d, and he heard our voices" he could no longer control himself, and continued with quiet sobs until the end of the service.

This was the last Passover Seder with my parents. After my return to the camp, I did not see them again. Nor did I hear from them again. But when I had returned to the camp, I had to describe everything anew. This time I could not control myself.

(Translator's Note: The next few paragraphs seem to have been told by Rushke (Shoshana) Yakhimovitch and perhaps the daughter of Khaim Kladovsky.)

Bitter herbs. Egg. Rushke, take me with you. Shank bone, karpas (a raw vegetable, usually parsley or celery), matzah. Chełmno . Gas chambers on wheels. Charoses. Wine. Everything, everything, I have forgotten nothing. Beautiful candlesticks with candles, a white tablecloth, covered matzah, everything, everything, just as it is supposed to be. Rushke, don't leave me behind. Everything so beautiful. Traditions, customs, clean without chometz. Kosher. Without memories, without bitter thoughts, without parents, without graves for a brother and sister, how can this happen, how can we understand this?

With these words, Rushke (Shoshana) Yakhimovitch began her description, her description of the last Seder she experienced in Pshaytsh (Przedecz) in 1942. I was sent to Gnojno, a hamlet not far from Inowroclaw (Inovrotslav). A ranch. From the autumn of 1940, I began to work there in the field picking potatoes, beets, guarded by savage, brutal Volksdeutsche with sticks, whips, and other instruments to beat stooped shoulders wet from rain. They acted with particular cruelty towards the Krel and Engel sisters. There was not a day or a night without beating them, accompanied by wild laughter. They took special pleasure in beating and kicking the unfortunate girls until they bled. They beat other girls too, but they mistreated these girls in an animalistic way. They had not dropped anything or done anything wrong. The truth is that they simply chose them as a scapegoat. Without any reason. That is how it was, because they were the rulers, the masters. As for culture, I believe they could not read or write. They spoke Polish poorly, and their German was not any better. That is how it was. The stick was in their hand. And they knew how to use it. After that, there was clearing the fields and carrying full sacks of produce on our backs. Then they harnessed

[Page 106]

us to the wagons because they treated their horses with respect. They kept us busy caring for the pigs, cows, and horses. To cut straw, to cook potatoes for the animals, from which we also ate a little, stealing food from the pigs. Not everyone had the means to buy food from the local peasants or trade a piece of clothing.

We lived like this for a year. Then they took us to Lojewo (Layove) camp. The guards there were a bit more humane. They did not beat us. The work there was also not easy. Perhaps it was more difficult. We excavated ditches, arranged wagons, transported the carts, which we had first filled with earth, and then poured additional earth on the road as appropriate, filling holes and puddles.

At this same time, that is autumn, 1941, they brought another group of thirty girls from Pshaytsh (Przedecz) to a camp in Tuczno, not far from us. Among the girls was Kayla Vishnivska. At about the same time, they brought a large group of men from Pshaytsh (Przedecz) to work in a sugar factory near Lojewo (Layove). We received very little food, and the men received even less. Many of them died from hunger and hard labor. The weak ones were sent to the hamlet Amze, which was near Inowroclaw (Inovrotslav), where they were shot by the German executioner. Among those killed were Yakov Pinkhas Rumer, Dovid Vishnievsky, Hersh Zielinsky, Shlamek Makovitsky, Moishe Raukh, Mendel Kviat, Dovid and his uncle Israel Khaym Zielinski, Maniek Raukh, and many others.

By the beginning of 1942, they began to liquidate the camps of Tuczno and Gnojno and sent everyone to the camp at Lojewo (Layove). Many youths arrived from the town of Radziejow. In Lojewo, the head of the camp selected Kayla Vishnivska as foreman of the girls (the elder Jew). We should write a second chapter about her, the good things she did. She organized a workshop for seamstresses, headed by Yetta Lntzitzka, for Pshaytsher girls in Lojewo; with ten girls, the work was not too difficult, and quietly they earned a bit of food which they gave to the starving men in the sugar factory. But with it all, we were anxious. We received bad news from our parents at home. Thanks to Kayla Vishnivska, I was able to be free for a week and go home. The others who went home with me for that bitter Passover were Khava Zielinsky, Feyge Pshedetzke, Tova Yakubovitch, Brayna Engel, Brayna Ofnbakh. We kept apart, in the event the Germans would capture one of us (we were not travelling legally), but we

[Page 107]

all arrived home. These were difficult days with our close ones for all of us. I found my mother and my eight–year–old brother Levi in the ghetto. They had been thrown out of our home. My family now lived in a small attic room at Avrom Fisher's. My father, Khaim Kladovsky, and my eldest brother had been sent to work a few weeks after I had been sent away, and no one had had any news of them since. I was told my father was killed working at the trains in Inowroclaw (Inovrotslav), but I later learned he was taken to the death camp **Amze** and murdered there. Tell me, my dear one, where is your grave? Where are your bones? When is the anniversary of your death?

My mother was hungry. She sold everything in order to send me packages to help me endure my suffering. My little brother became small and weak from these problems. He had begun to have a speech impediment. When I left to return to camp, he accompanied me. On the road, he asked, Lushke, take me with you. Lushke, I don't want to die. They will take us all to Chełmno where they will gas and burn us. Little brother, how can I? I have no idea what will happen to me. But Lushke, I don't want to die.

Every Passover I hear Levi's voice. Lushke, I want to live. Lushke, Lushke, Lushke.

I want to live.

Quiet Courage

by Y. L. L

Translated by Roberta Paula Books

In our story, we honor this great act of Yakov Yakubovitch of blessed memory.

On a weekday between Yom Kippur and Sukkos, they dragged all males over the age of fourteen out of their homes, brought them to the new market, and organized them in a semicircle. At the opening of the circle stood three men dressed in gabardine coats with raised collars and, on their heads, Tyrolian hats with feathers. Beside them was a small table covered with white paper, a razor and a scissors.

Almost all the Jewish men in town were assembled, with the Rabbi in front and, beside him, his devoted companion, the half blind

[Page 108]

elder – Itche the Shammes. The men varied in age, ranging from fourteen-year-old children and younger ones who did not want their fathers to go alone, to older men whom others helped by taking them by the arm. There was no shortage of helpers.

The scene was unnatural as they surrounded us with a thick wall of mockery and derision. They stood in their high shiny boots and stared at us with their colorless eyes, pale narcotic faces and thin lips.

They were our fate.

They were the ruling race.

All the Jewish men were gathered. Men went to search for those in hiding. After about a half hour, one of the three began to shout. He began to explain the inferiority of the Jews. He used words that a person from the lowest cultural standing would be embarrassed to have in his lexicon.

He ended by telling the farmers and workers that the filthy Jews, parasitic dogs, will be made to be productive.

A group of girls from Pshaytsh (in Polish, Przedecz) at forced labor

[Page 109]

These pigs will have to work all over the world for the victory of the northern ruling race. He shouted in that manner, with staring dead eyes, for approximately twenty minutes and ended by announcing that he will now introduce hygiene to these filthy bastard dogs. He called forward a local barber from among the Jews and ordered him to cut off beards, but only on one side. Soon the Jews looked as if a disease had distorted their faces. They, the gentlemen, rolled with laughter. They jumped and clapped their hands on the weapons at the sides of their pants. They summoned an old Jew who looked wretched with grey hair hanging from his half-beard. They placed him in the middle of the semicircle and again began to shout that he is an ugly, uncultured, filthy parasite. At first that Jew stood there embarrassed and sad. But then he began to smile. The German asked him angrily, what are you enjoying? His answer was excellent – we should say a memorial prayer (kaddish) for your culture.

Luckily the executioner did not understand the Yiddish answer. However, he did catch the word culture and became even angrier and took some of those who were assembled to the pump. He ordered two to turn the wheels, meaning to pump the water, and one of the Jews had to stand under the pouring water. When he was soaking wet, he was replaced by another. The wet man was forced to go to the other Jews, who were ordered to do gymnastics. They had to run, jump, and lie down on the ground. They made our Rabbi haul heavy planks of wood from one corner of the market to another. Here we see the ugly, audacious act carried out by a wild Jewish scoundrel (according to them). The eldest son of Itche Yakubovitch the tailor, the twenty-six-year-old Yakov, went to one of the gentlemen and with tears in his eyes asked if he could replace the Rabbi at this difficult work. For this exceptional crime they made Yakov lie down on the ground, and they beat him with a stick on his bare back twenty times, and then he had to do difficult gymnastics. They brought Yakov home wet and bloody where he lay in bed for a week.

This is how these gentlemen taught culture and productivity until late at night. When they themselves were finally tired and hoarse, they let the tortured, beaten, and exhausted Jews go home.

[Page 110]

Lament for a Town that is No More

by Pnina Leah (Zemelman)

Translated by Leon Zamosc

Edited by Roberta Paula Books

[Ed. Note: It is interesting that, although the poem is entirely in Hebrew, Rabbi Zemelman's daughter nonetheless uses the Yiddish name Pshaytsh to refer to the town – the name my father always used.]

The war is over and I am on my way home ...
After all the terrible suffering, I am going home.
Thousands roam the roads, lonely, worn out, exhausted.
The brutal war ended yesterday,
and today everyone is returning home ...

Every mile, whether by train or car
on my way home,
seems too slow, an eternity.
My beloved town Pshaytsh[1]
floats before my eyes all the time,
its houses, its residents, the place where I was born, the daughter of the rabbi.

Warm was my home, blessed with children,
four boys and four girls,
pure, innocent, and cheerful without end,
my righteous mother and my father the rabbi, can it be that they are gone?

About two hundred families, all of whom I knew by name.
Craftsmen, shopkeepers, petty traders,
Making a meager living but with dignity.
Can it be that they are all gone?

The train stops - Krzewata! Kłodawa!
Passengers get off the train, nobody recognizes me,
I feel soothed ... I grew up here and was still a child when I left,
it was a long way to go, but my town is in front of my eyes.
My town Pshaytsh[1] ... Oh, how I have loved you!
And it seems that all the rumors were untrue.

Because my town exists, it looks calm and whole.
The Christian Church is still here, Gothic and complete.
No. Nothing has happened, and I run to Pshaytsh.[1]
But what do I find? It is a town of the dead.
Shop after shop with the shutters closed, where are their owners?
I walk through empty streets and empty houses,

[Page 111]

on my way home - to my home!
From a distance I see it, standing on its own, somebody lives there,
Flowerpots on the windows, red like blood … Blood!

No! These are not my mother and father…
I knock on the door, hesitantly, with fear in my heart.

An evil woman appears.
What do you want? Who are you looking for?
She asks in a sharp voice that stabs my heart.
Are you the rabbi's daughter?

***Translator's Footnote*:**

1. Przedecz in Polish

The rabbi's residence and the Beis Midrash stood in the place where the fence is currently.

[Page 112]

Translated by Jerrold Landau

"How did you succeed in enduring the war? And you are still alive."

"No! this is not your house, Go away!" And she slammed the door in my face…

I lean on the wall – the common wall with the *Beis Midrash*…

The *Beis Midrash*; Like an enchanted word before my eyes. There, life constantly bustled – day and night. There they studied, there they prayed. Guests and poor people came there. It was the nerve center of Jewish life in the town…

Now – quiet, as if in a cemetery, pervaded there. The worshippers, the scholars, the communal activists are already no more. They all ascended on the stake in sanctification of the Divine Name and the nation. Everything ended and passed away.

My head is dizzy. I cannot focus – where am I? No, I did not weep. The tears were frozen in my eyes. Only a sharp pinch in the heart and suppressed anger. With a lowered head I leave my house… forever. I move from street to street, from house to house, with agony and anger. I knew them all by name. I knew them so well; we were like one family…

Here the yellow Itzi lived – a precious man and communal activist. From here, his emissaries went out in clown costumes on Purim to collect money for the poor. Here was the charitable fund, here was the Ludovy Bank, here the old market, and there the house of Reb Itshe *Shammes*. His voice announcing, "Go to the Synagogue!" still echoes in my ears.

Here, pure, wholesome Jewish life bustled, and is no more.

Again, I am here, passing by every house in the outskirts of the town, and calling all by name. However, wicked gentiles come out in their place. One question is on their mouths, "How did you survive? You are still alive…"

Accursed is the city upon whose streets the Jews were tortured and degraded. I recall my father of blessed memory – so pure, standing before the congregation in the beautiful synagogue that was burnt and is no more. The words emanated from his mouth*: Shema Yisrael*! The congregation that he loved and loved him responded after him. Dark, irritating thoughts overtook me, and I wanted, wanted, wanted… I fled from the city for it was empty of everything. It does not exist anymore for me. Behind me pursues the voice… How were you saved?!

The voice of gentiles – they did not extend a loving hand…

25.9.1962

[Page 113]

A Collection of Memories

by Y. L. L

Translated by Roberta Paula Books

Thrown away, sometimes it is possible to have oneself there between dangerous landowners hunting, catching fish, and other diversions, amplified by alcohol and blood, perils, and dangerous deeds, according to the customs of the wicked.

In those days, we looked at our town as a place ensnared in limitations, backward, with a difficult life for the hardworking masses, with few exceptions. A life circumscribed by laws and traditions which had been around since prehistoric times.

Today, decades later, we look through the mirror at our memory and see things totally differently. Even the forests, water, swamps with peat trenches, take on a different appearance. It could be that we understand it in a different way, or simply romanticizing the past makes everything nicer. However, the facts that we endured shed yet another light on the past.

Before me lie reminiscences written by three people: Yakov Topolsky, who stirs up the past of the cheerful years from 1900 until the outbreak of the murderous period; and Moishe Mokatov and Yitzkhak Loyn, who recount more facts from 1923- 1938. I don't need to agree with memories adorned with ideological flourishes from passionate hearts, nor with the complexes carried from the environments where they lived and spent their youth. However, in all this material, we see splendid characters, serious people, and kind, positive thinkers, thirsty for a renaissance which they stubbornly brought to town.

We see people who try to find a solution for the Jewish masses -- who are tied up by the endless persecution, state laws and other restrictions that are not at all simple.

Life in Pshaytsh (Przedecz) passed slowly, wearily. On summer evenings, cattle return home from the fields with a lazy, satisfied stride across the narrow streets. Leaving here and there some (Turkistanish energy) material on the stones, night comes closer, the shepherds crack their whips, the fathers rush off to Minchah (late afternoon prayers) and return home after Ma'ariv (evening prayer), when they have received all the latest news of the town. The wars evaded our streets, yet our town suffered.

In the furrows of the nearby villages where the Christians

[Page 114]

dug sand for the city folk to put on their floors, they found skeletons in cholera cemeteries from the Turkish – Russian war.

In the years 1917-1918 there was a typhus epidemic in town which, from nearly every family of the general population, claimed the life of at least one member. Even if there was no front line in town there were victims. Rulers changed, here there were Russians, over there, Germans, each with its persecutions. They always managed to find a spy who knew nothing, but was obliged to give up his soul. In those days people did a bit of business, worked a bit, smuggled a little and many were hungry. The worst economic time was the end of the First World War and the beginning of independence.

In the early years of the 1900s, journeymen came to work in Pshaytsh (Przedecz). They were from other towns. They belonged to the Populist movement ("Naradniye Vale") and tried to attract new members. But thanks to the Rabbi at that time and other religious Jews they did not succeed. A similar process was initiated by the Langnoz brothers in 1906, when they tried to establish a Zionist organization. Our pious parents were afraid to awake the Messiah. Although the study house, synagogue and smaller houses of prayer were always full with worship, new ideas did not cease to bubble. Thus, the idea of our own home, as well as far left ideas, remained.

Perhaps, when our parents were young, they hid Heine's poems in their Gemorah (Talmud), as many of our fathers were able to recite his work by heart. But they wanted to protect us and thought it better not to talk about it. I should not be revealing such a secret.

Every Friday night bright candles burned in the small windows. Beside them were the bent heads of our mothers covered in kerchiefs. They covered their eyes with their hands but we often saw hot, pained tears roll through their fingers. Saturday mornings, our mothers would walk on Synagogue Street in long dresses, our fathers holding their children by the hand. The child would carry his tallis (prayer shawl). In past days and on the holy Sabbath, we would offer praise to our creator.

Time dragged on slowly. There were weddings, funerals, and children to be reared. We were occupied with Gemorah, benevolence, scythes, and hoes, and we created new things. In Sarajevo, a shot falls, Kaisers fight, and soldiers fall. Hunger came and brought epidemics. Many people have become homeless.

[Page 115]

Many Jews came to Pshaytsh (Przedecz) from Łódź and other cities. We found places for them to sleep. Also, a kitchen to prepare food with newly collected funds. It was not a lot, but we were keeping people alive. Many families remained in town, including various professionals, and also scholars, and others. At that time the first library was founded on Jewish Street. Among the organizers were Yakov Topolsky and Ruzhie Mokotov. Lectures were organized. Also, an amateur drama club. New books were purchased with the funds collected from membership fees. Momentum grew to build a home for the library. A Zionist organization was founded under the imprimatur of the current rabbi. Things had to loosen up. But the library stayed and continued its activities. A primitive hospital was led by Itche Vayden with considerable assistance from Mrs. Mokotov. Her husband Yitzkhak Mokotov also devoted himself to the cause. In 1922 Rabbi Goldshlag left town to take on the position of rabbi of Sherpetz following the death of his grandfather, who had been the rabbi there.

During that year they began to consider candidate for a town rabbi. They listened to sermons, analyzed, considered, weighed, and measured. Our parents had a hard time making the decision, until they finally agreed to hire the young rabbi Rabbi Yosef Alexander Zemelman, the son of the rabbi of Drobin. I must add this was a good decision. They young rabbi turned out to be a highly intelligent, worthy man. On the day of his arrival, the entire Jewish town went out to greet him. A few youths on horses decorated with a variously colored ribbons kept things in order, wearing masks of the Tsar's Musketeers and other generals, including Cossacks, but all with Jewish hearts. Musicians were at the head of the group. There was such a feeling of holiday and cheerfulness. Thanks to the energetic and good organizing, everything took place uninterrupted. The rabbi was a kind, understanding man. The town became more moderate and more interesting. There was now a desire for knowledge. People began to read more. We received daily newspapers in Yiddish and Polish. The rabbi often invited young people for discussions on political topics as well as literature. He had a good pedagogic approach, although it was not always followed.

In the early spring of 1924, an agricultural training camp was established under the auspices of the General Zionists. Practically all the young people in town participated to some extent, learning how to work the fields of our future Jewish home.

[Page 116]

People worked enthusiastically on the large plot of land belonging to Khaim Zumer and Mirl Frank. Everyone carried up water. We also applied a full measure of fertilizer. The most beautiful flowers grew there. We were elated with the amount of fruit grown in autumn. The whole village bought radishes (new moon turnips), cucumbers, potatoes, tomatoes, rhubarb, parsley, and other vegetables. The young people worked every afternoon, and the entire day Sunday. At night they guarded against mischief makers, all voluntarily. The young people included: Yakov Topolsky, the Engel brothers, Gavriel Levin, Leyb Khudtsky, Hersh Zielinsky, Pinkhas Zikhlinsky, Menakhem Ravsky, Yitzkhak Bur'nshteyn, Yakov Hersh Vayden, Meir Lvkovitz, Khaim Aron Urbakh, Khaim Alter Iglinsky, Yekhiel Ofenbakh, Ezriel Skavransky, and many others. This truly positive organization was like the life of a summer bird, but only for one summer. Maybe had there not been such an abundant harvest of fruits, the successful training camp would not have collapsed so quickly. However, for one spring, summer and fall the Jewish youth showed they were capable of prodigious work.

In those times, there was economic progress. Tailors and shoemakers had greater success. A tailor – shoemaker "cell" was formed under the regulations of "Izba-Ziemieshlnitsa". They distributed journeymen and master diplomas. They had a professional commission. From all the neighboring towns came candidates to join from surrounding towns. With the money that came in, they rebuilt the Psalm Society (Khevre Tilim) building and formed a financial aid fund. The chairman of the cell was the hat maker Gershon Leyzer Haltrikht.

By 1927 we begin to see communist leaflets in our village and surrounding hamlets. The same year, a strike broke out among the shoemakers, tailors, and hat makers that lasted a few days. It felt like a strong jolt of electricity. A while later, a needle union was formed, with a Sholem Aleichem library. The following were among the organizers: Mikhl Shapiro, Nokhem Danielsky, Binyumin Tsanskovsky, Moishe Levin, and Esther Goldman. In 1929 the Young Mizrachi (religious Zionists) was founded. The majority of its members were young men from the local Yeshiva founded by Rabbi Zemelman. At that time, there was also stepped-up activity in the Polish streets. It was difficult to go out on the streets late at night. there were not organized activities, but the work of spreading information with collaboration and gossip was fruitful. It was especially difficult for the town's merchants, orchardists, for the poorest Jews in town.

[Page 117]

In 1932, Betar (a Revisionist Zionist youth group) was founded. People came from the central organization to give lectures. People also came to give courses in Hebrew. We played chess and ping pong; they organized outings to the hamlets to familiarize us with agricultural work. Quite interesting were the discussions led by the chairman, Shloime Yisaskhar Engel. He was an intelligent man who devoted his life to association work. He knew a lot, read a lot, and had a special way of planting a love of construction work in these passionate hearts. He would often say, no one will do the work for us. We must build a home and fight for a home with our own hands. Thanks to his efforts, three youngsters learned carpentry. Two of them live in Israel: Moishe Mokotov and Khaim Zikhlinsky. This was a time of great unemployment in Poland, including Jews with higher education. They wandered from town to town giving lectures and artistic performances. Among others who also came to us was the Doctor of Philosophy Foyglzon. He would recite poetry from Yiddish writers and translations of foreign authors. In one of his presentations, he said: "Jews, we must strive to emigrate from here, because Jews here will undergo a great tragedy".

In 1934 Fishl Topolsky organized a proper Poalei Zion (Workers of Zion) organization, and Mikhl Shapiro founded HaShomer HaTzair. They carried out their work in the same premises. They were highly intelligent people. They worked together in a united front with the needle workers union and did exciting cultural work. There was something on every evening, like a living evening newspaper. Question and answer evenings, singing, dancing, a drama club, public book readings and Hebrew learning. Those most active were: Fishl Topolsky, Tusyeh Yakhimovitch, Feyge Flatzker, Esther Goldman, Moishe Levin, Dovid Sayka, Levi Shveitzer, Soreh Haltrikht and others. From the proper Poalei Zion and HaShomer Hatzair membership, sadly no one survived. According to the recollections, we see there was worthwhile work happening on the Jewish street. Everything was destroyed, together with so many precious lives.

Consider a man like Hersh Lipman Perele. A tall, slim Jew with an aesthetic black beard and passionate black eyes. He walked quickly and held his head high. He would often say: "I am proud to be a Jew". He taught boys Mishna and Gemorah (Talmudic biblical interpretation). He put so much good will into his efforts. This fine and wise teacher had the patience to explain a passage three or four times, until we really understood, because our heads were,

[Page 118]

at the moment, in the yard where Yehoshua Isaac had just scored a goal.

Let's talk about Hershie Buf, who brought us chickens every week. There were such fine people among us. I remember when Hersh Lipman was sick, and we needed to bring him oranges. We didn't have any. Two boys went by bicycle to another town to bring the fruit for the patient. Or the hardworking Krel family, that worked so hard for a piece of bread. But when it came time to sew a suit for a poor groom for free, they did it with love.

Who did these good people disturb? Who?

One Tombstone Remains

by Y. L. L

Translated by Roberta Paula Books

All the laws were broken at once, all the odiousness of life, of humanity. Murderers freely roamed the streets, with hatred and mockery from all directions. There was nowhere to hide, surrounded by a sort of absurdity. Beatings were visited on Jewish heads without limit or pause. They shot people in the middle of the street, hanged them in the center of the marketplace, took them to useless work. Our children were dragged from our homes and sent who knows where. From some we receive an occasional letter, from others there is no trace. There is not a moment of rest. They burned down the synagogue and forced some prominent men, led by the rabbi, to sign a paper that said we had burned down our own holy building. And then we had to pay 50,000 zloty to the commandant of the town for the crime that had never been committed. When Moishe Hersh Danielsky and Dr. Diament handed over the money, which had been so difficult to collect, he said: Yes, this money is for the government, and now I want the same amount for me. There was not a drop of pity from anywhere. The helpless, unarmed Jew was surrounded by outstretched, blood thirsty hands. There was neither day nor night, even our children in the course

[Page 119]

of a day became adults, maybe in the course of mere hours. The schools were closed, religious schools, forbidden, it was an overexertion to come together, they were in no mood to play. They wandered around quietly with inquiring eyes, but there were no answers. The German prescription was already starting to work, a mandate for euthanasia "death without pity". There were various experiments at injections that they would need for their vicious military people, all connected to the annihilation of people of inferior races. What could you call this plan of one nation toward another? Perhaps one day a genius doctor will provide a diagnosis for this cruel psychosis and perhaps clarify these times, defend, or find an excuse or a reason why the world was silent until now? Who is guilty of this? Three-year-old children in 1940 already knew what was happening at the Chełmno camp. And for these blood suckers, this wasn't enough. Not only did they physically exterminate, but they annihilated and erased every trace of the Jewish people.

In the summer of 1940, the German miscreants, with the help of Polish volunteers, destroyed the Jewish cemetery. They promised pieces of tombstones to take as building materials for those that helped.

The Jewish cemetery in Pshaytsh (Przedecz) had existed for over 600 years. The first graves predated the 13th century. There were graves with an old patina for which you could not even decipher to whom the grave belonged, sunk deep in the ground, not able to know who had found eternal rest there. There were thousands of graves with various tombstones, some of sandstone, limestone, grey granite, and white and black marble, shining like mirrors and streaked with gentle red and green veins.

Dozens of young men from the Christian population scampered joyfully, like jackals, to grab this work. First they crossed themselves and recited, as usual, a short prayer for each effort and, while they worked, jokes fell from their mouths about what they found at this place of rest, as they banged away with their tools on the stones and said with a smile: "you Jews stuffed yourselves with enough fat geese and chickens". The Jews had to listen to this as the Germans forced them to harness themselves to wagons piled high with tombstones and take them to be stored in Khaim Zamer's garden. All the stones were pulled from the ground with cruelty, the field was plowed from end to end, no remnant of a cemetery remained. Only one tombstone remained, even though they planted potatoes there.

[Page 120]

Barely three hundred years ago, a great Jew lived here. Mothers passed on the story to their children. This was the time of the unfortunate "Liberum Veto"[1], when each Polish nobleman felt he was king of his fiefdom. The peasants were bound to the land and lived on the land. The peasant had the same worth as an ox, and like an ox, he had no rights. In the nobleman's palace, alcohol and honey flowed freely. When one nobleman overthrew another, he killed his whole family and all of his peasants. He stole the land because he was stronger, and the deceased ostensibly did not show him enough respect. In these bloody free times in Poland, a strong man came to town and chased all the Jews from their homes, as he was looking for a scapegoat and wanted to demonstrate his skill at killing people. He gathered everyone at the plaza of the Holy Florian and had the Jews line up in a long row. Facing them was a row of Christians. In the middle of the two rows, he placed a brilliant, respected Jew and said: Now, with one slash of my sword I will behead this man. Whichever side it falls will be the side he belongs to.

What horrible crime did the man commit to merit such a punishment? The Jews of Pshaytsh (Przedecz) had created an Eruv (boundary) within which they could carry objects on the Sabbath. He headed this committee.

At the very moment this nobleman, this murderer, lowered his sword on the man, a pregnant Jewish woman ran out of line and caught the man's head in her apron. The Jews gave him a Jewish burial. Within a short time, a small tree grew at the head of his grave. It grew into a large, thick, wild pear tree. It was as if the tree wanted to protect the grave of the old man with its branches. It served as a tombstone. This tombstone of many years ago remained.

Winds howl, sometimes from the west, sometimes from the east. The large branches are covered with flowers or leaves, or in winter they are bent and twisted from the snow.

These times are also twisted. The stones, the tombstones were divided up. The workers received some of them for the physical work they did in liquidating the Pshaytsher (Przedecz) Jewish cemetery. They used the remaining head stones to pave the streets of town.

The tombstone stands and the branches are as twisted as the times.

Translator's Footnote:

1.   The *liberum veto* (Latin for "free veto") was a parliamentary device in the Polish-Lithuanian Commonwealth. It was a form of unanimity voting rule that allowed any member of the Sejm (legislature) to force an immediate end to the current session and to nullify any legislation that had already been passed at the session by shouting, Sisto activitatem! (Latin: "I stop the activity!" or Nie pozwalam! (Polish: "I do not allow!"). In place from the mid-17th century to the late 18th century, the premise of the rule was: since all Polish noblemen were equal, every measure that came before the Sejm had to be passed unanimously.)

[Page 121]

Why?

by Y. L. L

In memory of Reb Khaim Tarner and family

Translated by Roberta Paula Books

"I have placed my rainbow in the clouds as a sign of the covenant between me and the earth". (Genesis, Chapter 9).

Like the echo of silver bells, the voices of young children escape from the small windows of the kheder (school for young children). Along the wall near the window is a long, straight table made from pine planks. Around the table are rough-hewn benches (not planed), and on them sit students ranging from four to twelve years old, repeating after the rabbi the words of the Hebrew Bible. At the head of the table, the Rabbi sits as his knowing look takes in the heads of the children being prepared for the difficult life of a Jew.

Nearby at a lower little table sit the three-year olds, called the alef beys (first two letters of the Hebrew alphabet) students.

The room was grey. There, the sun never peeked in. Two small windows opened toward the western side of the world. They were partially blocked by a horse stable. Between the windows and the stable, a small path led to the well where the surrounding neighbors drew water, the same well where the baker Klodawsky got the water for his bakery.

In the deep darkness of the well, one could hear an uninterrupted churning, as if many people were talking at the same time, which left us anxious and curious. We were convinced that in the cold, deep darkness there were thousands of devils and spirits lying in wait for our souls.

In the middle of the courtyard, which was surrounded by small houses where the artisans lived, was a post used to tan leather. Surrounding this place, shaped by the feet of horses and people, was greasy soil strewn with sacks filled with leather mixed with salt and hair. A strong, unpleasant smell emanated from this place. The smell from the horses' stable was like perfume in comparison to this smell.

On a summer afternoon, the sun sometimes shone on the working people. But in the kheder where the small children

[Page 122]

became familiar with the first words of the prayer book and Khumesh (Hebrew Bible), the sun never shone, as it was blocked by the horses' stable.

The entrance to the kheder was in a dark, narrow corridor. The floor was made from clay, which turned into hills and valleys, especially during the winter. The fact that the students did not break their hands and feet was a miracle from heaven.

G-d said, "I have indeed seen the suffering of My people in Egypt. I have heard how they cry out because of what their slave drivers do, and I am aware of their pain. I have come down to rescue them from Egypt's power. I will bring them out of the land, to a good, spacious land, to a land flowing with milk and honey" (Exodus, Chapter 3). The voices of the little children ring together with the bass of the Rebbe, filled with love and devotion.

Across from the door was a white, tall brick oven which, in the summer, was used only for cooking and in the winter, to heat the room.

G-d spoke to Moses saying, "I have heard the complaints of the Israelites. Speak to them and say, 'In the afternoon you will eat meat, and in the morning you will have your fill of bread. You will then know that I am G-d, your Lord'". (Exodus, Chapter 16).

Form the oven, parallel to the window, was a closet with kitchen utensils. There was also a closet for clothes. The room was divided in two, and the other half was completely cut off from daylight. That half was the kitchen and dining room etc. … When the sun was still high in the sky, it was dark in both rooms, and they had to use a kerosene lamp even though the windows were kept perfectly clean by the Rabbi's wife.

"Suddenly, he saw G-d standing over him. G-d said, 'I am your father, the Lord of Isaac. I will give to you and your descendants the land upon which you are lying.'" (Genesis, Chapter 28). The children's voices rang with rapture and with the beauty of promise.

The floor of the kheder looked like a mosaic: parts were wooden boards, and parts were clay. The boards were washed almost every day, but the part that was clay, especially in winter, liked to sweat or freeze, depending on the temperature outside and the heat of the oven.

Even here in the room, the floor was not ideal. Intentionally or unintentionally, there were hills and valleys. It would happen more than once that a 4–5-year-old boy would doze off during the Rabbi's dvar torah (explication of a Biblical passage). When a friend beside him on the bench would give him a shove or

[Page 123]

the Rabbi's loving voice would awaken him, he would be startled. Often the child would burst into tears or wet his pants, and then the Rabbi's wife would wipe his tears, wash, and calm the frightened child with motherly warmth.

"These are the foundations which Solomon laid for building the house of G-d: the length, according to the old standard of measurement, was sixty cubits and the breadth, twenty." (Chronicles 2, Chapter 3). The voices of the children rang out like the singing of birds, out to the yard where the hard-working people straightened their bent backs and looked toward the sky, as if they saw angels in heaven singing these songs of praise, together with the children.

A few generations of Jews had sat in this dark, sad room at the simple, long table as they were shown the way toward heartfelt love for the Master of the Universe.

For many years, at the head of the table sat the Geller Rebbe, a short, broad man with a wide patriarchal beard. Slowly, word by word, in his bass voice, he instilled in the children's small heads words of love to the Creator of the World.

Every morning, he opened the school day with all the children standing on their little feet saying the familiar Morning Prayer, "Modeh ah-nee lifanecha, Melekh chai v'kayam, she-hechezarta bee nishma-see b'chemlah rabbah emunasecha." (I give thanks before you, living and eternal King, for you have returned my soul to me with compassion; abundant is your faithfulness.) In the evening, at the end of the day of learning, everyone recited the Kriyas Shema, reciting "May the angel who has redeemed me from all harm bless these boys. May they carry on my name and the name of my fathers, Abraham and Isaac. May they become teeming multitudes upon the earth".

Each year, Reb Khaim Tarner also recited the morning prayer service during the Days of Awe (the ten days from Rosh Hashanah to Yom Kippur) in the House of Study, where he prayed all his years. When he would approach the podium in his kittel (white linen robe worn on special occasions), wrapped in his prayer shawl, people felt he was actually G-d's messenger.

Please accept my prayer as coming from a regular old man with a pleasant appearance and a full beard and a pleasant voice and involved in the common good for the people. However …

However, in this holy house, it was never joyful as the sun never peeked in.

Also, there was generally not enough bread to satisfy our hunger. But the hearts of the two magnificent people laughed with great joy when they heard the silvery voices of the small children sing out the praises of the great Name.

The Rebbe, Reb Khaim and his wife Malke had tears of joy in their loving eyes, and quietly sang along with the children:

[Page 124]

"And God created man in his image, and in the image of G-d he created man and woman".

And the Rabbi's wife Malke, in her clean, patched dress, always overworked, but always with a warm smile. For many years she cared for the children with motherly love.

Reb Khaim derived pleasure from his former students, who now sit in the House of Study and study biblical interpretation.

These magnificent people were exterminated. These beautiful, magnificent people do not even have a grave. The grass at the cemetery does not even sing them lullabies.

Only my spirited words praise the worthy Tarner family. Whoever reads this will remember these people and say:

"Magnified and sanctified be G-d's great name" (From the mourner's prayer)

God of mine, I call upon you, as a sinning Jew I praise you. Tell me, great G-d, why? Great one, why? Almighty, One and only, why, just one.

And why? Eternally, Eternally,

Why? Why?

W – H – Y?!

Memories of My Father's House

by Esther (Zemelman) Burg

Translated by Marshall Grant

I am recording the memories of my dear family, my parents, brothers and sisters, who perished in the Second World War at the blood–covered hands of the Nazi beasts.

And now, while documenting my childhood memories, I still find it hard to believe that everything that happened between then and now really took place, and even though my memories are a still a bit vague, I still feel and sense my family experiences from my parents' home.

We were eight children at home: four brothers and four sisters. I was the oldest, then came Leah, Yehoshua, Yoel, Nehemia, Adele, Chametza and Yankele, my parents' youngest. I lost them and they are no more; of my large family, only my sister Leah and I survived.

In my dreams, I see myself together with my dear family in our house and in our small town. It was like all other Polish towns – there was nothing exceptional about it.

[Page 125]

*Mrs. Esther Burg (Zemelman) in the Holocaust basement in Jerusalem, next to the memorial
to the fighters and heroes of the Warsaw Ghetto*

But in my eyes, the town was the symbol of beauty and prosperity. That was where I grew up and was educated, that was where my world was, that was where I dreamed my childhood dreams.

I remember when I was just three years old, my parents, of blessed memory, decided to send me to a *cheder* to learn the alphabet with the teacher known as Dar Ga'ala'ar Chaim. He was much older than the students. After I completed my studies in the *cheder*, my parents sent me to study in *Beit Ya'akov*. This was a school affiliated with *Agudat Yisrael*, founded by Ms.

Sarah Shnerer, and it mainly taught Tanach, a little Hebrew, home traditions and laws. The teacher at *Beit Ya'akov* was Mrs. Hirschberg. I loved and adored her very much. She had a pleasant personality and was very dedicated to her students.

After Mrs. Hirschberg moved away, a new teacher arrived. She had completed a seminar for certified teachers in Krakow. This was my aunt, Esther Zemelman, my father's sister. I completed my studies at *Beit Ya'akov* and reached the age at which children began their schooling. I was happy. It was the happiest day of my life. I felt "big" – ready for first grade. My first teacher was Mr. Jaczinsky, and I was almost seven years old. For the first time, I loved and adored someone other than my family, and I trusted him completely. After him, there were other teachers and my admiration went from teacher to teacher. I was especially captivated by Mrs. Pavashinsky, who was the wife of the school's principal.

For a while I studied at the old school. I was so happy when they began building a new school in the town. It was a beautiful and unique school, and one of the most beautiful buildings in the town. Later, I was hugely disappointed

[Page 126]

when I heard the government didn't have sufficient funds to completely finish the building. I was heartbroken when, for the first time, I learned that my beloved homeland, Poland, was poor.

Now, when looking back to the days of my youth, I see how much I loved Poland and how I believed it was my only homeland. I didn't feel the antisemitism surrounding me … I didn't feel what my "Polish brothers" did to me and my family.

I remember September 1939, the beginning of the Second World War. The Nazi monsters invaded Poland and in just a few days they entered our town. Persecution against the Jews began immediately. My father, the town's rabbi, suffered the most. I remember the tragic morning when they took my dear father from our home and sent him, with other prominent Jews in the community, to clean the streets; with Poles standing around them jeering, their eyes filled with satisfaction and happiness. There was more than the humiliation and embarrassment. They shaved the beards and *payos* of every Jew in the city. They ignited our beautiful synagogue and made my father sign a declaration stating that it was he, my father, and several other local Jews, who burned the synagogue down.

He was later sent to the ghetto. This is the street we called the *Alter Mark* (the Old Market) in Yiddish. This is where most of the residents were blue–collar workers and small–business owners. It was in these small homes that all the town's Jews had to crowd together.

The Nazi scourge stole our belongings. They closed Jewish shops, prohibited Jewish children from going to school, and there was no one to resist the cursed Nazis. My father's noble soul revolted when it could no longer endure the suffering of his city's brothers and the destruction of the community he loved with all his soul and with all his might. He was unable to help. He then escaped to Warsaw and made it to the Jewish ghetto. My father calls for revolt and revenge. He calls for Jews to rise and revolt against the Nazi enemy. With his life under threat, he goes to the "Aryan" side and resides as a "pure Aryan". He contacts leftist Polish partisans. He later made the same trip back to the ghetto with guns and ammunition. He held secret meetings inside the bunkers. He speaks with skill as he describes the horrific scenes of the destruction of our small town and other communities with passionate rhetoric.

My father calls for revenge and offers a plan for the uprising. He takes it upon himself to provide weapons and ammunition and was fairly successful in doing so. When the Warsaw Ghetto uprising began, my father was among the first combatants involved. Witnesses said that they last saw my father when he was emerging from a side street with a few other yeshiva students who attacked, with grenades and guns, a group of S.S. soldiers who had entered a Jewish house in order to set it on fire. My father and his group threw grenades at them and shot their pistols at them. The Germans also threw grenades and shot back with their rifles. This was the battle in which my father and the yeshiva students fell. This was the last piece of information concerning my dear father, as told by Hillel Seidman, in his book *Warsaw Ghetto Diary*.

The murderous Nazis continued to destroy the Jews in gas chambers even after the Warsaw Ghetto revolt. The destruction was faster after the fall of the ghetto, and the Jews were slaughtered and killed by the millions. Five years after the Warsaw Ghetto uprising, the War of Independence broke out in Israel, a nation striving to achieve independence in its homeland. On the 5th of Iyar, 5738; May 15th, 1948, the establishment of the State of Israel was declared, together with a bloody and costly war. The best of Jewish youth paved the path to the state's independence with their lives. This is where the remnants of the Holocaust gathered, here in the State of

[Page 127]

Israel, and we are confident that a second Holocaust will never occur. However, we must remember the soldiers who stood on the front line and fought for the establishment of Israel and died in the line of duty. They carried the flame of revolt in the Warsaw Ghetto and risked their lives against the Nazi animals. One of its founders and spiritual leaders of this revolt, and who actually took part in the combat, was my father, the late Rabbi Yosef Alexander Zemelman, the rabbi of the town of Przedecz, may God revenge his soul.

My Father Mikhl Hersh Naymark

by Simkha Naymark, Sao Paolo, Brazil

Translated by Janie Respitz

We were orphaned at a young age, since our mother Frimet passed away at the most beautiful time of her life. Our father was left with six young children. The older ones were not old enough to help care for the little ones or to help run the household. Our father was busy all day trying to earn a living. He was forced to look for another housewife. After looking for a long time, he married a widow named Rokhl who had a child from her first husband whose name was Hersh Leyb. Although she was a good wife to my father and a good housewife, we kids could not make peace with the fact that

A glance at the old market street photographed by
Mr. Simkha Naymark when he visited Przedecz in 1965

[Page 128]

another woman took the place of our good mother. This is the reason why at a very young age we looked for a way to be independent and leave home. We were very fond of our father and very proud of him. His house was always filled with people, Jews and Christians who would come to consult with him during times of trouble.

My father's advice was taken with the belief it would lead them in the right direction. Reb Mikhl Hersh always evaluated all matters to provide a way out of a difficult situation.

Not only did people from Przedecz come to my father for advice, but they also came from surrounding towns and villages, directly to the "good Jew" in search of help at a difficult time.

A few years ago, after my visit to Israel, I went to Poland to visit my birthplace, Przedecz with the hope of finding a relative or a friend alive. Unfortunately. this did not happen. When I came into contact with the town's Christian population and walked through the streets of my hometown, many citizens stopped me and with admiration called out: "This is the son of Mr. Naymark".

In a discussion with these people, it was brought to my attention that not only people from Przedecz, but also people from the surrounding towns and villages came to Mr. Naymark looking for help. Until this day, they remembered my father's name with respect and were not patronizing.

My father made a name for himself as the perpetual defender and often the judge of hundreds of suffering people, never differentiating between Jews and Christians or poor and wealthy.

My honest and good father, whom everyone respected and admired, was tragically killed together with his family. In those times, Hitler and his German barbarians, with the help of some of the Polish Christian population, began to annihilate the entire Jewish nation.

Luckily the plans of these barbarians were not realized, even though they killed one third of the Jewish people.

With this remembrance, I would like to erect a monument, a symbolic tombstone for my family which was tragically murdered. Most of all my unforgettable father, as well as the fathers and mothers who were sent to the gas chambers, hanged on gallows, and faced other forms of death. We will eternally honor

[Page 129]

the memory of the six million Jewish martyrs, among whom were my brothers, sisters, uncles, aunts, nephews, and cousins.

With deep respect, I remember my stepmother who shared the same fate as my father, as she was his devoted life partner in the most difficult moments of his life.

Memories

Translated from Hebrew by Marshall Grant

In the beginning of 1939, our bakery in Przedecz was closed by order of the authorities. My parents began to look for other sources of livelihood, and they found a bakery for lease in the city of Kleczew, and we moved there. The involvement of my father, of blessed memory, in the public activities of his hometown of Przedecz was part of his life. He was involved in the community's life and institutions, so the separation from his natural surroundings was very difficult.

Nevertheless, we became used to the new location and it seemed we had found our place.

But the atmosphere was toxic in Poland during those months, as was the way the Poles treated the Jews. Anti-Semitism erupted, and the concern was things would get worse if war broke out, and this weighed heavily on us, and on all Jews, especially those like us, who were new.

From my brother, Moshe in Israel, we received letters often. We were aware of the riots being suffered by the Jewish community there, and our concern was understood. My parents, may they rest in peace, would often say, if only we could be together with him in *Eretz Yisrael* – but it was a dream that never came true.

On September 1, 1939, the war broke out, and the boots of Nazi soldiers stomped over Poland, destroying cities – and it was the Jews who suffered the most.

The Germans entered Kleczew on the night of *Rosh Hashanah*, the new year, and on the holiday the next day the Germans took the Jews to the city's market to bully them so that the Jews would understand who now ruled the city. The torture and degradation had begun, and while getting used to the new situation, life continued.

Official prayer houses were not closed down, but Jews were not allowed to come and pray in public.

In the summer of 1940, the Nazis began the eradication of Kleczew's Jewish population, and transferred the Jewish residents to Zagórów. The Germans obtained vehicles, carts, and horses to transfer the exiled and their few belongings, which, while not a lot, still held much value for them.

I will note one small detail. When we left Kleczew, we left behind a half-ton of flour in a storage room, and when we arrived in Zagórów we received special permission from the Judenrat, with the approval of the German authorities, to use a car to bring the flour to us in Zagórów. We lived in a sort of ghetto for almost a year, and in the summer of 1941, all the younger people who were able to work physically were sent to the Inowroclaw and Farkash labor camps.

About two weeks before *Rosh Hashanah*, the expulsions from Zagórów began. The expulsion was carried out with complete thoroughness. All the Jewish residents and all the refugees who had arrived were rounded up and forced to pay four

[Page 130]

German marks for travel costs. They were then given medical checkups to verify that they were indeed able to work.

In the Farkash labor camp, I received a letter from my parents in which they notified me that they and the children were being sent to a work camp, and that in the next letter, they would notify me of their new address – an address I never received.

It was unbelievable how the Germans misled and deceived the Jews, how the masses believed every promise, every good word. The exiled were unable to believe that Germans had created a reality that was their worst nightmare – the work camps. Jews from Kleczew and Zagórów believed, when they were taken in terribly overcrowded trucks to the killing valley in the forests of Kazimierz, they believed when they were told that they were being taken to labor camps, they believed when the Germans brought them to the buildings with the sign "Special Jewish Bathhouses for Disinfection and Washing" appearing on them.

They believed that in their final moments a miracle would occur.

But the miracle never happened.

A month passed and we did not receive any letters with the promised new address. A man from Kleczew, who was in the Farkash labor camp travelled with permission to Zagórów to find out what had happened to his loved ones, to find out where they had been sent.

He was never seen again.

And nothing has been heard from him since.

And no news has been received from them. From snippets of news that were collected, it turns out that some of Jews were murdered - some were shot, and some were poisoned in trucks from hell. Amongst the Jews from Kleczew who were brought to Zagórów and sent to the valley of death, was also my father, Mendel Wolf Belinski, my suffering mother, Sarah Belinski, my two sisters: Briana 25 years old, Balatzia 16 years old and my brother Laybel 13 years old. "May their souls be bound in the bond of life," may G-d revenge them. From all those expelled from Zagórów to the forests of Kazimierz, no one survived.

In the Inowroclaw labor camp I met several people from Przedecz, Moshe Rabeski, Moshe Tchenaskowski, Hirsch Zingarman, Itsche Weidan, Moshe Aharon Weidan, Lev Chodotzki, and others, from whom I heard about the suffering of the Jews of Przedecz and the surrounding cities.

Of course, as a result of the lack of food we were forced to occasionally buy food outside the camp, but those who were caught faced a bitter fate. Asher Roznekrantz was caught with several potatoes in his pocket and sent a nearby camp for punishment. This camp had all the horrors from hell, and for those in this forced labor camp, their lives would sadly end there.

From the Farkash labor camp, I was sent to the Adkova labor camp at the end of 1942. There I met the brothers Shlomo and Eliezer Makovitzki, Yomtza Shlifkovitz, and Moshe Aharon Yacoboveski. Shlomo Makovitzki died in Adkova due to malnutrition. In February 1943, I was transferred to Andrychów where I met Azriel Skovronski and Monish Sayka, who worked on the construction of railroad tracks.

In Birkenau I met the Angel brothers, Arieh Lev Pe'er-Danski, Pinchas Rauch, the Danialeski brothers, who are now in the United States, and the Tapalski brothers.

The Sonderkommando operated in that camp, and at the end of 1944, a group organized itself to rebel

[Page 131]

and blew up the crematorium. Among this group's members was Hirsch Tapalaski. After the explosion, all members of the revolt were killed by the Germans.

From Birkenau I was sent to the Jaworzno camp, where I worked mining coal. From there, with the retreat of the German army, I was sent all the way to Blechhammer labor camp. Here I broke through the brick wall that surround the camp and made it to the forest, where I remained until the liberation.

Immediately upon my release in January 1945, I returned to Poland and twice visited my city of Przedecz. The city was desolate. I walked on its streets, I looked for remnants of Jewish life, and I didn't find any. The synagogue was burnt down, the *beit hamidrash*, where I had spent many hours of my childhood for prayers and study, was deserted. Not the sound of prayer, and not the sound of study was heard. And the Poles looked at me in wonder, as if I had returned from another planet. Could it be? Did Jews still remain? They were astonished, they were concerned for they may have to return Jewish assets and homes to their rightful owners. I paid full price for the bread I bought from our former friend, Doshak.

And then I left Przedecz forever.

Germany was defeated but was still fighting. Liberated Poland established its military right away. I enlisted because I was looking for revenge against the Germans. I saw scores of Germans with their families in Lower Silesia who had become refugees overnight. They left their homes, their possessions, with bundles on their shoulders, they left everything and were expelled to the crumbles of Germany. It was little retribution.

It was clear that our loved ones and our friends, who were murdered by Nazis after being humiliated and tortured in a way that history had not yet known, could not be brought back, and we couldn't save them.

I meant to travel to Israel. In 1948 I arrived in Italy, where I underwent additional military training in preparations for my conscription in Israel. In January 1949 I arrived in Israel, and after disembarking I was immediately sent to a military camp for conscription to the IDF. This was a day of celebration for me, as after so much suffering, I was wearing the uniform of the Israel Defense Forces. Forty-eight hours later, I received a furlough to visit my brother and his family, who lived in Ramat Gan. I was excited. However, my brother was not at home. He too was in the military. But after just half an hour, there was a knock on the door and my brother appeared with news of his release. Overwhelmed with emotion, we stood embracing and weeping for several minutes, both of us in IDF uniforms. My brother was about to be released after taking part in the War of Independence, while I was taking my first steps in Israel in an IDF uniform.

I was overcome with emotion and spiritual uplifting that I will always remember.

I was serving my country.

[Page 132]

Memories of My Father's Home

by Reuven Yamnick

Translated from Hebrew by Marshall Grant

Dedicated to the beloved memory of my dear parents, brothers and sisters who were murdered by the Nazis and their associates during the Holocaust.

My father, Shmuel Halevi, *shokhet* (ritual slaughterer) and cantor, of blessed memory.
My mother, Sarah Rachel Albert, of blessed memory.
My brother, Yaakov Yitzhak, his wife, Leah, and his family, of blessed memory.
My brother, Shalom, his wife, Malka, and his family, of blessed memory.
My sister, Chaya Devora, her husband, Yisrael Mandlboim, and her family, of blessed memory.
My sister, Royza Leah, of blessed memory.
My father, Rabbi Shmuel Yamnik, of blessed memory, was a *shokhet* (ritual slaughterer and examiner) and cantor in our town of Przedecz for more than 40 years. He lived his life with holy adherence to *Derech Eretz* (treating others with respect) and Torah, as said by Rabbi Eleazar Ben Azaria, "If there is no Torah, there is no *Derech Eretz*, and if there is no *Derech Eretz*, there can be no Torah, because it is *Derech Eretz* that supports the Torah, it completes it". This is the way he educated his children, to love the Torah, to love the People of Israel, to love the land of Israel, and to be civil and courteous to his fellowman.

My father was born in Rawa Mazowiecka to his father, Rabbi Yehuda Halevi, the *shokhet* and cantor in this city, and to his mother Beyla, on the 23rd of Elul, 5632 (September 26, 1872). He was named Shmuel on Sunday, on Rosh Hashanna 5633, when the *maftir* of Shmuel the Prophet was read (this I heard from my late father).

My mother was born in the city of Grodzisk, near Warsaw, to her father, Rabbi Yehuda Albert, and her mother, Rivka, in 5642 (1882). My father, as a young yeshiva student, was accepted to the position of *shokhet* and cantor in our city of Przedecz in 5650 – 1900, by Rabbi Moshe Chaim Blum, who later became the rabbi of Zamość, near Lublin. My father later became the *shokhet* under Rabbi Yehoshua Heschel and Rabbi David Goldschlak, the latter would become the rabbi of Sierpc. My father continued working with Rabbi Yosef Alexander Zemelman, the last rabbi of the town during the Second World War, who fell fighting the Nazis in the Warsaw Ghetto.

My late father was studious, devout, modest, humble, and goodhearted; he was hospitable and loyally served the community of Przedecz. He enjoyed the fruits of his labors, loved Israel and was a follower of Amishnov Hassidism. He frequently visited the Great Rabbis (*Admorim*) Rabbi Yaakov David and Rabbi Yosef. He studied with Rabbi Yaakov David, who was the last *Admor* in Amishnov, and before that the rabbi of Żyrardów, near Amishnov, and in the city of Grabów near Koło (not far from Przedecz). I remember when the *Admor*, Rabbi Yosef, visited his son, Rabbi Yaakov David in Grabów. On a Friday in the 1930s, my father decided to travel to Grabów for Shabbes and welcome the Rabbi. He leased a wagon and we left. For some reason we traveled on a dirt road;

[Page 133]

it was very muddy (it was right after the Passover holiday), and the horse could barely pull the wagon. We were concerned that we could desecrate the Sabbath. After a tumultuous journey, we were able to reach Grabów in time, and even managed to dip in the *mikveh* (ritual bath). Later, when my father met the great rabbi, he said, "Shmuel, I knew you would come – and I even asked here, has Shmuel the *Shoichet* from Przedecz arrived yet?" And that is how we leisurely spent the Shabbat with Rabbi Yosef. My father was a friendly and pleasant person. During World War I, a large number of Jewish refugees arrived in our city after their escape from Łódź. They were escaping the hunger that prevailed at that time in the larger cities, and many found refuge in our city. Everyone did the best they could to help refugees and their families and provide shelter in their homes. My father was no different; he gave one of the two rooms we used for bedrooms to a refugee named Fried, a cobbler

Rabbi Shmuel Yamnik
Shochat and Cantor

Mrs. Sarah Rachel Yamnik
his wife

by trade. Despite the apartment's congestion from the many small children in the family, he was very satisfied that he could help a Jewish refugee recover financially by sharing the apartment and enable him to go out and work to earn a living for his family. They owned a hand–operated mill for grinding flour. He also sporadically worked as a cobbler, and he was able to somehow survive. After the war, when the refugees returned to Łódź, we visited this family several times – they lived at 12 Wolborska Street. There were times when poor Jews came to raise money to go to Israel, and my father would accompany them to wealthy Jewish homes to help them with the fundraising. Among them was a young Jewish man from the city of Złoczów whose business had burned down and was requesting to come to Israel, and who was eventually successful in doing so. This man was

[Page 134]

well known in our city, and I often saw him leading prayer sessions as the cantor, chanting the first *Selichos* prayers. His business would often take him to our city, and he was pleasant to listen to. After he decided to move to Israel, he came to our city to collect money for his journey, and my father helped him as best he could. After the war, when I came to Israel as an illegal immigrant, I met this pleasant man and he shared many good memories of my father: his character and his hospitality. In our city, my father served as the ritual slaughterer and examiner, the mohel, cantor and Torah reader in the synagogue every day of the year. He would sound the shofar on Rosh Hashana and lead the High Holiday prayer sessions. On Yom Kippur, he would lead the *Kol Nidrei* and *musaf* prayers, and if the rabbi was unavailable, also the closing prayers. His voice was strong and pleasant, and he made sure his voice would also be heard in the women's section. After being accepted to be the ritual slaughterer and examiner in our city, he served together with the old cantor, Rabbi Shabtai Kotak, who was then the cantor and *shokhet*. When Rabbi Shabtai passed away, my father worked by himself for a long period of time until a replacement was found. Graberman was from the German city of Fürth and a good cantor, but he never imagined remaining in Przedecz. He expressed many times that this was only a transition point for him. And sure enough, after a short time, he moved to Szydłowiec as their cantor and ritual slaughterer and examiner. That again left my father alone in his position until the community was wiped out by the hateful Nazis. When he worked alone, he worked very hard, for many hours a day and without any time restrictions, from early morning until late at night. At sunrise, he was already on his way to the slaughterhouse – to slaughter the cows, and then the chickens. There were no limits to how long he would work, just morning to night, and he always fulfilled his position with loyalty, without complaints or grievances. This is because he knew that the holy work needed by the city rested on his shoulders as there was no one else to help him. For many years the city did not have a designated slaughterhouse for cows and chickens and each local butcher had their own in their yards. We had a small slaughterhouse for chickens in our yard. And just several years before the outbreak of the Second World War, a large and official slaughterhouse was opened by the local Polish Authorities in the yard of Rabbi Haim Zomer. This was very advanced for those days, with more conveniences for the butcher and slaughterer. There were also better sanitation conditions with constant supervision by a Polish veterinarian. There were specific hours in the morning allocated for the slaughter of cows and specific hours for chickens. When the chicken slaughterhouse was in our yard, it was very popular, especially when the women would buy chickens in the market and immediately come over to slaughter them. It was the same on Wednesdays and Thursdays before Shabbes or during the week before a holiday. The yard was full of women and children who brought their chickens for slaughter, and there were even times people had to stand in a long line. In the week before Yom Kippur, during the 10 days of repentance, the demand was even bigger because each person brought *kappores* (traditional atonement ritual in which a chicken is ritually used and then slaughtered) and each brought several chickens for food. During these times the slaughtering work would continue until late in the evening. The night before the day Yom Kippur eve began, my father walked with the *shammesh* (synagogue caretaker), Reb Itche Kovalsky, to homes who adhered to the tradition of waving a chicken above the heads of the home's residents in the morning before the holy day. And so, my father was busy all night with the slaughter of *kappores* until the sun rose in the morning before Yom Kippur eve and he would return home tired and exhausted. However, there was still a busy day ahead. There was no more slaughtering work, but he had to prepare for the holy day and lead the prayers in the large synagogue, on the morning before Yom Kippur eve began. He went

[Page 135]

to the synagogue for morning prayers, and after eating and resting shortly, he went to the mikvah and prepared for his day of holy undertakings. In the afternoon, he went to synagogue for afternoon prayers, and after the pre–fast meal, he blessed the children and went to the synagogue to lead the *Kol Nidre* prayers. The next day, on Yom Kippur, he prayed the morning and *musaf* (additional) prayers with the choir, composed of the Vishinsky brothers, Herschel, Zelig, Simcha, all led by their older brother Reuven. All had sung in the past with the old cantor, Rabbi Shabtai Kotek. My brother, Yehoshua, and myself were helped by him (I don't understand this – how were they helped by him? Is this what you meant?) during the high–holiday prayers.

My late father was an enthusiastic Zionist. At that time, this was courageous and risky for a devout Jew, especially a religious representative such as the *shoichat*, but he was unwavering in his desire to move to Israel. However, he never realized his dream and sent my brother Yehoshua to a *Hapoel Mizrakhi* kibbutz to be trained, as was done in those times. After several years of training, he received his certification and moved to Israel in 1935. His education for the love of Zionism was provided by my father. In his youth, in the house of his aging father, Rabbi Yehuda Halevi, he joined the *Agudat HaElef* Group that purchased land in Israel in the village of *Ein Zeitim* near Tzfat, with the hope of immigrating with his family and settling in Israel. However, the Group lost much of its capital in unsuccessful investments carried out in connection with the estate. It disbanded, and only three hundred people continued with this task, my father among them. It eventually completely disbanded, and all the efforts and funds he invested were lost; all that remained were the documents and receipts he held for the payments made, but he was never able to move to Israel.

During Nazi control, kosher slaughtering was completely forbidden, and anyone caught carrying out this practice would be put to death. My father endangered his life more than once by secretly going to Jewish homes with a knife under his arm to quietly slaughter the hidden chickens and provide them with kosher meat. This continued until the curtain fell on the Jews of Przedecz, and together with the entire community he had served for more than forty years, he was sacrificed, along with my mother. All the Jewish men, women, and children were destroyed and burned in the Chełmno death camp. We will always remember our loved ones, their lives, and their deaths. May God revenge their pure and holy souls; may their memories be blessed, and their souls bound in the bundle of life.

And now a few words about my late brothers and sisters.

My brother, Yaakov, lived in Lublin, near Włocławek. His trade was hat–making and he owned a store where he sold head coverings and brimmed hats. His wife, Leah, was a housewife, and they had two children, a daughter, Rozsha, and a son, Yehuda, the infant. He was respected in the city, a member of the community's administrative committee, devoutly religious, and his opinions were respected. When the Nazis entered Lublin, they began harassing the Jews just as they did everywhere else, and then the shipments to the death camps began. He escaped with his family to Węgrów, where my sister lived, and from there they went to the Warsaw Ghetto. They suffered all the hunger and pain afflicted the Ghetto. We do not know if he had been sent to Treblinka or died in the Warsaw Ghetto during the uprising. May God revenge his soul.

My brother Shalom lived in Łódź, at 5 Dravanbaska Street, with his wife, Michela, and their four sons. He owned a grocery store and was sent by the Nazis to Poznań, where he suffered from hunger, violence, and forced labor in stone quarries and road–masonry work. He died there, in the camp in Poznań. His wife was sent in a shipment to the death camp, his children were

[Page 136]

sent to a children's institution in Łódź for several months. After its destruction by the Nazis, the institution's children were sent to the death camp. May God revenge their souls.

My sister, Chaya Devora Mandlboim, lived in Węgrów, with her husband, Yisrael, and their only son, Reuven, where they owned a sewing shop. When the ghetto was razed by the Nazis, they were sent to Międzyrzec and from there to the Treblinka death camp. May God revenge their souls.

My sister, Royza Leah (Rozsha), died before the war on the 7th of Adar, 5697 (February 18, 1937). May her memory be blessed, and her soul bound in the bundle of life.

Royza Leah (Rozsha) Yamnik

[Page 137]

Memorial to My Daughter, Whom I Never Met

by Yitzhak Levin

Translated from Hebrew by Marshall Grant

Fate dropped us into the city of Bielawa. This was a city in the Republic of Bashkortostan and served as its capital. In June 1942, we were expelled from Chelyabinsk, where we were classified as "unwanted" because of our Polish descent. We were declared as "dangerous to the regime" and forced to leave the city within eight days due to the transfer of ministries from Moscow to Chelyabinsk. Despite the fact that the city had two high schools and was close to the Aksakavah train station, its streets were not paved and there were no sidewalks, no sewage system, no electricity, and water was pumped from a spring inside the city.

Most of the homes had one story, and the city in general looked very neglected. To rent an apartment was almost impossible. It cost quite a lot to find small living quarters with a family, and this was beyond our means. We had no choice but to enter a *kolkhoz* (collective farm) bearing the name *Nadezhda Krupskaya*, named after Lenin's wife. The kolkhoz was eight kilometers from the city, and that is where we worked for housing and a bit of food.

In August 1942, I was conscripted into the Red Army, which enabled my wife to find work in the city's only factory. She rented a small place with a family whose husband had been sent to serve on the front. The entire home was one room without any services or furniture. My wife had to sleep on the floor on a straw mattress. Rain dripped through the roof, and the entire structure would sway in stormy weather.

My wife was pregnant then. On February 17, 1943, our daughter was born and I received notice from my wife through a letter she had written me. They called her Izza. On her birth certificate, which had two languages, Russian and Bashkir (a Turkic language), it was written that Izza Izakobanna was born on February 17, 1943, the daughter of Yitzhak Shulimovitch Levin and Dvora Izralubanna from the Taub family.

After her maternity leave came to an end, my wife returned to her usual job, working 12 hours a day. During the workday, the baby was in a baby house, *Yasla* in Russian, and there they were obligated to feed our daughter, provide medical and general care, and a mattress and blanket for the baby. My wife was forced to buy these things from her own money. The institution held her ration card. Twice a day, my wife went to the Yasla to breastfeed the baby, but a woman who labors physically 12 hours a day and who does not always eat properly is unable to nurse, so she had no choice but to buy milk and other necessities in the free market as a supplement to baby food, all from her very limited wages.

So why was the baby losing weight?

The institution received enough food, but the baby's appearance deteriorated from day to day. She was so weak she often caught cold. Her system lost its power to resist. And the caretakers, they prospered, and so did their families – much of the baby food also made its way to the open market. The authorities never discovered a thing. Was the reason that the baby food had been stolen in such a successful manner that the method was never revealed? Or were they not interested in uncovering such a cruel, criminal act. The fact is that the baby house received the food and the babies went hungry.

[Page 138]

In August 1943 our daughter passed away, and I never met her. She died in the hospital.

In the last week before her death, my wife sat next to her bed day and night. There were no means to save her life, not even medicine was given to her – it was sent to the wounded soldiers. Then, my wife, while sitting next to the baby's bed, fell asleep from exhaustion and when she awoke, *Izzika*, was no longer alive. My wife bought a coffin for her, and brought her to the cemetery by herself. She was so exhausted she was unable to dig a grave for her daughter, and she had no money to pay for someone else to do it. The cemetery is located in a hilly and rocky area. She found an unused area, put her daughter in the coffin and covered the grave with broken rocks and clay. The rocks and clay were so sparse, there wasn't enough to properly mark the location as a burial site.

Those reading about this true event should think for a moment and enter the heart of the mother and the hearts of many other mothers who experienced a similar fate…

Hinda

by Yitzkhak Levin Israel

Translated by Roberta Paula Books

The last time I saw her was August 1939, one month before the beginning of the end. I don't know when she was murdered. I only know she is gone.

When she was six, her parents registered her in the private Hebrew school in the town where she was born, Koło.

The same year that she began learning, it could even have been on the first day, the calamity flared up that destroyed people, especially Jews.

Perhaps you, Lushia, can answer the question of why they did this.

Permit me dear child, my beloved only sister's daughter, to use the name your parents called you by at home, which I know you can't use. I don't even know where your grave is, or your little body. No, I cannot think about it. However, you do not leave my thoughts. Your mother was called Frayde Libe. Her maiden name was Levin. Your father was Yekhiel Meir Hayman. They worked hard their entire lives. I am convinced that in their lives, which were cut off so early, they never wronged anyone. They were members of the General Zionists. They got a blue and white little dress ready for you to wear to school. With your light blond braids with blue ribbons, you loved to jump rope, like most other children. When your little feet jumped, your white braids decorated with roses also jumped. Today is the first day of Passover 1973. Do you know, Lushia,

[Page 139]

how long it has been since I have seen you like this? Already thirty-four years. You would be turning forty. You, my child, have been gone thirty-four years …

Thousands of people, smart, educated, with eminent names and fancy titles, and scholars, have written hundreds, thousands, maybe millions of books about the war. They have searched and are still searching for reasons to explain the mass murder. There have already been thousands of trials against these murderers. Thousands of these murderers have been punished with arrest and sentences ranging from one year to life,

After much effort I received a photograph of my extended family. In the photo from right to left are my uncle (my father's brother) Moishe Levin, his daughter Leah, and his son Sender who in 1939 left for the occupied territories of Soviet Russia.

but after a short time, they were quietly released. I continue to ask how the entire world remained silent and allowed you, dear child, to be murdered. Was the whole force of the world in agreement with this terrifying murder? Was the whole world weaker than one country, Germany, which had about 60 million citizens? Answer me, leaders of all countries. I have the full right to pose this question.

[Page 140]

In 1943, he was seriously injured while serving in the Red Army. Today he lives in Russia. A sick man, an invalid. Standing beside Sender is my aunt Yetta. Seated on the table are Khanele and Abbale. The pious Jew sitting on the left is Aunt Yetta's father. He died before the war broke out. He was lucky. However, the Nazis desecrated his grave.

My father was a pious Jew. He sold kitchen utensils. He would travel to fairs with his wife. They slept together in the same bed only one night a week, the Friday of the Sabbath, as well as on the nights of holidays. He was not a wealthy man.

When the murderers entered Koło, they divided the Jews into three groups. One group was sent to Izbica in Lublin province. Among those sent were my sister and her family, my uncle Moishe Levin and his family, and that is all.

Little girl, Lushia, how much suffering did you endure?

Lushia, what was your fate?

Lushia, where is your grave?

One of Many

by Y.L.L Shlomi

Translated by Roberta Paula Books

I'm telling you. What luck, you hear. What luck that, in the diaspora, there were two days of compulsory rest. Of course, first of all was Shabbes, the Sabbath. And Sunday was Sunday. On Shabbes, our mothers actually rested. Friday? No. Fridays, the work was doubled. A half a day for a whole day's work, if not more. However, Sundays, beginning on Motzi Shabbes (Saturday night, after the Sabbath has ended), they did the household work for the entire week. Washing, drying, ironing, mending, darning, and embroidering in a great variety of color work. Naturally, our mothers had to work with our fathers for their means of support. They had to go to the market. They also went to the hamlets with their husbands to acquire various goods from the farmers and then return and sell the goods to the large merchants. They would leave late Sunday night, or early Monday morning when it was still dark. They carried two baskets in each hand and a pack on their backs. They bought chickens, geese, ducks, eggs, butter, and leather hides, as well as other hamlet products. Some hamlet merchants owned a horse and wagon. Sometimes they would buy a calf. Among those on foot was the

[Page 141]

Bialaglovsky family. But when you asked about the Bialaglovskys, nobody knew who you were talking about. However, everyone knew them as lame Khaye and blind Yosef. I would like to tell you about them.

In our town, everyone had a nickname, including them. During the last years before the war, they lived with Aron Tarantsik in a place in one room on Warsaw Street (a nice name). They changed apartments often because they didn't have money to pay the rent.

Except for adversity, they possessed nothing. Grown children don't count. They had three surviving children. Their oldest son, Gutman, was an apprentice tailor. He caught a cold walking in the rain to Izbica one night to find work. His illness grew worse, and he developed tuberculosis. He died when he was nineteen years old. Their daughter, Yokheved, was now the eldest at home. She left to work for a family as a maid. The youngest son, Lipman, sold newspapers. There was another small boy at home.

From all good fortune, except suffering, they had nothing.

From Monday to Thursday, this husband and wife would walk through the hamlets every day in order to earn what was barely a living wage.

Fridays, Khaye would prepare for the Sabbath, and Yosef would go out on the road.

Ay, ay! He would often sigh. At least on Friday he could rest his ears a bit. She has such a gift of gab that she talks twenty-four hours straight. Yes, my Khaye, we should live so long, loves to talk. And even if I don't know what she is talking about, I have to listen until my head explodes. Yosef was blind in one eye. The eye was obscured with some blue, some white, intertwined with red veins. It did not look very appealing. I don't remember which eye it was, left or right. I could have been the right. Yes, the right eye.

A tall Jew, with broad shoulders, thin, with a heavy, lurching gait, he walked through the streets and lanes in worn out shoes. In summer through the dust, and on rainy days through the mud. Beside him dragged Khaye the lame one. She had a peculiar gait. On one foot, she was of normal height, on the other, like a twelve-year old child. She did not sway from side to side, nor did she lead with one foot. She was just little, and then big.

When did this happen to his eye? It was not from a beating. He may have been born that way. We also don't know when Khaye

[Page 142]

began to limp. I believe they were both like this at their wedding. However, before that, she could talk, rapidly and at great length, without stopping. If they gave a talking competition in Pshaytsh (in Polish, Przedecz), she would surely win first prize. She was never lacking in something to say. She was the newspaper for the whole town. She was never short of topics or, by no means, words. She knew everyone and everything from every which way.

They never complained about their fate; whatever G-d gives is positive. The youngest son began to walk with his parents. Everyone worked daily from quite early in the morning until very late at night. He, a blind man, and she, lame. The daughter, away working as a maid. Lipman was no longer selling newspapers; he was now working for a hat maker. They each had grey, dusty faces, exhausted, never fulfilled. They accepted their fate with a sort of religious resignation, with devotion to the one that chose them.

Even though they had little time to sit on school or kheder benches, it must be said, with no opportunity or possibility to study, they were able to read Yiddish and Polish, and they loved to read.

Their difficult life, their pure, difficult life, was cut off in the gas chambers. Do not forget about them.

I Am Not an Exception

by Yitzkhak Levin

Translated by Roberta Paula Books

Oisada, according to nomenclature, is a place too small to be a city and too big to be a village (dorf). The town of Drobin, in the Plotzk region, was such a place. Not grown and at the same time overgrown. We lived there from the beginning of 1937. The center was the marketplace. That is where the church and town hall were. All around the four cornered plaza were homes with businesses, plastered with stones. Sherptser Street, where the rabbi lived, was paved, as well as Plotzker and Ratzoynzer Streets. The other three or four streets were sandy in the summer and very muddy in the fall. Beside the church, there was a square they called a park, with benches where couple could sit unnoticed. The synagogue was on

[Page 143]

Mrs. Royza Taub Padro, of blessed memory,
and her daughter Dvora, the wife of Yitzkhak
Levin, who lives in Israel

Zalisher Street. The bottom part was built of brick, the top part was wood. There were two libraries, one on the Jewish Street and one behind the headquarters of the fire fighters. There were few readers. There were no theater performances, movies, or public readings, at least in the years I lived there. Buses passed through two – three times a day.

We lived there from the beginning of 1937. The few weeks before the war broke out, we were nervous, and life was intense. There were open meetings and gatherings every day, often two or three times a day. This depended on the mood of an important man or woman. The same sentences were repeated "Strongly connected is ready". Not a button from a soldier's uniform. France is with us. The first

[Page 144]

time they gathered, people shouted and sang with them. The last days before the war broke out, people just shook their heads. On August 31st, the police and municipal leaders disappeared. The citizens organized self-defense only at night. On the 1st and 2nd of September, the town was bombed a few times. Civilians were killed, children. Individuals and groups of Polish soldiers appeared to be without leadership and without weapons, nothing except for small guns, and those who were last to be mobilized didn't even have that. Another group of soldiers stopped in the forest before our town on the way to Plotzk. They were bombed, and they were all killed. Among them were eight Jewish soldiers who were in the Polish army, mobilized shortly before the war and returning one at a time. However, the pious, learned Jew Yeruzlimsky did not return. He fell. The soldiers told about the bitter battles near Kutno, Gostynin and other places. They all repeated the same word, "treason". They sold us out.

Many took their families to neighboring villages. Others hid in cellars. It became very quiet. The Nazi army was coming through on its way to Warsaw. Soldiers grabbed people for work, mainly Jews. They arrested the rabbi and the priest. The teachers from the school were forced to clean the streets. Those arrested were freed, but then forced to clean the streets as well. They didn't permit us to gather in the House of Prayer. Jews gathered to pray in private homes.

They transformed the synagogue into a hospital for wounded Polish soldiers. They placed horses in the church. Warsaw fell. Among the lightly wounded was someone from Ukraine. He knew the language of the occupiers. Every day, he reported the conversations of the Polish soldiers to the Germans. The commandant of the hospital … I heard one of these reports when I was brought to work at the hospital. They took the sick ones away somewhere. They took over the hospital with the help of Jewish forced laborers. The building materials of the appropriated synagogue were distributed among the Christian population.

Together with the help of the Polish population, especially the wife of the local chimney sweep, they robbed Jewish business and private homes. The first victims were the clothing store owned by the Naymark family and the food wholesaler Finklshteyn. Things worsened for the Jews day by day. It is hard to be seen on the street. Big and small non–Jews pointed fingers and yelled "Jew". The Germans beat and swore with the most horrible dirty words. We must remove our hats for every German soldier.

[Page 145]

They tore off someone's ear. Another's beard was torn off with his skin. Every new day was worse than the previous day. New edicts every day. On the eve of Yom Kippur 1939, we saw three people walking in green civilian suits with Tyrolian hats on their heads. With piercing eyes, they examined everything. The next morning, Yom Kippur, the rabbi and his assistant went from house to house telling everyone to come to the marketplace. When everyone was gathered, these three men stood by a table covered with white paper. On the paper were a razor and scissors. After a speech and some yelling, we all learned that we were not human, we were a type of animal, parasites etc…

Then they called on a Jewish barber to cut off our beards, but only one side, as you would cut a four cornered paper from one corner to the other. The faces of the shaved Jews looked distorted. Some Christian women looked out their windows and cried, but most of them laughed. When the cutting was over, they made us do drills, run, fall, roll on the stones, and jump like frogs. Among us there were older people like the old ritual slaughterer, the old Warshavsky, a Jew of around 80, the tubercular sick tailor Fedru). This lasted for four hours. Two days later, they gathered all the men between the ages of 15 and 45, Jews and Christians, and locked us up in the church. We remained locked up there for two full days. Once a day, they permitted relatives to bring us food and allowed us to go out and relieve ourselves. But once a day is not enough. The first ones to dirty the place were not Jews. On the second night of our confinement, they ordered that all residents were to remain in their homes the following morning. The windows must be totally covered and anyone who looks out will be shot. The next morning, they actually took everyone in covered trucks to a field near the town of Sherptz (Sierpc in Polish), approximately 26 kilometers from Drobin. There, they made us sit with our hands on our necks. All around us were shiny machine guns manned by soldiers of the Wehrmacht. After sitting for two hours, they took us to a factory building called "Sherptzianka". The first three days, we received only water to drink. On the fourth day, Jews from Sherptz (Sierpc in Polish) brought us baskets of bread. In order to get permission

[Page 146]

to bring us food, they told us they had to pay two silver coins, each worth 10 zlotys. It is hard to forget the good deeds that people did, but it is even harder to forget those who wanted to transform us into animals.

Many among us, Christians and Jews, became very nervous due to hunger, their eyes bulged and their faces filled with blood. Many wailed like children. When a middle-aged soldier took away the baskets of bread from the Jewish women, he brought them to the large factory, where we were 2,000 men squeezed together. Slowly, with a pocketknife, he cut the bread and threw it to us. Forgive me readers, but I cannot find an appropriate way to express what took place. Many of us fell upon the bread, tumbling over each other. A pile of people rolled on the floor, tearing at one another and biting. This was, after all, the third day of hunger. The Jewish women brought a lot of bread, but the German with his helper beside the machine gun loved to watch us fall upon and fight each other.

Among others who did not want to provide any pleasure to the Germans were me and my two brothers. Due to fear from all the noise, we hid behind a wall. Everyone received bread. When he saw not everyone was prepared to fight, he gave everyone a piece in their hand.

Later on, they gave us food cooked in the military kitchen made with produce brought by Jewish women. Many of us were beaten. When you grab your food and don't eat in a normal way, many became ill and could not sit in a position that the cultured guards demanded. Therefore, they were beaten.

Now tell me, who is the animal?

Once every two days, they took us like sheep to a field to empty ourselves of natural needs. We were surrounded by armed soldiers. Besides guns, they had cameras and filmed the entire procedure.

After two weeks, a German in an Air Force uniform came to give a speech. He spoke in a mixture of Polish and German and told us they wanted to take us to work in Germany, but, since our friends the English and French were bombing the trains,

[Page 147]

they regretted to have to send us home. The next morning, a pastor came who spoke Polish. He handed each of us a document with our name on it. A few men remained, and I do not know their fate. They were Polish soldiers who had been captured by the Germans. Among them was a Jewish boy from Lubin in the Vlatslovek (Wloclawek in Polish) region, and the guard from the township of Drubin, because the Germans had found a broken gun behind the roof of his house.

It was raining. We three brothers with documents in our pockets headed home on foot. No one said a word during the twenty-six-kilometer walk. We were deep in thought, each in his own thoughts, but similar as if we talked about them out loud. What's doing with our sister in Koło? How are they living there under these circumstances? Our mother and youngest sister? Our experiences in the temporary camp told us a lot. The "Brown Book", published a few years previously, was familiar to us. We already knew about Dachau and other educational institutions in fascist Germany. Many Jews who had been chased into Poland told us, but we could not foresee everything. The most important was the collaboration with Russia, and how the western countries wanted to rid Europe of communism.

We arrived home with a confirmed plan. Our older brother Gavriel left for Warsaw. He believed that in a big city it would be easier to get lost in the crowd. A few days later, my other brother left for Warsaw with a Soviet destination. I remained with my mother and sister Esther. I received work replacing glass in the church. All the panes had been broken during the bombing. I worked for a month, and when I finished the church was active again. They prayed to God and quietly sang. When the priest paid me the 220 zlotys he owed me, he told me I should take the opportunity and go to Russia because here there will be no life for Jews. That is what I did.

I went with my wife, mother, and sister. Also travelling with us were Rivka Rizuv, Pikhas Zayde and Leybush Pctrikoz. All three were born in Drobin. We arrived in Bialystok without much difficulty. It was noisy with a lot of red flags. Business went from hand to hand. There were no pogroms, and no one grabbed you for forced labor. But there was much hatred among the local Christians and Jews toward us. Not everyone, but many. There was a shortage

[Page 148]

of work, a shortage of food. There was no money. The black market ate up everything. We found our brother Moishe. He was recruited to work and left with our mother not knowing where. We were not familiar with the geography of Russia. It was enough that they told us we would receive a place to live, work and food. At that time many were being recruited and returning from various places in Russia. They told of a difficult life and even more difficult climate. Ignoring this, in mid-December we were recruited for work. On January 17, 1940, we arrived in the city of Tzielavinsk, on the border between Europe and Asia.

We worked in construction. It was freezing cold, and we worked outside without appropriate clothing. But the worst was the shortage of food. We stood in line half the night for bread.

During February and March, many Poles passed through Tzielavinsk. They had escaped from Magnitugursk where they worked at digging stones. Like birds, they were attracted to warmer places and easier conditions. A young man from Drobin with the family name Prost told me that my brother Moishe and my mother were living in Magnitugursk. I wrote to them and they came to me without a permit. However, my brother did not want to remain in Russia. "I never imagined how life would be in a socialist order", he said. On May 9th, 1940, they left. I did not go because I did not have the money for a train ticket. I will not recount here my later experiences, perhaps later. After a while I established correspondence with my brother in Warsaw, with my sister Frayde Libe and her husband Yekhiel Meir Hayman and their daughter Lusha (Hinda) and my sister Sheyne Feyge who I lived with. I knew they were sent form Koło to Izbitsa past Viepshem. I received letters from them until the war broke out in 1941.

In 1944, when we entered liberated Lublin, I saw Majdanek. Someone who had been recently mobilized told me no Jews from Izbitsa had survived. I could not believe it, even though I was sure he was telling the truth.

By the end of January 1945, my military unit was in Warsaw. We were delegated to clean the Belvedere area of mines. I went to Praga, 4 Targuva Street where my brother Gavriel had lived before the ghetto. A female guard met me at the gate. She saw that I was a Jew. Who are you looking for? She asked. The Tsaytunger family, my aunt, and my brother Levin I responded with a happy smile. They all left long ago to Treblinka.

[Page 149]

What kind of place is that? I asked. That is a death camp, she responded. That is where they finished off so many.

Two years later, when my wounds healed, I was released from the military hospital, but this is not important. A month later, my wife returned from the Soviet Union. I learned that a large portion of Jews from Drobin, including the mother of my wife Royza Taub–Fedru and her seven-year-old son Moisheleh were sent to Piatrekov Tribunalsky ghetto, where they died from a Typhus epidemic.

We remained in Bidgashtsh. I looked in many places for Jews. I was in Drobin. We decided that after the war we would write to a Christian in town who would provide us with addresses of those who survived. He told me that just before the war broke out in 1941, he received a letter from my youngest sister in Bialystok. She told him that she and my brother Moishe were living and working there together with our mother, and things are going very well. He burned the letter and did not respond. A few years later I went a few times but did not receive any news.

I searched with the help of newspapers, radio, visited many places, asked hundreds of people. I looked at the faces of people passing in the street, stopping strangers, and pored over lists of survivors.

I'm still searching…

My Family, of Beloved Memory

by Moshe Belevsky

Translated from Hebrew by Marshall Grant

My father, Mendel Wolf Belevsky, the owner of a bakery, was born in the city of Przedecz on January 18, 1882, to his father, Avraham Simcha, and his mother, Frieda Rachel (Brostovesky). My late father was active in the local community, a member of the bank's management committee, and for years he was the *gabbai* (synagogue caretaker) and member of the *Chevrei Kaddisha* (ritual undertakers). He also served 15 years, until we left Przedecz in the spring of 1939, as the *gabbai* of the yeshiva, together with his friend Itsha Weidon. The worked closely together in managing the *Bikur Holim* Group and he was a *Mizrahi*activist and an enthusiastic supporter of *Tzi'rei Mizrachi v'HaShomer HaDati* (the Young Mizrahi and Religious Guard) branch in our city. The children, especially the boys, received a religious education that emphasized the love for the people and land of Israel. This is how he worked, significantly contributing to the yeshiva led by Rabbi Zemelman, who was one of my teachers. My father was a supporter of the Rabbi from Skierniewice and travelled to visit him at least once a year.

[Page 150]

Dealing with public issues was considered by my father to be very important, and this heavily influenced my mother, Frieda Rachel.

In addition to the bakery managed by my grandfather, my grandmother had an additional profession as a midwife, as it was defined in those times. Everything she earned from midwifery for wealthy families she gave to the infant's mothers who had little. Even if she was not paid, she gave from her own pocket. When not working as a midwife, she took the time to prepare jams, sweets, and beverages, and would take them to the newborns' mothers who could not afford it.

My grandfather once turned to her and said: Rachael, what are you doing? If you continue with your generosity, we will, God forbid, after the age of 120, leave this world without even having enough for burial shrouds and we will have to enter the true world in garments that we don't even own. The next day, my grandmother went out with the bakery's daily earnings, and bought white cloth. She worked days and night and sewed a burial shroud for herself and my grandfather. When she finished, she turned to my grandfather and said: My dear husband, we now have shrouds for ourselves, and now, can I continue with my "bigheartedness", as you call it? You must know, you are my partner in heaven. My grandfather remained silent, which fully expressed his consent to their partnership. They lived long and meaningful lives.

The Belevsky Family

Standing: Brayna, the daughter of blessed memory; Moshe, the son, and his wife, Liba, who live in Israel
Parents are sitting: the late Mendel Wolf and his wife, Hanna Sarah; between them, their son Chaim, who lives in Israel
Sitting below: the late Baltzia and Label

[Page 151]

My father had two brothers, the elder was Lipman Belevsky, and the younger Pinchas Aharon Belevsky, both of whom moved to live in Sompolno with their families in 1928. They were active in the community until its annihilation by the Nazis.

The three brothers, together with a large part of their families, died in the Holocaust. I moved to Israel in 1933, my brother Yosef Chaim, who survived the Holocaust in work camps, arrived later. The members of my family, my father, Mendel Wolf; my mother, Hannah Sarah; my sisters Brayna and Baltzia, who were active in *Beitar*; and my brother Label, may god revenge them, all perished.

From my Uncle Lipman Belevsky and his large family, from his married sons and daughters, only two grandchildren survived the Holocaust. They both live in the United States.

My uncle, Pinchas Aharon, his wife (my aunt) Zipora, and their married daughter Frieda Rachel, the namesake of my grandmother, with her husband, and two sons, Moshe and Dov, all were murdered in the Holocaust. Their son Avraham Simcha survived the camps during the war and has lived in Israel since 1949.

My mother of beloved memory, Hannah Sarah, from the Komiskovsky family in Sompolno, was the only sister to six brothers. She worked hard to provide us, the children, a religious education. She had a noble soul and was known for her deeply religious beliefs and hospitality. She paid especially close attention to settlement efforts in Israel. Every Friday, prior to lighting the candles, she put her donation in the collection box of Rabbi Meir, who was known to have had experienced a religious revelation, and then she put her coins in the blue JNF box.

All six of her brothers were known as gifted Torah scholars in the 1930s: Noah the eldest, Mendel, Meir from Sompolno; Yehuda Leib, Avraham from in Slupca; Bezalel who lived in Babiak. Most of the children were married. There is no way I can describe in words the personality of each one of them, but I can say: Torah, education and *Derech Eretz* (treating people equally) were equal in value. They were established financially, they gave their children the best education, all were enthusiastic *Hasidim* who followed Rabbi Skierniewice and often travelled to spend time with him.

In the 1930s, there were attempts to organize and buy a shared property in Israel for the entire family, with the goal of eventually moving to Israel. Some of them already had children in Israel. Immigration to Israel began in 1923 and continued until the riots of 1936. These bloody clashes shattered dream of my large family. Then the war broke out and the Nazi henchmen destroyed everything in their path. My six uncles and aunts, and most of their sons, daughters, and grandchildren, perished in the Holocaust.

May these lines bear witness to their blessed memory. May God revenge their lives.

A small part of the extended family survived the Holocaust in the camps and reached Israel shortly after it was established

[Page 152]

Testimony to My Family, Who Were Here, But Have Since Gone

by Moshe Mokotov

Translated from Hebrew by Marshall Grant

Despite the fact that the author of these lines is a son and a brother of a family that has been sentenced half to death, and half to life, I will objectively discuss the members of my family who were murdered.

Those who knew my father, Yitzhak Mokotov, would identify and agree with me that he was a dear person, from every aspect. He was one of the city's providers. The city's less fortunate were always welcomed, and they always found someone to whom they could voice their problems. As a child, I never understood why they visited so frequently. My father fulfilled the mitzvah of welcoming a bride with loyalty and happiness, and no less than a dozen couples were married in our city, with my father taking care of all the wedding arrangements. Here is where I need to add that my mother

Yitzhak Mokotov and his daughter, Bronka

enthusiastically supported him and his selfless efforts. She was the one who prepared the list of what was needed for the wedding. I still remember something my father would say to my mother, "What happened, Ruzsha, you have no list for me?". That was what he would ask her.

The readers of this book will surely remember the horses we owned, and a servant named Banashek, who would take care of them.

[Page 153]

This man, Banashek, would fill the storerooms in our yard with coal and peat. Wood was gathered by the guard living on the property, a tall and simple non–Jew named Piatcak. I was told this man "inherited" our apartment and began living there after Przedecz became "Judenrein" … When winter approached, my mother would prepare a list of the needy, which grew from year to year, and give it to my father. Together with Banashek, my father would make sure that the homes of needy Jews would have wood for heating. It took about a week to complete this act of generosity. Banashek then would fill the storeroom with an assortment of essential items needed for the harsh Polish winter. For months I waited with excitement for the coal to arrive. When I was a child, these were "holidays" for me, even though I would come home dirty, and more than once I was lectured and reprimanded by the heavy hand of my father.

My father's business relations and attitude towards the Christians gave him a reputation in the city and its surroundings, and more than once, these relationships contributed to various issues related to the city's Jewish citizens. He was always welcome in *Magistrat*. I remember once that my father did not hesitate to call the city's mayor (Bormisht) Novkovsky to come over at night when the city's stamp was required for a certain document. My mother was not only a housewife, but she also had her own "private matters". She was one of the founders of the city's library and managed it for many years. Another board member – Mr. Yaakov Topolesky, is certainly remembered by this book's readers when he participated in a memorial evening for the holy souls of our city, in the hall for Polish emigres in Tel Aviv. There isn't anyone in our city who doesn't remember the dear

Itche Wayden, or the blond Itche as he was also known. He was not well known because he was a tailor for women. I believe his reputation was based on his service as the gabbai of *Bikur Holim* in our city. My mother worked together with this Itche, and she donated much of her time to this institution that was nothing but primitive, but it was critical to our needy city. Mr. Itche often visited our home for business not related to tailoring. When Purim approached, as was his habit, he arrived to present his original plan to my mother for donations. Two young men would wear identical costumes and visit Jewish homes, with bells in their hands, and request donations for charity. The people made these donations without saying a word and were then issued receipts. I don't think any of the city's survivors have ever forgotten this scene. The sound of the bells from a distance told us children that the goodhearted young men in costumes had arrived, and it made us get up and leave the *Shulchan ha'aruch* prepared for the Purim meal. It was the height of the evening for all the city's children.

The Purim meal always makes me sentimental. It was on this evening, right before the meal, that my sister, Baronka, was born. Everyone knew this sweet girl with pigtails. When we came to Israel in 1935, she became just like all the other girls her age, a "sabra". She was cute and well–behaved, quiet and serious for her age, and carefully chose her friends. On Rehov Shlomo Hamelch in Tel Aviv, there is a national religious school and it still exists today, but unfortunately only the school still remains and each time I pass it, I look with grief and sadness at this building, which provided me with some of the best times of my life. The school's principal at that time was Mr. Yehiel Shtrauch from Włocławek. He was also the principal when I studied at the Hebrew gymnasium there. Many people knew this wonderful girl Baronka,

[Page 154]

and I was told she grew into a tall young girl, who was exceptionally beautiful. This was after my family returned to Przedecz to liquidate the last of their possessions. I was also told that Rabbi Zemelman, who gave *Tanach* classes in Przedecz's only school, would often use her as an example before his students.

I have a family member who emigrated to Melbourne, Australia. She told me that when Baronka was with the rest of her family in the Warsaw Ghetto, she had a chance to save her life. A Christian, who knew my younger sister, asked, and even begged her to leave the ghetto and come over to the Aryan side. Her response was: I will leave my father? And she perished with her mother… Yes, I have reasons to be sorry; and how!

Most of our belongings were distributed among non–Jews whom my father had worked with. In order to finally liquidate his business, my family returned to Poland. I remained here supporting my father's efforts to keep his English [visa] valid. It took my father more time than he planned to liquidate his business. In order that the visa would remain valid, and at the recommendation of the Consulate General, my mother arrived there by herself. This was two weeks

Bluma Zukerman (Mokotov), her husband Hanik, and their daughter Galila

before the war broke out. Shaul Makovitsky also travelled with her. Both arrived at the Tel Aviv port due to the riots of 1936–1939 (which is the reason the Tel Aviv port was opened). Friday, September 1st, 1939, was a black day for the Jewish people: Poland's Jews, three and a half million strong, its beautiful sons and its magnificent Judaism were destroyed in this war. In the beginning it was terrifying, and the level of concern rose every day. We did as best we could to prevent our family from becoming separated, but it seemed the distance worsened daily. The Italian consulate was in Yaffa, and every Shabbes I would travel there to give the Consulate General letters and documents that would be sent to my father

[Page 155]

Red Cross form that was received in Israel from my father Itzhak Mokotov

[Page 156]

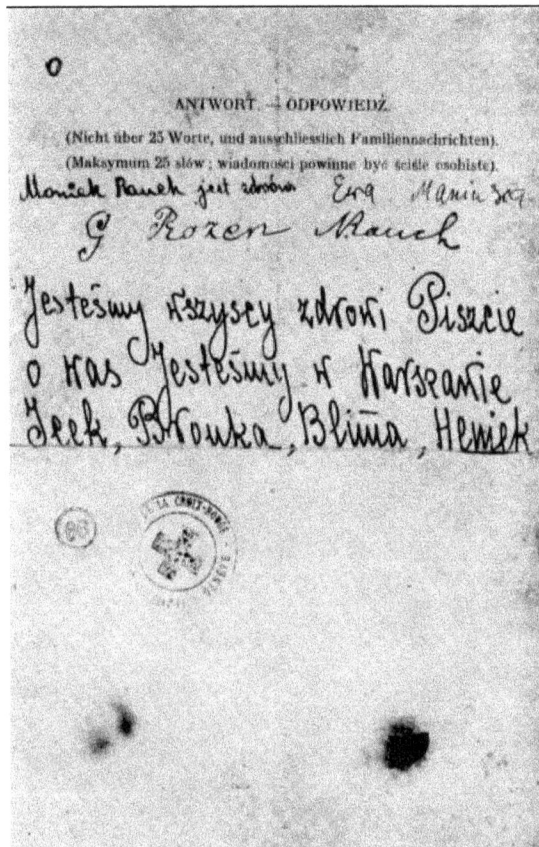

to help him leave Poland. This all was sent through the consulate's "diplomatic post", and from my father's response that I received (via Romania), we understood the documents had reached him. Again, there was a glimmer of hope that motivated us to double and triple our rescue efforts. And then, the last of our hopes were dashed. Italy declared war on England. The last bridge, over which the two families separated by the war were to be reunited, had collapsed!!

And then, everything that happened, happened to everyone….

There is a woman living in Jerusalem named Chava Appel–Rozneka. She met Meila Orbach–Brand, also from Jerusalem, as a young girl. Both women told us that my father, together with Meila's brother, Haim Aharon, leased an airplane when the war broke out in an attempt to leave Poland. Who knows if this is accurate or not, and in fact, what importance does it hold now?

I cannot complete the testimony of my family without mentioning my eldest sister – Blumka. She was four years older than I. When she completed the local school, she left Przedecz for Warsaw, where she studied in a girls' school named after Pearla Lovinska. My parents decided to nurture her musical talents. Even while in grade school, she was given violin lessons by a musical artist who, if I am not mistaken, lived near the "old market."

Bluma Mokotov and her daughter, Galila
Tel Aviv, 1936

[Page 158]

We called him Langa, and I can see my sister and the violin in her hands, but I am not sure which is larger – she or the violin. It appears that her talent was significant, and she continued to take music lessons with the church's official pipe organist (*Organista*). Over time, my father managed to bring a piano home, which, of course, caused a stir in Przedecz. And from then on, music could be heard in our home. Four hands were also heard when the *Organista* would visit and play music with my sister. I would like to note one small event that typically characterized my sister Blumka. One night, we were disturbed in the middle of the night by quiet notes from the piano. We were scared, and then surprised when we saw Blumka in the living room, sitting at the piano with a candle next to her. She was playing a selection pianissimo over and over so she would remember it by heart. My sister returned from Warsaw and travelled to Wloclawek for a short time to study accounting. This education contributed to her efforts to assist my father manage the books of the business operated by him and my uncle, Neta Wasserzog. She was one of the many enthusiastic supporters of Zeev Jabotinsky. It is interesting that such a small city, such as Przedecz, could be so vibrant with politics and political parties. I think the large number of its political parties encouraged her to find ways to immigrate to Palestine. I was told that more than once she was seen in a crowd, with a sign in her hand near "the Club" or library when a guest speaker would appear. The evenings were usually exciting … there was no lack of people with opposing opinions, and heated engagements were a sure thing. Her intention of immigrating to Palestine introduced her to a young man from Warsaw, Nehamia Zukerman. They eventually married and immediately went to Palestine. Their daughter, Galila, was born after their arrival.

In addition to my father and sister of blessed memory, I would like to add several more members of my close family who are an inseparable part of this story. My grandfather, Binyumin, and his wife, Golda. I was just a child, no more than five or six years old, I remember very large straw baskets in their home. These baskets were to be used to pack their possessions, and they were planning to immigrate to Palestine. They were among the first Mizrahi activists at that time. We were all devastated when he became ill and passed away in a Koło hospital at the age of 56. The fate of my family could have been different if my grandfather had not left us at such a young age. My grandmother moved into our home and for the rest of her life my father treated her fairly and with respect. For all intents and purposes, she managed the household.

The beginning of the end started at the church and ended in Chełmno … My aunt, Chava Rauch, my mother's sister, and her two children, Moniak and Marissa, together with her husband Mordchai. Their end was the same for everyone. My uncle, Yaakov Wolf Rozen, and his wife, Rayzel and their three daughters, left Przedecz for Łódź. There, it appears, they met their horrible fate. My uncle, Avraham Rozen, died an "honorable" death. He was fortunate in that he was taken by the Angel of Death. He was buried in Kłodawa in an unmarked grave.

May this testimony, which I dedicate to my beloved family, respectable people who always tried to help others, serve as a memorial for their memory.

May the memories of all the victims from our small city, and those of all Jews who were murdered, be blessed.

With great love, the son–brother,

Moniak

[Page 159]

Father's House

by Leah Zemelman Pnini, Jerusalem

Translated by Marshall Grant

Through the wall of forgetfulness that is closing in on me, and through a veil of serenity I did not want – in the dead of night I hear my brother's cry – a terrible cry, "You have sentenced us to destruction!" So, with great respect, I sit to provide testimony. Listen and read, my Jewish friends in Israel and the Diaspora, and those children of families, of thousands of families, naive and honest, who were murdered, and their blood cries to us, "Live on our holy country as a free nation, a nation that never knew the Diaspora, and the nation of murderers will be forever vanquished."

My family was normal and simple: four brothers, four sisters, an honest mother and my father, the rabbi.

My father was born in Drobin, where his father, my grandfather, served as rabbi.

He was appointed as the rabbi of Przedecz at a very young age. The city's younger members went riding on horseback to receive the rabbi at the city's entrance. He was slim, accompanied by a woman who was almost a little girl herself, and in her arms, my sister, Esther, who was eight months old. This is how the people of Przedecz, with singing and dancing, welcomed their rabbi as they paraded through the city's streets leading to the synagogue. It was there he spoke to both the Jews and Poles, as one, and his soul felt connected to Przedecz.

My father received many offers to serve as a rabbi in a larger city, such as Siedlce and Nasielsk. Nasielsk was my mother's birthplace, but my father, as I mentioned before, felt connected to Przedecz, and cutting those ties was impossible. I heard much from my father about how his emotion needs were never fully fulfilled, but despite these feelings, it was not enough to make him leave the city he felt so affiliated to. He would serve as the city's rabbi until the Nazi soldiers began destroying and killing the Jews, when he escaped to the Warsaw Ghetto. The community in Przedecz had about 250 households, most of them craftsmen such as tailors, cobblers, hat makers and leather workers. There were also small businessmen and even a few who were larger.

From the aspect of development, our city certainly lagged. It was only in 1928 that electricity finally arrived to the city. A radio was a luxury that only a few families were able to enjoy.

I remember as a young girl waking up in the dark to the sound of the merchants loading their goods on a horse–pulled wagon before departing, going from city to city, selling their wares in a market for their livelihood. The city's residents were not rich, but they earned their living honestly.

I took an active part in the daily life of our city, for example: one night the shokhet (ritual slaughterer and examiner), Shmuel Yamnik, entered our home. By the way he was a distant relative of our family. He arrived with the butcher, Michael Hersch Noymark. He was poor and miserable and cared for by a larger family. He made his living by going from village to village buying calves for slaughter, and then sell the meat to the population. This man was very concerned, because the question surrounded the issue of whether the calf was kosher. My father didn't sleep the entire night. I heard him pacing in his library, trying to find a way to not to make the calf unkosher. For the butcher, it was a question of life and death. When I woke up in the morning, I could tell by my father's smile that the calf was saved. And that is how my father lived in the community, he felt their suffering and their joy, until the disgraceful Germans came.

[Page 160]

The Arrival of the Germans to Our City:

I will never forget the day the Germans took my father, and here I want to answer those who claim that the soldiers did not take part in the annihilation of our people. By the way, in our city, there were almost no Nazis, everything was carried out by the soldiers. On Rosh Hashanna (the New Year), most of the community was gathered in the main synagogue, and the others in smaller synagogues and yeshivas. In the middle of the prayer service, it was Yom Kippur, the Germans entered the synagogue. I stood and watched my father with admiration, wrapped in a *kittle* (white prayer robes), his face covered with a *tallis* (prayer shawl), completely focused in prayer. The Germans took him outside and shaved him. I ran after him. They gave him a wheelbarrow so he could clean the street. Many city residents tried to take the wheelbarrow away from him, but the Germans kept them away with the butts of their rifles. I moved closer, despite the beatings I took, and he looked me in the eye. I have never seen such extreme pain in his eyes. He was paler than usual; his face was white where he had had his beard since his childhood. It was as if he was naked, I saw his distress and there will never be forgiveness for his shame. Again and again, I tried to reach him, until I understood, despite my young age, that my father wanted to be alone, and he was ashamed of his nakedness. Before the war began, my father would write in the *Moment* and *Togblat* newspapers under the pseudonym, Yossela. And even then, with an almost prophet–like vision, warned what was about to take place.

Additional Text

Two years after the Germans established themselves and wreaked havoc in the city, a German resident came and notified my father they were planning to arrest him, so he had no choice but to leave his home and the city he loved so much and escape. He suffered terribly as he went from village to village on his way to Warsaw. Here, with a weapon in his hand, a weapon as his shield, a weapon of fiery belief, a weapon to attack, a weapon made from molten lead, he fought for the honor of his family and his people, and he will always be in my heart.

My father, the rabbi, fell in battle on the fourth day of the uprising of the Warsaw Ghetto, may God revenge them. His heroic death in his fight against the Germans is described in *The Warsaw Ghetto Diaries*, by Hillel Seidman. My mother, brothers and sisters tried to escape and save themselves. The children were young, aged 3 to 12; six people in all. My sister and I were taken to the camp.

I will never forget the day I came home from the Lojewo camp (Lavoye in Yiddish) on a furlough. My brother, who was three years old at the time, told me the dreadful news: "there was a death camp named Chełmno and they wanted to take us there, everyone, but I wouldn't let them kill me – I will escape, I want to live." This is what a three–year–old boy told me. I stood silent and held him as he calmed down. He was the one who told me about Chełmno for the first time. You didn't run away, my dear brother, and there you were led, and it was there you were burned. According to rumors that reached me, my brother tried to run away, but the Polish henchmen caught him and handed him back to the Nazis. They took everyone else, and we remained alone, just my sister Esther and myself.

There are no flowers on my brother's grave, as there is no grave. Only one eternal question remains: why did they do this to us?

And let everyone come and demand justice for their childhood and teenage years that were abruptly taken from them, and for their adulthood, into which they will never grow and mature.

And let my brother Yehoshua come. He was eleven years old at the time. He had a promising future; they said he was a genius due to my grandfather. He would often stare at me with his wide gray eyes. And let Yoel, the redhead, come, and let

[Page 161]

Nehemia, the hero of the house come, the healthy and smiling child; and let Uda (אודה) come, she was so beautiful, and I remember how I brought her to the camp to save her. The little girl wandered around among us, and we missed home. She would eventually return, only to depart on a route in which there was no return. And let Chuma come and demand her childhood, she was just six years old and such an angel.

And let Yankele come, my youngest brother, three or four years old, a master chess player. I remember the Commissar would come to play chess with him, and we would sit in the house shaking with fear that something bad would happen to the boy. My younger six brothers and sisters, all pure souls, were taken, never to return. Along with my dear mother. And a day will come when I will feel that I must tell the story of my city and I will return to tell it, and everyone will come and appeal to me, "Don't forget me", and I will return and fight the fight for their lives. I want to put this in writing, how you were so beautiful and so humble, and how I loved you so much. But I know this can never be done, because I loved you too much, all of you – every street and every person in the city, the old, the young, the infants.

Itche the Blond was quiet man; he was not well educated and not very wealthy. He was a tailor for women's attire. I had a feeling that Jews of this kind disappeared a long time ago. Each one of us has the duty to remember them and include them in the history of the Jewish people, because these figures have disappeared and are no more. And here he stands before you – a woman's tailor, husband to a paralyzed wife, never giving up and never letting his pain show. He never had children, and every day he sewed and in the dark of night helped others. He was the *gabbai* (caretaker) of the yeshiva, of *bikur cholim*, and also for a charity and book repair foundation. He did not make speeches; they were strange to him. He was a man of action. He collected money and distributed it to the needy, modestly and secretly in order not to embarrass them. He was economically responsible and lived within his means. I remember how, on Purim, he would send two of the older boys dressed as clowns to collect money as donations. No one dared to reveal their true identity and the city's residents contributed and gave money to the best of their abilities because they knew what it was for and where it was going.

I can still hear the bells' ringing going from house to house and Itche waiting for them. I was a young girl of ten, sitting at a sewing machine, waiting with him in the hope of being sent on a delivery. In the meantime, until the boys returned, he would sit and entertain me with wonderful stories told by the great rebbes (*Admors*) from Skierniewice and Kotzk, and the hours happily passed. Itche would tell exciting stories by candlelight until the boys returned with the donations. Itche would count the money and send them on their way. He would divide the proceeds into piles and then run to distribute it. It was explicitly forbidden to wait until the next day to enact the *mitzvah* – tomorrow would be another day. He was a well-known and humble person, a product of those times, and who knows if we will witness anyone similar in our generation who is able to continue his efforts.

There is much more to be said about my late father, about the significant role he played in the city's daily life and about his heroics in battle.

The heavens to which he prayed are witness; G–d in heaven, in whom he believed, is witness; as in the soil and land he worked so hard for in peaceful times, only to be halted during the war. And here is a young daughter commemorating her father, the rabbi, with eternal admiration. The respect and love transcend words.

Let history commemorate and remember, and let it tell the story of my father's righteous and pure life; and we will continue, and we will be satisfied, and we will live with what you have built.

[Page 162]

My Family of Blessed Memory

by Fishel Goldman

Translated from Hebrew by Marshall Grant

The members of our family included my father, Yehiel Goldman, my mother, Sarah Lantzitzki, two brothers and two sisters.

When the war broke out in September 1939, my brother Michael Hirsch was conscripted into the Polish military and was taken prisoner under unbearable conditions. According to the testimony of Abba Buks, who was also a prisoner, but escaped, the Germans began to eradicate prisoner of war camps around the end of March 1940 by shooting the inmates. The camps were located near the city of Bielsk Podlaski. When the Jews of the city heard that the Germans were murdering Jewish inmates, they tried to pay a ransom for their rescue, but to no avail.

On April 28, 1940, we received a letter from the Bielsk Podlaski community saying that my brother, after being killed by the Germans, had been brought to a Jewish cemetery for burial.

Those in the prison camp remembered two more residents of our city, the brothers Hanan and Monish, the sons of Lev Klodawski, and they too were murdered. According to Abba Buks, who was together with them, they stood embracing each other as they were killed by the Germans. According to Buks, the soldiers were from our city, and before they carried out their task they suggested (to Abba Buks) that they run and save themselves and said, "you have a family, run away!"

And thus began the problems in our city, like every other city in the vicinity. Jewish families were thrown out of their homes and sent to a Jewish ghetto, with just a few of their household belongings, in the vicinity of "the old market". Even before this expulsion, the ghetto was already suffering from overcrowded housing.

After being expelled from their homes, those exiled were also disconnected from their means to make a living and had to make do in any way possible, selling household items for example, the few that remained after being transferred to the ghetto.

Some of the younger men, and a few of the older ones, were already in labor camps. Those remaining in the city, me among them, were made to work at various tasks of forced labor. The supervisors were "our friends from yesterday" and would often use whips to urge us on in our work, men and women as one.

In August 1941, I was sent with a group of young men and women to a labor camp. After two days of travel in cars intended for cattle, we arrived in Tuczno, a camp near Inowrocław. My two sisters were there. We worked for three months in a sugar factory under the supervision of Polish policemen. We worked hard, but the conditions were relatively bearable.

From Tuczno we were transferred to a camp named Yanikovo, and our situation became worse. The camp's main cook behaved cruelly towards the inmates, and every day he would murder 5-6 of them. Twice a week, we would be called out in the middle of the night to be counted. The snow was a half-meter high, and we were made to stand half an hour, sometimes an hour, without moving. Of course, the next day some of the prisoners were sick, which is when the killer again used his gun. He would say this is not a hospital, it is a labor camp. The inmates who were able to go to work were beaten until they were bleeding. Some of them escaped but were caught and brought back - to be hanged, an act carried out in public. All the inmates were made to wake up in the middle of the night, stand

[Page 163]

and witness the execution. One of those hanged, before the noose was tied around his neck, shouted out loud, "Let freedom live!" The Polish murderer approached him with an axe and split his head open. You wanted freedom, Jew, well now you have it.

After the war, I was the sole witness in the Polish court where the murderer was tried. He was sentenced to 25 years in prison. The judge told me that if there had been one more witness the murderer would have been sentenced to death.

My sisters were in the Leawa labor camp. They advised me to escape from the Yakshitz labor camp, where I was now held, and I went to them. The camp commander concealed me for two weeks until the searches for me stopped. I would then go to work regularly with all the inmates, and in May 1942 we received shocking news, the destruction of Przedecz's Jewish community and the destruction of all the Jewish residents by poisoned gas in the Chełmno death camp, among them my father Yehiel Yosef Goldman, my mother, Sarah and my sister Yatka, who had been previously released from the camp and sent home. My G-d avenge them.

In October 1943, I was sent to Auschwitz, where I received number 144324. Accounts of the horrors of the Auschwitz death camp could fill a book – the torture, degradation, cruel beatings, marching to work escorted by bloodthirsty dogs and … the orchestra. I was in Commando 101 and lived in Block 27. In January 1945, four days before the liberation of Auschwitz, the Germans moved us to the Gliwice camp. On the way, along the Czech border, the Christian population threw us loaves of bread. After four days of travel in which no food was distributed, I took a chance, as others did, and jumped from the slow-moving train to catch a loaf of bread, however the Germans shot at us with their machine guns. I was slightly injured in my forehead, and I was unable to enjoy the bread. We continued the journey to Gliwice. We stayed for 12 hours. The more the Russians advanced, the Germans pushed us forward, Oranienburg, Flossenbürg, and others.

[Page 164]

Rukhele the Dairywoman

by Y. L. L.

Translated by Roberta Paula Books

You live in a town, and it seems as though you know all of the people: all the people, all the stones, every tree, every building, everything. Not on purpose, you observe your neighbors from near and far, at weddings, funerals, circumcisions, Bar Mitzvahs, on holidays and on the Sabbath, on a regular workday. You have compassion for the sick, the old, the poor, and those who don't know what to do with themselves. You know everyone's nature and cries, sadness, joys, and laughter. You have no doubt that in the simplest person, exhausted from hard work and poverty, lies the highest level of humanity, heroism, intelligence. The highest level of true humanity.

In the wooden house which belonged to Vishnivsky, whom we called the hunchback, lived the widow Rukhele, the milk seller. Her husband had died a year after they were married. She was left with a small child and no means of support. That's when she began to sell milk and dairy products to the Jewish homes. She was the only dairywoman in our town. Winter and summer, she filled her buckets early in the morning with milk and hung tin pails which held a half liter each. She sold cheese and sour cream too, but there were not many customers for them since cheese and sour cream were luxury items for so many. She was bent under the burden of her two buckets. Her child grew up. She guarded and took care of him day and night. His every step and breath were her whole life. Watching him grow filled her black eyes with joy. Years passed quickly, and the boy grew up and started working. With his first earnings he found a better place to live at the tanner's Vishnievsky. The small house stood between the houses of Zikhlinsky and Mordkhai Ber Vayden. Life was now easier. The widow no longer had to work so hard, and it always felt like springtime in their tidy, clean house. There was a great feeling of honor and respect between mother and son. It was rare to find such a family. Rukhele began to dream about leading her son to the wedding canopy and eventually becoming a grandmother. How beautiful it would be to have a grandchild. And for sure, her son would have a son. And he, may he live long

[Page 165]

would be named after his late grandfather, of blessed memory. Her heart swelled with joy. She imagined taking the little boy by his small hand to walk in the sun, in the fresh air, and then taking him to Kheder (elementary school), and then, she imagined, getting nervous that he was late returning home.

Poland was shrouded with a dark, barbaric night shrouded. "They" grabbed young people from their homes and took them to a faraway black abyss, to hard labor camps. Her son was also taken by these murderers. It was dark and cold in the house. She cried all night and did not eat, so that she could send packages to the camp. Her life now consisted of waiting for letters. Suddenly this was taken away as well. She stopped crying. She thought and contemplated. She became silent and small. Once in a while, she spoke briefly with the housewives. The Christians liked her. They felt the pain of her motherly heart. From time to time, the youngest daughter of her Christian neighbor brought her a glass of tea or milk. She made the lonely woman eat and drink and tried to distract her.

Three times, "they" looked for her, and each time the Christian girl said that she had gone away, that she was not here, that she didn't know where she had gone. They were very meticulous. They did not leave anyone out. The unhappy woman sat on a low bench in the corner of her room, staring at one spot. From time to time, she smiled to herself. We thought she had gone mad, said the girl.

The woman sat and recalled the details of her life. Bit by bit, she re–experienced her life. When she had been a little girl, her mother would be annoyed with her. She played a lot but didn't study enough. Unintentionally, she had broken something. Her engagement, her wedding. She could hear her mother's happy cries, her father's sighs. She remembered the blessed time of her pregnancy, the first signs of life in her womb. First, she lost her parents and then, her husband, the father of her little orphan. She watched her child grow, how he laid in his cradle and kicked his little feet. The first time he had said the child's prayer which she had taught him. How he went to Kheder and first learned Khumash (Torah), followed by the commentaries of Rashi, and the sun continued to shine for her.

[Page 166]

She almost broke out in laughter. Yes. Once I did not tell the truth. That is when a poor family's youngest daughter became ill. Every day, she brought milk for the child but told them that Francisca, the Christian woman, was paying for it. Otherwise (she defended herself) they would have not taken the milk from me. It was also possible that they understood. So what, I once told a lie. May God forgive me. The main thing is the child survived. But for what? She catches herself. That is not important. It is always a good deed to fight death. God is merciful, righteous, the one and only.

However, today we must stop. She took the measure of her house, the walls, the furniture, her son's sewing machine, everything, all her possessions, for the last time.

The whole time she sat lost in thought, the neighbor's daughter stood in the vestibule. When Rukhl Shveitzer opened the door of her home, the entire Christian family came from the other side and stopped her. You can't go. They don't know about you. You must remain with us. The unhappy woman, Rukhl Shveitzer, was very surprised, but she controlled herself and replied that she had to go, that she could not remain. A Jew in the house meant death for all the other inhabitants. I can't and won't bring danger to anyone. It would mean death for everyone. No, no, I will go now. I will go with everyone, with the whole town. I must not remain. I must go with everyone, I must. I'm going.

[Page 167]

Moishe Yakhimovitch of blessed memory

Translated by Roberta Paula Books

15 Sivan 5732 (May 28, 1972)

Today, six weeks after the death of our fellow Pshaytsher (landsman), Moishe Yakhimovitch, z"l, with the permission of his wife T. L. Yakhimovitch, we are attempting to edit the memoirs written by the deceased.

We want to try to present his sad experiences of the war years in the spirit in which he wrote.

In April 1942, we intensely recognized the approaching liquidation of Pshaytsher Jewry (Przedecz in Polish). In the neighboring towns, the ghettos no longer existed. All their Jewish inhabitants had been sent to Chełmno death camp, which was situated between Dabie (Dambie in Yiddish) and Koło.

While in a village where I had found a hiding place for my family, I learned that the Nazis had sent all the Jews from Pshaytsh (Przedecz in Polish) to Chełmno death camp. Among them were my beloved father Aron Dovid, my sister Krusa, my wife Rokhl, and our two small daughters Yazda and Mala, may their memories be blessed.

I could no longer show myself in the region. I had been hiding in the garage of the Christian, Drabyolo, for six weeks. The Christians told me, in detail, about the liquidation of the Jewish population of Pshaytsh (Przedecz in Polish). They further told me that Shmuel Abba Abramovitch, who had been hiding with a Christian shoemaker, had been handed over by him to Henkl, an ASA (Sturmabteilung) man, a local German.

Similarly, Menakhem Ravski had been captured by a local German, Friedrich Henebauer, who killed him in Jakubowo (Yakobov in Yiddish) forest.

The surrounding peasants trembled about their own fate and asked me to leave the area. I ran from there to the village of Debina (Dembina in Yiddish), near Kłodawa. I thought I could hide there for a short time. However, I felt like an animal being stalked by hunters for its fur. Every rustling sound terrified me. I slept in the fields on the haystacks. For days I did not eat or wash. My nerves were shot to the nth degree. I considered surrendering to the hangmen, but something inside me made we want to live. My goal was to survive and to tell the world of the horrible betrayal perpetrated by the Christian population, resulting the destruction of Polish Jewry.

[Page 168]

One night I stole a bicycle and left for Inowroclaw (Inavaratslav in Yiddish). From there I went to Lojewo (Layove in Yiddish), a camp where many girls from Pshaytsh (Przedecz in Polish) had been sent.

After four weeks in the camp, I was chosen as the head of a group in the camp. At that time, I established a workshop where approximately fifty people worked. It is important to mention this because none of the workers in my workshop died, on account of the relatively good conditions they had thanks to this work.

It was an open camp, into which we were permitted to bring food. Also, thanks to this, we were able to live.

Sometime around July – August 1943, the head of the camp informed me that the camp was soon to be liquidated, and that all the people would be sent to Poznań to clean up the city after it had been bombed.

However, I overheard that they were sending all of us to Auschwitz. When I told the people in camp, some managed to escape, me included.

This was Shabbes (Saturday), the 30th of August. That same day, I arrived at a farm not far from Lojewo (Layove in Yiddish). Here, too, there were several girls from Pshaytsh (Przedecz in Polish). Suddenly, before daybreak the next morning, September 1st, I noticed a truck approaching. I didn't have a chance to warn anyone, and I ran off by myself to the field. The following were in the camp: Ruzhe Topolsky, Esther Danielsky and Tobche Danielsky, the two daughters of Kasriel Yakobovitch, Soreh Nekhe Haltrikht, Pesia Danielsky. In the field, not far from the camp, I found a shovel and started working. Then I heard the loud screams of the girls as they were being beaten by the Nazis. This was their final journey. They were sent to Auschwitz. Not one of them returned. The screams of these girls as they were being sent off prevent me from forgetting the past.

I then went to hide with a Christian in a village not far from Lojewo (Layove in Yiddish). I stayed there for one week. When he saw I wasn't leaving, he threatened to report me to the police. I told him I would find another place, but that I would return in eight days to get my things which I had hidden with him when I was in the camp. When I returned to collect my belongings, the police were there waiting for me. They tied up my hands and feet and sent me to a jail in Muntfa.

[Page 169]

Until 12 o'clock that night I was held in a guarded room where they questioned me about different things. Then, they threw me into a room in a cellar, locked the door and left. I felt these were my last hours.

Once again, I made up my mind not to surrender to death. I used all my strength. I struggled to free myself from the chains restraining my hands and feet. My hands and feet were bleeding after I freed myself, but I didn't feel anything. I broke the window with a piece of iron, which I had found in the cellar, and ran off to the Christian who earlier had turned me over to the Germans, to get the money I had left there. I told him they had freed me, but when I heard the police were chasing after me again, once again I was forced to run. I later learned that the Germans put a bounty of 500 marks on my head.

As I was running, a peddler chased me with a wagon and wanted money. When I gave it to him, he demanded no less than that I should go with him to the gendarmerie. I struggled with him, and I argued, and I got a good beating, but I tore myself away from his hands. Escaping via a deep ditch, the Gentile could no longer chase me. Before the war, this gully had been the boundary between Germany and Poland. I went into the water to hide from this Gentile.

Afterwards, I had to remove my clothes to dry them on the grass. I hid myself naked in a pit in the forest.

Meanwhile, the Christian informed the school children in the area and, together, they began to search for me in the forest. They actually passed right by my hiding spot but did not find me.

Once again, I saved myself from death.

I went to my former camp commander, Patik, in Broniewo (Broynyeve in Yiddish), who had helped many Jews. I asked him to prepare papers for me so that I could live as a Christian. Baltzia Goldman had received such papers. Unfortunately, he was no longer able to help. He told me he was considered suspicious, and the Gestapo was looking for him.

However, he gave me a place to sleep in the loft of the barn.

That night a young Christian apparently wanted to kill me.

[Page 170]

He looked for me but did not find me. When day broke, he left. But I heard him scream that he would kill me yet.

Later, Patik's wife came up to me and brought me food and a rope for me to hang myself. When she left, her husband entered my hiding place and brought me an address in Paproć (Paprotch in Yiddish) of a good friend of his who would hide me. After a week during which she had hidden me, the Christian took me to her sister in Inowroclaw (Inavaratslav in Yiddish). I hid there in a cellar, together with Baltzia Goldman, until the end of the war.

During the year and a half in hiding, we worked for the Christians. I made boots, and Baltzia knit various pieces of clothing. For a bowl of soup in a dark, wet cellar, we paid with hard work. I contracted tuberculosis of the spine. For two years after the war, I lay in a cast. Thanks to the care I received from my wife Baltzia, whom I married after we left the cellar, I survived.

I would like to state that our two sons were the last Jewish children to be born in Pshaytsh (Przedecz in Polish). Today we all live in Israel.

My wish is that my story serves as a warning to the world that there should not be any more wars, any ghettos, any camps, or any racial hatred.

[Page 171]

Reb Itche Kovalsky "The Shammesh"

by Moishe Bilbasky

Translated from Yiddish by Roberta Paula Books

Reb Itche the Shammesh (beadle or Rabbi's assistant), that is what he was called in town. A last name was not needed, since no one would have used it, and no one would have recognized whom they meant.

Reb Itche the Shammesh was something of a scholar, albeit a very modest man. Because of his profession, it is probable that he did not want to display his knowledge. He did not want to embarrass the important men in town, who were proud of their more limited education.

Reb Itche the Shammesh was the center around which revolved all Jewish life in town. Often it seemed that, without him, people would not have known what was going on in town.

He was the steady companion of the Rabbi. Wherever the Rabbi went, Reb Itche accompanied him, whether it be a weekday, Sabbath, or a holiday.

Friday at lunchtime, the Rabbi and his shadow would inspect the Eruv in town (a wire boundary within which Jews were permitted to carry objects on the Sabbath) to make sure it had not been harmed, G–d forbid, during the week. More than once, he noticed that the Eruv was ritually unsuitable and there was not enough time to repair it before the Sabbath, and the town was left without the Eruv. Right after lunch, the Rabbi went to the mikveh (bath house) to ritually immerse himself in honor of the Sabbath. Reb Itche was beside him. The Rabbi left the ritual bath. Reb Itche the Shammesh hurried home to grab a wooden hammer, then ran to knock on Jewish doors so that people would hurry their preparations in honor of the Sabbath.

Now came the last few minutes before the Sabbath, and once again Reb Itche was at his post, but now dressed for the Sabbath in his velvet hat and his long delicate kaftan, perhaps his wedding garment. Once again, he ran through the town. Standing on his tippy toes, in every street corner he called out C – A – A– A – N – D – L – E – S, light your candles! He shouted so loudly that even in heaven they could hear that Jews were preparing to welcome the "Sabbath Queen".

When he had finished this task, he walked with slow steps. It was already Shabbes, and everyone knows "do not take heavy steps" (an admonition not to exert oneself on the Sabbath). Reb Itche walked slowly, step by step to the Rabbi's house and waited with humility for the Rabbi to finish, and they enter the synagogue.

The streets came alive. In every Jewish window

[Page 172]

Sabbath candles burned brightly. One could see, through some windows, a woman with a covered head hiding her face in her hands and blessing the Sabbath candles. The tenderness and gentleness of the Jewish mother could be felt at that moment, in the glow of the Sabbath candles on our mothers' faces.

Fathers with children carrying prayer books came out of each house and headed toward the synagogue, or the house of study, or the Khevre Tilim ("Society of Psalms") to pray. A mood of holiness settled over the town. Laborers, craftsmen, country peddlers who had worked hard the entire week and carried the burden of earning a living on their bent shoulders. You see the "neshome yeseyre" (additional soul) that each Jew possesses to give honor to the Sabbath.

And Reb Itche accompanied the Rabbi to synagogue with his slow steps, and one sensed that he, indeed, Itche the Shammesh, was actually G–d's messenger, with his knocking on doors, with his calling "light the candles", he played an important role in the holy Sabbath atmosphere that now settled over the town. And if the Eruv was in fact damaged, he would stand in front of the prayer house, the Society of Psalms, between the evening service and the Kabbalah Shabbes (prayer service for the welcoming of the Sabbath), with a red handkerchief tied around his neck, calling out "it is forbidden to carry".

The prayer service to welcome the Sabbath ends and everyone goes home. Once again Reb Itche accompanies the Rabbi to his home. Heading home from prayers, every Jews wants to approach the Rabbi to wish him a Good Sabbath, Rebe. And adds Good Sabbath, Reb Itche.

Saturday morning, Jews wake up and recite the Torah portion twice, then the translation once (in other words, the custom was to read the weekly portion twice in Hebrew and once with the Aramaic translation of Onkelos), sometimes also have a bite to eat with a glass of something warm and wait for Itche Shammes's call. And then he appears, with his slow steps, and soon one hears his familiar call: "T–o t–h–e S–y–n–a–g–o–o–o–o– ... –gue!"

And the Jews go into the synagogue. After Shacharis (the morning service) and before the Torah reading, his job is to sell the Aliyes (the privilege being called up to the Torah). With a bang of his hand on the reading desk, he calls out: "ten grosheyne for a koheyn, twenty grosheyne for a koheyn, and so forth". He does not say groshen as one does all week, but grosheyne, with a "shenye" (a change in pronunciation) to honor the Sabbath.

After prayers, of course he accompanies the Rabbi home again, to his residence, which borders the house of study. And there, from time to time, a warm reception awaited him. His son–in–law, Reb Elijah Walter, a learned Jew and a fine prayer leader, would recite Sabbath blessings there before the lectern! Or Sabbath of the new month. Some Jews who were still sitting in the House of Study waiting for him would say: "Ay, Ay, Reb Itche, everyone enjoyed your son–in–law's service today. He was amazing". And the modest Reb Itche would shake his head. May G–d see to it that he was the real messenger and may G–d accept his prayers on behalf of all people

[Page 173]

of Israel. And a special prayer "He will redeem us soon and gather in our exiles from the four corners of the earth".

And when Reb Itche came home and told everything to his wife, they both lifted their hands toward heaven and whispered a prayer to the Creator of the universe. Beloved G–d, we ask you not to disturb our bit of pleasure, as this is the only bit of light in our difficult labored life.

Reb Itche and his wooden hammer had another task. Before Rosh Hashanah, when Selichos (the prayers of repentance) are recited every morning, Reb Itche knocked on Jewish doors before dawn to wake everyone for Selichos. The prayer house filled with people praying. On Rosh Hashanah and Yom Kippur, wearing his white kittel (white ceremonial robe), with his glasses perched on the tip of his nose, he was the community's messenger from the synagogue up to G–d.

To supplement his income, he provided Pshaytsher (Przedecz) Jews with a certified lulav (for Sukkos) and of willow branches for Hoshana Rabbah.

On Chanukah, when Jews would come to synagogue for evening prayers, Itche Shammesh was also at his post. He was the one to light the Chanukah candles, accompanied with a blessing using a very special melody.

One day before Passover the Rabbi, accompanied by a large portion of the

The street from the old market where the Shammesh Reb Itche Kovalsky lived.
Standing in front are Simkha Naymark and his wife on their visit to Pshaytsh (Przedecz) in 1965.

[Page 174]

local gentry, went to the river to draw "mayim shelanu", water which would stay overnight for making shmura (watched) matzah. Reb Itche lugged the large wooden bucket. And, while drawing the water, singing took place, chapters from Hallel. Reb Itche carried the heavy water bucket, but every few steps someone took over in order to take part in the good deed of bringing water for the shmura matzah.

Shavuot, the holiday of the giving of the Torah, Reb Itche decorated the synagogue and the house of study with greens, as is the Jewish custom. He did this with such devotion, as if he was actually preparing to receive the gift of Torah.

Understandably, when a legal question was brought before the Rabbi, his task was to bring the litigant to the Rabbi. He remained at his post, ready to carry out any mission, until the end of the litigation.

At meetings of the community council, his job was to carry out all assignments.

When there was a wedding in town, Reb Itche, in the name of the host, invited the guests.

G–d forbid when someone died, Jews wanted to fulfill the good deed of accompanying the deceased to his eternal rest. Reb Itche ran through town calling out for people to attend the funeral. During the funeral, he ran through the crowd with a collection box saying, "righteousness shields from death".

When the dark clouds of the German fascist occupation fell on Poland, the sky over Pshaytsh (Przedecz) darkened as well. Reb Itche was worried about how the institutions of the Jewish community would continue to exist when he, Itche the

Shammesh, would not be able to fulfill his role. It was already the days of repentance when he would wake the people. Would they be permitted to leave their homes in the middle of the night? The occupiers had begun to show who they were. They had already taken away the key to the synagogue, all the community institutions and Jewish organizations were closed. People were afraid to pray in groups, even in private homes. Every day brought new edicts, with their hardships. Jews were being kidnapped for forced labor and were beaten. Half of their beards were cut off. The Rabbi was forced to carry heavy planks of wood while Reb Itche, his companion, had to stand at a distance and watch.

The nights of repentance. Reb Itche looked at his orphaned wooden hammer. Reb Itche and his hammer could no longer carry out their task. But how could we not say the prayers of repentance. Reb Itche scrambled into the yard, and from there into the yard of his neighbors, Avrom Fisher, Shimshon Zielinsky. At the second yard of Khaim Yosef Zielinsky, Yisroel Khaim Zielinsky he tapped lightly on their doors and asked them to come with him to say the prayers of repentance. They comprised

[Page 175]

a half quorum of Jews. By the light of a small candle sitting on the floor, his son–in–law Reb Elijah Walter began Ashrei (an adaptation of Psalm 145 as an alphabetic acrostic) "Happy are the people who dwell in your house". When he came to the passage "G–d is righteous in every way, and faithful in every deed", he broke out with such a wail, joined by all those praying with him, and all said after that "The Eternal protects all who seek G–d in love, but will destroy the wicked." And each of them ended the chapter with "We will bless G–d now and forever, Hallelujah". Each one of them felt that he was the messenger for all Jews, and at that moment Reb Khaim Yosef the saddle maker said with a broken heart "On your doors we knock, compassionate one, don't turn us away empty from before you" (from the prayers of repentance). Reb Avrom Fisher continued the prayer: "We approach (relying on) your name. Lord, act for the sake of your name because of your name's honor". (This and quotes that follow are from the penitential prayers, called Selichos.)

They continued with the penitential service, and Reb Yisroel Khaim the tinsmith continued, his voice breaking, "From the beginning until now, we are exiled, killed, slaughtered, and butchered. We remain a tiny remnant among the sharp thorns. With the fearsome wonders of your right hand, we will be saved for eternity. For we trust your abundant mercy," followed by Reb Shimshon Zielinsky: "May our pleadings be acceptable as we stand (before you) during the nights. Turn (toward us) favorably, as with a burned and consumed sacrifice. Magnify your miracles, you who does greatly." A few youths from the neighbors arrived and everyone together "Hear our voices, Lord, our G–d, look and have mercy upon us, and receive our prayers with mercy and favor." The heavy steps of soldiers could be heard outside, patrolling the town, and Reb Itche, now totally broken, stood up, forgetting about the new situation, and began to chant "Hear our voices, Lord, our G–d. Look and have mercy upon us, and receive our prayers with mercy and favor" And he said this prayer with such a moaning, it was like two thousand years of Jewish suffering in exile, all the pogroms, slaughters and inquisitions lying on his bowed shoulders. With that, he opened his private Holy Ark, the old dresser where he kept all his ritual items, his prayer shawl and phylacteries, his kittel (white ritual robe), the synagogue's shofar (ram's horn), the synagogue key and his orphaned wooden hammer. They should all bear witness to the fact that, even in these difficult times, Jews were saying the prayers of repentance. And with the spirit of tradition. And when he came to the passage "Do not cast us away in old age. When our strength fails, do not abandon us", he wept along with everyone else.

And they continued like this until the service was completed. "Help us, G–d of our salvation, because of your honored name, and save us, atone our sins for your name's sake".

In the above-mentioned dresser, well hidden in a corner, lay a small package bound with a white string. Once a year, Reb Itche and his wife opened it, aired it out well, and carefully tied it up again. Shrouds. When the time comes that they are called to the world of truth, they should not, G–d forbid, be buried in an unfamiliar shroud…

Itche Kovalsky the Shammesh, his son–in–law Elijah Walter, Avrom Fisher the tanner, Shimshon Zielinsky the tailor, Khaim Yosef the saddle maker, Yisroel Khaim the tinsmith and their sons, who assembled to recite the prayers of repentance, with a few others who risked their lives. With great respect

[Page 176]

we must remember their names. With this deed, they were the first in town to raise the flag of resistance against the Nazi occupation.

Reb Itche the Shammes could not find his footing after they took away the key to the synagogue. His heart told him that the murderers did not want only to kill the Jews, they wanted to annihilate every trace of Jews and Jewishness. The synagogue was in danger. And what would happen to the Torah scrolls? But he convinced himself that, under the circumstances, in the event G–d forbid of a decree to burn the synagogue, there would be more glory for the Torah, since the holy books, too, would go up in flames. The holy letters would reach the Divine Throne and demand a fair trial for "Am Yisrael", the Jewish people, the people whom you chose. He believed that each attempt to rescue the books would cost Jewish blood. Maybe that was their intention. Any (rescued) books would be disgraced and mocked. In fact, the barbarians did burn down the synagogue, the night of Shmini Atzeret. In other years, on such a night, all houses of prayer would be packed. Itche remembered how he would be busy in holiday preparations. The holiday mood would have captured young and old. But today transformed the night of Shmini Atzeret into a "night they will be made to cry" (a reference to the lamentations recited on Tisha b'Av to commemorate the destruction of the temple in Jerusalem), they had to mourn the destruction. And the entire world remained silent.

Reb Itche became unwell and dispirited. The synagogue, the blessed sanctuary, and the holy books were burned. He stood in the corner at his private Holy Ark and asked the master of the universe for salvation as he recited the prayers for the seventh day of repentance.

When the Nazi criminals laid their hands on our community in town, the Pshaytsher (Przedecz) Jewish community was liquidated through the final annihilating deportation to Chełmno on April 24, 1942, the 7th day of Iyar. The Jews were gathered in the local church in the last hours of their lives. Reb Itche the Shammesh sensed his obligation and called out to everyone: "Jews, let us say the Vidui (the confessional prayer said by Jews before dying)."

And with these holy words, Sh'ma Yisroel (Hear O Israel) on his kosher lips, Itche the Shammesh shared the same fate as all the other Jews from Pshaytsh (Przedecz) on their last journey. May the Lord avenge his blood. Let his memory be for a blessing.

[Page 177]

Rabbi Zemelman – The Person and the Personality

by A. Talmid

Translated from Hebrew by Marshall Grant

I hold in my hands the book, *The Warsaw Ghetto Diaries*, by Hillel Seidman. This is a new version of the book released in New York in 1957, which follows the first version published in Tel Aviv in 1946. It can be assumed that the thousands of copies are not only in private libraries but also in many universities, and the historian who researches the Holocaust will certainly find interesting information with historical significance between its pages.

Among the book's content is a record of Rabbi Zemelman, who fought in the Warsaw Ghetto and fell fighting the Germans.

While reading the book, I asked myself, how will our sons, who serve in the IDF, appreciate the brave actions of Rabbi Zemelman and his call to rebellion, to purchase arms, and finally, his call to take up arms and fight the Germans. A battle from which he never returned.

Our young soldiers have made heroism a habit during their IDF service. Many have fought in two or three major wars, and others in the smaller ones after the Six–Day War. They have shown tremendous courage, and thanks to their heroic actions, the

IDF is where it is today. Can they appreciate the heroism shown in the Warsaw Ghetto by such a distinguished man as Rabbi Zemelman?

I asked myself this question, and I have written my responses down on paper. I remember the day that Rabbi Zemelman and his family arrived to accept the position of rabbi in our city. It turned into a celebration! In the early hours of the afternoon, all the city's residents put on their nicest clothes. In the evening, the city's leaders also turned out, supported by the entire Jewish community. There were two young men in costumes riding on horseback at the head of the group who went to receive the rabbi and his family. Upon entering the city, the rabbi alighted from the carriage carrying his family, and as he started walking, the parade began. The rabbi was led under a *chuppah* (wedding canopy), together with the city's leaders, to the synagogue. There was an honor guard on both sides of the chuppah, with all the other Jewish residents gathered around. Following the festive *ma'ariv* (the evening prayers) led by the cantor and *shochet* (ritual slaughterer and examiner), the rabbi was presented with his official rabbinical documents and appointed by the head of the community to his position. He gave a sermon on behalf of the occasion. Of course, it was in Yiddish, but he then spoke in Hebrew, which the rabbi spoke well with an Ashkenazi accent. The crowd was overjoyed. The surprise of the evening came when, after he saw municipal officials and police representatives from the *bima*, he acknowledged their presence with a speech in Polish, which surprised everyone. There were loud rounds of applause that actually shook the walls of our beautiful synagogue.

He called Ya'akov Tapolsky to the stage and thanked him for the honor guard. Zemelman then expressed hope that he would enjoy the full cooperation of all segments of the population in the future, just as he had been awarded on that day.

As if to endorse this wish, the rounds of applause seemed to go on forever; in fact, our synagogue had never witnessed such an ovation.

[Page 178]

Immediately after beginning his tenure, Zemelman worked to develop the Jewish religious institutions that were, at that time, haphazardly operated. They were expanded and placed under public supervision that he himself led. These efforts resulted in the establishment of *Beit Ya'akov*, a girls' school, the city's second institution, which touched many students. The best teachers were recruited from the city and outside of it, and the results were extraordinary. Whether day or night, voices could be heard from the schools, learning holy scriptures, "singing" the *Gemara* and *Tanach*. The rabbi did not only serve as the principal of the educational institutions, he himself taught lessons to the older students. In fact, thanks to rabbi's efforts and organization, winds of change began to be felt in the city, and in many respects, an awakening had begun.

I had the privilege to be one of his students, and I remember how he was interested in all facets of life.

He was well liked by the public with his courteous behavior and distinguished demeanor. He befriended the wisest students and the city's most humble; no one was too important or insignificant. He always respected those younger than he with his Torah and wisdom and would always be prepared to share the beauty of Jewish beliefs. In every one of his speeches, he always tried to emphasize the content and philosophy of traditional Judaism. He tied the love of the Torah to the love of the Jewish people.

He was so powerful that even the most mundane conversation became an incredible experience just by hearing his voice. He spent every free moment studying the Torah, in fact it can be said that he never stopped. He wrote interpretations of the Torah and corresponded extensively with the most eminent rabbis in Poland concerning his opinions. He was also well respected among the local Christian community and made friends with many. The city's leaders and clergy were sympathetic to his problems. Every year, he would travel for two to three weeks to Ger and spend time with the *Rebbe*, whom he deeply admired. Upon his return, he would share his experiences with anyone he encountered, which enabled him to find a common language with some of the youth who were not regular visitors to the synagogue. He heard their problems and their paths to *tikkun olam*. He would argue with them endlessly, but with mutual respect.

Chess was another field in which he was knowledgeable, and in his spare time, he would play with his students or other acquaintances in the city.

His wife, a *rebbetzin*, in her own right, had a gentle soul. She made her home with comfort and tenderness; she eagerly helped him, and her only request was to stand by the side of her respected husband.

It was not unusual to see lights on in their home at two or three o'clock in the morning while preparing an answer that had to be provided the next day. The shokhet had found impurities in a cow that had been slaughtered and brought the question to the rabbi. The rabbi was looking for a way to make the cow kosher, because he knew the shokhet's dire financial situation. It continued for almost the entire night. When he had to deem a cow unkosher, it was like part of his heart had been torn away.

The celebration of the *sauda shlishis* (shaleshudes in Yiddish, the third Sabbath meal) on Shabbes became well known throughout the city. Jewish students would memorize what they had learned so they could participate in the Talmudic discussion held during the meal.

Politically speaking, he was affiliated with *Agudas Yisrael*, and as part of this organization, he supported efforts for the settlement of Israel. It was not easy for him to come to terms with the fact that some of his students established *Mizrachi Youth* (Tze'erei Mizrachi). It was the time of the *Tarpat* riots (1929 in Palestine), the destruction of Hebron's Jewish community in *Kiryat Arba*, and the brutal murder of tens of yeshiva students by the Arabs.

[Page 179]

When his former students were collecting funds for the JNF (Jewish National Fund), they went to his house as well, and the rabbi warmly accepted them. There were some reservations, however, and he explained that as a member of Agudas Yisrael, he could not contribute, but he sent them to his wife, who gave a substantial contribution.

I will note a small, but important, detail. He was never a physically strong man.

The years went by, and he took care of the community and provided for their spiritual needs. His dedication was complete. More than once, he was offered positions in larger cities, with a larger salary, but Przedecz was his city, and he would not leave. With every ounce of his soul, he was dedicated to the community and its members.

Then the war broke out, and the Polish friends became enemies overnight. It was with their help that the Germans began to harass the Jews.

The Germans did everything they could to humiliate him, and thus break the community's spirit of resistance. He was made to work in forced labor in the market square so he would be seen by the city's Christians and Jews. When a Jewish man begged the Germans to let him work instead of the rabbi, he was beaten so severely he began to bleed. While this was seen by the rabbi and the others present, the worst humiliation was when they shaved the rabbi's beard, and the beards of all Jews in the city. Of course, they did not do this gently, and it can be assumed that this was the moment the seeds of revenge were planted and began to grow in Zemelman's heart.

The night of *Shmini Atzeres* (a Jewish holiday) arrives, and it is this of all nights that turned into a night of lament. The synagogue was ablaze, curfew was being enforced in the city, and several of Przedecz's Jews take their lives into their own hands and visit the rabbi's home. They pleaded, "Rabbi, please, let us try and save the Torah scrolls from the burning synagogue, no matter what the cost. Why did the Nazis choose the night of Shemini Atzeret of all nights to turn into a night of destruction?" The rabbi was moved by their very presence in his home and by their willingness to make such a holy sacrifice, but he ordered them not to do anything at this time. "This is the time to protect our lives. The Germans are planning a bloodbath, and it is unlikely the Torah scrolls can be saved. We are commanded to respect the Torah, but we are also commanded to save our lives. The very fact you came here under the threat of death is greatly honoring the Torah. In the situation we find ourselves in, the biggest honor will be when the holy parchments and letters will rise in flames to the heavens and will stand before the holy throne, and in their presence, they will remember and acknowledge the holy communities, which died a martyr's death."

The rabbi turned and faced the corner and stood there for a moment. When he turned around, tears could be seen falling from his eyes. He said, "Friends, I have known you for years, and we have not always agreed on everything and we have had our differences, but your willingness to sacrifice yourselves shows how devoted you are to Judaism, and how the treasures of our people are dear to you. We are all praying that "our eyes behold your return to Zion with mercy". It could be that Saul's suffering ended in exile, but let us all now promise, in this significant time, that if, with G-d's help, we stay alive, we will remove the chains of exile, we will return to our homeland and fight for a Jewish state in the Land of Israel. We will collect the holy letters from our Torah that rose to the heavens engulfed in flames, and we will carry them through the ocean of Jewish tears created from 2,000 years of diaspora. And with these letters, weakened by fire and water, we will write new Torah scrolls, we will build beautiful synagogues, and this will be so very magnificent, a sight the world will have never before seen."

[Page 180]

The atmosphere in the room was almost charged with electricity. Those present were all deeply moved and agreed with the rabbi's words. They said, our teacher, our rabbi, we are with you!

And the synagogue was in flames…

All the participants remained in the rabbi's home until the morning, as he had instructed, in order to not needlessly risk their lives.

When they departed, he turned to them and said, my friends, we will cling to life and pray to our fathers in the heavens that we will be worthy to revenge the *Amalek* of our times, how they tortured us, the people of Israel and everything sacred to Judaism. This is a calling to impose the revenge of God on the Nazi vermin, and only then will we be worthy and be entitled to celebrate our holidays in the Land of Israel.

The day after the holiday, the rabbi, accompanied by his oldest son, Yehoshua Elimelech, went to where the synagogue once stood. They broke into tears, and the rabbi begged for forgiveness and compassion for not trying to rescue the place of worship and the Torah scrolls within. It was his respect for the synagogue that influenced him – he did not want tens of fatalities as the Nazis had planned. "My dear son, we follow the sanctity of life, therefore we must plan for the day we can take revenge for all that has been inflicted on us and our holy sites. This will be divine revenge of today's *Amalek*. We will be the messengers, and we will restore our pride and splendor."

On that same day, the rabbi was made to sign, under threat and humiliation, that he and his congregants were responsible for burning the synagogue. He also took upon himself, under the orders of the Nazis, to pay a fine.

The rabbi, despite the humiliation he suffered, was time and time again required to approach the military administrators and try, for the good of his community, to postpone one of the upcoming decrees against the Jews. There were times he succeeded, but everyone knew it was only a temporary postponement. The Nazi monster had not abandoned its plans.

Yes, the Nazi machine continued to destroy and kill. Tens of youngsters from his community were sent to labor camps, two of the rabbi's daughters among them. It was forced labor, punishment camps. Some were able to send letters, others were not. News arrives about the youngsters, most of them tortured or murdered while working. Older people are also sent to labor camps, and no family in the city remains completely intact.

Half of Przedecz's Jews are in labor camps. The others are made to leave their homes and move to the ghetto. Helpless and defenseless, the Jews succumb to their fate and leave the homes they have lived in for decades and leave for the ghetto. Everyone is humiliated; they are hoping for a miracle while clinging to their instinct to live. Their husbands, sons, and daughters are in the labor camps, and they are waiting for a letter, a sign of life. No one knows who has the better fate: those who remained, or those who were sent away.

This is the way they lived, in the harshest of conditions, with a unique stubbornness in their belief they would again live in comfort and their children and relatives would return from the camps. They planned for better days.

But as it turned out, it was all for naught.

On the 7th of Iyar, 5702; April 24, 1942, the Jews of Przedecz are destroyed. They are sent to the valley of death, infamously known as Chełmno. They are asphyxiated in the vans of death.

And here I hold before me *The Diaries of the Warsaw Ghetto*, by Hillel Seidman. The book

[Page 181]

describes life in the Ghetto, the horrors they experienced, being sent to the labor camps, and the arrests. Community leaders convene, including the *Admorim* (khasidic term for rebbe) and other rabbis to discuss the situation. The urgent issue at hand was whether the Germans were actually planning to destroy Warsaw's Jewry. The largest concentration of Jews in Europe? There are optimists, and there are pessimists.

The optimists: our strength is in our numbers. Half a million people. They wouldn't dare! Warsaw is strength! They will have to take this influence into consideration. There are many Christians who want the ghetto to remain, and there are Germans who want the Ghetto to remain. The German tax office receives 25% of the value of the goods that enter – as a "gift". The Commissar also receives huge sums of money and other gifts from the community for various measures of relief. And secondly, the soldiers: if the Ghetto is destroyed, they will be sent to the front. And last but not least, the Ghetto produces a great deal, it is an important economic hub, and it is inconceivable that the Germans will want to eliminate it.

And on the other side were the pessimists: yes, they will dare! The Nazis are capable of anything. They are not to be believed; the Germans don't take anything into consideration. We are in great danger, and we need to think about how to rescue ourselves. The pessimists prevailed.

And then there were proposals: to collect great sums of money and bribe the Gestapo. To collect gold and offer bribes. A proposal is made to send a delegation to the Governor–General; others suggest opening new factories to produce more, and in this way prevail.

Mr. Yosef Kennigsburg, who recently arrived from Lublin, where he miraculously survived the expulsion, provides chilling details of the destruction there. He asks us not to succumb to their deceptions. We need to immediately adopt any means of survival available. A proposal is made to secretly send a delegation to Switzerland and to appeal to international public opinion from there. England must recognize all the Jews, at least until the war is over, as citizens of Eretz Yisrael; America must take us under its wings; the Pope must be asked to issue a special appeal.

But what can be done when we are locked in jail? How can we send an envoy to Switzerland when anyone who crosses the street faces the penalty of death? Our brothers abroad will not understand, at least this time, the huge danger of annihilation, nor will the world's conscience be shaken. Little by little, the participants become pale as they understand that all the rescue plans are unfeasible and cannot be achieved. We are helpless, we are lost.

And we read on (Ed. Note: in *The Diaries of the Warsaw Ghetto*, by Hillel Seidman):

- The Gestapo's expulsion preparations.
- A campaign for the annihilation of Warsaw's Jews begins.
- The Ghetto is surrounded, *Aussiedlung* [evacuation] order issued.
- Mass expulsion to the *Umschlagplatz*.
- Czerniaków (head of the *Judenrat*) takes his own life.
- There are 7,000 victims a day.
- Hunger kills many; there is a massacre on Nowolipie Street.
- The *Small Ghetto* destroyed.
- Janusz Korczak leads his students to their fate.
- The brother of the Munkatch's rabbi returns from Treblinka and provides accounts of mass killings.

[Page 182]

- Distressing news from surrounding villages.

Meaning, up until now has been a factual description of the harsh conditions suffered by the Jews in the Warsaw Ghetto. From the chapter titled, *Rabbi Zemelman Calls for Revolt and Revenge*, page 153:

> *Among the village refugees who now arrived in Warsaw is Rabbi Zemelman, Przedecz's rabbi. He also tells of the destruction of rural Jewish communities, both large and small. That rabbi is an activist in the Aguda and a talented scholar, who tried to make contact with left–wing Polish partisans. He would sneak over to the Aryan side and behave as if he belonged there and would return with weapons and ammunition. His calls for revolt were met with firm resistance.*

> *Today I heard Rabbi Zemelman speak in a secret meeting in "the Bunker". He is a talented speaker with fire in his soul; he describes the inconceivable scenes from the destruction of Jewish communities. He calls for vengeance, "Great is revenge that is given between two names of God", referring to the Talmud's definition of "a God of retribution".*

> *He also proposes a detailed plan for an uprising, and he takes it upon himself to provide arms and ammunition.*

> *He does not just demand action from others, he acts himself. Today, for example, he provided the Defense Committee 12 pistols and several boxes of bullets.*

When he went on a mission to purchase weapons, he did it as if he was hearing the tortured cries of his children, of his saint–like wife; the cries of the hundreds of children from his community, and of every Jew in Przedecz; the cries of millions of Jews across Europe who are being tortured and cruelly murdered; the cries of our fathers in the heavens. Oh, compassionate God above, for your holy name in this world, we will inflict our vengeance.

He demanded our blood be avenged from our nemesis. Please, God, do not let our sacrifice be in vain, pursue and destroy them.

Rabbi Zemelman saw himself as a divine messenger to take revenge, in His name, for what the Nazis have inflicted on us.

He visited the rabbis and *Admors* and demanded they also call for revolt and vengeance. "I was told that he visited a meeting of the *pioneers*, the core of the insurgence, and he captivated their young minds. Last week there was a heated exchange between him and Bund representatives who instructed that the insurgency wait for a sign from London and their socialist comrades on the Aryan side. And it was Rabbi Zemelman who proved all this was all an illusion, all in vain".

In other words, it was Rabbi Zemelman who first initiated the uprising and reprisal in the Ghetto among religious and other circles. When asked the questions, "Rabbi, with empty fists we will rise up against the Germans? Can a tight fist overcome them?" He proved they would fight with more than a tight fist. He slipped to the Aryan side and returned with arms and ammunition. I am sure he witnessed divine miracles.

It is hard to imagine that here there are groups organizing to fight the Germans, groups of hungry and depressed boys, most of whom have lost a large part of their families – but they are not humbled. Their souls are prepared to fight the Nazi animals, and this, Zemelman considered a present–day miracle, a miracle from the heavens.

Then an announcement appeared, signed by many officials, including the President of the Jewish Council,

[Page 183]

Engineer Mark Lichtenbaum, calling for the Jewish population to volunteer to travel to Poniatow and Trawniki, near Lublin, for work. They were promising the volunteers would work in good working conditions.

The Jewish National Council convened and decided not to encourage travel. The Gestapo local collaborators have betrayed us in the past, we will not move from here. The rabbis, with the active participation of Rabbi Zemelman, issued a declaration calling on the population not to travel. The slogan: Our Numbers – Our Strength. Any separation, any division weakens our opposition, and it is treasonous to the memory of our loved ones, and it is treasonous to ourselves.

This policy was successful; the Jews are not volunteering to travel. Nevertheless, those hungry and starving were prepared to leave. The Jewish Resistance Movement, together with the rabbis, and again, with the active participation of Rabbi Zemelman, create a special fund from monies aggressively collected from the city's affluent to support the needs of those who were able to persevere and not have to travel due to hunger.

But the fateful hour was approaching. The holiday commemorating our freedom began, and so did the revolt. When it became apparent the Germans were planning to destroy the Ghetto, the password was given: armed opposition and revolt, courage under fire.

The battle for the Ghetto had begun.

In the uprising's headquarters, people gather for the *seder*, haphazardly, with the participation of Rabbi Zemelman. He asks, "Would anyone be as wise as to express his interpretation given by the freedom fighters in those times and conditions to the phrase, '*Why is tonight different from all other nights?*' Can we feel the excitement when they said, '*Pour out Your wrath upon the nations that do not acknowledge You, for they have devoured Jacob and laid waste his habitation? Pour out your anger and destroy them from beneath G-d's heavens*'." The seder continues, they are wonderful times. The fear of death is replaced with another feeling, of Pesach and resistance, holiday and struggle.

And the battle for the Ghetto has begun.

The commanders of the uprising give orders to open fire, and the results that evening were that no Germans were to be seen on the streets. It seems that they too are afraid of the angel of death, especially when hundreds of their comrades had already been injured. They know that every home has a Jewish soldier lying in wait for them, and they retreat.

The soldiers also continue to take action in the post called "North". One of the commanders there is Rabbi Zemelman.

And the Polish partisans, who promised to join when the insurgence began? They idly watched the battle from the side.

No delusions, no help from anyone.

And the Ghetto is in flames. The Jewish solders, among them Rabbi Zemelman, face the overwhelming Nazi war machine with extraordinary bravery. This is not a battle of equals. This is a battle of modern weaponry against the spirit of bravery, against soldiers who left for battle chanting "God is a God of vengeance, and the God of vengeance appeared". This is the story told about Rabbi Zemelman's last battle, and the one in which he fell. May God revenge his soul.

"Rabbi Zemelman and his comrades stood strong in a bitter and stubborn battle; they fought bravely, with heroism and sacrifice, and paid with their lives".

That is the way they fought, as heroes, as grandchildren of the Maccabees, and we have achieved a Jewish nation

[Page 184]

in the Land of Israel following the years of Holocaust and heroism, achieved through a bloody war. It was the uprising in the ghettos, a spark that burned and became a flame, that ignited the hearts of other soldiers in Israel: the heroic IDF soldiers who have bravely fought in the wars of our lifetime and who promise that another Holocaust will never happen again.

It was Rabbi Zemelman, the rabbi of Przedecz, who was one of those who lit the spark that would become an inextinguishable flame.

This is how Rabbi Yosef Alexander Zemelman sanctified G-d's name during his life and in his death. He has been promised a place of honor on the long list of Israel's heroes.

May his soul be bound in the bundle of life.

[Page 185]

The Reciting of the Kaddish

by Rabbi Itzhak Yedidia Frankel

Translated from Hebrew by Marshall Grant

By generous permission of the Great Rabbi, Yitzhak Yedidia Frankel, for the memorial book dedicated to the innocent Jews of Przedecz

We have just completed the memorial service next to the monument commemorating the Warsaw Ghetto. The monument lies on the corner of Ganesha-Dazika streets, in front of the military prison. In the past, the square was the center of Jewish activity. The intersections of Nalewki, Pawia and Dezalna Streets were filled day and night with vibrant Jewish life, full of energy and activity. And now - there are only the walls of the military prison; only they remain as testimony to the destruction of Warsaw in those days.

The entire area was a mountain of rubble, and no two bricks remained cemented together. Over the last few years, apartments for workers have been built, and on the "*Umschlagplatz*", a granite memorial has been erected, representing the struggle, uprising and destruction.

The Mute Memorial Cries Out to All

The abandoned memorial stands mute and cries out to all.

It was to this memorial that Jewish delegations flowed from around the world to pay their respects and admiration to the Jews who heroically gave their lives in the uprising of the

Translation from Polish: In this place, on the 8th of May 1943, the commander of the Warsaw Ghetto uprising,
Mordkhai Anielewicz, died a heroic death, together with his staff and tens of soldiers who took part in the revolt against the German murderers.

[Page 186]

Warsaw Ghetto twenty years ago. At 4 p.m. this Friday, the Sabbath evening of the *Shmini* Torah portion, we arrived in the thousands to the memorial's square and waited for the ceremony to begin. Lines and lines of Polish policemen separated the official delegations that had arrived from around the world and the curious spectators who began to gather from every direction.

An armed Polish battalion has gathered in the center of the square. Members of government have arrived, as have prominent Jewish educators and international delegations, which have brought 237 flower wreaths to be laid at the base of the memorial. The delegation from Israel has also arrived, including Dr. Adolf Berman. The Polish and international press are also present with their radio and television teams.

We stand at attention and listen to the notes of the Polish national anthem "Poland is not yet lost, so long as we still live". Yes… Poland is not lost… but Poland's Jewry? Our heart is torn to shreds as the military officer speaks about those who have fallen fighting fascism, and then requests that all anti-fascist forces unite in the common struggle against its resurrection. Our hearts raged and overflowed; God in the heavens, what is going on here? Did we come to a memorial service for Polish soldiers who died in battle? Is this also the way its Jewish fighters of Warsaw fell? Were there not cries of revenge and *Shema Yisrael* that could be heard? And the whispering of *I Believe*?

A Jewish Mark has been Left on the Ceremony

Finally, the general ends his speech by calling, "Respect their memory!". The soldiers presented their arms, and everyone was silent. Hearts beat strongly and shook. I left the line I was standing in with determined strides towards the memorial. And when I reached the military officer, I gathered all my strength, and the strength of many other pure souls that filled the space, and I screamed

Rabbi Yitzhak Yedidia Frankel saying Kaddish

On the left, in the beret and wearing medals, Mr. Yitzhak Zanderman, the Chairman of the Israeli branch of the Association of Disabled Veterans of the War Against the Nazis.

[Page 187]

a scream that shattered the surrounding silence: ***Yisgadal v'yiskadash sh'mei raba!*** [Exalted and hallowed be G-d's great name] The pen cannot describe what transpired at that moment. From all sides there was crying and wailing and many even joined the saying of the Kaddish prayer. We stared in the direction of those gathered around the square, beyond the lines of the Polish police. Hysterical cries and screams were heard from there. It turns out that the crowd was Jewish, a crowd that cannot recognize its own members on any other day. Today, however, it was this tragic Kaddish that broke the ice, and all the sorrow and pain that had accumulated in their hearts could finally be released.

The military commander, government officials and the entire diplomatic corps, from the East and the West, all remained at attention. Their faces become pale as Poland shook from cries and lament.

This was the Jewish mark left at this official ceremony, integrated into the official texts that would come later. From this moment on, let every person in Poland know that this is our memorial service, and for that reason alone Jews from all over the world have come to commemorate their brothers and sisters who fell in the uprising and struggle in the name of God.

On Route to Mila 18

We leave the square; the police open a corridor through the crowded throng that have come to see us. An old, handicapped man, sitting in a wheelchair, insists with his words and a glance that we approach him. We come to him, and he grabs my hand and covers it with kisses and tears. The eyes of all those around us are puffy and red. Under the ice, warm springs of repressed and expecting Jewish souls have been discovered. We march from the square towards Mila 18, where Mordechai Anielewicz, the commander of the uprising, and his comrades fell. This visit was not part of the official plan, but the Israeli delegation unexpectedly decided to go there. The other delegations marched after us.

We arrive at Mila Street, which no longer really exists. Somehow, at some time, a few new houses were erected among the rubble, but Mila 18 and its surroundings are still in ruins and desolate. The bunker built with reinforced cement that served the commander of the uprising protrudes from the ground. The names of the fallen are etched in the concrete in Polish and Yiddish. "Here, on May 8, 1943, the last of the soldiers fighting the Germans fell after lighting the flame of revolt on April 19, 1943". And the names appear:

Mordkhai Anielewicz, the commander of the uprising, Arie Wilner, E. Fondiminsky, Mira Fuchrer, Lev Grizlatz, Sara Żagiel, Lejb Rotblat, Berl Braude, Szyja Szpancer, Haim Akerman, and others.

The bunker's block of concrete protrudes from the pile of ruins we have all climbed together. We stood in silence, feeling that we were standing on the "Masada" of European Jewry. Fear and trembling engulfed us as we lit a fire as a memorial flame for the fallen, where the ground was soaked with the blood they shed. I said the prayer *Maleh Rachamim* (prayer for the souls of the deceased), "please, do not be silent or show restraint when the blood of Israel is shed like water - Oh land, do not cover their blood until retaliation and revenge are delivered".

[Page 188]

My lips whispered Psalm 142, when David was in the cave of prayer, "My voice cries out to God." I said the Kaddish in a broken voice and looked around. I saw my Jewish brothers there, and they were just like me, with their heads bowed contemplating the holiness of the ground on which they stood. Before me stood Stimson, an English cleric from London, the head of the Jewish Friendship League, who arrived with a Jewish delegation from London. He approached me, and with tears in his eyes, and he looked away; there is no repentance and no forgiveness for these horrific crimes! Including those who stood by and let it happen.

Welcoming the Sabbath in Warsaw's Only Synagogue

The clock shows 6:30 p.m., 15 minutes until the *Shabbes* (Sabbath) candles must be lit, according to Warsaw time. I am rushing to reach the only remaining synagogue in Warsaw before Shabbat arrives. It is located at 6 Twarda Street, and no one knows or can explain what caused the Germans to leave this synagogue untouched after they had completely demolished and left no remnant of any other synagogue in Warsaw, or in Poland for that matter. I travel in the Ambassador's car, which brings me to my destination: the route from Zamenhof to Twarda Street, now named Craiova Army Street. It is destroyed and deserted, except for the square that used to be named Dzerzhinsky Platz. A statue of Dzerzhinsky stood in the middle; he was ethnic Polish, one of the founders of the October Revolution.

A Polish general, disabled veteran from the war against the Nazis, next to the memorial during the Kaddish prayer

[Page 189]

Up ahead are the former offices of the Finance Ministry, which currently houses the Warsaw Municipality. The previous municipality building on Tatralani Platz was completely destroyed; the entire area around the Tatralani Platz and Bielańska Street was turned into a barren desert.

We pass Dzerzhinsky's square towards Twarda Street; along the way, everything is abandoned, scorched earth. The façade of building number 6 no longer exists, and only the Nożyk Synagogue, located in the yard, remains completely untouched. I enter the synagogue, everything is exactly as it was back then, except for the minimal lighting and emptiness projecting a mood of depression and heartbreak.

It is getting late by the time a minyan (prayer quorum) gathered. The minyan was composed of officials from the Warsaw community, whose job it was to oversee the kosher kitchen next to the synagogue, and to guard the synagogue and the cemetery on Ganesha Street. After the prayers, we went up to the kitchen and recited blessings with wine from Israel and celebrated the Jewish commandments.

Standing Proud Through the City's Streets

I decided that on Saturday morning I would approach the Jewish delegation and anyone else who, in the name of Israel, would be willing to march with us, together, to the synagogue through the streets of Warsaw, completely outdoors and under the sun. This way all the gentiles will know that "Joseph still lives" and that the Jews are marching proud and erect through Warsaw's streets! Everyone who heard my offer willingly and enthusiastically accepted: the Israeli delegation, and those from

England, France, the USA, Mexico and more, including those from neighboring countries: Czechoslovakia, Hungary, and East Germany. The Israeli ambassador decided, together with his employees, to join us as well. It is interesting that Dr. Darin, a *Mapam* (left wing political party) member, and Ruzka Korczak, a former partisan and currently a kibbutz member, were the first to warmly accept my offer.

At 10 a.m., under the bright sun, we walked down Jerozolimskie (Jerusalem) Avenue and Marszałkowska Street; more than 100 Jews from all over the world, among them, Mr. Banet Janner, a British Member of Parliament, Mr. Harry Lundy, Rabbi Heschel, Rebbe Amos from England, a French admiral and officials of the Joint (the Joint Distribution Committee) in Europe. Elderly Polish men and women watched the rare event, and many even crossed themselves; they thought that these were the Jews who had been sent to Auschwitz and who have now been resurrected.

Dancing Among the Ruins

The Sabbath welcomed the Hebrew month of Iyar, and as it was my mother's yahrzeit (anniversary of death), I led the morning prayers. I asked Rabbi Katz from Bratislava to say a few words to those present. Even though he initially declined, he later accepted my request and rose speak, and these were his short words: "This week, in the *Shmini* Torah portion, we read, 'And Moses spoke harshly unto Aaron, and unto Eleazar and unto Ithamar, his sons that were left'. Dear brothers, we are the sons that are left. And we ask that you not be angry at us if your eyes see things that are unthinkable or if you are unable to understand our words. We ask God for better days." Immediately after him, the writer of these lines [Ed. Note: e.g., Rabbi Frankel] returned to the pulpit and began, "In the *Shmini* Torah portion it says, 'And let the whole house of Israel bewail the burning

[Page 190]

which God hath kindled.' This is why we came here, to bewail the burning which God hath kindled." After me, Dr. H. Shashkas, from the USA, gave an emotional speech. People held hands and flags flew, and then they spontaneously began singing the song: *And We Were Dispersed Among the Gentiles.*

Hand-in-hand and shoulder-to-shoulder, we lift our feet, and we cry our tears, and again and again we sing, "And we were dispersed among the Gentiles", Jews from the East and West, from one side to another. And we were dispersed among the Gentiles… This dance became a release from all the emotional tension, a sort of purification and elevation. It echoed in our ears for hours to come.

With G-d's help,

I have hereby written my notes on [illegible] and I hereby authorize you to print them, and to print the picture.

By the way, I have left out the two rabbis: Rabbi Goldberg from [illegible] and **Rabbi Zemelman**, may God revenge their souls, [illegible] - **Przedecz was so very fortunate to have such an esteemed and respected rabbi.** [Bold type added by Editor.]

Respectfully yours, [illegible]

[Page 191]

Testimony of the Writer Hillel Seidman[a]

Translated by Jerrold Landau

On page 153 of his book "Warsaw Ghetto Diary,", the accomplished writer Hillel Seidman portrays Rabbi Zemelman's reputation and role in the Warsaw Ghetto uprising.

"Rabbi Zemelman Calls for Revolt and Revenge."

"Among the refugees of the town who have now come to Warsaw, there is also Rabbi Zemelman, the rabbi of Przedecz. He also tells about the annihilation of the Jewish communities, small and large, in the outlying cities. That rabbi, Aguda activist, and great scholar attempted to forge connections with the left-leaning Polish partisans. He snuck over to the Aryan side, stayed there like a pure Aryan, and brought guns and arms to the ghetto. With great enthusiasm, he called for resistance.

Today, I heard Rabbi Zemelman speaking in a clandestine meeting in the bunker. He spoke with great talent. With the full fire of his soul, he described the scenes of atrocities of the annihilation of Jewish communities, and he called for revenge. "Great is revenge, for it is found between two letters." [he said], basing it on the Talmudic explanation of "A L-rd of revenge is G-d". [Psalms 94:1].

He also proposed a detailed plan for an uprising. He took it upon himself to provide arms and weapons (which had already happened, incidentally even then, on a large scale). Not only did he speak finely, but he also acted finely. For example, today, he gave over 12 guns and several crates of bullets to the committee. He visited all the rabbis and *Admorim* [Khassidic Rebbes] and demanded that they also call for revolt. I am told that he visited a group of pioneers [*chalutzim*] who formed the central kernel of the resistance and enthused the very young pioneers. Last week, sharp words were exchanged between him and the Bund forces, who had said that they must wait for a sign from London, and their comrades the Socialists from the Aryan side. He proved that all these excuses – are for naught…"

The last time we heard from Rabbi Zemelman of blessed memory was mentioned on page 257 of the aforementioned book.
"From the burning house on 17 Mila Street, a group of armed Yeshiva students emerged with hand grenades and Molotov cocktails. Rabbi Zemelman and Rabbi Reuven Horowic joined them, as they ran in the direction of Zamenhhof and Kopieca streets. Along the way, they saw S.S. groups and excavators who were going from house to house and setting them on fire. The lads (most from the minyan of Gerrer Hassidim on Nolawki 19) immediately entered the gate of the house at 44 Zamenhof, from where they threw hand grenades and Molotov cocktails at the Germans, and the Germans threw hand grenades back at them. The person who told this story does not know what happened after that because it had become too dangerous to see what was happening.

[Page 192]

This is the last we hear of Rabbi Zemelman, Rabbi Reuven Horowic, and the groups of Yeshiva students. Several other people who were saved from the ghetto (Berish Erlich, Rabbi Meir Zemba, and others) who are currently in Landsberg near Munich served as eyewitnesses to the aforementioned facts."

We further bring a few more citations from that same book "Warsaw Ghetto Diary," from pages 241, 248, 251, and 256, where the name of the hero Rabbi Yosef Aleksander Zemelman, may the memory of the holy be blessed, is mentioned.

Page 241: "The Rabbis – to whom many asked for their advice about whether to remain in the ghetto or to volunteer to travel to Poniatów and Trawniki near Lublin to work in the German enterprises under good conditions – commanded them to remain in the place and not to go voluntarily, for it was the ruse of the Nazis to bring the Jews out willingly and transport them to the gas chambers of Treblinka. Among the rabbis who entered the Yeshiva on Kopieca Street, where Rabbi Menachem Ziemba lived in the dwelling of his nephew Yitzchak Ziemba, there was rabbi Goldszland of Sierpc (who was once the rabbi in the city of Przedecz before the arrival of Rabbi Zemelman), Rabbi Ber of Zduńska Wola, Rabbi Treistman of Łódź, Rabbi Zemelman of Przedecz;" and several other rabbis mentioned in this book.

Page 248: "On 21 Zamenhof Street across from Kopieca Street at the central command of the party, a Passover Seder was conducted. Present were Rabbi Reuven Horowic (an activist of Mizrachi, the rabbi of Olek), Rabbi Zemelman of Przedecz (from the Agudas Yisroel youth), the Rodal brothers, Aniliewicz, "Tusia", Yosef Kenigsberg, his son-in-law Simcha, and others. The Rabbis did not preach, but rather uttered slogans calling for persistence and battle."

Rabbi Goldszlag describes the Passover Seder at the home of Rabbi Menachem Ziemba on 7 Kopieca.

Page 251: "The Jewish fighters remain on guard in a state of readiness. A reinforcement arrived from Muranowska, where the "Northern" sector command was located, and from Świętokrzyska, where the "Southern" sector command was located. Rabbi Reuven Horowic, Rabbi Zemelman of Przedecz, Ajchenbaum (a Revisionist who escaped from Majdanek to Warsaw), and a group of *chalutzim*, including Meir Tajlblum and Yitzchak Szcrabti, and others stood at the head."

Page 256: "The head command of the "brigade" worked on Mila 21, where Mendel Kirszenbaum, his daughter and son-in-law Birenbaum, Aleksander Landau and his daughter (who fell when she tossed a bomb at a German captain on the sixth day of the revolt), Rabbi Zemelman of Przedecz, Rabbi Horowic, Nachum Rembo and his wife, Anielewicz, Tyusia, Kaminer, the son-in-law and daughter of Dr. Sziper, and others were found. They directed the battle in the Zamenhof-Muranowskia-Kopieca sector. In the meantime, the sounds of explosions and flames approached, and the smoke could already be felt. The situation became unbearable. What to do? To move to another place? To where?"

And thus, we come to the end of the sad ghetto tragedy, when we brought Rabbi Zemelman out of the battle from the house at Mila 17 which was burning. A group of S.S. men were going along, and the threw grenades and Molotov cocktails. After the battle, we heard no more news of Rabbi Zemelman. He certainly fell there as

[Page 193]

a fighter among the thousands of other fighters in the Warsaw Ghetto, and one of the great leaders of the Warsaw Ghetto uprising against the German Nazi murderers who killed and annihilated 6,000,000 Jews, the best and finest of European Jewry. Above all, he smuggled weapons into the ghetto at the risk of his life. May his great and holy memory be etched in all the survivors of Przedecz and spread through the entire world forever. May his holy member be blessed, and his bravery and holiness never depart from our midst."

Now we bring a personal letter of appreciation from that same writer, Hillel Seidman, who lives in America. He, who personally knew Rabbi Yosef Aleksander Zemelman of blessed memory and his great traits, writes about him and his great personality and activity, especially for the Yizkor Book:

"Rabbi Zemelman was a young man, a great scholar, full of energy and enthusiasm – a holy flame burned within him, for all the martyrs of Israel as well as for the Land of Israel. He was among the leaders of the Agudas Yisrael youth, for which he worked with enthusiasm and dedication. In the conventions of the movement, he appeared as an orator forged of flames of fire. He did not relate to the troubles and aspirations of the nation with indifference – rather, he was completely consumed with the love of Jews. We knew the man and his manner of speaking, and we learned to appreciate and love him. He was always involved with activities and ideas. He made demands upon others, but he served as an exemplary model. He was always the Nachshon [1], ready to jump into any sea.

Indeed, the vast majority of Agudas Yisroel youth gathered around the Land of Israel. That means that their desire was for *aliya* and the upbuilding of the Land, and they also wanted to join *hachsharah* [organizations for *aliya* preparation] and to obtain certificates for *aliya*. Indeed, Rabbi Zemelman of blessed memory was among those who expressed these aspirations without reservation or hesitation, without circumlocution. The atmosphere immediately warmed when he rose to the podium of the conventions, for they knew that his words would be fiery and lofty.

He still stands before the eyes of my spirit with the full enthusiasm of his fiery soul as he expressed himself with his logical words accompanied by a plethora of honest emotion, for the man was true to himself. He never cowed before anyone, and he was not afraid to express his opinion – against the opinion of the hesitators and hemmers and hawers. He did not give up, especially regarding matters of the Land of Israel.

Along with this, he fought for the independence of Orthodox Jewry against all who plotted to be its representatives unjustly and without any rights – that is, the assimilationists as well as the secular Zionists, who trampled over the heads of the holy nation. This battle especially came to expression at the time of the elections to the communal councils, city councils, Sejm, and senate (Polish parliament). At such times, the battle heated up in its full strength, and Rabbi Zemelman was, as always, one of the chief fighters. Then, at the end of 1942 and the beginning of 1943, after the great killing when only few were left, we found out that Rabbi Zemelman of Przedecz was wandering about the city – in the ghetto and in Aryan neighborhoods – calling for resistance and revolt. Many youths gathered around him, and he stood at the head of a strong, close-knit group that later participated in the uprising. They all fell in battle.

[Page 194]

Other details on his activities in the underground and the uprising are not known to me, since I was already imprisoned by the Germans during the time of the uprising in April 1943, and the information reaching me was perforce choppy. I only remember that Rabbi Yehuda Leib Orlian, who had been the head of the Beis Yaakov seminary in Krakow and was then in Warsaw, told me a great deal about the activities and words of Rabbi Zemelman. He astounded us as a man of the uprising, since not only rabbis, but also the vast majority, was not inclined toward such.

Another surprise for me was the fact that after the Holocaust, the historians of the uprising did not see it fitting to give prominence to the activities of Rabbi Zemelman. It seems that the inclination to forget the role of an Orthodox rabbi in these events was increasing. Even the discoverers of the Hassidic "uprising" that did not take place skipped over this wonderful personality.

I knew him well since we were comrades in outlook, especially with regard to the Land of Israel, and I very much held in esteem his good nature, generous traits, great strength, and willingness to go to battle for the sake of his nation.

May his memory not depart from us."

Hillel Seidman

Such was the man – such was Rabbi Yosef Aleksander Zemelman, the final rabbi of the town of Przedecz (Pshaytsh), and one of the heroes of the Warsaw Ghetto.

May his soul be bound in the bonds of eternal life.

Editor's Note:

 a. The prolific writer Dr. Hillel Seidman died August 28, 1995, in New York. He wrote "Warsaw Ghetto Diary", which was published in Hebrew, Yiddish and later in English.

Translator's Footnote:

 1. According to Jewish tradition, Nachshon the son of Aminadab, leader of the tribe of Judah, was the first to jump into the Red Sea, even before it split.

[Page 195]

On the Grave of My People

Translated by Janie Respitz

This is an excerpt from the book "Ash and Fire" by the poet Yakov Pat. We are bringing you this excerpt from the book about the destruction of the Warsaw ghetto after the uprising by the heroes against the beastly German murderers, the murderers of the Jewish people. Practically with bare hands, these last Jewish fighters in the Warsaw ghetto fought the murderers as they did not want to be led like sheep to the slaughter. One of the heroic ghetto heroes was the rabbi from Przedecz Rabbi Yosef Alexander Zemelman of righteous blessed memory. This great scholar and leader, with his gentleness and kindness illuminated our town. He had a bubbly nature just like Rabbi Akiva of blessed memory, who during the days of Bar Kochba witnessed the destruction of the Holy Land. He called for an uprising against the Romans and did not allow them to submit to slaughter. This is what Rabbi Zemelman did when he called upon ghetto Jews to fight the Nazi animals. He died a hero, fighting, as we will soon describe.

Therefore, we are presenting the above-mentioned excerpt from the book:

On the Grave of My People

Today I was at the grave of my people for the fourth time in the former Warsaw Jewish ghetto.

I went to say goodbye in silence, perhaps for the last time, to my former Jewish Warsaw. Four times I climbed through the massive ruins of our people. The first time, I was very nervous to go deep into the destruction. When I returned the second time, I crawled and ran up and down the hills, in the depth of this large area where the upheaval of our history had transpired. The third time, I spent hours walking and searching for remnants of my ten years on the streets of Warsaw.

The fourth time, I went to say goodbye, in order to take the largest grave of the Jewish people into my eyes and heart, to be able to always see and feel it.

And now, at night, a few hours before I leave Warsaw, I write these lines and would like to recite psalms just as our fathers and grandfathers did, with a candle at the head of a corpse. Where will my help come from?

Until today, the world has not seen such a powerful, cruel, miserable, and dark scene. It is a sea of destruction. Dead waves are thickened over the sea. All the streets of Warsaw have become one immense, gigantic memorial of generations past. These streets no longer exist: Nalevky, Muranov, Dzhike, Pavyie, Smotche, Gensha, Francisca, Shvientoyorske, Navalipiye, Mila, Karmelitzka. Nothing has remained, just emptiness. Mounds of destruction jut out, iron rods, stones piled higher and higher, and lower down are shallow ditches, crazy peaks, and wild fantastic figures of demons. I stand in a deserted field that once was Krashinsky Place.

My companion, the captain of the ghetto fighters and the great grandchild of the Vilna Gaon Mark Edelman, tells me: "this is where the ghetto battle began", and points to another field of destruction. "This is where we placed the mines when the Germans were approaching".

I stood on a mound of ruins. When the Ghetto was burned and destroyed, the Nazis built a concentration camp on the ruins for Jews from Greece who they brought there. These Greek Jews were slaves, tortured skeletons

[Page 196]

who died here, one after the other. The dead lay on these hills of extermination for days and weeks, while under the hills lay thousands of Polish Jews who still lie there until today. We are at the gate of the former brush shop in the German slave factory about which more will be written. One of the world's most dramatic stories. This is where the decisive ghetto battle took place. This is where young Jewish heroes killed 300 Germans; this is where Jewish youth threw their lives up to heaven. Like angels - the mother recounted, throwing stars from the sky into the night. I walk and walk. I climb up and down the hills, stand for a while with my head bent. Until today, lying under these huge ruins is the fighter and martyr Mikhl Klepfish, one of the heroes of the ghetto, who already weaves through Jewish legend, whose grandmother took slippers and Shabbes candles with her to Treblinka. There are no greater or holier words that can and must be whispered: "Magnified and sanctified be G-d's great name"! (From the mourner's prayer, Kaddish).

And this is how the poet describes the great destruction of Warsaw Jewry, the great heroism Jewish youth displayed fighting against the Nazis as they fought until their last breath and fell between the burning and falling buildings. Although it appeared that the end of the great destruction was nearing, the Jewish heroes of the ghetto did not allow themselves to be led as sheep to the alter. The Nazis paid a price for their victory in the Warsaw ghetto. Thousands of Germans were killed by the Jewish heroes.

And we, the survivors and refugees from Pshaytsh (Przedecz), must remember that one of the heroes in the Warsaw ghetto who excelled in bravery and fought, encouraged, and called others to battle against the Nazi beasts was our unforgettable rabbi from Pshaytsh (Przedecz), Rabbi Yosef Alexander Zemelman, of blessed and righteous memory. He is mentioned in many periodicals which have been published over the past years, especially underlined in the diary of the writer Hillel Zaydman "Diary in the Warsaw Ghetto". Behind the large mound of ruins of the Warsaw ghetto, among the thousands of Jewish heroic fighters, lies the holy body of the great hero, the rabbi from Pshaytsh (Przedecz), Rabbi Yosef Alexander Zemelman, of blessed and righteous memory. We, the survivors from Pshaytsh (Przedecz), whisper the words:

"Magnified and sanctified be G-d's great name!"

[Page 197]

The sole large tree that remains in the cemetery as a silent monument. Photographed by the family of Dr. Prof. Brand in 1966.

Our comrade Simcha Neumark and his wife Hela standing in the area of the cemetery in 1965.

[Page 198]

Tushya Yakhimovitch Calls for Revenge

by Y.L.L Shlomi

Translated from Yiddish by Roberta Paula Books

I've been thinking for a while about answering your letter, dear Nishra. I could not bring myself to write because until now I was not able to answer your question as to whether I have adjusted. There are various explanations. For people who have not experienced anything in their lives, we can call it getting used to a new place, a job, an apartment, society and so forth. For me there is a second meaning. I understand that you want to know if I have forgotten what I endured, meaning the camps, the camps, the camps.

No, and once again no!

I have been living in the richest, luckiest country in the world these past ten years, and I have not forgotten. I am sure that everyone who went through this swamp

A monument at Birkenau – Auschwitz in memory of the Jews murdered there
Photographed by Dr. Brand 1965

[Page 199]

of vile murderous hatred will never forget. There are some people who want to rid themselves of horrible thoughts by living a happy life, but this does not mean they have forgotten. There are those that mull over everything. Every day, they go step by step through their terrible experiences and wonder how it all happened and how they managed to survive. For each of us who went through this, something has remained that does not want to go away. Sometimes it hurts more and sometimes less, but it never goes away. There is always something from that time spent in hell.

I received your letter on the anniversary of my last conversation with Tashya, the beginning of the second half, on December 1944. You, Nishra, did not know her, but it seems to me that I knew her. Up until 1941, we lived in a small town where everyone knew each other. I was twenty-five years old, and she was a few years older than me. During this entire period of shame on the world, we were together, and I did not realize that such an extraordinary, pure person existed.

Our last chapter, as you know was "Auschwitz". It was near the end. The insurrection was dying, the Red Army was already at the Vistula. Bits and pieces of news were reaching us, but we were still generally isolated. Understandably, we were Jews, dirty thieves, and add to that, killers of God. This came to us through the burning ovens and furnaces, through hundreds of transports of Hungarian Jews, through daily shootings of captured soldiers, through the uncovering old mass graves and the burning of half rotted bodies, in order to erase their sins, to cover up their tracks, through the stinking smoke and thick flames.

The last days, we were in the same barrack. The last nights, we slept on the same bunk. Lying next to me, she said: you know, tomorrow I am going to the "sick house", which meant to die. I shouted with anguish, look at what is going on around us, it won't last much longer. Don't be a child, she replied, and don't try to console me. This is not the place for that.

It was a strain for her to speak. She was very weak. Her feet were swollen.

[Page 200]

It took great effort for her to move from place to place. In the opposite corner of the barrack, there was a separate, small room for a Christian or someone pretending to be a Christian. That evening, she took in two to three women, and they quietly sang Christmas Carols. The melodies were not foreign to us. We could even recognize the words through the slats. It was not our religion, but it reminded us of the past.

I haven't eaten for a week, said Tashya, I just drink and drink. My insides are burning. I know I will not be fooled when I die in the gas. I want to die conscious. I want to look, for the last time, at the face of he who wears death's head on his hat (Totenkopf, skull and bones), he who is called doctor.

The singing brought us back. It reminded us of times past that will never return. No one was left in our town Pshaytsh (Przedecz). We believed our lives would be normal. That sons would stand at their parents' graves and recite the mourner's prayer, and that their daughters would sit Shiva and cry together. Now we don't even know the dates of death for our loved ones or whether anyone still exists in this world. With great effort, she spoke these words. It was difficult for her to breathe. She continued to speak slowly. She was afraid she would not be able say all she wanted. Every one of her words felt like a stone on my heart and remained forever.

As soon as they entered our town, all the non–Jews avoided us. For every small thing, a piece of bread or another life necessity, we had to pay dearly. Not with money but with gold and other goods. They often robbed us of all we had or blackmailed us.

There could not be any talk about resistance. They laughed in our faces, and from the start we were sentenced to annihilation. In the early days, the pharmacist Grushtzinska came to me and asked me to sew dresses for her daughters. I believed I would receive some products from her for my work, a bit of medicine, a piece of soap, but no.

[Page 201]

She gave me some pieces of paper with which I could not buy anything.

Our life wasn't yet miserable. We earned every piece of bread honestly. We made an effort to keep the cultural activities in town going. We really lived decently. They put an end to everything. Do you remember, little girl, our evenings at the needle society and how we taught older people to read and write. How much light there was then, in our work and in our dreams, and now there is nothing. But you can't kill decency. They will kill thousands more, but they too will be killed.

Then humanity will blossom again, and you my child …

Don't forget little girl, that when all of this will end – you will not build anything on this ground.

This is our cemetery. Run away, and wherever you will be ….

Do you hear me -- you should tell all and delete nothing! Do not be ashamed, they should be ashamed. They wanted to lead the world to a sort of wildness and in large measure they succeeded, but they remained the wild ones. Perhaps things would have been different had people united against the beasts. But everyone thought he would live through it and feared taking the risk. This is what the murderers enjoyed. Killing individuals and the masses.

I am not talking now about us Jews.

Yes, little girl, under the mattress are three pieces of bread. I gave two to the commander so that she would free me tomorrow.

A few words from the Christmas Carols continue to ring out. You hear the camp asleep. However, in addition to the two of us, there was the noise of the flames from the chimneys, but the there was also smoke from the bodies of the Musselmen (a slang term used amongst Jewish concentration camp prisoners to refer to those suffering from a combination of starvation and exhaustion, as well as those who were resigned to their impending death), from the heat bursting the skin, hands and feet moving, ash, ash. And pieces of bones.

Do you hear, they are already sounding the roll call. You stay alive to tell the story. This is how the night passes.

From that day on, when I put a piece of bread to my mouth, I hear the words from those Christmas Carols, and I remember those three pieces of bread. It could be thanks to those pieces of bread that I survived. And now I tell the story. But the only people who believe it are those who lived through it.

[Page 202]

Memories from the Days of the Holocaust

by Reuven Yemenik

Translated by Sara Mages

When the Holocaust, which destroyed thousands of Jewish communities and most of the Jewish population, descended on the magnificent European Jewry, in that black period I lived in the city of Sompolno near Koło. The Germans entered the city on the morning of Rosh Hashanah 5700. In the early morning hours, we prayed in private homes and guards stood outside during the blowing of the Shofar for fear that the Germans would notice us. All the private prayer houses were filled to capacity. Everyone, men, women, and a lot of youth, felt the fear of judgment of that day and knew what those damn Nazis were capable of doing. Everyone prayed in tears and emotions and felt the meaning of the requests - "*Zochreinu L'chaim*" ["Remember us for Life"], "*Unetaneh tokef*[1] *Mi Yichye*" ["Who shall Live"], etc. On the first day, and also on the second, the prayers were held without interruption because the Germans were still busy with their arrangements and their organization in the city. After the prayer we went home separately so as not to attract the attention of the Germans and the Polish informers. The Jewish stores were open by the order of the temporary German governor.

On the Saturday after Rosh Hashanah the Germans started to catch Jews in the streets and also from their homes for forced labor. They brought them to the courtyard of City Hall and sorted them for various jobs in the city and outside it. It is important to know that then, at the beginning, before the establishment of Jewish committee and a Judenrat, absolute lawlessness prevailed in this area. Those who were captured went to work, and those who managed to hide remained at home until a Jewish Committee was organized under the leadership of Mr. Plotzki the owner of the flour mill. Later he became the head of the Judenrat and the mediator between the Gestapo and the Jews. The organizer of the work was a Jew named Vart. The Jewish Committee, who had a special building for its operation, prepared lists workers. Those, whose names appeared on the list, were notified the day before that they had to report for work in the courtyard of the Jewish Committee building. From there each person was sent to work in the city for the "Volksdeutsche" [ethnic Germans] or outside the city in excavation, cleaning the roads and more, and woe to the man who didn't report on that day. He was brutally beaten by the Gestapo and was forced to work for a long time even if his name wasn't included in the list. Here I have to describe the fifth day, the day before Yom Kippur Eve which, at that time, fell on the Sabbath. On this day, in the afternoon, the Gestapo announced that all the Jewish men must gather in the market square in front of the City Hall and those, who wouldn't appear, will be shot. The fear was great because no one knew what these murderers plotted to do. At the fixed hour, hundreds of men, young and old, gathered in the designated area. No one was missing. The Germans searched all the homes but couldn't find anyone. A high-ranking Gestapo officer stood on the tall steps of the municipality building and next to him stood many "Volksdeutsche" and the new German mayor. Various papers were scattered on the table. The Gestapo officer held a whip in his hand and S.S. men, who held machine guns in their hands, surrounded the Jews. We were sure that that they will be given an order to kill all the Jews, but silence prevailed, and the Gestapo officer started to address the Jews: "Your dignity has ended, from today you will work with shovels and pitchforks,

[Page 203]

those who own a store, or a business must liquidate it within a short period of time, and all of you will work for us the Germans. Damned Jews! Up to now you've cheated us and sucked our blood and bone marrow." Now he poured a heap of scorn, insults and curses on the Jews who stood quietly in their disgrace without uttering a word. A member of his entourage, a "Volksdeutsche," pointed at a Jew by the name of Gershon Czerniak hy"d. He was a highly respected rich Jew who owned an iron shop in the market. The Nazi told the officer that this Jew cursed Hitler's name. The officer consulted with the new mayor and asked for his opinion. The latter replied that he knew Czerniak and that he was a decent and honest man. Then the Gestapo officer said that he respects the mayor's opinion, and if not - he would have ordered to kill the Jew on the spot and ordered the Jews to scatter and run to their homes... The Poles, who stood around the market, laughed about what had happened to the

Jews and accompanied them shouting, swearing, and cursing. The Jews were saved this time. The Germans broke into the homes and with brutal beating looted everything in sight - furniture, household items, blankets, clothes, furs, and everything of value. From the shops they've looted fabrics, shoes, foodstuffs, tobacco, tea, and rice, and left the Jews naked and destitute. They moved the Jews to small, crowded apartments and gave their apartments to the "Volksdeutsche." They also took the business, shops and warehouses from the Jews and gave them to the Germans. The suffering reached its peak, there was nothing to live on and the Jews starved. There were constant searches and Jews were abducted for workday and night. In the winter of 1940, the Jews worked in cleaning the railway near the city of Konin. We worked for two days, day and night, without food or drink. We only ate what we had brought with us. The Jews sold the property that they had managed to hide to their Polish neighbors - jewelry, clothing, or merchandise from the stores that the Germans closed or seized. The Jewish Committee organized small food rations of milk and sugar for the Jewish families. There wasn't a designated ghetto, but the number of apartments was reduced, and the crowding and the density were great. The transports to labor camps in Germany began in the summer of 1941. The first transport of several hundred young and old men to a labor camp in Germany took place in the month of Tamuz 5701- August 1941. Everyone gathered in the courtyard of the Jewish Committee and the Jews, whose names appeared on the list, were sent accompanied by policemen and "Volksdeutsche" to the train station in the city of Sompolno. Women and children stood around the train station's fence and their heart-rending cries accompanied their loved ones who were sent to the labor camp. The transport left for the nearby city of Koło where they slept on the Great Synagogue's floor. From there they we were sent to Posen [Poznań] and to other camps. The second transport, that I was in, left on 9 Av 5701 [22 August 1941] and took the same route as the first. On the next day, at dusk, we arrived to Zbąszyń camp near the old border of Poland and Germany where the German Jews, who were expelled from Germany in 1938, were being held by the Germans. We were there for a day and met part of the first transport from Sompolno. On the next day the Germans carried out a selection - some stayed in Zbąszyń and some were sent to the labor camp in Buchwarder-Forest near Posen. There, we met a large group of Jews who arrived at the beginning of the summer from Łódź. They held the various jobs in the camp like the deputy of the camp's leader,

[Page 204]

the heads of the barracks, the kitchen managers and the cooks, the leaders of the work outside the camp, the distributers of the work in the camp, clinic, in the barrack of those who peeled potato and more.

The Jews, who arrived from Sompoln, also received a number of jobs because the camp's population has grown, and the number of meals increased. The situation of the veteran Jews, who came from Łódź, had improved because the newcomers from Sompolno and other cities in the Koło district like: Kłodawa, Dambia [Dąbie] received food parcels from home. The Jews from Łódź didn't receive food parcels because of the great famine in the ghetto. Most of the time we didn't eat the food from the camp's kitchen, and the Jews from Łódź received more food from the kitchen and also a portion from our food parcels. Most of the work was done outside the camp in the construction of the Reichsautobahn [the German motorway] which was called R.A.B. in short. The Germans wanted to build a fast road, a wide road with a boulevard in the middle, from the city of Danzig [Gdańsk] through Posen [Poznań] to Berlin. The Jews leveled the ground which passed through forests, fields, lakes, rivers, villages, and cities. We worked from dawn to dusk with wheelbarrows and wagons. We uprooted trees and rocks, worked in the sand and in the earth, in the swamps and in the water. It was a hard work under the supervision of the evil German foremen, under blows, insults, curses, and shouts. The Jews returned to the camp in the evening tired and exhausted and received a meager food ration of thin soup of potatoes and carrots, and a piece of bread with or without margarine. They got up at four in the morning for black coffee and a little bread and left for work at five under the supervision of the foremen. It was a labor camp without the S.S. only elderly Germans maintained the order at work and in the camp, but the camp was surrounded by barbed wire. The commander of the camp was a German named Stupengel who wasn't mean or cruel. Unlike in other camps, he didn't beat or cursed and was better than the others, but there were two cruel German foremen there. The first was Resel who was cruel and sadistic. Almost every day a Jew, who was beaten and tortured by him during the hard work, was brought back to the camp. The second was Novek. He didn't hit but he forced the Jews to work fast and didn't let them rest for even one minute. Working for him was like the hard work in Egypt. The Jews worked without rest and ran with wheelbarrows full of dirt, sand, and stones. On the first day I worked for the cruel Nazi Resel, but when I saw the brutal blows that he had inflicted on the Jews I moved to work for Novek without anyone noticing it. Before sunrise, when it was still dark outside, I joined those who worked for Novek and was saved from his cruel blows. A few weeks later I became ill at work, and under the recommendation of the camp's doctor I moved to the potato peelers barrack where I worked under the supervision of a Jew named Kroshinsky from Sompolno. On Chanukah of the same year, 5702 -1942, the Germans brought two Jews from a nearby camp - an adult named Yakov Friedman from Zychlin and a teenager named Neta Piaskowsky from the city of Bełchatów. The Germans accused them that they walked out of the camp to ask for food and hung them in front all the people in the camp.

In 5702, before the holiday of Passover, they transferred us to Küstrin camp about sixty kilometers from Berlin. There, we worked in a factory that manufactured cardboard, paper, oils, and turpentine. The first shift worked from six in the morning to six in the evening, and the second shift from six in the evening to six in the morning. Relatively, it was an easier work than the work in the previous camp. On Passover, of that year I received a package and a letter from

[Page 205]

my parents. It was the last letter because on 7 Iyar 5702-24 April 1942, they were taken by the Germans to the Christian Church and from there to Chełmno extermination camp. Then, the Germans liquidated the remaining Jews in the city of Przedecz. May the Lord avenge their blood. On 16 Shevat 5702, I received the last letter from Sompolno. They wrote me that everyone was taken to the big movie theatre near the train station, and from there they were sent for extermination in Chełmno. From Küstrin-Neustadt we were transferred to Fosstenbürg near the Oder River where we worked outside the camp until August 1943.

On Passover 5703-1943, after the Warsaw Ghetto uprising, the Germans decided to liquidate all the open camps and transfer the Jews to camps that were surrounded by an electric fence and were under the strict observation of the S.S. We were transferred from Fursstenberg camp through the Liibbenau camp to Auschwitz where everyone received a tattooed number on his arm. I received the number 142047 with the Jewish mark, which was half a Star of David, below the number. In Auschwitz I was in the Krentin Block from August to the end of September 1942. I was transferred to Birkenau where the crematoriums and the gas chambers were located. From Birkenau I was transferred back to Auschwitz and from there I was sent to Jaworzno camp (here, I have written a lot about my life in these camps, but this isn't the place for it). In Jaworznom most of the prisoners worked in the coal mine. The rest, about six thousand Jewish, Russian, and Polish prisoners worked in the construction of a huge power plant which was supposed to serve the entire district of Silesia, but the Germans didn't finish the construction of this plant. On 15 January 1945, when the Russians got closer the city of Krakow and to Auschwitz, and Auschwitz was also bombed, the Germans liquidated the camp, took most of the prisoners with them and retreated to Germany. Only those who managed to hide, and the sick remained. After a long walk, through impassable roads, forests, and fields we arrived at the city of Beuthen and from there to Blechhammer. We stayed there for three days and then we were sent to Gross-Rosen - a terrible camp with all the cruelty of the Nazis. We walked under the strict observance of the S.S. who shot those who lagged a little, and the entire road was littered with the bodies of Jewish prisoners. In March 1945, we were transferred from Gross-Rosen to Buchenwald concentration camp. From there I was sent to Berga an der Elster labor camp to work in the quarry. I was there for about two weeks. After I became seriously ill, I was sent back to Buchenwald together with other patients. On Wednesday, 28 Nisan 5705, 11 April 1945, American soldiers captured the camp, and I was liberated on that day. After the liberation we were transferred to the city of Landsberg. A year later I moved, together with several hundred Jews to Italy, and from there I sailed on the illegal immigrant ship *"Kaf Gimel Yordei Ha'Sira"*[2] to Eretz Yisrael. The British caught us in the middle of the sea and transferred us to a detention camp in Cyprus. After six months in Cyprus, I was transferred to the detention camp in Atlit and later to Kiryat Shmuel near Haifa. After I was released from there I built, with G-d's help, a new home and a new life in Israel.

Translator's footnotes:

1.   The *piyyut*, or sacred poem, "*Unetaneh tokef kedushas hayom*" ("Let us proclaim the sacred power of this day"), is recited on Rosh Hashanah and on Yom Kippur.
2.   "*Kaf Gimel Yordei Ha'Sira*" - the "23 Who Went Down at Sea." The ship was named in honor of the 23 members of the "*Haganah*" whose launch disappeared at sea during a mission to Tripoli, Lebanon, in the service of the British Army against the Vichy French Forces.

[Page 206]

Shabbes in Town

by Moshe Bilevski

Translated by Sara Mages

Dedicated to the memory of
My father Mendel Wolf Bilevski z"l
My mother Chane Sara z"l
My sister Breina z"l
My sister Balzia z"l
My brother Leibel z"l
Who perished in the Holocaust, hy"d

In general, it's possible to say that Przedecz was a city of workers and small trades who worked hard all week for their livelihood.

When Friday afternoon arrived, it was possible to feel the change in the atmosphere. The Sabbath Queen is approaching!

Each family prepared its own challah and baked it in the bakery. Families, their income being limited, ate what they ate during the week and tried, for the honor of the Sabbath, to prepare food that would bring a spiritual atmosphere to their home. Obviously, there were families who lived comfortably and were able to afford large, expensive fish, and there were families who could barely afford sardines at a cheap price, but still, they ate fish for the Sabbath.

It's Friday afternoon, the housewife, with the help of her older daughters, is still busy with the last preparations. The men go to immerse in the *mikveh*.

The last hour before the beginning of the Sabbath is approaching, and the cholent is taken from most of the Jewish homes to the bakery. And here is Itche Kowalski, the town's *Shammes* [beadle], and with a wooden hammer in his hand he knocks on the doorposts of the houses to speed up those who are late with their final preparations for the Sabbath.

A tremble passes through those who haven't yet finished, fast, or G-d forbid, I will desecrate the Sabbath.

And now the *Shammes* is calling - "Light the candles!" He stands on his tiptoes at every crossroad so it would also be possible to see and hear in the high heaven how a Jewish community is welcoming the Sabbath, and it's also a sign that all the preparations have reached their end.

The appearance of the town has changed, and peace and moderation reigned all over.

The housewife is wearing her Sabbath dress, and her head is covered with a scarf. She lights the Sabbath candles and blesses them with great deliberation. Now, the men and the boys are leaving the house dressed in their Sabbath clothes, some in the direction of the synagogue, some to Beis HaMidrash and some to "*Hevrat Tehillim*" [Psalms society], for the *Kabbalas Shabbes* [welcoming the Shabbes] prayer. The streets come to new life, to life of serenity and gentleness. With darkness the Sabbath candles shine through the windows. Oh! These Sabbath candles, how much magic

[Page 207]

and how much soul were in them. A sea of tears was shed by our mothers of blessed memory when they lit the candles. They prayed for the welfare of the home, for livelihood with dignity and the health of all the family members.

It happened, that during the *Kabbalas Shabbes* prayer in Beis HaMidrash one of the latecomers whispered to someone that the light was still on at the barbershop. Immediately, a number of worshipers rushed to the barbershop to punish the desecrators of the Sabbath, but by the time they arrived it was already dark in the shop and the worshipers returned to Beis HaMidrash.

The prayer ended. At times, Reb Itche the *Shammes* appeared and with a hand clap on the *bimah* announced that the *eruv*[1] is faulty and it's forbidden to take an object from place to place, or, that there are guests in town and it's necessary to invite them for a meal. When the *eruv* was faulty, the children had to bring the *Tallis* or the *Siddur* to the synagogue, and also bring the cholent from the bakery. In addition, not a single guest was left without a Sabbath meal. The worshipers returned home. After the blessing of *"Gut Shabbes"* [good Shabbes] they start with the prayer - *"Shalom aleichem malachi ha-shalom"* [peace upon you the angels of peace], the same angels who accompany every Jew on his way from the synagogue. At the end, the Sabbath prayer, which praised, the housewife, wasn't forgotten - "A woman of valor, who can find? Far beyond pearls is her value."

The additional soul, which entered to dwell in every Jewish home on the Sabbath, is noticeable. The table is covered with a white tablecloth and on it are the candlesticks with the flickering Sabbath candles, the two challahs are covered with a special napkin, a wine bottle and the Kiddush Cup which was inherited from a father or a grandfather. All these factors created a festive atmosphere at the house. After the Kiddush, the family atmosphere was also felt at the table and during the meal, because for a large part of the townspeople it was the first meal during the week that the whole family sat together and savored the meal with Sabbath songs.

At the end of the meal, and after *Birkas Hamazon,* the youth finds himself in meetings of the various associations. Some in *"Tzeirei Zion"* which conducted an extensive activity among the youth, some in *"Betar"* or in the Jewish library, and some walk together around the town.

They get up on Sabbath morning and the father reads *Shnayim mikra ve-echad targum*[2], and revives his heart with a cup of hot tea. And now they hear the voice of the *Shammes* calling - Enter the Synagogue! The little children want to sleep a little longer, but the *eruv* is faulty, and they have to bring the Tallis to the synagogue. There were also a number of early risers who came early to the Beis HaMidrash. Some study a chapter from the Talmud and some read a chapter from *Ein Yaakov*[3]. At any rate, the voice of the Torah is sounded most of the hours of the day.

Until 1925, there was still a place of prayer for the Ger Hassidim in a rented apartment in the yard of Reb Yeshayahu Zelinski's house, but for financial reasons they were forced to close it. There was no shortage of problems in the *Parshas* [Torah passages] " *Bechukotai*" ["By my decrees"] and "*Ki* Thavo" ["When you enter"], and during the reading of the *Tochacha* [verses of rebuke] they honored one of the wandering poor who agreed to be called to the Torah for a financial compensation. But, if he didn't agree, the *Ba'al Koreh*[4] blessed the *Parshas* and read it to himself quietly. In 1928 the *Ba'al Koreh* was Reb Chezkel (Yechezkel) Mordchai Lenchitzki. The worshipers gathered in Beis HaMidrash for a prayer, but he was missing. They started with the *Shacharis* [morning] prayer, maybe he was late and will arrive by the time of the Torah reading, but the boy was missing. Someone whispered that one of his sons locked him

[Page 208]

in his home to prevent him from reading the *Tochacha*, and to avoid all kinds of misfortunes which were caused by it. After the delay in the reading of the Torah, they found someone who was willing to be called to the Torah for a fair monetary compensation. In addition, he was also given a cart of firewood which was promised to him by my father, Reb Mendel Wolf Bilevski, who was the *Gabbai* of Beis HaMidrash, and Reb Itche Weiden, z"l. Since then, Reb Aharon David Yechimovitz was honored with the reading of the Torah.

Occasionally, the rabbi delayed the reading of the Torah. As we know, the delay of the reading on the Sabbath was a very important way to solve unique and important community issues. When the rabbi, who usually prayed in the synagogue, appeared in Beis HaMidrash for the Sabbath prayer, we knew that something important was at stake. And indeed, after the *Shacharis* [morning] prayer the rabbi climbed on the *bimah* and informed the worshipers that he was forced to delay the reading of the Torah because there was a deficit in the education budget, or another important matter such as *Hachnosos Kallah* [helping a poor bride] and demanded the participation of the worshipers to cover these expenses. Reb Neta Weszrzog stood up , as was his custom in such cases, and promised to cover the deficit. The entire congregation joined him and promised to help to the best of their ability. Then, it was allowed to continue with the reading of the Torah and the prayer service.

In the winter, Orbienski, the blind cemetery keeper and the town's "*Shabbes Goy*" [Sabbath Gentile] passed from house to house on the Sabbath and turned on the heaters that warmed the houses on the Sabbath. On his back he carried a sack and in it he kept the slices of challah that he received from the Jews for his trouble. On the next day he received his payment in cash.

In the afternoon the youth gathered again for activities in the various Zionists organizations. The adults used the time for a short nap because - "It is a joy to rest on a Sabbath."

A large crowd came to Beis HaMidrash for the *Minkha* [afternoon] prayer.

In "*Hevras Tehillim,*" where most of the craftsmen prayed, chapters of *Tehillim* were read before the *Minkha* prayer. The cantor, who passed before the Holly Ark, was Mr. Michael Hersh Neumark who had a unique tune for the *Minkha* prayer.

All the town's scholars came to the traditional third meal at the rabbi's house. The rabbi uttered the words of the Torah and the ritual slaughterers, R' Shmuel Yamnik and R' Eliyahu Walter z"l, conducted the singing during the meal. The Sabbath ended with the *Ma'ariv* [evening] prayer, the lighting of the *Havdalah* candle and the blessing of "*A Gut Voch*!" [a good week], and life began to ferment again for a week of new worries.

When we came home from the Beis HaMidrash after the *Ma'ariv* prayer, we found our mother z"l on the doorstep whispering the prayer - the plea that is recited at the conclusion of the Sabbath and before the *Havdalah* blessing.

"God of Abraham, and of Isaac, and of Jacob, protect your beloved people Israel from all hurt, in your love. As the beloved holy Sabbath goes away, that the week, and the month, and the year, should come to us with perfect faith, with faith in the sages, with love and attachment to good friends, to attachment to the blessed Creator, with belief in your thirteen principles of faith, and in the ultimate redemption, may it be soon, and the Resurrection of the dead, and in the prophecy of Moses, our teacher, may he rest in peace." Amen!

Translator's footnotes:

1. *Eruv* - a perimeter usually strung on the utility poles (often rope) that combines separate pieces of property into one large parcel. It enables the Jews to observe the traditional Shabbes rules and allowing them to carry children and belongings anywhere inside the perimeter.
2. *Shnayim mikra ve-echad targum* - "*Twice the Torah and once translation*" is the Jewish practice of reading the weekly Torah portion in a prescribed manner. In addition to hearing the Torah portion read in the synagogue, a person should read it himself twice during that week together with the translation.
3. *Ein Ya'akov* - a compilation of all the Aggadic (lore) material in the Talmud together with the commentaries.
4. *Ba'al Koreh* - master of the reading - is the person who reads the Torah from the scroll in the synagogue.

[Page 209]

The Trial on Synagogue Street

by Yitzkhak Ben Shalom

Translated from Yiddish by Roberta Paula Books

From time to time, I walk through the town where I was born. I will tell you about one of these walks.

The Trial on Synagogue Street.

This happened a while ago, but it could have been yesterday, I can't say exactly when, I could have happened day in and day out.

It could also have happened only in my imagination. The memories churn in my head, and I can't seem to free myself from them.

A grey darkness fell upon the town, together with a stillness. It was so unusual that it rang in my ears. We heard nothing, not even the quiet conversations of the trees nor the gentle song of the wheat and other plants. The nightingale did not sing even though it was its time. There was no sign of life; however, from time to time a bat's sharp whistle cut through the light air. The town sleeps calmly. The old wooden houses stand quietly. The town sleeps, soon you will

Photo: "Synagogue Street" Simkha Noymark stands on the street corner during his visit to Przedecz in 1965.

[Page 210]

strain your ears and hear the breathing of sleeping Jews after a long day of difficult work. I approach the small houses. I stride through the streets and look inside. The shutters are broken, the windows removed. The doors are gone. Everything inside is either broken or stolen, the floors and ceilings are torn apart. Even the winter oven and the kitchen are destroyed, and feathers from pillows and blankets are strewn all over. Fear peers out of every corner without face or form, just eyes of various colors and various ages, congealed in suffering and dried out, looking at you and shouting without a voice, without words, they speak, they shout, they – they.

Be quiet for a moment. From afar, we can hear footsteps, a sort of song. A man strides in the middle of the street in worn out shoes and is saying something; no, he is singing, yes, he is calling.

This was Itche the Shammes (the rabbi's assistant). He is walking in the middle of the street because the sidewalks are paved with tombstones. He walks lightly as if he is swept through the air and sings. He is talking as if he is singing in his light, raspy voice. He sings the partisan hymn "Never Say This is Your Final Road".

As this reverberates, people begin to appear in the streets. Entire families float about, as well as individuals from all the streets, from German Street, from church Street, from Khatch Street, from the market and the old market, hundreds, thousands stride from all around. There are now millions, and all are heading to Synagogue Street. People, men and women. Old and young, and young mothers with small children in their arms, quietly filling the width of the street in an empty space near the where the synagogue once stood. Everyone is looking and waiting for someone.

Pessi the blind woman approaches, led by the blind Tzeria.

Yes, yes, I know. I just want to say we have to put on trial the reason for the hatred of our people, this is what I want to remind everyone, said the blind Pessi.

Many people are standing, six million people, broken, with split open heads and torn breasts, without hands and feet, and squeezed heads. All are with burned bodies. No one is dancing here. No one is singing here. They stand deep in thought and stubbornly, quietly scream, don't forget us.

[Page 211]

The dead song of hope rings out, "Never Say This is Your Final Road".

Three middle aged people appear with grenades in their hands; it appears they died in battle; they are the leaders of a battle. Among them is an older Jew; he is absorbed in his task. His hands are on his shoulders and his mouth is moving as if he was talking.

Itche the Shammes suddenly bangs the podium and says: Jews, be quiet. The trial is about to begin.

And then:

The Jew standing in the middle stretches out his right hand and begins with these words: I have been elected to be the chief judge. I believe we are all judges, chief judges. Everyone here knows me. I lived a life of toil, like the majority of Jews, working hard for a piece of bread, for a bit of food. I lived on the street of the old market. I spent my life fulfilling good deeds, like all other Jews. All my life I judged and was a mediator for those who needed justice. My name is Mikhl Hersh Noymark. When the strange murderers brought Yom Kippur to our town, they placed me in the middle of the market and mocked me, since they wanted to humiliate the entire Jewish people.

Looking at the house of VolksDeutsche where a small group of Judenrat leaders were gathered, he turned to them and said – don't stand apart from everyone. We will not put you on trial for the problems you caused due to your weakness and belief that causing pain to your brothers would protect your small lives. No – no – we will not try you. We will not even harm your lives; we only have pity for you.

Then he turned to everyone and continued: they strove to annihilate the Jewish people and to burn the Jewish heart. But as they burned bodies, hearts became stronger. We can put them on trial and pass judgement, but on whom? Here, we must try an entire nation that, for its entire modern history, continued to bring trouble to humanity, to culture. But how can we put a nation on trial when the whole world remained silent. With this silence, they are accomplices.

Can we try the whole world?

[Page 212]

Too often when times are difficult, the Jews are blamed?!

Too often, the physically weak are blamed! He stretched out his right arm and continued:

May Jewish blood remain a stain of guilt and shame on all who actively and passively murdered people. May the continuous fire of all the burned synagogues burn the conscience of all who took part!

May the nonexistent ash of our burned corpses arise as a strong free nation in a free Jewish state and be a sign that "the strength of Israel will not be false".

The sun comes up, flaming blood shining on our cemeteries, from the cities and towns where Jews lived and built.

A stillness, a deathly pallor in the captured lands.

[Page 213]

My Town Przedecz (Pshaytsh)

by Reuven Yamnik

Translated by Janie Respitz

Przedecz Street
Photographed by Simkha Naymark in 1965

I knew my town
Tied together with thousands of threads
I knew the fathers, the mothers, the children
Until the day they disappeared.

I knew the sincere Jews
Honest hard workers who labored tediously for a piece of bread,
They lived in poverty, but quite happy
And continued to weave the Jewish golden chain.

[Page 214]

I knew the small houses
Embracing as if dancing together
The simple Jews from their small prayer houses
Looking affectionately upon holidays.

And the clean tidy little houses
With white sand covering the floors
And the brass candlesticks with their Sabbath candles
Which our mothers blessed silently with tears.

I knew my town
With a blossoming youth and high culture
With exuberant energy to live and create
With souls as clean and pure as nature.

I knew my town
In times of hatred and hostility
From boycotts to picketers, from stolen livelihoods
From anti – Semitic placards and assaults in the streets.

I knew my town
In the years of tears, blood, and destitution
When the Nazis stole and murdered
And chased old and young to their deaths.

I knew my town
When it bled from open wounds
When our dearest and closest ones called for revenge
And the murder in the day they disappeared.

[Page 215]

I knew my town
Small, pious, calm and hearty
From all our nearest and dearest only a bit of ash remains
After the extermination in the abyss of hatred.

I knew the small Jewish children
Their voices rang out like silver bells
They too were brutally exterminated
In the fiery tongues of the crematoria.

Let my sad song serve as a monument
On the ashes of the innocent victims
And a reminder of a depraved world
That killed children and women without pity.

We must build a new life in our own land
A place that will protect Jews from hatred

Where there will no more senseless victims
And will take revenge for the innocent spilled blood.

May the blood of our beloved martyrs
Never be forgotten
And their last call – Hear O Israel!
Shall be heard eternally.

[Page 216]

The Tombstone

by Y.L.L

Translated by Janie Respitz

I want to believe that the index finger on your right hand did not sarcastically mock the imprisoned women. I want to believe that your children risked their lives to toss them a piece of bread. I want to believe that there were many good deeds. If not, why did you erect the tombstone? On the anniversary of their deaths, surely you bring flowers and wreaths, just as you did the first time … you did it beautifully that time. A marble slab with an inscription. This is the grave of 67 Polish citizens of Jewish descent. And from money collected from the villagers, nice, really nice.

On the other side of the stone slab lie skeletons of brutally murdered Polish citizens of Jewish descent.

From where do you know the important resident from the village Yanikov near Inowrolaw (Inavratslov in Yiddish)? Huh, from where? The skeletons are without names. Only a small hole at the bottom part of their skull, without documents, without names, without guilt. It could be that among them there was a citizen from rich America, from mighty Russia, cold Finland, from the province and the small town Przedecz. I believe this is the grave of the conscience of the whole world which remained silent.

Yes, for sure. This is the grave of my and your sisters, mothers. Until today somewhere there is a man or woman searching for his or her mother. He lights a candle on a designated day of the year and looks into the glow of the small bloodied flame and asks, mother, where are you? Where are your remains?

You should have inscribed the following on the cold stone:

This is the grave of the murdered conscience of the world.

Then, in a few years, the stone will be able to tell the story.

[Page 217]

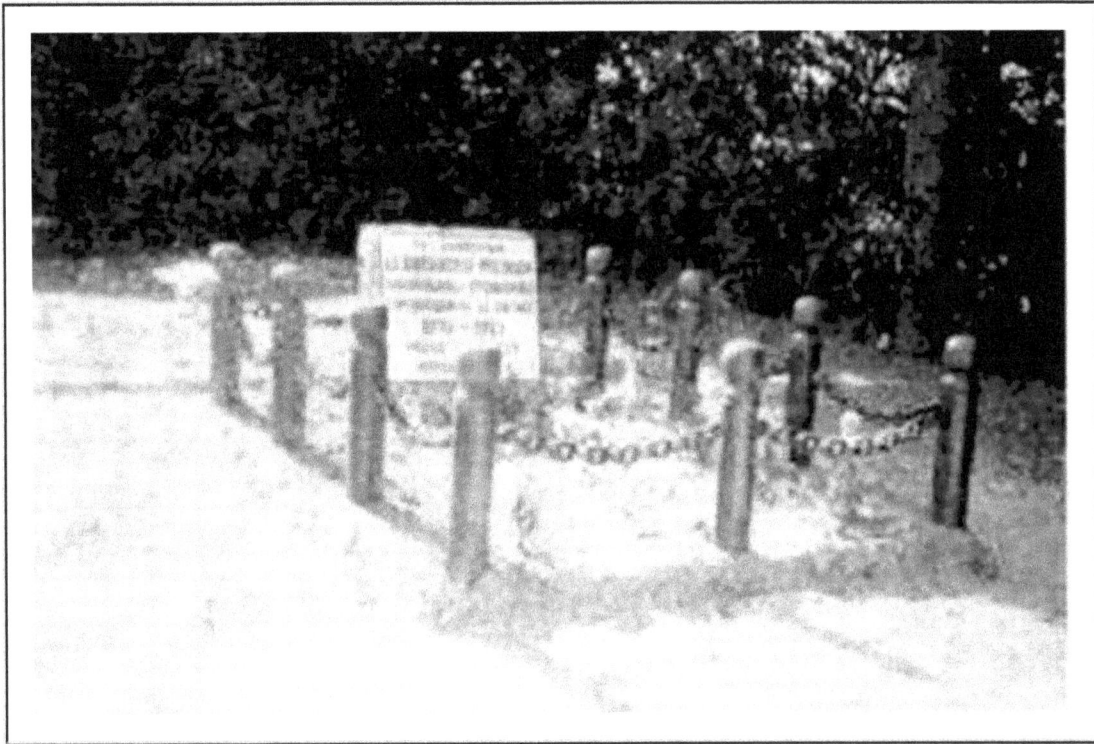

Translated from Polish: Here lie 67 Polish citizens of the Jewish people, martyred during the years 1939-1945 by the German executioners.

[Page 218]

Young Mizrachi and Hashomer Hadati

by Moshe Bilavsky

Translated by Jerrold Landau

Let these lines be included in the monument that we are erecting in the form of a Yizkor book in memory of the Jews of Przedecz who perished in the Holocaust.

I will begin with memories from the period following the arrival of Rabbi Zemelman to our city in 1923.

His first activity immediately after his arrival was the founding of a modern *cheder* with teachers who were knowledgeable in Torah, including two from outside our city who succeeded in gathering a sizable portion of the youth of our city within its walls.

Top row from the right: Itshe Danilski, Binyamin Zichlinski, Shmuel Zielinski, Yaakov Pradanski.
Second row from top: Nota Grinblat, Leibush Asch, Moshe Czanskowski, Hela Jakubowicz, Michael Hersh Goldman, Hersh Zingerman, Zalman Danilski, Hersh Topolski, Yaakov Zichlinski, Sala Izbicka, Tova Danilska.
Seated: Yetka Danilska, Miriam Rabski, … Rumek, Mala Orbach, Yitzchak Leibish Offenbach, Liba and Moshe Bilski, Beila Ekert, Mala Frenkel, Mania Rauch, Rana Fiszer.
Sitting in the bottom row: Heniek Rauch, David Zielinski, Shmuel Leib Ofas.

Reb Mordechai Yehoshua Perla especially stood out from among the local teachers. He was local to the city, an expert scholar, with a splendid countenance, a scholar who had no stain on his clothing. He had a teaching permit, but did not have rabbinical ordination. The subjects he taught included Talmud

[Page 219]

and Yoreh Deah [1]. His classes were a pleasure for his students. He was especially loved because he went beyond the limitations of the other teachers, and also taught us Nach [2], which was considered a heretical subject in their eyes [3]. In general, all of our studies were at a very high level. It was a great honor for us to draw forth Torah from his mouth, and his name went before him throughout the entire area. He was always clean and neat. He attracted the attention of everyone when he walked through the street. People looked at him with awe and reverence. His clean clothing always added to him charm and imparted an aura of levelheadedness and splendorous honor. All the residents of our city recognized him and revered him for his great objective of disseminating Torah to his students. He was revered by his listeners both for his personality as well as his learning methodology, which was accompanied by wonderful melodies. It was an honor to be counted among his students. His brother Reb Hersh Lipman Perla also taught us. It is painful for me to note that both of them perished in the Holocaust along with their wives and all their children. May G-d avenge their blood.

At that time, there were also a number of lads from outside the city who came to study with us. They lived under the Esn Teg [daily rotation of meals] system – that is, a considerable number of the householders invited such lads to eat with them one day a week. This is how the lads were sustained. They also served as examples and spokespeople for the local students. There was a special class for the choicest students given by Rabbi Zemelman of blessed memory, held in the Beis Midrash daily between 11:00 a.m. and 2:00 p.m. There were no exams, but all the students were present at the rabbi's third Sabbath meal [Shaleshudes], where they were tested orally by the rabbi and the scholars of the city.

In essence, the test was also for the questioners – that is, they too wanted to prove their scholarship.

The preparations for the test took place on Thursday night. The students would remain awake all night and prepare for these tests in the Beis Midrash building. Marks were not given for these tests.

During that period, we worked on an effort to enrich the library of the Beis Midrash. We used that library for our studies. The effort was called Tikkun S'farim.

Every Friday, two lads from our group, aged 13-14, went out to the houses of the city to collect donations for Tikkun S'farim. This author, as well as my friend Yehoshua Yamnik who currently lives in Haifa, were the trustees of this effort. There was a senior trustee above us – Itshe the Yellow [der Geler Itshe]. The donations were collected from all the residents of the city. Some gave more and others. The donations were of 5, 10, or 15 groszy. Every week, the money was placed into a wooden box, stored in Reb Itshe Vajden's – Itshe the Yellow's – house. The keys to the box were solely in his hands. Book were purchased according to need, and torn books were rebound.

One day when we came to the Beis Midrash for the Mincha and Ma'ariv services, one of the worshippers, a former communal administrator, approached me. He had also been the gabbai of the Beis Midrash for many years. He asked me to come to his house after the services with my friend Yehoshua Yamnik for a significant conversation.

We did not know what was awaiting us in that discussion. We went to him and sat at the table where the head of the household was sitting.

Our host who was sitting at the head of the table stood up without uttering a word and paced back and forth in the room. We looked at each other, and realized that something was bothering him, and it was hard for him to find the words.

We sat quietly. We were silent and waited for what was to come.

[Page 220]

Finally, after long minutes, he approached the bookshelf that adored his room, took out a Gemara with a splendid binding, and brought it to the table where we were sitting.

He placed the Gemara on the table, sat down, opened it, and sighed. He began his conversation with us in a quiet, restrained voice. We felt that tears were choking his throat. He said, "Since I am down to a loaf of bread, I am forced to sell these books for the livelihood of my family. I received them from my father-in-law as a wedding present, as was the custom in those days. I am forced to part with them, but under no circumstance to distance myself from them. Therefore, if you have the possibility of purchasing them for the library of the Beis Midrash, I am prepared to sell them for below their value. I will thereby attain two things, a sum of money to sustain my family, and, with G-d's help, at appropriate times, I can also peruse them within the walls of the Beis Midrash. However, I ask one thing of you, that the public should not know that I have reached this state."

We left his house silently, with a promise to give him a response within a few days. We set out to the house of the rabbi. We told him what we had just heard. At first, the rabbi was astounded. However, he finally told us that if indeed the situation has come to this point that he was forced to sell his books to sustain his family, we should make every effort to acquire the books for the Beis Midrash, and G-d will help us. He opened his wallet, took out five zloty, and said, "This is my share."

We agreed with the seller on a price of two hundred zloty, and to wait until the money was collected before we carry this out. The gabbai of the Beis Midrash, my father of blessed memory Reb Mendel Wolf Bilewski, and Itshe Vayden of blessed memory agreed to renovate the bookshelf from the Beis Midrash fund.

The sum was collected, and the purchase took place. The seller parted from his books with tears in his eyes. We brought the books, which included the entire Babylonian Talmud in a fine leather binding, to the Beis Midrash with our own hands. Here, the satisfaction of all the Jews of the city, that is the donors who felt that they were partners in this enterprise, was felt. However, our joy was tempered by sadness that a man who was one of the honorable people of our city had reached a position where he had to sell his books to sustain his family.

During the Shacharit service the next morning, the rabbi called me and my friend Yehoshua over to a corner of the Beis Midrash, and said, "You should know that the thought barely left me the entire night that one of the families of our city has reached such a situation."

Now I can state that these were the books of Reb Hersh Pradanski. No remnant of his family survived the Holocaust.

One day when we came to the Beis Midrash in the morning, we found the doors of the bookcase inscribed with the words of the Gemara "Don minia veika beatra." That is, learn from the books and return them to their place. This was the work of our friend Reuven Yamnik.

Here I must note that Reb Hersh Pradanski was one of the great scholars of the city. The pathways of the Talmud and halachic decisors were clear to him, and he walked in their light all his life. To our sorrow, the scholars of our city did not understand the needs of the times and the desire of the youth to free themselves from the fetters of the exile.

During that period, we were cut off from all the vanities of this world. We were not even allowed to read newspapers lest they influence our way of thinking. We were forced to read the newspaper in secret, hidden within the folios of the Gemara or Yoreh Deah. When the rabbi left the room for a few minutes, the newspaper appeared on the table, and someone read the news or the article aloud.

[Page 221]

A Shana Tova greeting sent from Przedecz by the members of Young Mizrachi to the member Moshe Bilavsky in the Land of Israel in the year 5694 [1934].

Translator's note: the form and style of this Shana Tova greeting is difficult, and the printing is not always clear. It is replete innuendoes, and written poetic style, and with acronyms and mnemonics. I did my best to translate it as much as possible. A[??] mark indicates that I could not make out some words or phrases.

The top has an acronym of the year 5694, embedded in the sentence: Let the Zionist idea take root through Torah and Labor.

Down the right side: Let the year and its curses end. Down the left side: Let the year and its blessings begin. [These are refrains from the *Achot Ketana* piyyut recited just before the Maariv service on the eve of Rosh Hashanah. See my commentary on this piyyut at: https://jerroldlandau.com/piyut5.php].

With blessings of a Shana Tova

For our friend Moshe Bilewski and his dear wife
The Land of Israel Haifa [embedded in an acronym: The seashore, in front of the city]

[Most of the rest of the lines follow an acrostic down the right side: Moshe Nechemia Bilewski]

We wish you with joy and gladness
That you merited to come to our land to the fruitful Land of Israel
Moshe, you should know that you have peace
Receive a blessing from us [??]
May it be easy for you in our native land
May your home be blessed in our native land
[??] you are in the dwelling of G-d
Let there be for you the covenant of labor and the Torah of Israel
Accept our blessing [??]
In the year 5694 take our wishes
Let them go up en masse to our native land [??]
To build our land, the precious land
With the idea of Mizrachi and the covenant of our ancient Israel
Pave up, pave up the route
Let this be a year of redemption
Let your names grow for blessing and praise

Wishing you from
The Mizrachi and young Mizrachi and Hashomer Hadati
Przedecz, 1 Tishrei, [??]
May our Dispersed make Aliya in the near future
Build your future on the mountains of Zion and Jerusalem, may you be inscribed and sealed for life!

Translator's footnotes:
1. One of the four sections of the Code of Jewish Law.
2. The Prophets and *Ketuvim* [Writings or Hagiographa] parts of the Bible, not commonly taught in a traditional *cheder* setting. There are several reasons for this – perhaps the most significant is that the study of these sections of the Bible were stressed by secularists, and the traditionalists tried to distance themselves. Another reason is that many verses of these books are referenced in the Talmud, so they should be studied in the context of the relevant Talmudic discussions. It should be noted that in the more modern Orthodox society, the study of the books of the bible flourishes.
3. An over-exaggeration. The books of the bible are certainly not considered heretical, albeit their formal study was frowned upon in the traditional *cheder* setting.

[Page 222]

The Establishment of Tzirey Mizrachi
(The Young Mizrachi)

by Moshe Bilavsky

Translated from Hebrew by Marshall Grant

Back in those days, in 1929, news began to reach us of bloody riots taking place in Palestine, mainly the massacre in Hebron, and we felt that we, with all our hearts, were with those there who were fighting the Arabs. We were not able to publicly express these sentiments, because that would reveal a breach in the wall of our Jewish studies. Torah studies still continued on one hand, but there were pages of the *Haynt* newspaper between Gemara pages, on the other. It was our friend, Ze'ev Rusk, who would bring us the newspaper he was able to pinch from his uncle, Netta Wasertzog. Even though it would arrive a day late, we could still follow the events taking place in Israel.

Then we came up with the idea that, along with our studies, we would dedicate ourselves to work for those in Palestine. However, the institutions of *Agudat Yisrael*, the organization we had grown up with, did not sufficiently provide us, the younger generation, what we desired. We had to venture into the "unknown", meaning the Religious–Zionist Movement.

Then Rabbi Katriel Fischel Tkorsh, from Wloclawek, visited our city. He currently lived in Israel and served on the Tel Aviv Rabbinate. His speech in the home of Mr. Leibish, a longtime Mizrachi businessman, excited us and we felt that this was the path we needed to take. The *Tzerei Mizrachi* (The Young Mizrachi) Movement was established. Later, The *Shomer Hadati* (The Religious Guard), consisting of younger boys and girls. Even though Rabbi Zemelman was angered by our decision, he took solace in the fact that we remained within the Religious–Zionist Movement.

Our first steps were to distribute pamphlets of the Zionist movement and to collect money for the JNF. Remember, at that time there was an agreement between the Mizrachi Movement and the JNF leadership that all the monies collected by the Mizrachi organizations would be used only to redeem land for religious settlements.

The JNF instructed us to collect 400 zlotys that needed to be collected that year, and I am proud to say that we surpassed this amount from the first year of our operations. The blue box was found in almost every Jewish home in our city, and almost every person called to the Torah knew that he had to donate to the JNF. A large part of the proceeds came from the sale of the JNF calendar and making deliveries on Purim. On the day before Yom Kippur, during the afternoon prayers, when almost every Jewish home was preparing for Judgement Day, we put a collection bowl in the prayer hall, along with all the other collection bowls, with the sign, "Redeem Israel". It was eventually filled with tens of zlotys, and it came from everyone, from all walks of Jewish life.

There was a special atmosphere when Simchat Torah came, and every male from the age of thirteen was called to the Torah. The message was that the donation for this important cause should not be the few *grushen* that one gives from his pocket for some common cause, but much more. This was a contribution for the redemption of the holy land in order to further establish a Jewish presence there. And God willing, maybe he or one of his family members will be one of those who benefits from these efforts.

The message reached every Jewish household in our city, and almost everyone who was called to the Torah on the Simkhas Torah holiday donated to the JNF and its efforts towards the redemption of land in Palestine. This was considered a huge achievement for the fairly new Young Mizrachi movement. The great contribution of many adults, supporters of the movement, must be positively acknowledged,

[Page 223]

in addition to the extensive assistance of the synagogue and study center.

While going around the city to collect donations for the JNF, we did not skip the home of the rabbi who had taught us in the past (and once said we had "left for an evil culture"). The rabbi warmly welcomed us but explained that he could not personally donate to this cause for obvious reasons. However, he referred us to his wife, who provided a generous donation.

The JNF representatives among us were Itzhak Leibish Ofenbach, Ze'ev Rusk and the secretary Moshe Tshanskavesky. In the winter of 1932, Moshe Tshanskavesky and his associates were recognized by the JNF head office for their accomplishments for the JNF. I will note the assistance of some of the adults who were members of other Zionist movements and were at our side to achieve this respected goal.

In the summer of 1931, a public meeting was held in support of the JNF, in which the JNF representative Mr. Bernstein from Warsaw came to speak. He described the situation in Palestine following the riots and the need to increase efforts to redeem the country's lands. For emphasis he added, "Rachel refused to be comforted, and wept for her children who were gone"; and then, "Rachel, our matriarch, cried on her grave for her children in the diaspora." And in order to enable more Jews to return to the Land of Israel, the first thing that was needed was the redemption of land there, and to redeem it with money from the people for the people. The contributions to the JNF increased.

I would like to especially note the Hebrew lessons given to us by I. L. Ofenbach in our hall. The lessons would take place three times a week, and almost all the young boys and girls attended.

On Shabbes afternoon, we would gather to further our Hebrew knowledge, in which we would extensively analyze the events that took place in Palestine in the previous week.

Almost immediately after founding the movement, we recognized that we still had a large amount of organizational work ahead of us, and the relatively high costs exceeded our means. We had no choice but to search for alternative sources of income. We began by distributing newspapers in the city: *Yidishe Tagblat, Haynt, Letste Nayes* and other newspapers written in Polish. The proceeds went to finance the branch's vast activities. Another advantage for taking this course of action was that many families, who had not had a newspaper in their home for years and were disconnected from current world events, were now reconnected. They knew they could buy a newspaper today without committing to buy one tomorrow. They bought a newspaper, which created gatherings in tens of households where the family members would read together. Many community members would gather at the afternoon and morning prayers and provide their own analysis of events taking place around the world.

The visit of Rabbi Litman from Koło

The visit of Rabbi Litman in February 1933 was deemed a great success. Attempts made by our supporters to hold his lecture in the synagogue were unsuccessful due to the rabbi's opposition. Rabbi Litman's lecture in our hall attracted a large crowd; tens stood outside the hall to listen to him calling to increase the efforts of the Mizrachi, the Young Mizrachi and the Shomer Hadati movements. He was a guest of the Ofenbachs and for the duration of the three–day visit, the house was overwhelmed with people coming to express their support of the movement. In the elections for the Zionist Congress that year,

[Page 224]

our movement won 70% of the vote in our city, and we credited this to Rabbi Litman's visit. This was Rabbi Litman's second visit to our city; the first time was in the summer of 1932, which also attracted large crowds who came to hear his lecture.

In 1932, I left the city and travelled to a training *kibbutz* in Blizyn. My parents opposed the idea, and even though my father was a Mizrachi member and was one of the most prolific supporters of our organization, he was not a supporter of my decision. He considered it a sort of adventure due to the slim chances of making *Aliya*. It was well known that the government in Mandatory Palestine only issued a very small number of immigration permits. However, when I arrived at the kibbutz, they sent me their blessing in a letter. My friends continued their efforts, and several more registered in similar training groups.

Then some members arrived at the kibbutz from Myszyniec. One of them was a cute girl, Liba Friedman, and after a short acquaintance we decided to marry. After we were approved for Aliya on behalf of the Center, we were married in February 1933.

In August of 1933, I made Aliya to the Land of Israel, and now I will describe my last Shabbes in my city. My uncle, Pinchas Aharon and Lipman Bilevsky and several other relatives on my mother's side came from Sompolno especially for that Shabbes. Of course, in the synagogue where I had prayed with my friends over the years, I was blessed by everyone there. Lunch on one hand, was cheerful – everyone was happy for me, and I, with G-d's help, was grateful for being able to receive such an opportunity. On the other hand, there was my parents' distress over their eldest son leaving them. I will always remember the melancholy and happiness in my mother's eyes, a mix of both joy and sadness. However, the thought that I was travelling to the Land of Israel, the land of my dreams, prevailed, and our house was a happy one.

In the afternoon, I went out with my friends I. L. Ofenbach and Ze'ev Rusk to say goodbye to the city's residents. I went to almost every home, and when we arrived at the home of Shmuel Yamnik, the city's *shochat*, he apologized to my friends and invited me into the other room. There he revealed his secret: his son Yehoshua, who had been a student in a Warsaw yeshiva, had left and was now in a training kibbutz. He asked me not to tell anyone because it could harm him and his livelihood.

On Saturday night, my friends surprised me and threw a party in a large hall at the local fire department. Almost all the city's Jews were there, which again proved everyone's support of our organization and its final goal of making Aliya.

We were sure our city was on the verge of massive emigration to the Land of Israel. However, for various reasons, only of a few arrived from Przedecz (in Hebrew, Pshedets). My friend I.L. Ofenbach spent five years in the training kibbutz but was never allowed to make Aliya; and in the end of 1934 my friend Ze'ev Rusk arrived. In the second world war, he was conscripted under an order of Supreme Council of the Jewish *Yeshuv* into the Jewish Fighting Brigade of the British Army. He fought against the Nazis on the Italian front and fell in battle. Eliezer Perlmutter also arrived; he was born and educated in our city. In the war of Independence, he fought and fell in battle defending Jerusalem. In 1935, my friend Yehoshua Yamnik arrived, and then the numbers dwindled. This appears to be due, to a certain extent, to the riots that broke out in Palestine in 1936 and continued until the beginning 1939, when the war broke out. These disturbances and the Aliya restrictions enacted by the government in Mandatory Palestine put an end to my years of efforts to bring my family to Palestine.

And that was the last chance for Przedecz's Jews.

These simple and honest Jews were nationally renowned; they were supporters of the building of the Land of Israel, in their subconscious they were avid Zionists, and felt all the pain felt by our brothers in Palestine.

Unfortunately, they were not able to see the huge miracle of Israel's resurrection when the Jewish state was established. Only a few remained after the war and moved to Israel.

Where are you, my dear parents, my sisters Brayna and Baltzia, my brother Leibel, my teacher and rabbi, Rabbi Zemelman, my fellow students and Zionist activists, all the residents of Przedecz: men, women, and children.

A cruel storm passed over Europe and took with it six million of our Jewish brothers, and you are dearest among them.

There is no longer a Jewish community in Przedecz (in Hebrew, Pshedets).

May their souls be bound in the bond of life.

[Page 225]

Interest Free Loan Society Fund

by A. Pshaytsher

Translated by Roberta Paula Books

Like every Jewish town in Poland, Pshaytsh (Przedecz) had its Gmiles Khesed (interest free loan society). Townspeople remember it having been active from 1905. Wars came and went, governments changed, headed by Russians, Germans, and Poles. In each of these circumstances, the loan society was an important factor in the town's economic life.

After the First World War, there was significant inflation and a kilo of bread cost thousands; unfortunately, the Gmiles Khesed had to close.

In 1923, economic life normalized a bit and Jews wanted to rebuild their lives. This would have been impossible without working capital loans for establishing a business. Thus, the desire to restart the institution. Thanks to a few substantial people, the bank was re-established and grew. Over the years, the fund was run by volunteers, without administrative costs.

This fund was particularly important. Anyone who needed a loan could come without ceremony or intervention by a clerk. Anyone could approach the administration and present his request.

For sure, we remember the years from 1923, on Saturday nights, right after the Havdallah service

[Page 226]

to welcome the new week, when Reb Moishe Topolsky, its leader, and other men of substance would come to the House of Study, sit at a long table, and receive requests for loans and payments on outstanding loans. For the most part, the requests were confirmed without ceremony. Understandably, this depended on the amount of money that had flowed in that evening. More than once, someone needed a special loan and there was not enough money in the fund. Sometimes members of the board reached into their own pocket to provide the loan – so that there would be no interruption in the functioning of the fund.

The foundational capital of the institution was raised from the wealthier community members, with a token contribution from the other members of the association.

This is how the institution helped all levels of Jewish society with loans, particularly small businessmen, artisans, and those who travelled to the villages to buy and sell goods.

In 1935-36, when antisemitism oppressed Jewish businesses, those who had needed Gmiles Khesed loans were hit especially hard and unfortunately were unable to pay their debts. The institution, which was limited in funds, was forced to stop its activity.

In 1937, with the help of young energy, the bank resumed its activity, aided by the central Gmiles Khesed in Warsaw, which was supported by the Joint, and was able to provide larger loans.

During this time, small factories were established to make socks, sweaters and other things which were supported by loans from the free loan society. The newly founded administration carried out intensive work which provided the institution with a solid base.

With the outbreak of the war in September 1939, the institution closed.

[Page 227]

Society to Care for the Sick – Itche Vayden

by Moishe Bilavsky

Translated by Janie Respitz

In town, there was a society to care for the sick (Bikur Cholim) headed by Itche Vaydman.

Actually, we could say that he alone was the society to care for the sick, as he was the person who took care of everything: raising money, sending a doctor to a patient in need, buying medication and taking care of the household of the sick person. If there was not enough money in the fund to pay the doctor or pharmacist, Itche Vaydman would make sure there was no delay in bringing a doctor or medication to the patient. You could also come to him to borrow a thermometer to take someone's temperature, a spray for an enema, and cupping glasses.

When someone was gravely ill, they not only called for a doctor but also a quorum of Jews to recite psalms and pray for a recovery. They would go to the cemetery and ask a deceased relative to intercede on behalf of the patient in the next world and send a full recovery. They spoke out against the evil eye. But these measures that did not require money, unlike a doctor or a pharmacist, which is where the Society to Care for the Sick played a role.

Itche did not know a lot of languages. He spoke a very broken Polish. He tried to talk to the Christian pharmacist in Polish, but when the Jewish doctor insisted on speaking only Polish with Jews, Itche, on principle spoke to him in Yiddish. "Jews talk to each other in Yiddish" he would say.

Revenue for the institution came mainly from someone wanting to say a prayer for the sick in synagogue, with a vow to contribute to the society. On the eve of Yom Kippur, after the evening prayer, a bowl was placed on the podium with a sign "Society to Care for the Sick", and all who came to pray donated. On Purim, when Jews sat down to enjoy the Purim feast, two people in costumes with bells came asking for money in the name of the Society to Care for the Sick. Again, Jews would donate to this worthy institution.

There is an expression "There is no poor community". From small donations, the society existed and provided useful services.

[Page 228]

When there was a deficit, Itche would close his sewing machine, give instructions to the young girl who worked for him, and would walk about town. He knew which doors to open, and when Itche Vaydman arrived he would receive the nicest donations for the Society to Care for the Sick. He also had a few women helping him with this sacred work.

There was also a "Linat HaTsedek" (guarding the sick). Spending the night with a sick person was among the good deeds performed in our town. Here there was no distinction between rich and poor. Doctors would leave the patient at home, so men and women felt it was a sacred act to spend the night with the patient and care for him. Itche Vaydman contributed to this as well.

The Sabbath Torah parsha Vayira is particularly sacred to the Society to Care for the Sick. In this parsha, the angels come to visit Abraham our forefather when he is sick. All pledges made on this day, whether in the synagogue or the Study Hall or the Psalm Society, would go to this worthy cause.

The burial society would joke with him that, after he had lived 120 years, they will take revenge since he was a spirited competitor! Their activity was thanks to the angel of death, whom Itche and the Bikur Cholim Society would often chase out of town.

Blessed be the memory of Itche Vaydman and of those who helped him in this sacred work.

We cannot end the memoir about the Bikur Cholim society without describing Itche Vaydman the person.

Itche and his wife Esther did not have any children. He ran a workshop for women's tailoring. The young women apprentices were treated by him and his wife like their own children. Above all he loved children. By nature, he was quick, a quick talker and walker. But when he met a child, especially a schoolboy, he would stop and have a chat, and you could really see how much he enjoyed this.

He spoke loudly, you may have thought he was shouting, but when you got close you could tell the words were coming straight from his heart.

He was no great writer, but everyone's needs were written deep in his heart. He had very little free time. He was also the manager (Gabe) of the House of Study, which was situated

[Page 229]

near his home. In the winter, when it was cold outside, snow or a frost, poor, destitute wanderers would come to town and spend the night in a hostel (Hachnose Orkhim) or in the House of Study. Itche would not go to sleep until he was sure the oven was good and hot, often doing it himself. He made sure these itinerants who had a difficult life would not suffer from the cold.

Everyone was familiar with his home. Anyone who needed a doctor, medication or those who wanted to donate in his holy work knew where he lived.

He was no great scholar, but he was passionately observant. People who had known him for a long time said that in his youth he had been an enthusiastic member of the Jewish Workers Party. However, he disagreed with their methods on how to achieve their goals and broke away.

Many people called Itche "Yellow Itche". He was a Loibitzscher Chasid. Two or three times a year, he would visit his Rebbe and return and tell about his visit and how he received a blessing from him to be healthy and continue in his benevolent work. This gave him courage, and he would return to his sacred mission with even more energy.

May the memory of Itche Vaydman be blessed.

For his deep, great love of people, his compassion for human suffering and his constant readiness to help those in need.

The murderers from the master race destroyed this great magnificent life.

May God avenge his death.

[Page 230]

The Ludovy Bank

by A. Pshaytsher

Translated from Hebrew by Marshall Grant

After the First World War, there was no banking institution that could assist merchants, tradesmen and shop owners who needed loans to continue their operations.

In general, the economic situation in those times was unclear. The frequent rise in prices drove many businesses to close.

When the situation improved a bit in 1924–25 and the zloty returned to a realistic value, the need for a financial institution was felt; an institution that could provide loans to the city's Jewish residents.

Even though there was a charity fund, whose loans saved Jews from hunger many times, it was based on philanthropy and limited to what it could provide in the face of the growing demand.

Members of the Ludovy Bank

Top row standing, L–R: Yaakov Wolf Klar, Itsche Weiden, Avraham Eliah Prochovesky, Lazer Zichlinsky, Herschel Vishinsky
Second row, L–R: Gershon Lazer Heltreich, Moshe Levkowitz, Haim Claudevsky, Kapal Saika, Moshe Tapalsky, Moshe Rauch, Nachum Ribinsky, Mendl Wolf Bilevsky, Yosef Tapalsky
Third row L–R: Esther Pullman (Sochachevsky), Moshe Aaron Weiden, Shabtai Oppenbach, Yehiel Tapalsky, Moshe Sochachevsky, Netta Wasserzog, Natan Skobronsky, Shimshon Zichlinsky, Hinda Toronchek, Wolf Rusk

[Page 231]

In 1926, the Ludovy Bank was established, and it was managed by Netta Wasserzog, Natan Skobronsky and Moshe Tapalsky.

Moshe Sachatchavesky headed the institution, which was a branch of *Dezenith*. Since it had provided a great deal of the initial funding, the bank was required to report its activities and submit annual reports for control purposes.

Loans of up to 500 zlotys were provided, all according to banking criteria, and with the co-signing of two city residents who were approved by the bank.

Since its establishment, the institution was located in the upper floor of the home of Rabbi Shmuel Abba Avrmovitch. The first employees of the bank were: Esther Sochachevska, Ze'ev Rusk and Hinda Toronchik.

The bank's activities included issuing securities, third–party payments, and, mainly, the provision of interest–bearing loans.

The bankers worked hard and faithfully fulfilled the objectives undertaken towards its members. There was vibrant activity every day; some paying deeds, some paying loans. There were instances, due to varying circumstances, when the deed or loan could not be repaid on time. The bank's administrators always gave an option to extend the payment deadline, and there were even times when a new loan was provided. In 1936, due to the circumstances of the time, the bank had to close its doors. It never succeeded in renewing its operations.

The Town Pshaytsh (Przedecz)

by Ruven Yamnik

Translated by Janie Respitz

Young memories, old dreams, do not stop invading your thoughts, and disappear and reappear in various episodes and experiences in this small town of our birth – Przedecz, or as we called it, Pshaytsh. Who among us does not remember the small Jewish town where we took life's first steps, where we planted the first roots of our future lives. Who does not feel it deep in his soul when he remembers or just says the word Pshaytsh and lets out a heart-wrenching sigh and a hot tear when we remember the barbaric way the entire Jewish population was annihilated by the Nazis and their collaborators. Unfortunately for us, the small remnants of the town that remain is not Jewish Pshaytsh, even though it continues to exist on the Polish map, but for us it no longer exists. It has continued its existence without any Jews …

[Page 232]

The town of Pshaytsh (Przedecz) is situated in the western part of Congress Poland, a part of Vlotslavek (Wloclawek) district in the Tarner province. It was a small, quiet town with approximately two hundred and fifty Jewish families, numbering approximately one thousand three hundred of the total population of five thousand.

The town stood off to a side, not on any rail line and not near any major highway. There have been Jews living there for about 700 years, but we don't have an exact date as we are missing official documents. In any event, it was the oldest town in the region. It received its order as a city from King Kazimierz the Great in the 14th century. During the same century, a fortress was built by the king on German Street, which served as protection for the king's military in town. The fortress later became

City Hall

[Page 233]

a German church in the 18th century, which we remember until today, with its large round tower and small windows all around.

The First Jews in Town

Where did the first Jews settle in Pshaytsh (Przedecz)? According to how the town was built, we can boldly say they settled on Synagogue Street. Those chased and tormented Jews that arrived built the most necessary Jewish institutions: the ritual bath, the society to recite psalms, which was their first prayer house, and the cemetery. This is how Synagogue Street came to be built. From the records of the burial society, we know that many Jews were brought from surrounding towns to be buried in the Pshaytsh (Przedecz) cemetery since the younger and smaller towns did not have a cemetery of their own. We remember there were very old tombstones in our cemetery, half sunken in the ground dating back to the 13th century.

The Environs of Pshaytsh (Przedecz)

The neighboring towns that bordered with Pshaytsh (Przedecz) were: Kłodawa, 8 kilometers away to the south and on the main railroad. To the east was the town of Dombrovitz, 12 kilometers away. It was a very small town with a few families. Their last rabbi was Rabbi Moishe Drakhman, of blessed memory, a son-in-law of the rabbi of Pshaytsh, Rabbi Berish Menkhe, of blessed memory. He came from Lubin, a small town near Wloclawek (Vlotslavek in Yiddish). To the north was the town of Chodecz, 13 kilometers away and to the northwest was the town of Izbica Kujawska.

The Villages Around Pshaytsh (Przedecz)

The villages surrounding Pshaytsh (Przedecz) were inhabited exclusively by Christians except for the village Ribne where a few Jews lived. There were large forests and there was a sawmill to cut wood that belonged to a Jew, Moishe Berman, of blessed memory. To the south was the village Gures which, in the hot summer months, served as a summer resort where Jews would rent rooms for their families from village farmers and spend a few weeks in the fresh air of the large pine forest. The children partook of many amusing activities.

[Page 234]

To the east and north of the town were long and wide wheat fields and large orchards with a variety of fruit trees. To the southwest were swamps created by the nearby Yedz River. We would dig out peat from the bogs and use it in the winter to heat the houses and the ovens.

The Yedz River

The western part of town, and a portion of the south side lay on the Yedz River. It was not a flowing river; it was stagnant water. The river was filled with a variety of fish and plants. Before Shavuot the boys would pick green reeds (tatarak) to place in the windows, as the custom was to decorate homes with greens for the holiday. What did the river not do for the Pshaytsher Jewish people, youth and children? ... on Rosh Hashanah after the evening service all the Jewish men and women, big and small left the prayer houses with their prayer books under their arms and went to the river to say "Tashlikh", when pockets are shaken out into the river to symbolize casting of sins. Before Passover the Rabbi and his Hasidim would go down to the river and draw water (called Mayim Shelaynu or "our water"), put it in a barrel and bring it to town to make Matzah.

Leyzer Zikhlinsky's House

[Page 235]

This matzah was baked with song and devotion. The water would stand in the barrel all night (that is why it was called "our water"), in other words, water that spent the night, so that it would not be too cold for making matzah. The barrel was covered with a white cloth to keep it Kosher for Passover.

In the winter, when the river would freeze, there were great expectations. The frost made the river look like a shiny table, and it was used as an ideal sports facility for sledding. We would chop a hole in the ice. Fish would jump out for some fresh air, and we would catch them in buckets. The river was calm, never stormy. We swam there in the summer. For the Jewish women, the river was a blessing. They would bring their laundry to wash and bleach in the river. The banks of the river were filled with women and children all summer long. The laundry, after washing and bleaching, was clean and white. They would bring food and drink for themselves and the children and spend many hours. The children played and their joyful laughter could be heard from far away. Their task was to bring water in buckets and spray the laundry spread out on the grass. There was no shortage of work, and mothers and their children were happy.

North of our town on the road to Chodecz, about 7 kilometers away was the village Szatki (Tseti In Yiddish). That was where the small railroad was which we called "clumsy", which connected the town to the city Wloclawek (Vlotslavek in Yiddish). The city merchants used the railroad to bring their goods from the city or to export their products and manufactured goods as well as wheat. Pshaytsh (Przedecz) did not have a big train. If one needed to travel by train, he had to go to Kshevate, a village just past Kłodawa about 12 kilometers away. That is where the large rail line was which connected our town to the rest of the world.

The Orchards and the Fruit Sellers

The orchards in the surrounding villages provided livelihoods for the Jews of our town. Right after Passover, Jews would rent the orchards from the Christians and moved there for the entire summer, until all the fruits were picked from the trees. They had to do this to ensure

[Page 236]

the fruits would not be stolen. They lived in wooden shacks. When the fruit was ripe, they sold it to merchants from the big cities of Koło, Łódź and others. Entire families worked hard all summer in the heat, rain, and storms. Living in these wooden shacks, they did not sleep or eat as they were used to, and with a bit of luck, scratched out a living.

Now let's take a walk through the town that once bubbled with Jewish life, raised beautiful Jewish children in an atmosphere of culture, love of life, with Jewish schools, prayer houses, ritual objects, workshops, and business which were all suddenly eroded by Hitler's deluge and cruelly extermination. We begin our walk at the home of our rabbi, the last Pshaytsher (Przedecz) rabbi, Rabbi Yosef Alexander Zemelman of righteous blessed memory. His house served as his residence as well as a courthouse and served as a beacon for all Jews of Pshaytsh (Przedecz).

The house was the second half of the House of Study and had served as the rabbi's house for previous rabbis; Rabbi Auerbach, Rabbi Blum, who later became the rabbi in Zamosc, near Lublin. After him it was Rabbi Goldshlak Yehoshua Dovid, who became the rabbi in Sherpcz (Sheps), and the last, Rabbi Zemelman with his wife and eight children. He had his private residence here as well. All community and religious matters were concentrated here, as well as all meeting of the synagogue council which handled all important matters like ritual slaughter, charity institutions, the ritual bath, the bank, the house of prayer, learning institutions as well as other issues. In the courthouse, judgements were passed involving established members of the community. The rabbi would make peace among them and settled their disputes. Here he would also answer religious queries about chickens and cattle, and would give a class on Torah commentary with the finest Yeshiva students etc. … In the yard they built a long annex with a few rooms and a Sukkah with a roof which could be opened with a string. The branches to cover the Sukkah lay on the floor all year, so it was always ready for the holiday of Sukkot. In the annex there was a school for girls called "Beys Yakov". It belonged to the Learning Institution for Girls founded by Mrs. Soreh Shenirer of blessed memory from Krakow and existed throughout Poland. Also in the annex was a Yeshiva (religious high school) for boys who studied with teachers and the rabbi. There were also boys from other towns who came to learn. They ate their meals in some of the wealthier homes. All day until late at night

[Page 237]

you could hear their voices coming from the House of Study and the Yeshiva. There was a custom to stay up all night on Thursdays and study until dawn when it was still quite dark. They would then go to Reb Mendl Wolf Bilbasky to buy a fresh bun and together have a feast. In the morning after prayers, they would go home, but shortly after would come to Rabbi Zemelman for a class from 11:00 – 1:00. In the evening before prayers and at night after prayers the boys would review the rabbi's lesson together in the House of Study.

Now we arrive on Synagogue Street which is inhabited almost exclusively by artisans. How many memories awaken in me about this street, even after all these years. Many young apprentices felt connected to this small street, which we called the "Synagogue Street". The oldest street in town was wide and short, paved with round sharp stones. The sidewalks were paved with the same stones, just smaller. The houses which were small and low with pointed roofs were crowded together as if they were old people being held up to prevent falling. Could you see such a street in other towns? The windows were small, the doors were low, and various sized shutters with spread wings from both sides.

House of Mordkhai Poyzner

The shutters were lacquered, painted in a variety of colors, brown, yellow, green, white and others. The air was filled with a variety of food smells: cooked stews and fried onions mixed with the smells of smoke from the high chimneys and the sounds of children laughing and crying, as well as noises from sewing machines, banging of shoemaker's hammers, because artisans live in these small houses. Hard working Jewish tailors, hat makers, saddle makers, shoemakers, fruit sellers, village peddlers, and many other Jews would worry about earning a living, staying healthy, marrying off their children, and other problems. In the evening when the air was heavy inside the homes, people sat on their front stoops or on benches. Women sat and talked with their neighbors. The men went to the House of Study for evening prayers, children played games. Some climbed the chestnut trees. Friday afternoon the Jews went to the ritual bath to immerse in honor of the Sabbath, and Friday evening and holidays Jews went to pray. Saturday morning and holidays, especially Rosh Hashanah and Yom Kippur the mood was elevated. Jewish women, our mothers and grandmothers, wearing wigs, long dresses, some still wearing their wedding dresses, went to synagogue with their husbands, carrying their prayer books under their arms. The men carried their prayer shawls and prayer books and during the High Holidays wore long white coats. You can hear the beautiful holiday prayers coming from the synagogue. On the High Holidays you can hear the choir as well as the blowing of the Shofar by the ritual slaughterer Reb Shmuel Yamnik. Children ran around the synagogue and filled the air with their little voices. You can hear the wailing of the women from the women's section of the synagogue as they ask God with supplications to grant them a good year, health, and livelihood. When the prayers ended, the Synagogue Street filled up with men, women and children walking home with the hopes God heard their requests for a good year.

Nearby Warshavska Street, which we referred to as House of Study Street, was also inhabited exclusively by Jews, mainly artisans and most of the Jewish institutions could be found there. Of course, there was the House of Study and the rabbi's home. In the yard was the Yeshiva, the Beys Yakov School for girls, the hostel, the Jewish court, and community house. The house of Reb Itche Vaydman was an institution unto itself, as it housed the Society to Care for the Sick, repair shop for holy books and other important things. The Ludovy Bank was also situated on this street under the management of

[Page 239]

Mr. Moishe Sokhochevsky and his staff, in the house of Shmuel Abba Abramovitch. Betar was also there, the Revisionist organization led by the hard-working activist Shloimeh Yisakhar Engel. Across the way in the large yard belonging to Khaim Zamer was the town slaughterhouse for cattle and fowl, a sanitary establishment for those times. Also, in Khaim Zamer's yard was the pharmacy of the Christian antisemite Grushtzinsky. The Jewish doctor Avrom Diament also lived there. The religious Zionist organization – Young Mizrachi – was also there. All the institutions were concentrated on Warshavksa – House of Study Street. All Jewish cultural, economic, and communal life in town flowed from this street.

The Market

We are now in the center of town, the marketplace called "Pilsudukiega Place". It was paved with small round stones and the sidewalks were paved with the same stones. To the north there were a few Jewish businesses including Leyzer Zikhlinsky's grocery store and Binyumin Frenkel's iron business. To the south was the City Hall, butcher shops and the Fire Hall. From there, the street led to the river. There was a water pump in front of City Hall. The pump had two large wheels which were turned in order to draw water. It was well known in town that this pump had the best water and people came from far away for this water. In winter, when it was very cold, the pump was wrapped with sacks and straw to prevent it from freezing. Often, this did not help. When this happened, we poured a few buckets of water from above and this helped to retrieve water.

City Hall was a two-story building where city council and administration sat. Jews were also represented in the administration. Next to this were the butcher shops which were rented by Jewish butchers – the brothers Khaim and Mordkhai Goldman. Next to them was the Fire Hall, which was also a two-story building. The upstairs was used for entertainment and cinema, and downstairs was used for firefighting equipment and the fire wagons.

Every two weeks, on Monday, there was a fair at the marketplace.

[Page 240]

The fair was loud and noisy. Artisans and merchants would display their goods. People from our town as well as nearby villages would come to buy and sell their goods.

During the Nazi occupation, one of the saddest events for the Jewish population occurred on this spot. This is where the cruel act took place of cutting of Jew's beards and forcing them to lie in the mud and pour water from the pump on their shaved heads. They ordered a Jew to stand under the pump and two others were forced to turn the wheels and pour water on his head. All the Jews there had to witness this. They kept them there, soaking wet, for the entire day. They were forced to run around and were tortured. Our Polish neighbors stood by and happily watched this spectacle. At the same spot, women and girls sat and picked the grass from under the stones, under the supervision of the VolksDeutsch. Here at the marketplace, Rabbi Zemelman was forced to carry heavy wooden planks on his shoulders,

Khotch Street
Photographed by Prof. Brand on his visit to Pshaytsh in 1965

[Page 241]

from the lumber warehouse on Chodecz Street.

There were other large and small streets, some with more and some with less significance, but they were all built in the same style. The population was mixed – Jews, Poles, and Germans who once all lived peacefully together, although always with a bit of envy of the Jews. However, this was not displayed until shortly before the Nazi war. This is when they started antisemitic schemes from the boycotts of Jewish businesses and slogans which included "Don't buy from Jews", "Beat up Jews", "Jews to Palestine" and others. They also picketed Jewish stores, not allowing Polish customers to enter. The Jewish economic situation worsened when the Jews who travelled to the villages to buy and sell, and there were many, were faced with horrible chicanery and beatings. Their livelihood was destroyed, as well as the fruit sellers in the orchards, as they were now forbidden to lease orchards from the Christians. At night their lives were at risk due to the thieves and thugs. Even in "good" times it was difficult for the village peddlers to earn a living. They left their homes before dawn when it was still dark outside and returned home in the evening. Their lives were more difficult than the lives of the market merchants. They had to walk far distances, often threatened by village dogs. Many were actually bitten. They endured bad weather, frost, snow, storms, rain, heat, and winds, as well as other problems they faced at the hands of the Christians in the villages, just to be able to eke out a living. Many times, they would only have dry bread for themselves, their wives and children … often it would happen that if the head of the family, the village peddler would get sick. His family would remain without food and destitute. This was how the majority of the Pshaytsh (Przedecz) population lived. When we remember it today, it is hard to understand how they lived. This is how things were until the outbreak of the war, when everyone was annihilated by a variety of cruel death methods. There were also middle-income Jews, merchants, businessmen, artisans, each with his own business, each with his own worries and never with any overabundance. They never strove for luxuries and helped each other out as much as possible. But for everyone, when the Sabbath and holidays arrived, they forgot the difficult days,

[Page 242]

the hardships of trying to earn a living. They went to synagogue or the House of Study to pray or to listen to the rabbi's sermon. At night on weekdays between the opening and closing of evening prayers they would listen to fine words and parables from a travelling preacher. Such individuals would come often to our town to collect money for an institution or sometimes for themselves, a needy bride, a ransom, or just to earn some money. The preacher would receive permission from the rabbi to go up to the pulpit. He would begin with the words "My teacher and gentlemen" or "Dear Jews". He would quote from the Torah, provide parables, and talk from his heart so people would support him. He would end with the words "Zion will be redeemed". He would go down from the lectern, take a candle and stand by the door. All the Jews exiting the House of Study would give him a donation. There were fine Jews in our town. They were hardworking, pious, and sympathized with another's hardships. They worked very hard in order to feed their large families. Start with our own Rabbi Zemelman, and around town according to where they lived, "Lovers are not separated in life and death". So it is that Jews lived here for hundreds of years, generation after generation passing from father to son, with religious feeling, love for the Land of Israel and hope for better times …

[Page 243]

Eili Eili – a Dirge

(Sung to the Tune of Eli Tzion)

Lament, lament, weep my soul
And shout out, o daughter of Israel
Raise a lament and wail
For a conflagration has consumed in Israel.

For the slaughter of the people that was premeditated
Tribulations of bereavement, rivers of blood,
No mercy for the old or young
For the binding [a reference to the binding of Isaac] of a pure sacrifice.
Lament, lament…

For the children, weaned of milk
Crushed upon rocks
And for their blood that flowed
In the open, outside, in front of their parents.
Lament, lament…

For the destroyed communities
And the destruction of the sanctuaries of G-d
Ignited in fire and flames
Splendid cities of Israel.
Lament, lament…

For generations that were cut off
The blood of parents mixed with the blood of children
In the vale of Auschwitz they were killed and perished
They ascended in the smoke of the crematoria.
Lament, lament…

For the prisoners, clothed in sackcloth.
Wasting away in their myriads
In Treblinka, Chełmno, and Majdanek
With nobody to gather their bones.
Lament, Lament…

Lament for the wagons crowded with people
Upholstered with sulfur and pitch
Overcome by thirst as their souls depart
They scream for water, but nobody provides.
Lament, lament…

For the girls who fainted
Women who took their own lives
With their pure hand, they perished together
And were not desecrated, their honor has ended.
Lament, lament…

For those frozen in the snowy fields
Many children in the bosom of their mothers
And for the martyrs who screamed out
Buried alive within the pits.
Lament, lament…

For the parchment scrolls desecrated
At the hands of the Nazis who blasphemed G-d
Torn up, ripped up, and left in filth
Among the garbage heaps, without a redeemer.
Lament, lament…

For the righteous ones, the modest of the world
The princes of the nation, the studiers of Torah
All were suffocated in the gas chambers.
The menorah fell and was extinguished.
Lament, lament…

[Page 244]

For the youth, the young ones of the nation
Girded for battle, with hands of rebellion
Against the evil ones, spillers of blood
Raising up flashes of flames…
Lament, lament…

For the rivers of blood and weeping
Revenge for the covenant is guarded in the heart
In the battle in the ghetto without fear
They extended their might, a pillar of bravery.
Lament, lament…

For the sanctification of the Divine Name and the nation
And for avenging the blood of the pure
They gave their lives in freedom
They fought and fell as heroes.
Lament, lament…

Raise up a dirge for the disaster of the nation
Full of agony, enveloped in destruction
Will hatred darken forever
And will light not spread out?
Lament, lament…

See G-d, arise, you shriveled ones
My heart fell, enemies arise
Listen to my prayer, bring refuge
Save my soul from the people of blood.
Lament, lament…

For the hero on the stage of eternity
As an eternal light shining with splendor
Everything drips of blood, the sacrifice to the demon
We will remember for ever and ever.

Lament, lament, weep my soul
And shout out, o daughter of Israel
Raise a lament and wail
For a conflagration has consumed in Israel.

———

The dirge *Eili Eili* was composed by Y. L. Bialer, a native of Warsaw and a survivor of the Holocaust. It was authorized in the year 5708 [1948] by the Council of Holy Communities of Poland for the Memorial Day of the Martyrs.

Translator's note:
For Leib Bialer, see http://yleksikon.blogspot.com/2015/01/yude-leyb-byaler-yehuda-leib-bialer.html . An official version of this dirge in Hebrew can be seen here: http://old.piyut.org.il/textual/english/329.html

I translated this *Kina* myself, as I have been unable to find an English translation on the internet.

This is one of several dirges [*kinot*] written for the Holocaust, and is often recited on Tisha B'Av. It was composed a few months after the conclusion of the war. I have written an extensive e-book on piyyutim [Jewish religious poetry], and this *Kina* is mentioned along with four other *Kinot* written about the Holocaust. See https://jerroldlandau.com/piyutKinot8.php [search the page for "Shoah"].

As noted in the note above, as well as in my work, this dirge was written in the style of *Eli Tzion*, perhaps the most famous of the Tisha B'Av *Kinot*. For the haunting melody see https://www.youtube.com/watch?v=Vl89waBrX_o

[Page 245]

Yizkor

El Maleh HaRachamim

Translated from Hebrew by Marshall Grant

Creator of the heavens and the earth, hearer of the cries of the desolate, judge for widows and fathers of orphans, do not let the blood of your people, the people of Israel, spill like water. Provide safe rest on the wings of the Divine Presence, amongst the holy, pure and glorious, who shine like the sky, for the souls of six million Jewish souls, among them the members of our Przedecz community and the surrounding areas; hundreds of men, women and children, who were killed and slaughtered and asphyxiated and drowned and burnt and buried alive by the despicable, wicked and horrific German Nazis in the gas chambers, in Chełmno, Auschwitz, Maidanik, Treblinka and other places; and in countries occupied by the Nazis. All were holy and pure, among them spiritual leaders, scholars and righteous, innocent, and honest, rabbis and their followers and scholars and students of Torah. May the Merciful One remember them and provide them eternal rest in heaven; may he protect them forever in the folds of his wings and will bind their soul in the bonds of life. God is their salvation, and he will revenge their revenge, and will remember their sacrifice. And may you provide their rights to the people of Israel. Earth, do not cover their blood, and let their cry have no resting place! It is due to them the remnants of Israel have returned to their homes, and these holy souls will be eternally remembered for their innocence, and let them rest in peace, and let the days until their resurrection come to an end and let us say amen.

ארגון יוצאי
עיר פשדיץ ופשייטש
(שטשיטשווע)
בישראל

The Organization of Former Przedecz Residents

[Page 247]

The Martyrs of Przedecz

Translated from Yiddish by Janie Respitz

Rabbi Yosef Alexander **Zemelman**
His wife: Bilha
Their sons: Yehoshua Elimelekh, Yoel,
Nekhemia, Yakov
Their daughters: Nekhama, Adel.

Our rabbi, Rabbi Zemelman, was a great personality. Besides being the rabbi in town and a Torah scholar, he was also proficient in general classic secular literature and politics. Even the Christian population held him in high esteem and respected him. He was a handsome man who earned respect. He was kind and was always smiling. The rabbi's wife was the mother of eight children. Small and thin, she was always hard at work. However, she always managed to find time to help those in need and listen to the problems of the women in town. There was not a family in town which she did not visit and help. Her heart was open to all who suffered, always with a smile and a kind word.

Vayden Itche
His wife: Esther

Itche Vayden and his wife Esther were a family without children. He found comfort in community and philanthropic work. He was an honest, pious Jew who served as the manager (gabbai) of the House of Study for many years, guardian of the hostel, active in the Society to Care for the Sick, repaired holy books and other community functions. His profession was a women's tailor. Every girl who apprenticed with him was treated as if she was his very own child, taking care of all her needs.

[Page 248]

Klar Yakov Wolf
His wife: Lola
Their daughters: Yadza, Khana, Mina

Yakov Wolf Klar, who lived in the same house as his family, owned a haberdashery. He was an intellectual and one of the founders of the Public Library.

Taranchik Aharon
His wife: Feyge
Their sons: Avrom Khaim, Rafael, Tuvia, Yoel,
Itche

Reb Aharon Taranchik and his wife had six sons. He operated a shoemaker workshop together with his own children and sold his goods in the market. His sons were intelligent boys who were active in the Sholem Aleichem Library. One of his sons, Yakov Meir lives in Argentina.

> **Bialogluvsky** Yosef
> His wife: Khaya
> Their sons: Avrom, Daniel
> Daughter: Yokheved.

Yosef Bialogluvsky and his family. Actually no one knew them as Bialogluvsky. They were known as blind Yosef and lame Khaya. They were village peddlers. All day long, they carried their goods in baskets and sold them to wholesalers. They had three children. Their eldest son Gutman died at age 18 of tuberculosis.

[Page 249]

> **Abramovitch** Shmuel Abba
> His wife: Rivka
> Their sons: Tuvia, Yosef, Mordkhai
> Their daughter: Esther

The Abramovitch family was pious and well off. They lived in their own house where he also had a leather business and other shoemaker accessories. He was the manager of the Burial Society. His children ran a boot stitching workshop. They were all active in the Betar organization. When the last Jews of Przedecz were being liquidated, he decided to hide at his former client's house, the shoemaker Ostrushka. However, this non–Jew delivered him into the hands of an S.A man, Henkl, who shot him. His daughter Yiskha Fuder lives in Israel.

The Abramovitch Family

[Page 250]

> **Bilbasky** Moishe
> His wife: Malka Soreh
> Their son: Shimon
> Their daughters: Yetta Khaya, Rokhl

Moishe Bilbasky was the son of Lipman Bilbasky. He and his family were traditional Jews. The children were raised in a nationalist spirit. He owned a food store and also dealt with fish and burn materials. With all of this, he was not a wealthy man, but he had a good heart and loved to do a favor for those in need.

> **Rozen** Soreh – a widow
> Her daughter: Ita
> Her son: Henekh and family

Soreh Rozen (whom we called "Kupkete" "Little Hat"), a widow who raised two children, worked very hard and travelled with her haberdashery goods to fairs and villages, and managed to earn a living. Her son Henekh married and moved to Izvitz, where he was a teacher in the kheder.

> **Yakhimovitch** Aharon Dovid
> His wife: Trayna
> Their son: Yitzkhak Leyb and his family
> Their daughters: Tashe, Krusa.

Aharon Dovid Yakhimovitch and his family. He was a shoemaker. He read from the Torah in the House of Study. He and his wife were very fine people. All of his children were active in the cultural life in town. His eldest son, Moishe, passed away in Israel.

[Page 251]

> **Buks** Arye
> His wife: Ruta. Their daughter: Hella

There were five people in the Buks family. They had a butcher shop and also dealt with livestock. Their house and shop belonged to them. He was a traditional Jew. He allowed his children, like most people in town, to receive a public education. He subscribed to a daily Yiddish newspaper, as he had the means and the time for this. Arye Buks, his wife and daughter were killed during the Holocaust. Their two sons, Yuzek and Yitzkhak, live in America.

> **Liek** Mendl
> His wife: Brayne
> Sons: Mordkhai, Dovid
> Daughter: Leah.

Mendl Liek and his family. A village peddler who, during the summer, together with his wife rented an orchard. Their eldest son Rafael had been a tailor. He caught a cold travelling to a fair and died at the young age of 18. Their daughter Leah was an intelligent girl who read a lot. Besides helping her mother with housework, she also did tailoring to supplement the family income. Their son Mordkhai Dovid was a quiet boy who also worked as a tailor. The youngest son Eliyahu helped his father with peddling. No one from the family has remained.

[Page 252]

> **Toronchik** Yosef Zelig
> His wife: Eta
> Their sons: Aharon, Tuvia

The young Toronchik couple and their two sons lived in their own home, which they received from their parents as a wedding gift. It was common in Poland that family members would marry each other. Yosef Zelig and Eta were not only husband and wife but cousins. We rarely see such a harmonious life as this couple led. They were very cultured people and spent a lot of time reading. He was a supporter of the left-wing worker's movement. He was a shoemaker by profession and worked at home. No one from the family was among the Jews of Przedecz who survived the Holocaust.

Yosef Zelig Toronchik

[Page 253]

> **Zielinsky** Shimshon
> His wife Rokhl

Shimshon Zielinsky and his wife did not have any children. He was a tailor. They raised their nephew Hersh **Zingerman** in their home. One of the rabbi's best students, and a member of the Young Mizrachi Organization. He strove to go to the Land of Israel but did not achieve this goal. He was killed in Poznań. Shimshon Zielinsky was a Jew with a permanent smile. He was always ready to help another, although he was not wealthy. He was religious and a supporter of the Mizrachi movement.

Fisher Avrom
His wife:
Their sons: Yakov, Moishe
Their daughters: Esther, Ronia, Masha, Pesa and her
family.

Avrom Fisher was a tanner. He had a large family and a food store. He was a Hasid. It was a nice, observant family. He provided all his children with a very religious education. His eldest son Mendl studied in the Yeshiva, his second son Yakov was very observant and knew the entire Book of Psalms by heart. He was active in Young Mizrachi. Reb Avrom Fisher was the manager of the Reb Meir Baal Nes Fund and collected money for the holy goal of settlement in the Land of Israel. His married daughter Pesa lived in Koło.

[Page 254]

Zielinsky Esther
Her sons: Yankl, Ruven, Nakhman
Her daughters: Khava Hindl, Gitl.

Esther Zielinsky was the wife of Khaim Zielinsky who lives in America. She was a passionate Jewish mother and together with her eight children lived in great poverty. They were all killed in the camps.

Zielinsky Yisroel Khaim
His wife: Shifra
Their sons: Ozer, Dovid, Sholem Aron
Their daughter: Ytke

Yisroel Khaim Zielinsky lived in the same house where he had his sheet metal workshop with his two sons. They sold their product at the market. They were very nice people and loved to do favors for others. His children were intelligent people and were all active in the Zionist movement.

Zielinsky Khaim Yosef
His wife: Esther
Their daughter: Soreh

Khaim Yosef Zielinsky was a saddle maker. He had a large, well-established family and was an active member of the Psalm Society. His children were intelligent people. One of his daughters was active in the workers' movement. The youngest daughter Khava lives in America.

[Page 255]

> **Ekert** Avrom
> His wife: Rivka
> Their daughters: Bayle, Khana, Frimet, Bronia

Avrom Ekert with his family. He was a tinsmith. Like the majority of the Jews in Przedecz we were also observant and supported Mizrachi. His daughters helped him in his tin business. The whole family were singers. Friday nights, you could hear the family singing beautiful Shabbes melodies.

> **Kovalsky** Itche the Shammash (Gabbai)
> His wife: Hinda Dvoyre
> Their sons: Nokhem, his wife and family.

Itche Kovalsky was the town's Shammes (Rabbi's assistant). He was an old, religious Jew with a white beard. He ran all the town's functions and without him no one would have known what to do. He directed all religious life in town. His wife Hinda Dvoyre was practically a doctor. When a child sprained a hand, they knew to go straight to Hinda Dvoyre. She would take some fat, rub it in and wrap it with a kerchief and all was good. She also made her own ointments. She was always in a good mood. She received everyone with a smile and a kind word.

Their son Nokhem lived with his wife and children in Sampolno. He was a hat maker. He was an observant man and one of the most esteemed in town. He raised his children in the spirit of traditional nationalism.

[Page 256]

> **Valter** Eliyahu
> His wife: Yekhet
> His son: Avrom
> Their daughters: Hinda Dvoyre, Khana

His son in law Elye Valter lived in the same house. He was a young man, a Khasid, a learned man in all secular subjects. He was a good prayer leader and had a beautiful voice that pleased not only the Jews from Przedecz, but those who heard him when he travelled to fairs selling his dry goods, where he used to be the distinguished emissary, especially with his prayers honoring the new month (rosh khodesh). In the Psalm Society, Reb Eliyahu would give a lecture every Sabbath before the evening service based on the weekly portion of Torah or from Ethics of the Fathers.

> **Vishnivsky** Ruven
> His wife: Gitl
> His mother: Khana Rivka
> His son: Hersh Meir
> His daughters: Feygl, Khava, Khaya Soreh

Ruven Vishnivsky, a hat maker. He was one of the choir boys under the old cantor Shabtai Kotek, of blessed memory, during the Rosh Hashanah and Yom Kippur services. Later he was a choir boy with the ritual slaughterer Yamnik Shmuel. He was one of the rebuilders of the Psalm Society. He was an intelligent Jew and passionate supporter of the worker's movement in town.

> **Vishnivsky** Khaya
> Her son: Shmuel Zalman
> Her daughters: Khana Gitl, Rodah, Khava Tova.

Khaya Vishnivsky was the wife of Hershl who lives in America. She was a devoted Jewish mother who was killed with her five children in the camps.

[Page 257]

> **Zikhlinsky** Dakhe – widow
> Her son: **Davinsky** Yitzkhak
> His wife: Genia   His son: Shloime

Dakhe Zikhlinsky (Davinsky) was a grain dealer together with her son Yitzkhak Davinsky, whom they called Yitzkhak the Lame. He was a very nice person. All his free time was dedicated to literature. He was a board member of the Public Library and a supporter of the Zionist movement. He also gave evening classes, without pay, teaching the Polish language to Jewish youth.

> **Vishnivsky** Yisroel Khaim - widower
> **Zikhlinsky** Yakov
> His wife: Hella
> Their daughter: Malka

Yisroel Khaim Vishnivsky had a food store. In his free time, he sat in the House of Study and studied Eyn Yakov, often with others. His son in law Yakov Zikhlinsky and his wife Hella lived with him were well educated and liked to discuss world politics.

> **Shveitzer** Rokhl - widow

Rokhl Shveitzer. Her husband died not long after they were married, and she was left with a small child and without a livelihood. She became a dairy woman. Even though she was not well off, she helped poor families who could not afford milk. She raised her son on her own. Many would have wished to have such a child. She was killed in the death camp Chełmno . Her son lives in Israel.

[Page 258]

> **Klar** Elazar
> His wife: Ella
> Their daughters: Bella, Khana

Elazar Klar was a tailor and the son in law of Yosef **Vishnivsky**. Like the majority of artisans in town, he sold his sewn goods in the market. He was a member of the Psalm Society.

Vayden Mordkhai Ber
His wife: Khava
Their married sons: Yekhiel, Yakov Hersh and their families

Mordkhai Ber Vaydman and his wife Khava had a food store. He was an observant man. His son Yakov Hersh was one of the founders of the Public Library and the drama club. Thanks to the proceeds of performances, the library was able to purchase new books and sponsor activities. A few years before the war, Yakov Hersh moved to Konin. One of Mordkhai Ber's sons, Yekhiel, lived in Łódź. He was an observant man and kept his house strictly kosher.

Kladovsky Elye Dovid
His wife: Brayndl
Their daughter: Y'tke

Elye Dovid Klodavksky was a tailor. He would travel to fairs to sell his goods. He was an observant man and very active in the Psalm Society. The family lived in constrained material conditions. Their son Zalman lives in Israel.

[Page 259]

Yakubovsky Kasriel
His wife: Khaya
Son: Avrom
Daughters: Frayda, Mikhal

Kasriel Yakubovsky was a custom tailor. He was a religious Jew. He prayed at the House of Study. Between the afternoon and evening prayers, he would study with Reb Leyb Lentzitzky. He had fine, intelligent children. His son Dovid was one of the founders of the Public Library. He died in America in 1972. Their son Moishe Aron, who was one of the founders of the Sholem Aleichem Library, lived in Canada.

Shimonovitch Herman
His wife and four children

Herman Shimonovitch was a son in law of the old **Shperke**. He lived in an attic apartment in the house of the Christian Lapatkevitch. He would travel to markets selling haberdashery. Later, he became a teacher, and his wife went to the markets. They had four children. They were a quiet family who were not involved in community affairs. Because of this we do not know their names.

Avigdor Yitzkhak and his family
Son in law of **Shperke**

Yitzkhak Avigdor was a son in law of the Shperke family. He was a tombstone engraver. In order to provide for his family, he also did book binding. This was a quiet, traditional family and cultured educated people. Unfortunately, no one from the Shperke or Avigdor family survived.

[Page 260]

> **Frankenshteyn** Ruven
> His wife: ...
> His son: Itzik
> His daughters: Tove, Frimet, Rekhl
> And family

Ruven Frankenshteyn, maker of ready to wear clothes. An observant Jew and the head of his family. Ruven, his wife and five children lived in poverty. Nevertheless, he sent all his children to kheder and to school. It must be pointed out that all his children were intelligent. One of his sons, Mendl, survived Auschwitz and lived in Przedecz until 1964.

> **Grinblat** Noteh
> His wife: Bella
> two children

Noteh Grinblat, his wife and two children lived in their own nice house. He was a grain merchant and a respected Jew. He was wealthy according to the standards of the town. He was a great supporter of Mizrachi and a member of the Board of Directors of the Public Bank.

> **Grinblat** Dovid
> His wife and family

Dovid Greenblat was the brother of Noteh Grinblat. They were both grain merchants. He was an honest man from a quiet, modest family. His house was open, and he supported poor people. They fulfilled the good deed of welcoming guests. Unfortunately, no one from either brother's family survived. They were killed in Chełmno .

[Page 261]

> **Frankenshteyn** Hersh
> His wife: Shprintze
> His sons: Mordkhai, Mendl
> His daughters: Malka, Frimet

The Frankenshteyn family rented one room under the roof of Noteh Grinblat. The room was dark, and the life of this family was dark. The father Hersh and his wife Shprintze left for the village on Sunday to buy and sell village products, and often would not return until Friday afternoon. There was often nothing to eat in their home. Furniture – a table, a bed – of course not. The family slept on straw on the floor, and during the winter covered themselves with their clothes. Often on market days you could see their two daughters collect spoiled produce the farmers had thrown away. The eldest son worked as a shoemaker, the eldest daughter took care of the house, but they all knew how to read and write despite the fact that they often could not go to school because they did not have shoes on their feet. This was a traditional Jewish family. No one survived. The Germans considered them to be parasites and thieves.

Linchitsky Yekhezkel Mordkhai
His wife: Rozhe
Sons: Eliyahu, Avrom, Hersh Leyzer, Noteh.
Daughter: Ita

Yekhezkel Mordkhai and his family lived in their own house. Together with his eldest son Hersh Leyzer he was a village peddler. Two other sons, Eliyahu and Avrom, ran a tailor workroom. Their daughter Ita was a women's tailor. Both workshops were in the same room. Despite this, they were not well off. They were a very observant family, simple honest people. Reb Yekhezkel Mordkhai read from the Torah for many years in the House of Study. In his free time, he studied Ein Yakov with other Jews.\

[Page 262]

Markovitch Wolf
His wife: Henna
Her son: Nokhem Zielinsky

Wolf Markovitch dealt in a variety of goods and rags with his stepson. In the 1920's, he married the widow Henna **Zielinsky** who had two sons, Hersh and Nokhem. Nokhem was a sick boy, and his stepfather treated him as his own son. Wolf Markovitch was a very smart and nice man. Like the majority of Jews in town, he was observant and a member of the Psalm Society. Even though he was not from Przedecz, everyone in town loved him very much.

Neklin Naftali
His wife: Hadasa and family
His brothers: Avrom and family,
Eliyah and family

Naftali Neklin was one of many Jews in town who honestly looked for different ways to earn a living and provide for his family. He was a village peddler, a glazer, a fruit seller, and a wagon driver. He had a coach that was put together with planks of wood, painted red, that squeaked when he drove it. He would take passengers in this coach to the train station in Kshevate (Ed. Note: a village just past Kłodawa about 12 kilometers away). From all of this, he barely earned a living, and like most people, he worked hard and went hungry. The last years before the war, he lived in Izbica. His son Mendl died in Israel around 1952.

His two brothers Avrom and Eliyahu were hairdressers and had a shop. In the years before the war, they left Przedecz but we do not know the exact details. They were all murdered by the Nazis.

[Page 263]

> **Levkovitch** Mikhal
> Shperke Elye his wife and family

Shapiro (Shperke), the parents died in June 1926. They left behind three daughters and a son. They lived in a fenced house. Their son Mikhal Shapiro and his sister remained in the house. Mikhal was a hat maker. He helped write requisitions for the Jewish inhabitants to various government institutions. He was one of the founders of the Needle Union, where he offered lessons in reading and writing without pay to young people who needed these skills. He also founded the Shomer Hatzair organization which functioned on a high cultural level. His brother Elye married and moved to Kłodawa, where he had a photography business.

> **Neklin** Moishe
> His wife: Soreh Gitl
> Their sons: Meir, Avrom, Lipman, Yosef
> Their daughter: Ella

The Levkovitch family was a big family. All six children were active in the Sholem Aleichem Library. Young workers often gathered in their home for discussions and to read newspapers. They would also sing worker's songs that were not always legal. Even though the parents were observant, they sympathized with the worker's movement. The young people loved the parents very much. Almost everyone in the family was a hard worker. They had a coach and four horses and took passengers to the train as well as heavy loads to Vlotslavek and grain from the grain dealers. Besides this, they had a Matzah bakery where, on the eve of Passover, they would bake Matzah with the Rabbi and the Khasidim with the special "Water that Slept" (Ed. Note: Mayim Shelanu – water drawn the day before and left to rest overnight, a requisite for making matzoh) which was brought the night before from the Yedz River. His daughter Dvoyre lives in Canada.

[Page 264]

> **Zielinsky** Hersh
> His wife: Khana
> Their sons: Moishe, Wolf

The **Nelkin** family was large, with ten grown children. They earned a living as village peddlers, hairdressers, tailors, glazers, wagon drivers and one was even a dance teacher. They all married and moved to other towns except the youngest daughter, Khana who married the glazer Hersh **Zielinsky** and lived in her parents' home after they died. She had two children. As well as being a glazer, Hersh played the violin at weddings. He also entertained the wedding guests with his beautiful singing voice.

> **Rivinsky** Mordkhai
> His wife: Yokheved Rekhl

Mordkhai Rivinsky was a son in law of Zalman **Buks**. He was a tailor who sold his wares at the fairs. As most of the artisans in town, he was traditional. He prayed with the Psalm Society. He died in a camp. His wife was killed in Auschwitz.

> **Bornshteyn** Leybush Mendl
> His wife: Zelda
> Daughter: Rokhl
> Sons: Ozer, Eliyahu

Leybush Mendl Bornshteyn was the son of Tuvia Bornshteyn. He lived with his family in Kłodawa. Leybush Mendl ran a large hat-making workshop and employed a few workers. Thanks to his good financial situation, he was one of the more esteemed householders in town. His children received a national traditional education.

[Page 265]

> **Miller** Hersh
> His wife: Rivka
> Sons: Sholem, Mordkhai, Gutman
> Daughter: one

Hersh Miller was a custom shoemaker, good at his trade. His eldest son, Sholem was an educated young man. All three sons worked with their father and helped provide for the family. It was a well-respected family. Being an observant man, he provided his children with a traditional education. He was a member of the Psalm Society and contributed money to its building.

> **Pshedetsky** Mikhal
> His wife: Gitl
> Their sons: Shmuel, Zelig, Khaim Yakov

Mikhal Pshedetsky was a tailor who repaired torn clothes. He sold the refurbished clothing at the market. Like all the tailors in town he spent weeks away from home. Even though he worked hard far from home all week in order to provide for his family, he was an observant man and would always be among the first on the Sabbath at the Psalm Society. As an observant Jew, he gave his children a traditional education. His dear devoted wife Gitl helped to maintain the traditional atmosphere at home. Their daughter Feyge lives in America.

[Page 266]

> **Noymark** Mikhal Hersh
> His wife: Rakhil
> Their sons: Hersh Leyb, Yakov
> Their daughters: Tauba, Malka, Khaya Rokhl, Blema

Mikhl Hersh Naymark (sometimes spelled Noymark), was a village peddler, a quiet butcher who slaughtered calves, goats, and sheep. He sold the meat at cheap prices specially for poor people. He prayed at the House of Study regularly. During the Sabbath afternoon prayers, he had the longstanding tenured position of leading the service. When it came to the line "You are One and Your name is One" he sang so beautifully. It sounded as if it was coming from deep in his heart. He was a smart and kindhearted man. He loved to build and rebuild. The people living in his houses did not have the ability to pay rent. Mikhal Hersh never demanded rent. He took whatever they were able to pay whenever they were able to pay. He was praised by everyone in town, Jews and Christians. He was always full of humor and loved to share witticisms. His daughter Golda died in Brazil in 1971. His son Simkha lives in Brazil.

His second wife Rakhil had a son from her first husband, Hersh Leyb Prakhovsky. He was a tailor who worked for another tailor. He was an intelligent young man and played an active role in the professional union and the Sholem Aleichem Library.

[Page 267]

Khava Klodavsky
Simkha Noymark's aunt

Bluma Noymark
Mikhal Hersh Noymark's daughter

Kayla and Bluma Klodavsky,
Simkha Noymarks's aunts

Khava Rokhl, Yakov, Malka, Tauba Noymark

[Page 268]

> **Noymark** Tuvia
> His wife: Shayna
> Their daughter: Frimet

Tuvia Noymark and his wife Shayna had two children. He lived in his own house. He had a horse and wagon, and every day he travelled to the villages and sold whatever he could. In order to earn a living, he worked very hard. He was an observant man, very smart, but quiet and did not get involved in any issues. He provided his children with a religious education.

> **Toronchik** Mordkhai
> His wife: Mindl
> Son: Yoel
> Daughters: Khaya, Tauba

Mordkhai Toronchik was a saddle maker and by nature a happy man. He loved to talk to people, particularly in the House of Study between afternoon and evening prayers, when Jews discussed all worldly affairs. He liked to convince his listeners that his opinions were right. He was an observant man and worked hard to earn a living. His wife helped out with business. They provided their children with a religious Zionist education.

[Page 269]

> **Tchanskovsky** Yitzkhak
> His wife: Masha
> Their son: Avrom
> Their daughters: Freda, Mikhl

Yitzkhak Tchanskovsky and his wife Masha had three children. He was Mikhal Hersh Naymark's son in law. He dealt in village products. He was a quiet, observant man who did not get involved in community matters. He lived a difficult, hard-working life and with great hardship provided for his family. However, on the Sabbath he was among the first to arrive to pray at the Psalm Society. Many families lived in Mikhal Hersh Naymark's house. It was small, low, with a slanted roof. In the yard there were small wooden annexes like many other homes in this part of town, which was called the old marketplace. The houses miraculously stood up and the biggest miracle was that a fire never broke out, which would have destroyed everything.

> **Shpringer** Motl – widow
> Her son in law – Stramsky Mordkhai
> His wife: Pese

The Stramsky family, Mordkhai, his wife Pese, and their small child lived in the same house as his mother-in-law, Motl Shpringer. Mordkhai, the son in law, was the sole provider. He would go to the market with a small valise which carried a little bit of merchandise, including children's toys and other inexpensive things that he would sell for 35 groshen each. He did not earn a lot from this. But he tried not to be a burden on anyone. This was a quiet family. On the Saturday afternoons that he was home, he liked to sit at the table with his family and read a newspaper or a book.

[Page 270]

> **Sokhchevsky** Moishe
> His wife: Miriam
> Their daughter: Regina
> Her husband: Leyb Ulezniko and three children.
> Daughter: Edzhe
> Her husband: Yakov Glassman
> Their son: Mark
> Their daughter: Miriam

The house of Moishe Sokhchevsky, of blessed memory was a bit bigger and longer than the other houses at the old marketplace. He was a well to do businessman with a dry goods store and was a custom tailor.

Regina and her husband Leyb Ulezniko

Edzhe Glassman (Sokhchevsky)

[Page 271]

He was the chairman of the Ludovy Bank as well as one of its founders. He was an observant Jew and a passionate Zionist. When an important guest came to town, he would stay at his house, and Moishe Sokhchevsky would take care of him. When Rabbi Zemelman first arrived in town as a potential candidate to become our town's rabbi, he spent his first Sabbath with him. When he was officially hired as rabbi, after the celebration in the synagogue the leaders of the community gathered at Moishe Sokhchevsky's for a reception until late at night. When the Keltz Rebbe visited our town in early 1930s, he too stayed at his house and led his Sabbath table there. His daughter Esther Pulman lives in Israel and his second daughter Sala Diskin lives in Paris.

> **Krauskopf** Kalman Yakov
> His wife:
> His son: Moishe
> His daughter: Soreh

In the yard of this house was the building that later housed the Sholem Aleichem Library. Kalman Yakov Krauskopf lived there with his family. He was a house painter, tall and thin with long hands similar to Don Quixote from La Mancha, not to compare. With a stroke of the brush, he could whitewash half a wall. On the white, he would paint the color the householder chose – gold, silver, yellow or red etc. … On winter days when he had no work he would sit in the House of Study beside the hot oven and tell stories about the red Jews on the other side of the Sambatyon, and about Leviathan and the legendary giant ox whose flesh will be eaten by the righteous in paradise. Small boys would gather around and swallow up every word he said with great curiosity. He never earned a lot of money.

[Page 272]

Goldman Blema Rokhl – widow
Her daughter: Esther

Blema Rokhl Goldman had a butcher shop in the marketplace in the building with all the butcher shops beside City Hall. She lived with her daughter Esther, who was a seamstress. She was one of the founders of the Needle Union and the Sholem Aleichem Library. She took courses in reading and writing and was a member of the drama club. She stood at the helm of the cultural movement in town.

Goldman Tuvia
His wife: Malka
Their son: Yosef
Their daughter: Feyge Miriam

Tuvia Goldman, like his brothers Mordkhai and Khaim, was a butcher. He was a member of the Public Library and dedicated a lot of his free time to its development. He was an observant Jew and a knowledgeable man. He provided his children with a traditional Zionist education. His wife Malka contributed a lot to this, as she was known to be an educated, knowledgeable woman.

Goldman Khaim
His wife: Shayne Brokha
Their daughter: Khana

Khaim Goldman was a butcher in partnership with his brother Mordkhai. This was a quiet, modest family. They were observant people. He, too, prayed at the Psalm Society. His home was pious and traditional. He, his wife and daughter were known in town as knowledgeable people.

[Page 273]

Goldman Mordkhai
His wife: Khaya Soreh
Their daughter: Kazer

Mordkhai Goldman was a butcher by profession. Like his mother Blema, he had a butcher shop in the marketplace next to City Hall. He was a pious Jew and prayed at the Psalm Society. He was on the Board of Directors of the Interest Free Loan Society (Bikur Cholim). He gave his daughter Kazer a traditional education. Wandering guests and poor people were always warmly welcomed in their home, receiving food and a nice donation.

Nimchovka Mendl
His wife: Pese

Mendl Nimchovka was a village peddler. He lived in a roof room (attic) on top of the house of Itzik Zingerman. He liked to get involved in community affairs and once was elected as a community council member. He also served as the representative of artisans on city council. He was a smart and nice person, and people enjoyed listening to his speeches and observations. He was also religious and a member of the Psalm Society. His wife Pese, even though she was a sick woman, did all she could to help the poor, even though she was limited in what she could do.

Buks Nakhman
His wife: Tzesha

Nakhman Buks was Zalman's son. He was a saddle maker. In order to avoid military service, he tortured himself a bit, and suffered from this all his years. He married and left Przedecz. He was a very knowledgeable man and often came to visit his father and family in town in order to fulfil the good deed of honoring your father.

[Page 274]

Rukhshteyn Khaim
His wife: Malka

Khaim Rukhshteyn was a tailor. The last years before the war, he worked as a teacher with small children in kheder. He was a good, pious, and smart Jew. He prayed in the synagogue. He had one daughter, Soreh Ratzeh, the wife of Leyb Khodetsky. By nature, he was a happy person and loved to tell jokes, which people enjoyed very much. In the House of Study, between afternoon and evening prayers, he would tell everyone the news of the day because he liked to read newspapers. Even though he was a poor man, no one noticed as he never revealed to anyone that he needed anything. His wife Malka was a great homemaker, and her home was always clean and tidy.

Zingerman Itzik
His wife: Sheva
His son: Hersh
Their son: Zingerman Avrom
Their daughter: Zigerman Miriam
Their daughter: Zingerman Khana
and their families.

Itzik Zingerman was a tinsmith. Like most Jews in town, he was observant and served as the gabbai of the synagogue for many years where he devoted all his energy. He had a big family, three sons and three daughters. They were all very cultured people. Five of them were married and lived outside of Przedecz. They had many grandchildren. They were all killed. No one survived from this beautiful family. The eldest son Avrom lived in Łódź. He and his brother-in-law visited Israel in 1935 and wanted to settle there. Unfortunately, he could not realize this goal and returned to Poland and was murdered with all the others.

[Page 275]

> **Raukh** Khaim
> His wife: Rokhl Leah and family.

Khaim Raukh was the eldest son in law of Itzik Zingerman. They lived in the same house. He was a chicken dealer, a wholesaler, taking chickens to Łódź. They had a very nice house. He loved to tell witticisms and jokes. He was an observant man and prayed in the synagogue.

> Khaim **Torner**
> His wife: Malka
> Their sons: Shmuel Hersh, Yehoshua

The Torner family was a cultured family. Reb Khaim was a teacher and taught almost all the children in town. His sons Shmuel Hersh and Yehoshua were members of the Needle Union. They were both tailors. They were very cultured people and read a lot. They were well informed in many areas. Their youngest son Arye lives in America.

> **Martshok** Shimon
> His wife: Royza
> Their sons: Yosef, Avrom
> Their daughters: Hinda, Tamar

Shimon Martshok was a village peddler and a fruit seller. He spent half a year in the villages and summers in the orchards where he protected the fruit he bought from the Christians. Most Jews in our town earned their living like this. Hard work but not a lot of money. He was a good, quiet observant man who did not get involved in community affairs. He worried about feeding his family and being able to provide a good education for his children.

[Page 276]

> **Kladovsky** Mordkhai
> His wife: Khaya Soreh
> His son: Moishe Aron
> His daughter: Yokheved

Mordkhai Kladovsky was the son in law of Blema Rokhl Goldman. He took over the bakery of his uncle, Levi Klodavsky. He was one of the founding members of the Public Library. His wife Khaya Soreh was also an active member of the library. They were quiet, observant people. Their children received a traditional and Zionist education.

> **Buks** Zalman – a widower
> His daughters: Mindl,?

Zalman Buks was a village peddler and a widower. When his youngest daughter Mindl was born, his wife died. He devoted himself totally to her and didn't sleep nights in order to be both father and mother to this child. He worked hard, but barely earned a living from this hard work. His daughter Mindl was very cultured and was a member of the Sholem Aleichem Library. His daughter Khava Leah lives in America.

> **Buks** Abba
> His wife: Rokhl and their family

Abba Buks was a village peddler. His wife Rokhl was the daughter of Yosef Vishnivsky. He worked hard day in and day out but barely earned a living. On the Sabbath he arrived at the Psalm Society very early and recited psalms before praying. He was killed in Auschwitz.

[Page 277]

> **Saike** Kapl
> His wife: Rivka
> Their sons: Monish, Yehoshua, Yosef, Khaim.
> Their daughter: Yudis

Kapl Saike lived on the right-hand side of the beginning of Synagogue Street. He was a saddle maker and had a big family. They had a very nice house. He was the gabbai of the synagogue, a member of the Ludovy Bank and, for a short time, was a member of the Board of Directors of the community. He was a happy man. His son Monish was an intelligent man, a good artist. His oil paintings hung on the walls of the synagogue. He was in various camps, including Auschwitz and Yavazne, and died shortly before liberation in Buchenwald.

From left to right: Moishe Toronchik, Itche Danielsky, Monish Saike, Itzik Danielsky, Shmuel Zielinsky, Pinkhas Raukh, Yehushua Saike, Monish Klodavsky

[Page 278]

Zielinsky Moishe
His wife: Soreh
Their son: Yakov

Moishe Zielinsky was Zalman's son. He was a tailor, but not independent. He got work from other tailors who would travel with their goods to fairs. Like most Jews in town, he was an observant and quiet man. He did not get involved in community matters. He worked hard until late at night in order to feed his family. When they rebuilt the Psalm Society building in 1928, he gave a lot of himself and was one of the more important members. He was also a member of the Interest Free Loan Society (Bikur Cholim). His wife Soreh helped to support the family by finishing and sewing merchandise until late at night. They provided their son Yakov with a traditional education, and he was a member of the Shomer Hadati (The Religious Guard) organization.

Naymark Mordkhai
His wife: Ita and their sons
Their daughter: Leah
Her husband: Miller Nokhem

Mordkhai Naymark was a shoemaker by profession. A pious simple Jew. They had four or five daughters. The eldest lived in Vlatslavek. She and her husband Avrom Rayzer were active in the worker's movement. Their second daughter was the wife of Mikhal Danielsky, who lived on Chotcher Street. Another daughter and her husband Nokhem lived together with her parents. Nokhem was an upholsterer by profession but could not earn a living at this in Przedecz, so he worked with his father-in-law as a shoemaker. All the daughters in the Naymark family were fine, intelligent women.

[Page 279]

Frankenshteyn Mordkhai
His wife: Khaya Soreh
Sons: Yakov Yehoshua, Simkha

Mordkhai Frankenshteyn was a saddle maker. He was an observant Jew interested in secular subjects. He was a member of the Psalm Society. He worked hard to earn a living. His entire family was killed in the camps.

Kladovsky Leyb
His wife: Mindl
His daughter: Krasil
His sons: Monish, Naftali, Wolf, Tuvia, Dovid.

Leyb Kladovsky was a tailor with a large family. He would travel to the marketplace with his finished clothing. He educated his children in a traditional Jewish spirit. His youngest son Monish and daughter Krasil were members of the Mizrachi movement and belonged to the youth movement Shomer Hadati. They subscribed to the daily Yiddish newspaper.

> **Saike** Bluma Rokhl – a widow
> Her sons: Abba, Dovid
> Her daughters: Khana, Golda Rivka

Bluma Rokhl Saike was a fruit dealer. She had two sons and two daughters. She was a widow. The whole family worked. Her eldest son was a saddle maker, the second, a tailor, one daughter sewed underwear and one daughter was married. They were intelligent people, well read and very active in the workers' movement.

[Page 280]

> **Zielinsky** Leyb
> His wife: Shifra
> Their son: Moishe
> Their daughter: Kayla

Leyb Zielinsky was the son of Moishe, the saddle maker. He had a wife and two children. He was a hat maker who worked for someone else out of his house. He was not active in any community institutions nor in any political parties as he had no time. He was busy with his hats from dawn until dusk and barely earned a living. He had confidence in his own hands and used them to work hard to earn a living. He did not lose courage. He loved life. He loved Yiddish folk songs. He sat at his sewing machine and sang old folk songs which many of us had already forgotten. Shifra was a good and tidy housewife and saved every penny. Their home served as a workshop. The dining room and bedroom were spotless. No one has remained from this beautiful family.

> **Frankenshteyn** Mashil – a widower
> His son: Avrom
> His daughter: Frayda

Mashil Frankenshteyn was a saddle maker, a widower. His wife died young, and he carried the burden of raising two children on his own. He had to work to earn a living, in addition to being a mother to his children. Nevertheless, he managed to give his children a good Jewish education. He was a quiet man, did not get involved in any matters. He was a member of the Interest Free Loan Society and prayed at the Psalm Society. He was an observant and modest man.

[Page 281]

> **Zielinsky** Hersh
> His wife: Genia
> Their daughter: Soreh
> Their son: Mikhal

Hersh Zielinsky was a rag dealer and, at times, a metal dealer with his stepfather Markovitch. He had a large place near his house where he kept his goods in a warehouse. He was a well-off Jew who prayed in the synagogue. He worked hard to feed his wife and two children.

Zikhlinsky Yakov
His wife: Soreh Yehudis

Yakov Zikhlinsky was a leather merchant. His wife was Soreh Yehudis, the daughter of Yisroel Klar. He was wealthy, elderly, observant, stout, and fat. One night in the 1920s, a few non-Jewish thieves broke into his house and beat him up badly, wounding his head with an iron bar, and robbed him. Miraculously, he survived because he hung on to the bars on the window and shouted for help. The murderers left him and ran away. He lay sick for several weeks. To show his thanks to God for his survival, and to symbolize the seven wounds he had on his head, he donated a seven branched electric chandelier to the synagogue, with his name inscribed on it. It was a beautiful fixture which illuminated the entire synagogue.

[Page 282]

Plotzker Avrom
His wife: Frimet

Avrom Plotzker and his wife Frimet were an elderly couple. They were very observant people. In his later years, he was no longer working and had married off his children. They took great pleasure in their children and grandchildren. His children supported them and provided everything they needed. He made sure to pray with a minyan (quorum) and was among the first to arrive at the House of Study for prayers. He gave out charity, and his wife Frimet knew which were the poorer homes that needed help and gave them as much as she possibly could.

Plotzker Frimet

Plotzker Avrom

[Page 283]

> **Khadetsky** Fyvush
> His wife: Yokheved
> Their son: Yosef

Fyvush Khadetsky and his wife, the daughter of Avrom Potzker, lived on Synagogue Street across from his father-in-law. He was a village peddler. It was a traditional family. He was not a wealthy man. However, they gave their son a fine education. They were quiet, modest people.

> **Kladovsky** Yekhezkel
> His wife: Esther Rokhl

Yekhezkel Kladovsky and his wife Esther Rokhl did not have any children. During the summer months, he rented an orchard, and he dealt with fruit all year long. His wife Esther Rokhl was energetic and was the kneader of the Matzah sweets for Passover. She was active in the society which provided someone to spend the night with a sick person and collected money and clothing which she distributed among the poor, of which there was no shortage in town. She also belonged to the Women's Burial Society. They were observant people loved by everyone.

> **Klar** Avrom Yosef – a widower
> His daughter: Soreh and her family

Avrom Yosef Klar was a widower. His daughter Soreh was a seamstress who earned a living sewing underwear and clothing. In his old age, before the war, Reb Avrom Yosef was supported by his son Eliezer. He was an observant man who spent many hours of the day in the House of Study studying Ein Yakov.

[Page 284]

> **Kazhimirsky** Mendl
> His wife: Frimet
> Daughter: Miriam
> **Kazhimirsky** Meir
> His wife: Brayna
> Their sons: Avrom, Yakov

The two brothers Mendl and Meir Kazhimirsky and their families. They were the sons of Bronkhie Frankenshteyn from her first marriage. They were handsome men, tall, the tallest Jews in town. They worked as small tradesmen in the village. They were not well educated, but they were honest, observant Jews and were always ready to defend Jewish honor against the non-Jews and gained respect for all Jews. They were proud Jews. They were married just before the war.

> **Kladovsky** Yakov Mordkhai
> His wife: Tauba

Yakov Mordkhai Kladovsly and his wife Tauba worked almost exclusively in the orchards. His wife Tauba tried to make some money as a fortune teller. She would read the palms of the women famers or use cards and she "knew" in advance what to say would happen to them and what had already happened with the farmer's family. When she was with one village family, she would ask about all the other inhabitants. This is how she became proficient in all their secrets. She did it all with common sense, as she was a smart woman. This is how some people earned a living in town. During the winter, when the roads were covered in snow and frozen over, she could not go to the village, so she worked as a cook for Jewish celebrations or mended socks and underwear for people.

[Page 285]

> **Vishnivsky** Khana
> Her sons: Dovid, Shmuel Zalman
> Her daughters: Gitl, Roda

Vishnievsky Dovid, Pshedetsky Shmuel Zelig, Hertzberg Moishe, Liek Mordkhai

Khana Vishnivksy was the wife of Zelig, who lives in America. She and her four children were killed in one of the German death camps. Her short life was tragically ended like all other Polish Jews. She was a good mother with a warm heart. She provided her children with a nice Jewish education even though earning a living was not easy. But her children received all that was possible. Her eldest daughter Kayla enrolled in Jewish activities in a camp in Inovartslav. She now lives in America.

> **Iglinsky** Khaya
> a widow

Khaya Iglinsky was an observant woman. She helped the wealthier Jews in town prepare celebrations. She was a very good cook. She was active in the Women's Burial Society and in the society that spent the night with the sick. Although she was a poor woman, she sympathized with those who suffered and helped as much as possible.

[Page 286]

> **Vishnivsky** Khaim Zalman
> His wife: Soreh
> Their son: Meir Hersh
> Their daughter: Dvoyre

Khaim Zalman Vishnivksy with his wife and children. He was a tailor who travelled to fairs. He was a happy man who always liked to say a kind word or tell a joke. He sang beautifully and was a manager of the Psalm Society. He was a supporter of the left-wing Zionist movement. There were always people who loved to sing and have a good time in his house. A lovely Jewish home.

> **Danielsky** Khava
> Her son: Danielsky Mordkhai
> His wife: Miriam
> Their daughters: Gutcha, Itke

Mordkhai Danielsky and his wife Miriam and his mother Khava. He was a village peddler and his wife Miriam helped support the family by sewing underwear. His mother Khava was a fruit dealer all year long and helped her son support the family. His brother Yisroel and his wife's sister Bashe live in Brazil. They were religious people and one of the finest families in town. He prayed in the synagogue and was knowledgeable in politics and was always able to tell everyone the news as he read newspapers and knew what was happening in the country and the world. He provided his children with a religious traditional education.

[Page 287]

> **Iglinsky** Khaim Alter
> His wife: Rekhl
> Children: two

Khaim Alter was the son in law of Khaim Yosef Zielinsky. He had a large table filled with haberdashery at the market. One could buy books, children's toys, sewing tools as well as other articles, all for 35 groschen apiece. He was well read and very intelligent. He was active in the worker's movement. His brother Yisroel lives in Haifa with his family.

> **Iglinsky** Avrom
> His wife: Hadassah
> 4 children

Avrom Iglinsky was the son of Khaya. He lived in Sompolna (15 miles NE of Konin). His business was bringing merchandise from Koło for the Jewish merchants. He had a horse and wagon and was on the road all week, busy with the orders the merchants gave him and large sums of money. He was an honest man and carried out his work with great precision. He was religious and on Saturday, his only day of rest, he was among the first to arrive for prayers at the synagogue. He provided his children with a very good Jewish education and his wife Hadassah was a woman of valor. She went to the merchants to take orders and money to give to her husband Avrom, all done with great accuracy. It was a lovely, honest quiet home.

[Page 288]

> **Vengrovsky** Yehuda
> His wife: Zelda
> Their sons: Rafael, Yitzkhak
> Their daughter: Malka

Zelda Vengrovsky nee Inglinsky and her husband Yehuda

Zelda Vengrovsky, the daughter of the Inglinsky family, married her husband Yehuda and lived in Wloclawek (Vlotslavek in Yiddish). He was a saddle maker. He worked hard to support his family, his wife and three children, nevertheless his children received a good Jewish education. He was a kind-hearted man and was loved by neighbors and friends.

> **Rivnitsky** Shimon
> His wife: Hinda

This family was known as Uncle Shimonye and Auntie Hiniye. Their children were already married, and this old couple bought gifts for their grandchildren. In their later years they were supported by their children. This was a religious home, and they lived a quiet modest life.

[Page 289]

> **Frankenshteyn** Leyb
> His wife: Brayne
> Their son: Mordkhai
> Their daughter: Frayda

Leybye Frankenshteyn and his wife Bronkhia lived in the second half of the building which housed the Psalm Society, together with their two grown children, a son and a daughter. He was a village peddler and his wife sold milk, cheese, and soured milk. She was active in the Women's Burial Society. They were very simple people with a welcoming home. In the evenings young people would gather in their home for a glass of milk or soured milk and discussion.

Mrs. Tauba **Yakhimovitch**
The widow of Reb Meir Leyb
Her Son: Shmuel Hersh. His wife: Soreh. Their son Meir Leyb;
daughter: Khana.
Her Son: Itzik and his wife; their daughter Mikhl; their son: Shloymeh
Her son: Mordkhai; his wife: Frida Bella.

Tauba Yakhimovitch was a religious woman. During the Nazi occupation, she helped those suffering when the official Prayer Houses no longer existed. The synagogue had already been burned down, the House of Study was taken over by the Nazis and turned into a tailor shop. This is when the pious kind Tauba Yakhimovitch risked her life and offered her small home for Jews to come and pray. She lived in poverty, however with the little she had she helped others. Her daughter Mania Himel lives in Israel.

[Page 290]

Fisher Moishe
His wife and two daughters

The Fisher family came to Pshaytsh (Przedecz in Polish) in the 1930s. They lived in Travinsky's house on Ziabe Street, which led to the Yedzhe River. Moishe Fisher was a religious man who dealt with tannery and leather. His wife and son Yakov Ber, who now lives in America, helped him with his work. They lived a quiet comfortable life. His two daughters were well educated children.

Pshedetsky Tzeria
Her sister: Soreh Piezhak

At the end of Synagogue Street in an attic in the home of the Christian Novovkovsky lived two sisters, the blind Tzeria and her widowed sister who earned a living selling fish. Their brother and his family lived in Wloclawek (Vlotslavek in Yiddish). The widow's son was a tailor. He was a kind and intelligent young man who left for Russia in the early 1920s. The two sisters lived a quiet modest life and were not well known in town.

Zumer Khaim
His wife: Guta
Their sons: Nakhman, Avrom

Khaim Zumer was once a wealthy man, a grain dealer. He ran an opulent household with an open door for the poor. He distributed alms and clothing. He was a kindhearted Jew. Unfortunately, he later became impoverished. Having nothing to do, he sat in the neighboring House of Study all day with the other beggars and told stories, thought, and smiled. He had a wife and two intelligent sons.

[Page 291]

Dr. Diament Avrom

Dr. Avrom Diament live in the house of Khaim Zumer. He was a kind and gentle man. He felt as if he had been born in Pshaytsh (Przedecz in Polish). He loved the Jewish population and used all his energy to try to help and heal. He provided culture to a portion of the youth and was a supporter of the left-wing worker's movement. He would often give lectures about medicine and culture in the Public Library. There were many who were interested.

Dr. Diament Avrom

[Page 292]

Skavransky Frimet – a widow
Her son: Yisroel Leyb
Her daughters: Esther Gitl, Ita, Masha

We are returning to Warshavsky Street or, as we Jews called it, the House of Study Street. On the right corner where you head down to the river lived the widow Frimet with her four children, one son and three daughters. She was the widow of the Hasid and great scholar Reb Avrom Hersh Skavransky of blessed memory. He was a teacher in Rabbi Zemelman's Yeshiva and died young. One day between afternoon and evening prayers he fell. They carried him home, but he was already dead. She then opened a food store where she barely earned a living. She had a very gifted son, Yisroel Leyb. Her daughter Esther Gitl was a seamstress and helped support the family. This was a very religious household which lived a difficult life.

Zielinsky Zalman
His wife: Pola
Their sons: Avrom, Dovid, Yosef, Ruven

Zalman Zielinsky and his wife Pola and four sons. This was one of the hardest working families in town. Whatever job he took, it did not work out. He worked hard until late at night and lived within limits. Zalman was a tailor, tried to do business in the villages, rented orchards. The last years before the war he worked as a carrier for the grain dealer Yehoshua Zikhlinsky. He would often be seen sitting on the steps of Leyzer Zikhlinsky's house waiting for work, together with the Christian carriers. This is a characteristic description of a small Jewish town in Poland.

No one remained from this fine Jewish family.

[Page 293]

Zikhlinsky Yosef
His wife: Shayna
Their sons: Yakov, Yehuda, Khaim

Yosef Zikhlinsky ran a hat making shop and had an assistant. He sold his goods at the market. He was a religious and knowledgeable man. He would often be seen sitting on the high steps of his house reading a newspaper. It was a nice welcoming house. His children were educated in a Jewish national spirit. His wife Shayna was the daughter of Yeshaye Zikhlinsky and was an intelligent well-read woman. She was good hearted and was an active volunteer in Jewish institutions. Their home was open to the poor. Their daughter Golda, today Grabinsky, lives in Israel.

Khodetsky Leyb
His wife: Soreh Ratza
Son: Mordkhai
Daughter: Esther

Leyb Khodetsky lived in the same house. He was a village peddler and a knowledgeable man. He sat on the board of the Public Library and was a member of the drama club. In the 1920s, when the Pioneer movement was founded, they created a training camp for pioneers in the garden of Khaim Zumer. He was one of the initiators of working the soil and planting. While in the Nazi camp in Inowrolaw (Inavratslov in Yiddish) he worked very hard on the trains and was killed between two train cars, that crushed him. His wife Soreh Ratza was also active in the library. She was murdered with her two children in Chełmno.

[Page 294]

> **Prakhovsky** Avrom Elye
> His wife: Dvoyre
> Their daughters: Gutcha, Motil

Avrom Elye Prokhovsky ran a tailor shop and hired a few workers. He sold their sewn goods in the market. He was a successful man but unfortunately his household received some knocks. His wife Dvoyre died suddenly of a heart attack, and shortly thereafter his youngest daughter Motil died. He was involved in community affairs. He was also a member of the synagogue council. If you needed a permit to slaughter a chicken in the nearby slaughterhouse you had to buy it from him. He was also the manager of the synagogue for a short time.

> **Chanskovsky** Avrom
> His wife: Rokhl
> Their sons: Binyumin, Shloyme, Moishe.
> Their daughters: Tobchiya, Khaya

The Chanstkovsky family. The head of the family, Avrom, died in 1932.

His widow remained with three sons and two daughters. Each of them was active in something different. Each according to his own interests. Binyumin and Shloyme were involved in the needle union. Moishe was a member of the Young Mizrachi movement and active in the Jewish National Fund and was preparing to move to the Land of Israel. He attended a pioneer training camp but never realized his dream. Their daughter Khaya was active in Betar. The whole family was intelligent and knowledgeable.

[Page 295]

> The **Levin** Family
> Father: Sholem
> Mother: Yokheved
> Son: Gavriel Wolf
> Daughter: Shayna Feyge
> Son: Moishe Yekhiel
> Daughter: Esther
> Their son in law: Yekhiel Meir Hayman.
> His wife: Frayda Liba nee Levin
> Their daughter: Hinda Shayna

Looking at one family in a small Jewish Polish town, one was sure they lived without any worries. The whole family had work. The father was an important Jew, learned, gave lessons in how to read and write in the following languages: Yiddish, Polish, German and Russian. He taught people how to write letters and foreign and local addresses for those who could not do it themselves. He taught young boys the depths of Jewish wisdom. He worked as a glazer; his wife helped him. His eldest daughter was a seamstress. She had a lot of work. The eldest son sold haberdashery at the market. The younger son was a tailor. The second and third daughters worked with the eldest as seamstresses. The youngest son worked with his parents as a glazer. They were all working, but there was little income as work was paid less than the standard of living and was not stable. This

Jew was knowledgeable in Yiddish and foreign classic literature. He loved geography. He knew a lot; however, he was not a great earner. He died at the end of 1931. The eldest married daughter lived in Koło. All three sons and the youngest daughter were active in the left wing, illegal worker's movement. From the whole family, the only one who survived was the youngest son Yitzkhak, who lives in Israel.

[Page 296]

Perlmuter Yehuda
His wife: Khaya
Their daughters: Gutcha, Trayna
His brother: Eliyahu

The Family of Yehuda Perlmuter

Yehuda Perlmuter was a merchant who sold sewing equipment and later had a food store. A few years before the war, he went to live in Kłodawa. His son Eliezer came to the Land of Israel in 1934. He got married and lived in Jerusalem. He was in the Jewish Brigade of the British Army, and, during the War of Independence, he accompanied transports of food from Tel Aviv to Jerusalem and was killed on the road by an Arab attack on the transport. His widow and children live in Jerusalem. Yehuda Perlmuter was a respectable Jew, sat on the synagogue council, and for a short time was manager of the House of Study. He gave charity and his house was always open for those in need.

[Page 297]

Ash Leybush Yosef
His wife: Bina

Leybush Yosef Ash and his wife had a store where they sold glass and kitchen wares. He was a passionate Zionist, a talker, and an activist. He was active in the Mizrachi movement and in the blue and white Jewish National Fund. He was a well-dressed man with an aesthetic appearance. The youth movements "Young Mizrachi" and "The Religious Guard" looked to him for leadership and advice. His wife Bina helped him in these interests.

Frank Mirl

Mirl Frank was a single woman in her twenties. She had a school that most of the children from town attended. She was a good teacher. She died in the 1920s, then two families of relatives moved into her house, the Ashs and the Chanstovskys.

Pshedetsky Miriam Leah

Miriam Leah Pshedetzky was a single woman who did business in the villages with a bit of haberdashery and brought village products back to town to sell. She was a quiet, religious poor woman.

[Page 298]

Bilavsky Mendl Wolf
His wife: Hene Soreh
Their daughters: Brayna, Baltzia
Their son: Leybl

Hene Soreh Bilavsky
Bluma Ratza Bilavsky

The Bilavsky Brothers
Lipman Bilavsky
Mendl Wolf Bilavsky

Mendl Wolf Bilavsky was a baker. He was an honest man and a passionate supporter of the Mizrachi movement. He served as manager of the House of Study for many years and was a board member of the bank. He gave charity and interest free loans. His wife Hene Soreh helped him a lot in his philanthropic activities. He provided his children with a religious national education. Their son was active in the Young Mizrachi movement and their daughter Brayna was a member of Betar. Mendl Wolf Bilavsky, his wife Hene Soreh, their daughters Brayna and Baltzia, and their son Leybl were killed by the Nazis in the Kazimierz Forest.

Their son Moishe and his wife Liba moved to the Land of Israel in 1933. Their son Yosef Khaim was saved from Hitler's hell and came to the Land of Israel in 1949.

[Page 299]

> **Bilavsky** Pinkhas Aron
> His wife: Tzipora
> His daughter: Frayda Rokhl
> His sons: Ber, Moishe Hersh

Pinkhas Aron Bilavsky was a baker and lived on German Street behind City Hall. In 1928 the family moved to Sompolna and opened a large bakery. This was a fine family with a welcoming home. They were one of the most respected families in town. Pinkhas Aron was active in community institutions, especially education. His wife Tzipora came from Bordovi and was a beautiful and intelligent woman. Their children received a traditional national education. Pinkhas Aron Bilavsky, his wife

Tzipora, their eldest daughter Frayda Rokhl who got married right before the war, their two sons Ber and Moishe Hersh were all murdered by the Nazis.

Their eldest son Avrom Simkha survived the horrible war years in German camps and came to the Land of Israel at the end of 1949.

Mendl Wolf Bilavsky
His son: Leybl His daughter: Baltzia Bilavsky, Pinkhas Aron, His son: Muniek.

[Page 300]

Bilavsky Lipman
His daughter: Soreh Yudis and her family

Reb Lipman Bilavsky was one of the oldest householders in town. He was a tailor, a religious Jew. In the early 1930s he moved to Sompolna where his daughter Khana Bialaglovsky lived with her family. Reb Lipman had 2 sons and 3 married daughters and grandchildren. Two grandchildren survived and are living in America.

Danielsky Mania – a widow
Her sons: Levi, Itche

Mania Danielsky, a widow, ran a large shoemaker shop. This was a wealthy fine family with an open door to those in need. She would give charity and interest free loans on a daily basis. Her son and daughter were well informed people. They were all Zionists. Her three sons Moishe Hersh, Mordkhai Wolf and Zalman live in America.

Tapinsky Peysakh
His wife: Soreh
Their daughter: Khaya

Peysakh Tapinsky and his wife Soreh who was the daughter of Mania Danielsky and the sister of Moishe Hersh, Zalman and Mordkhai Wolf who live in America. He was a leather merchant and had a good Jewish heart. He did a lot for the poor and needy. His door was open for all who suffered. His wife Soreh was also known for her good heartedness. Their daughter Khaya received a traditional education.

[Page 301]

Rivinsky – a widower
and his family.

Nokhem Rivinsky was a well-dressed man with a small black beard. He prayed regularly at the House of Study. Between afternoon and evening prayers he liked to discuss the news of the day with others. He was a smart, well-informed man, but very religious. Occasionally he liked to pray at the cantor's pulpit.

Danielsky Yakov
His wife: Brayna and family

Yakov Danielsky was a shoemaker. He was the son of Mikhal Danielsky and the son in law of Nokhem Rivinsky. He had a workshop and sold his goods and the market. He was a religious Jew who prayed in the synagogue. He gave charity and supported charitable institutions. He was a quiet and nice person. His wife Brayna was also nice with a kind Jewish heart.

Danielsky Levi
Levi

Levi Danielsky was the son of Mikhal Danielsky. He was a partner with his brother Yakov in the shoemaker workshop. Like his brother, he too was a religious, knowledgeable man. He also prayed in the synagogue, gave charity, and welcomed guests. He was a supporter of the worker's movement and supported its activities.

[Page 302]

Zikhlinsky Shimshon
His wife: …
Two children

Shimshon Zikhlinsky was a boot stitcher. He was a passionate Zionist and supported the Mizrachi movement. He was one of the founders of the Public Library. He, his wife and two children whose names we unfortunately do not remember were murdered in Chełmno .

> **Kladovsky** Kayla – a widow
> Her son: Avrom
> His wife: and children

Kayla Kladovsky dealt in used clothes and helped her son in his leather and hide business. She was active in community affairs. She knew every household in town and knew what they needed. Despite her limited means, she helped others as much as she could. Her son was a quiet, nice person.

> **Kladovsky** Hersh Leyb
> His wife: Leah
> His children: …

Hersh Leyb, Kayla's second son, also lived here. He was a hat maker. He was by nature a happy person. He was a traditional Jew and the son in law of Leyb Kladovsky. He was a member of the Public Library and the drama club at the library. It was always joyful in their home. They often sang Yiddish folk songs.

[Page 303]

> **Zielinsky** Eliyahu
> His wife: Rekhil
> His son: Shmuel
> His daughter: Frayda

Eliyahu Zielinsky was a tailor who took his goods to sell at the market. He was a religious Jew who prayed in the Psalm Society and was among those who helped rebuild it. He was a community activist and for a time sat on the Jewish community council. He ran a respectful household, and his children received a fine education. They were good, knowledgeable people, active in the Public Library and the drama club. In the 1920s he tried his luck and moved to Brazil to improve his financial situation. Unfortunately, things did not work out and he returned and rebuilt his former tailor workshop.

> **Pardansky** Hersh
> His wife: Esther
> Their sons: Arye Leyb, Yakov
> Their daughters: Mala, Dvoyre, Soreh.

Hersh Pardansky was learned, religious, well informed, and well read. He had a nice aesthetic appearance. During the period that there was a small Ger Hasidic congregation in town, he would go there to pray. In the 1920s, he had a large haberdashery store where the whole family worked. He ran a respectable house and gave charity. His wife Esther was also known to be supportive of the needy. Unfortunately, due to high taxes, he had to liquidate his business and lived off what his children earned from their work. His children had received a good education. They were all well informed and intelligent people. His youngest son, Yakov, was active in Religious Guard movement.

[Page 304]

Zielinsky Ruven
His wife: Tzipora
Their son: Isar
Their daughter: Khana

Ruven Zielinsky was the son of Elye Zielinsky of blessed memory. His wife Tzipora was the daughter of Isar Morgnshtern of blessed memory. They were working people. He was a tailor and active in the cultural life in town. They were members of the Worker's Movement. A few years before the war they moved to Łódź.

Ruven Zielinsky and his wife: Tzipora nee Morgnshtern

[Page 305]

Rokhl **Morgnshtern** – a widow
Her sons: Shloime, Shaul, Arye, Ziskind.
Her daughters: Pola, Hinda Lutka.

Shloime Morgnshtern

Rokhl Morgnshtern lived on the corner of the marketplace at German Street and City Hall with her small children. This is where she had her grocery store. She was the widow of Reb Isar Morgnshtern of blessed memory who died in his in 20s on the day of Yom Kippur. She was left with small children. She worked hard to support her family and raise her children. She was a very kind woman, observant and donated to the needy. She educated her children in a national religious spirit. Her son Yisakhar survived the difficult Hitleristic hell with its forced labor camps. He was the only member of the family to survive. He lives in America.

[Page 306]

Vishnivsky Simkha
His wife: Tzeria
Their daughters: Yetta, Malka, Kayla

Tzeria Vishnivsky, Simkha's wife.

Simkha Vishnivsky was a tailor. He was one of the Vishnivsky brothers who were all good singers and were choir boys with the old cantor Reb Shabtai Kutek of blessed memory. Later they sang with the ritual slaughterer Reb Shmuel Yamnik of blessed memory, whose choir they helped with their beautiful voices during the High Holidays and other holidays in the synagogue. Simkha was a religious Jew, well informed and well read. He was by nature a very happy man and loved to give nice little speeches. In the 1930s he moved to Sompolna where he had another tailor shop. Together with all the other Jews in Sompolna, he was sent to the camps in Poznań and died there. His wife Tzeria helped him support the family by sewing and purchasing yarn and buttons. She and their children were also killed by the Nazi murderers.

[Page 307]

Yosef **Rozenberg**
His wife: Leah Danielsky
His sister: …
Nokhem Danielsky
His wife: … and his family

The two Danielsky sisters lived in one house. One of the sisters married. Her husband Yosef Rozenberg had a shoemaker shop. They raised Nokhem Danielsky the son of Mikhal Danielsky. Nokhem was orphaned when his mother died and these two sisters raised him. When he got married, he moved to Sompolna. Nokhem was an intelligent and well-read man. He was active in the left-wing worker's movement. He was a tailor by profession. He was one of the organizers of Yiddish lessons to read and write in the needle union. He also gave lectures on the history of the labor movement.

Perle Mordkhai Yehoshua
His wife: Khana
Their sons: Pinkhas, Meir

Mordkhai Yehoshua Perle was a widower. He was educated in Rabbi Zemelman's yeshiva. He was a great scholar and a wonderful explainer. He was always well dressed and read passages with his students from the highest levels of holy books. His attitude toward his students was more like a father than a teacher. Everyone in town respected him. It was an honor to be his student. Before the war he moved to Kalisz and taught students at the Yeshiva of Reb Zalman Yankilevitch of blessed memory. Rabbi Yankilevitch moved to the Land of Israel and became a member of the Knesset (Parliament) under the name Ben –Yakov in the Agudah Yisrael party.

The two sons of Reb Mordkhai Yehoshua Perle studied in the Yeshiva and were known to have sharp minds.

[Page 308]

> **Borenshteyn** Tuvia
> His wife: Malka
> Their sons: Yakov, Zelig, Hersh, Yitzkhak.
> Their daughter: Tauba

Tuvia Borenshteyn sold used goods, rags, iron, copper, brass among other things. He went to the villages and traded his used goods for plates, glasses and toys or money. He worked very hard to feed his large family. He was religious, like the majority of the Jews in town. It was a lovely warm home. Three of his children, Yitzkhak, Yakov and his daughter Tauba, were active in the needle union. When his children grew up, they helped support the family and their financial situation improved. One sun Yosef survived and lived in Pshaytsh (Przedecz in Polish) until the 1960s, and then wandered away.

> **Rusak** Moishe Aron
> His wife: Rokhl
> His daughters: Soreh Yudis, Esther, Royza.
> His son: Kasriel

Moishe Aron Rusak was the secretary of the Jewish community. He was a well-dressed Jew and a passionate Zionist. He was active in Mizrachi and was a good speaker. He was well informed and well read. This is how he raised his children as well. His son Wolf was a member and one of the founders of "Young Mizrachi". He attended a pioneer training camp and, in 1934, moved to the Land of Israel. They made him a goodbye party at the hall of the fire station. Reb Moishe Aron was hopeful that he and his family would have the honor of settling in the Land of Israel too. Unfortunately, they did not live to see this. Once in the Land of Israel, Wolf volunteered in the Jewish Brigade and, together with the English, fought on the Italian front. He fell in battle. Their daughter Tzesha has been living in Israel since 1935 and his son Yisroel of blessed memory lived out the war in Russia under very difficult conditions. He later came to Israel and died there.

[Page 309]

> **Haltrikht** Gershon Leyzer
> His wife: Luba
> His sons: Itzik Mordkhai, Yerakhmiel Noyakh
> His daughters: Yente Gitl, Soreh Nikha, Khana Kayla

Gershon Leyzer Haltrikht

Now we will describe the Jews who lived on Klinski Street. This is where Gershon Leyzer Haltrikht, the hat maker, lived with his wife and five children. In the 1920's he was the master craftsman in town. He was authorized to hand out master and journeymen letters after a professional exam for tailors, hat makers and shoemakers. Part of the money he received for distributing the above-mentioned letters (diplomas) was spent rebuilding the Psalm Society as well as creating a free loan society for the many artisans. Gershon Leyzer was a traditional Jew and quietly supported the worker's movement. He loved to read newspapers when the children were growing up. This is what it was like in his house as it was with most Jews in town. Three of his children worked with him at his trade, nevertheless they had financial worries. More than once, they had to ask themselves where they would find the money to buy what was needed for the Sabbath. The eldest daughter Soreh Nikha was an active member of the Sholem Aleichem Library. Yente Gitl and Yitzkhak Mordkhai belonged to the Shomer Hatzair movement. Unfortunately, no one from this family survived.

[Page 310]

> **Raukh** Yehuda Leyb
> His wife: Rayza
> His son: Itzik

Yehuda Leyb Raukh was a chicken dealer. He and his wife were both intelligent and religious. He gave his son a traditional education. He was the son of Avrom Raukh of blessed memory. He was a quiet man who did not get involved in community affairs. He ran a large business, sending chickens to Łódź and other cities. He had his own horse and wagon. In his younger years, he was a member of the Public Library.

> The **Kladovsky** Family
> His wife and two children

The Kladovsky family lived next door. He was a custom tailor and the son in law of Avrom Raukh, a respected family. They did not get involved in community affairs and that is why we do not remember their names.

[Page 311]

> **Raukh** Efraim
> His wife: Ruzha

His brother Efraim Raukh was his partner in the chicken business. He was also a traditional Jew. We do not remember the names of his children. There were seven brothers and two sisters in the family. Six brothers and one sister lived in Pshaytsh (Przedecz in Polish). One brother, Yakov Raukh, lived in Koło and had a large wholesale food business. Unfortunately, no one from the family survived.

> **Marchak** Khava – a widow and
> her family.

Khava Marchak was a widow with three children. Her husband died in the 1920s. After he died, she opened a food store on the corner of Kłodawa Street, which she took over from her father-in-law Moishe Marchak. As a single mother with small children, she could not run the business. She gave it over to someone else and moved with her children to Wloclawek (Vlatslovek

in Yiddish) in the 1930s. She was the sister of Reb Yehuda Perlmuter of blessed memory.

> **Shmuel** Khaym
> His wife: Khaya and his family

Khaym, Shmuel, his wife Khaya and their children lived in the same house as Khava Marchak. He was the son in law of Reb Kalman Rapaport. He took over the food store from Khava Marchak. He was a well-dressed young man and a Ger Hasid. He came from Leczyca (Lintshits). He spent his spare time in the House of Study learning. He and his wife gave charity and welcomed guests.

[Page 312]

> **Danielsky** Gershon
> His wife: …
> His sons: Tuvia, Itzik, Ezriel, Mordkhai
> Leyb
> His daughter: Leah

Gershon Danielsky with his wife and children were the only Jews who lived on the long Kłodawa Street. He was the only Jew in town who worked the land. He also had a food store and a passenger car which he used to drive people to Łódź. This was a fine, respectable family. He was a religious Jew and they all worked hard. He was financially well situated. One son and his daughter lived in England.

> **Danielsky** Moishe
> His wife: …
> His daughter: Taubche

Moishe Danielsky was a chicken dealer. He was a religious nationalist Jew, a great supporter of the Jewish National Fund. He was a quiet man, knowledgeable and well read. He ran a lovely traditional home. They gave their only daughter Taubche a good traditional Jewish education. She was a member of the Young Mizrachi organization and was an intelligent young woman.

> **Zikhlinsky** Gutman – a widower

Gutman Zikhlinsky was an old religious Jew. His neighbor was Yakov Danielsky, and there was hardly any difference between these two men. Gutman also sat in the House of Study and read Ein Yakov. He did not work. He was supported by his son Shimshon.

[Page 313]

> **Zikhlinsky** Ezra
> His wife: Bluma
> Their sons: Aron Sender, Yosef
> Their daughters: Malka, Bayla

We now arrive at the street which led to the villages Orkusheve, Dzivie and the town of Dombrovitz. Ezra Zikhlinsky lived on this street with his wife Bluma and their beautiful, large family. He had a horse and wagon and dealt in village products. He was a religious respectable Jew. He had his own house and a piece of land where he grew vegetables and fodder. The whole family were productive people. Two sons were tailors, and one son was a carpenter. One son was a hairdresser. The girls sewed underwear at home and the youngest son was still at school. With all this and with great effort they barely earned a living. In order to improve their financial situation, they rented their house and moved to Łódź where the situation had somewhat improved. They were quiet calm working people and lived according to Jewish tradition. From this family, three sons survived. Hersh and Khaym live in Israel and Fishl lives in America.

> **Danielsky** Yakov
> His wife: Shurka

Yakov Danielsky and his wife Shurka lived a few houses down. He was an old religious Jew. He would often sit in the House of Study and read Ein Yakov. He did nothing to earn a living. He was supported by his children. He loved to tell stories of his past experiences and tell witticisms. He was loved by the younger generation who loved listening to his stories.

[Page 314]

> **Marchak** Yehoshua
> His wife: Berta His son: Yakov Ber
> Daughter: …

We now arrive at the house where Yehoshua Marchak lived with his wife Berta and their children. He was a well to do grain merchant. He lived in a fenced in house without neighbors. He gave charity and was a quiet, religious man. His wife Berta was an intelligent, religious woman and their children were raised in this spirit. No one from this family survived.

> **Topolsky** Yekhiel
> His wife: Nekha and their children

Yekhiel Topolsky lived in the same house as did his brother Moishe Topolsky and his family. He was a tanner. He lived in the Land of Israel for a few years but returned. He was a supporter of the Mizrachi movement. He had a wife and children. This fine quiet family was killed in Chełmno .

> **Ekert** Efraim
> His wife: Gitl
> Daughters: Bayla, Mindl
> Son: …

Efraim Ekert, a tailor, and his wife and children lived in the same house. He worked hard to earn a living and travelled to fairs to sell his sewn goods. Efraim was a member of the Psalm Society. This was a quiet, modest religious family.

[Page 315]

> **Topolsky** Moishe
> His wife: Miriam Leah
> Their sons: Yosef, Yitzkhak, Hersh
> His daughters: Khana, Ruzhe
> His married daughter: Graydans Khava.
> Her husband: Eliezer and 3 children

Topolsky Ruzhe, Bilavsky Brayne

Khava Graydans nee Topolsky

Moishe Topolsky and his large family lived in the same house. He was a businessman well respected in town. He was a member of the board of the Jewish community – a councilman. He was a member of the board of the bank and was head of the Interest Free Loan Society. He was a tanner, turning raw material into leather. His son Yosef was one the founders of the Public Library. He was an intelligent and knowledgeable young man. His son Hersh was one of the rebels in the extermination camp Auschwitz – Birkenau where he was active with others in an attempt to blow up the crematorium. He died there. He was an active member in Young Mizrachi. His son Yitzkhak and daughter Ruzhe were members of Betar. His daughter Khava married and moved to Inyeve. The eldest son Yakov survived the camps and lives with his wife in America.

[Page 316]

> **Topolsky** Fishl
> His wife: Genendl
> His daughter: Luba and three more children

Fishl Topolsky, Moishe Topolsky's son, lived on the next street over. He was a boot stitcher by profession. His wife Genendl was the daughter of Yeshaya Zielinsky. Fishl was a founder and chairman of the Labor Zionists. He was an intelligent and well-informed young man. His wife was a member of the Public Library. They too found the same fate as all other Jews form Pshaytsh (Przedecz in Polish) and were killed in Chełmno together with their small children.

Topolsky Fishl and his wife Genendl nee Zielinsky

[Page 317]

Sokhachevsky Gavriel
His wife: Esther
Their son: Feyvish, his family and two more daughters

Feyvish Sokhachevsky had a food store together with his father Gavriel. His two sisters sewed underwear. Gavriel, his father was a religious man. Even though he lived far away from the House of Study, he would go there every day to pray, arriving among the first. His son Feyvish was also a religious young man and a supporter of the Mizrachi movement. This was an honorable quiet family. There were also two sisters, but unfortunately, we don't have exact details about them. No one survived from this family.

Fisher Mendl
His wife: Zelda
His son: Yeshaya Hersh and his family.

Mendl, the son of Avrom Fisher and his wife Zelda, the daughter of Reb Mordkhai Binyumin Davidovitch. was a boot stitcher by profession. His wife Zelda was a hat decorator and had a women's hat store. Mendl was a Torah scholar and studied for years with Rabbi Zemelman. He was a quiet and modest young man. He did not get involved in community affairs and worked hard to earn a living for his family.

Rozen Yakov Wolf
His wife: Reyzl
Their daughters: Bina, Sala

Yakov Wolf Rozen had a food store. He was a supporter of the Mizrachi movement. He was a quiet, modest man. He did not get involved in community affairs. His wife and children helped out in his store. He was one of the most active founders of the Public Library. They gave their children a religious Zionist education.

[Page 318]

Yamnik Shmuel – ritual slaughterer
His wife: Soreh Rokhl
His daughter: Royza Leah

The ritual slaughterer Reb Shmuel Yamnik lived in his own house with his wife Soreh Leah and their daughter Ruzhe. He was a kindhearted Jew. He was learned and educated in many fields. He was a ritual slaughterer and performed circumcisions in Pshaytsh (Przedecz in Polish) for more than 40 years. His daughter Ruzhe died young in 1937. His two sons Ruven and Yehoshua live in Israel and one son Leybush lives in Brazil.

Yamnil Sholem
His wife: Malka
4 children.

The second son of Reb Shmuel Yamnik – Sholem - lived in Łódź with his wife Malka and four children. He was sent to a camp in Poznań and was killed there. His wife and children were also killed by the Nazis. When there was an action in Łódź, his four sons died a martyr's death.

Mandlboym Yisroel
His wife: Khaya Dvoyre nee Yamnik
Their son: Ruven

The daughter of Shmuel Yamnik married Yisroel Mandlboym from Vengrov. They had a haberdashery store. They had a son Ruven. They were killed in a Nazi camp after they spent a long time in the Mezrich ghetto.

[Page 319]

Yamnik Yakov Yitzkhak
His wife: Leah
Their son: Yehuda Hersh
Their daughter: Ruzha

Yamnik Yakov Yitzkhak and his wife Leah

Their son: Yehuda Hersh

His son Yakov Yitzkhak Yamnik lived in Lubin – a hat maker and active in communal affairs. He was a member of the community board of directors, he was a councilman. He and his wife Leah and their two children, their daughter Ruzhe and son Yehuda Hersh, were killed in Treblinka where they were sent from the Warsaw ghetto.

[Page 320]

> **Goldman** Yekhil Yosef
> His wife: Soreh
> His son: Mikhal Hersh
> His daughter: Itka

Now we come to a house which was inhabited only by Jews. The first to live here was Reb Yekhil Yosef Goldman with his wife Soreh and family. He was a baker. He had his bakery in the yard. He also made ice cream. For this purpose, he had a big hole with ice beside the bakery, filled in the winter months. His son Mikhal Hersh who helped him with his work was a member in the Mizrachi movement. He was killed serving in the Polish army when the war broke out in 1939. His daughter Yeske was killed in the camps. His son Fishl and daughter Balche live in Israel.

> **Yamnik** Shulamis nee Fridman
> Her daughter: Bayla Tziporah
> Her son: Khaim Yehuda
> They were murdered in Chełmno with all the
> martyrs from the city of Sompolna. On the
> 16th of Shevat, 5710.
> February 3rd, 1942

> **Bilavsky** Blema Ratza

In the same house right across lived a single woman Blema Ratze, a widow who performed a variety of good deeds helping families and single people.

[Page 321]

[Ed. Note: At some point the authors seem to progress from one house to the neighboring house, from one block to the next block.]

> **Danielsky** Esther Rokhl
> Her son: Shimon Leyb
> Her daughters: Krusa, Yetke, Gitl

Mrs. Esther Rokhl Dielsky now lived in a shop in the same house where Reb Berish Menkhe of blessed memory had once lived. She was a widow with four children, one son and three daughters. Her son Shimon Leyb was a shoemaker and was the breadwinner of the family. Her daughters also helped out as much as possible. This was a quiet, modest family, observant people who worked hard to feed themselves.

> **Radzievsky** Leah – a widow
> **Radzievsky** Yekhiel Yakov
> His wife: …
> and family.

In the dwelling that led out to the courtyard, from the same house had lived the widow Leah Radzievsky who cooked lunches and other meals there and rented out beds for Jewish travelers. Her stepson Yekhiel Radzievsky was a teacher and lived in Dombia near Koło.

> **Torner** Menashe
> His wife: Gitl
> His daughter: Dora and another daughter.

Menashe Torner was the son of Reb Khaim Torner. His wife was Gitl, and they had two daughters. He was a custom tailor, a quiet, honorable man, a hard worker, supported his father with all that was possible and did favors for the needy.

[Page 322]

> Rabbi **Drakhman** Moishe, Rabbi in
> Dombrovitz, son-in-law of Reb
> Berish **Menkhe** of blessed memory.
> His wife and family.

Rabbi Moishe Drakhman was from Lubin, a town near Włocławek (Vlotslavek in Yiddish). He was the son-in-law of Berish Menkhe of blessed memory who brought him to live with him and his only daughter. He was a great scholar. He taught the older Yeshiva boys for many years in Przedecz and was later hired as Rabbi in the nearby town of Dombrovitz. No one survived from this family.

> **Pozner** Mordkhai
> His wife: Miriam
> His son: Mikhal Hersh
> His daughter: Itka
> His brother: Elye

On the floor of the same house lived Mordkhe Poyzner with his wife and children. Beside the house he had a food store, together with his mother and his brother Elye. Mordkhe Poyzner was a quiet man. He was not involved in community affairs. In his youth he was one of the first Zionists in town. He was one of the founders of the Public Library and an active member.

> **Raukh** Mordkhe
> His wife: Khava
> His son: Moniek
> His daughter: Manya

Mordkhe Raukh with his wife Khava and two children, his son Moniek and his daughter Manya. He was an employee of the partners in the grain business Notte **Vasertzug** and Yitzkhak **Mokatov**. He was a supporter of the Mizrachi movement. His home was traditional, and he educated his children in this spirit.

[Page 323]

> **Romer** Pinkhas
> His wife: Tzipora
> His son: Meir and family
> His daughter: Sale and family

Romer Sale and her daughter

Romer Meir with his wife and daughter

In the second house lived Pinkhas Romer. He used to have a manufacturing business. Like the majority of Jews in town, he was also a religious person. In his younger years, he was active in the Zionist movement. His son Meir was the only young man to complete public high school. He was an intelligent and well-informed man. While in the Polish army, he was preparing to become an officer and, for a short time, served as a factory officer. After he married, he left for the estates where he was a teacher in a public school. Pinkhas Romer's daughter Sale was an intelligent woman.

[Page 324]

Rozen Binyumin
His wife: Gusta
His son: Avrom and family

Mrs. Rozen Gusta,
Her granddaughter: Brinka Mokotov
Her great granddaughter: Galila Zukerman,
the daughter of Bluma Mokotov

Binyumin Rozen

Binyumin Rozen and his wife Gusta had a grocery store. He was a passionate Zionist, one of the first to be active in Mizrachi. Already in the 1920s, he was preparing to move to the Land of Israel to realize his life's goal. However, he got sick and died during an operation in the hospital. His wife went to live with their daughter Ruzha Mokotov. His son Avrom took over his father's business. He was also a Zionist and an active member in Mizrachi. After he married, he moved to Kłodawa.

[Page 325]

Goldman Yakov Meir
His wife: Yekhle
His daughter: Khava
He died in 1940 at age 82 and was the last to
be buried in the local cemetery.

Reb Yakov Meir Goldman was a rich man, a scholar and a very well respected, imposing figure in town. He was tall, with a nice white beard. He was a member of the board of directors of the Ludovy Bank, an influential person. He had an iron business in the house which he later gave to his son-in-law, Mendl Kviat, and his daughter Dora. He was a personality. He would often pray at the pulpit on the High Holidays. He would go for morning prayers to the House of Study and often be the one to lead the first Selichos service. On Simchat Torah, after prayers, he would make a large reception for everyone who came to pray in the House of Study. He died in 1940 during the war and was the last Jew to be buried in the cemetery. He had three married sons who lived outside of Przedecz. They were Mendl, who lived in Brisk Koyavsky with his wife and family, his son Elazar, who lived with his family in Łódź, and his son Wolf who lived with his family in Kłodawa.

Reb Yakov Meir Goldman and family at the Bar Mitzvah celebration of his grandson

[Page 326]

Khava Pretzol née Goldman and her husband

> **Mokotov** Yitzkhak
> His daughter: Bronka
> His daughter: Bluma
> Her husband: **Zukerman** Henyiek
> Their daughter: Glila

Yitzkhak Mokotov, his wife Ruzha, and their family lived in the same courtyard. He was a rich Jew, a grain dealer with his partner Reb Notte **Vasertzug** of blessed memory. Their door was always open for poor people and those in need. He would host a large reception after prayers on Simchas Torah. This was one of the finest families in town. In 1935, he and his family, together with his partner Notte Vassertzug and his wife Esther, moved to the Land of Israel as capitalists and later returned to Poland to cash in debts from Polish landowners and others. Yitzkhak Mokotov, his daughter Bluma, her husband Henyiek and their child, as well as his daughter Bronka remained and were killed by the Nazi murderers. His wife Ruzhe and their son Moishe and his family live in Israel.

[Page 327]

> **Klar** Yisroel – a widower
> His daughter: Malka
> **Haber** Yisroel – his son-in-law
> His wife: Krusa
> Daughters: Mirl, Yekhle
> Her Daughter: **Yakhimovitch** Rokhl
> Her Daughters: Yadzia, Mala

Haber Krusa née Klar

In the second part of this house lived Yisroel Klar, a widower. He owned a haberdashery business and lived with his daughters. His daughter Malka left for Russia in 1939, and we never heard from her again. His daughter Krusa also lived there with her husband Yisroel Haber, a custom tailor, and their two daughters. Reb Yisroel Klar was an observant Jew. He was among the first to arrive for prayers at the House of Study. After prayers, he would remain to read Ein Yakov. His two daughters Krusa and Malka were intelligent women, members of the Public Library, and they ran the haberdashery business. Yisroel Haber was a good custom tailor, an intelligent and quiet man. He was a supporter of the worker's movement.

[Page 328]

Rokhl, the eldest daughter of Yisroel Klar, lived on the same floor with her husband and their two daughters Yadzia and Mala. They had a shoe business. No one from this family survived.

> **Kviat** Mendl
> His wife: Dora
> Their son: Yitzkhak
> Their daughter: Ella

Mendl Kviat was the son-in-law of Reb Yakov Meir Goldman. His wife Dora and two children. He took over the iron business from his father-in-law. He was a modern Hasidic young man, a good businessman, always busy in his shop. They gave their children a good religious education. He was not involved in community affairs.

> **Rozenkrantz** Hersh
> His wife: …
> His son: Asher
> His daughters: Mina, Yetke

Hersh Rozenkrantz lived in the wooden house next door with his wife and three children, Asher, Mina and Yetke. He was a watchmaker and a goldsmith. In the 1920s, he was active in the Zionist organization. He was a religious Jew and a quiet person. He was not involved in community affairs. His children received a traditional education, and they were active in the Mizrachi youth organization The Religious Guard.

[Page 329]

> **Urnbakh** Avrom Wolf
> His wife: Soreh Nekhle
> Their daughter: Matil

Avrom Wolf Urnbakh, the son-in-law of Kalman Rappaport, with his wife and their daughter. He had a manufacturing business. The business was run by his wife Soreh Nekhle, while he spent most of his day learning in the House of Study. He was a Hasidic young man and on the High Holidays travelled to his Rebbe in Ger.

> **Rappaport** Kalman
> His wife: Khana
> His daughter: Drezil

Rappaport Khana, the wife of Reb Kalman, née Aurbakh

Reb Kalman Rappaport lived on the corner of the market and Kilinsky Street with his wife Khana and their children. He had a large grocery store, wholesale, and retail. Even though he had a large business, he came to the House of Study every morning and night and was often seen studying Gemore after prayers. He was a scholar and made a great impression with his beautiful white beard. He gave a lot of charity and on the Sabbath would always have a guest for a meal. His children also received a religious education. His son Moishe lives in America and his daughter Baltche lives in Australia.

[Page 330]

Aurbakh (Auerbach) Soreh – a widow
Her son: Khaim Aron

Aurbakh Soreh nee Ayman.
The wife of Reb Avrom Shloimeh of blessed memory.
Daughter of Reb Leml and Bayla.

The widow Sara Auerbach lived in the second half of the house with her two grown children, her son Chaim Aron and her daughter Mala [Ed. Note: a diminutive for Esther Malka], may she live long. Her husband Avraham Shlomo of blessed memory died young. He was a rich man, observant and very well respected in town. He was a grandson of the former Pshaytsher rabbi, Rabbi Chaim Auerbach of blessed memory. Reb Avraham Shlomo was a member of the community council and very active in all community affairs. After his death, his wife ran his manufacturing business with the help of her son Chaim Aron, who was also a chess champion in town. He was an intelligent, well-read young man. [Ed. Note: According to his descendants, he was a textile manufacturer, and his untimely death was attributed to tetanus.]

Mrs. Auerbach ran a fine, Jewish household. She provided her children with a traditional national education. She was known for welcoming guests and supporting the needy. Chaim Aron was killed in the Poznań extermination camp. Her daughter Mala, the wife of Professor Brand, lives in Jerusalem.

[Page 331]

Aurbakh (Auerbach) Khaim Aron of blessed memory and his sister Mala, may she live a long life.
(Playing chess).

> **Danielsky** Manya – a widow
> Her sons: Moishe, Azriel
> Her daughters: Regina, Pesia.
> Her son-in-law: Izbitzky Hersh
> His wife: Shaindl
> Their son: Shloime
> Their daughter: Sala

This is where Mrs. Danielsky lived. She had a tavern and a restaurant. Her son Azriel was a tailor and also loved to play the violin in his spare time. Her son Moishe helped in her business. She had three daughters. Pesie, Regina and her husband Pivke lived together with their mother. They were members of the Public Library and were active in the drama club.

Also in the same house were her son-in-law Hersh Izbitsky with his wife Shaindl and their two children Shloime and Sala. This was a traditional family. Their daughter Sala was a member of the Religious Guard organization. No one survived from this large family.

[Page 332]

> **Perl** Hersh Lipman
> His wife: Golda
> Their daughters: Rivka, Khaya, Ella
> Their sons: Avrom Zalman, Mordkhai, Mendl

The second half of the house was inhabited by Hersh Lipman Perl's family, which included his wife Golda and their children. He was the son-in-law of a religious woman who was called the "Rishishitz" because she came from the town of Rishishitz. She had another son-in-law in the town of Lubin near Włocławek (Vlotslavek in Yiddish), a rich Hasid with his wife Shaindl. Together with her son-in-law Bunim and her daughter she went to the Land of Israel in the 1920s. They remained there for a short time and then returned to Poland. Reb Hersh Lipman Perl, of blessed memory had a manufacturing shop. He was observant and a scholar, a Ger Hasid, and educated his children in this spirit. He also taught in a small congregation of wealthy people and taught the children Gemore.

> **Davidovitch** Mordkhe Binyumin
> His wife: Khava
> Their sons: Avram Zalman, Yisakhar Leybush
> Their daughter: Rokhl

His brother-in-law Reb Mordkhe Binyumin Davidovitch lived in the same house, along with his wife Khava and their children. He had a haberdashery and was also a watchmaker. He was a scholar and loved to use expressions from the Torah and offer ingenious explanations. He was held in high esteem by Rabbi Zemelman and was one of the most important participants at the table of the third Sabbath meal. He often took part in discussions about Torah with the rabbi. His son Avrom Zalman and daughter Rokhl were in a Nazi labor camp and were shot there. Their son Yehoshua Isaac lives in Israel.

[Page 333]

> **Goldman** Avrom
> His wife: Trayna
> Their son: Heniek

Avrom Goldman lived in the house next door, the son of Yakov Meir Goldman with his wife Trayna, the daughter of Moishe Sokhatchevsky, and their children. Avrom's business dealt with iron and building materials. He had a great sense of humor. He was a traditional and intelligent man. His wife was one of the founders of the Public Library. Their house was open to the poor and those in need.

Their daughter Sala and her family live in Israel. Their second daughter, Ronia, and her family live in America.

> **Aurbakh** Yitzkhak Yosef
> His wife: Khava
> Their son: Avrom
> Their daughter: Malka Royza

Reb Yitzkhak Aurbakh of blessed memory lived in the same house. He was a blond young man, a scholar, and a Hasid. He ran a manufacturing business. He also was a teacher in Rabbi Zemelman's Yeshiva. However, with all this, he was not a wealthy man. He was quite poor. His son Avrom learned in a Yeshiva outside of Przedecz and received his teaching permit just before the war. His daughters also received a religious education. Reb Yitzkhak Yosef was an intelligent man, quiet, well read, very observant, and the family lived practically in poverty.

In the evening, Reb Yitzkhak Yosef would sit for hours in the House of Study learning Gemore and Torah, sometimes alone and sometimes leading a larger group that took part in his teachings. He was one of the most admirable, honest men in town.

[Page 334]

> **Ravsky** Moishe
> His wife: Roda
> His sons: Daniel, Menakhem, Shloime
> His daughters: Soreh, Miriam

Moishe Ravsky and his family lived in the same house. His wife Roda was the daughter of Lipman Bilavsky. They ran a hat shop with their sons. Their daughters also helped out. It was one of the nicest workshops in the region. It was a happy household. They were always singing while they worked. Reb Moishe was an observant and quiet man. His wife Roda almost always travelled with him to fairs. The children were provided with a national, traditional education. Their daughter Soreh was an active member in the Religious Guard organization. Their son Menakhm was shot in 1942 by the local Nazi Volksdeutsche, Henebauer. Their son Avrom Yakov lives in America.

> **Danielsky** Mikhal
> His wife: Tzirl
> His sons: Ben-Zion, Vova, Shmuel
> His married son Nokhem and his family:
> Daughters: Geula and another daughter.

Reb Mikhal Danielsky lived in the house next door. He ran a shoemaking workshop with his son. He was an observant Jew active in the Burial Society. All his sons were active in the professional union and the Sholem Aleichem Library. They were intelligent and well-read.

[Page 335]

> **Shlipkovitch** Binyumin (Yomtche)

The bachelor Binyumin (Yomtche) Shlipkovitch lived in the same house. He sold stockings and socks in the market. He brought the goods from Łódź or Alexandrov. He was an orphan without a mother or father and lived in great poverty. His father Reb Shmuel Yehuda of blessed memory was a teacher who taught small boys Chumash and Gemore in his own home. He died before the war.

> **Toronchik** Binyumin
> His wife: ...

> His sons: Moishe, Shloime Dovid
> His daughters: Hinda, Frayda

The Toronchik family with four children lived in their own home. In the 1920s, the family ran a food store. At that time, there was another daughter who was sick, and her illness ate up their income. None of this helped, and the girl died. Binyumin Toronchik was an observant and loyal Jew and raised his children in this spirit. Shortly before the war, their eldest son Moishe received his teaching permit from a Yeshiva in Warsaw. The younger son also studied in a Yeshiva. Their daughter Hinda was active in the Public Library. She was an employee at the Ludovy Bank. Their older daughter worked far from home. Let these words serve as a monument for this beautiful, nice family.

[Page 336]

> **Zielinsky** Nakhman – a widower
> His grandson: Heniek

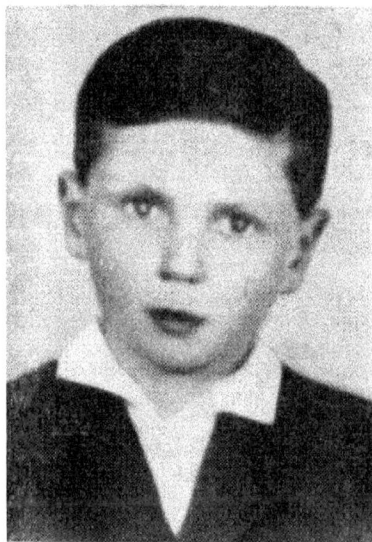

Heniek Zeliensky son of Avrom Ozer, may he live a long life

The old man Nakhman Zielinsky lived on Stadalne Street. He was a tailor who sewed loose robes, warm kaftans, pants, silk coats, and suits for children. He sewed well. He was an observant Jew. His son Avrom Ozer lives in Paris, his daughter Basha lives in Brazil and his son Khaim lives in America. Avrom Ozer's son Heniek was killed by the Nazis in the Łódź ghetto. When there was an Action in the ghetto to take all small children, young Heniek was among those who died a martyr's death.

[Page 337]

> **Skobronsky** Nosn
> His wife: Taube
> Their sons: Ezriel, Yoel.
> Their daughters: Hella, Rivka.

When the war broke out, almost everyone in the Skobronsky family was grown up. This was an interesting, intelligent family. The children illuminated this household. There were no special political party affiliations in this home, but they were all supporters of Zionism. This was a traditional Jewish family. The head of the family ran a grain business with his younger son. The older son Ezriel died one day after liberation from Buchenwald from exhaustion. He was an employee in Łódź. He was one of the most intelligent young men in Przedecz. He read a lot and knew a lot. The eldest daughter Hella was married and lived with her husband in Khatch. Rivka was on the board of the library until the outbreak of the war. Two sons from this family survived, Khaim and Yakov, who live in America.

Feyntukh Shimon
His wife: Bronia.
Their daughter: Regina.

Shimon Feyntukh, his wife Bronia and their daughter Regina lived in the second house. He came to Przedecz in the 1920s and lived there until 1938. He left and we do not know any details about this family.

[Page 338]

Yakubovitch Itche
His wife: Kayla
His sons: Yakov, Notte

Yakov Yakubovitch

Itche Yakubovitch lived in the same house with his wife Kayla and their family. He was a good custom tailor for men. He was always in a good mood, a happy man. He loved to say something nice and tell a good joke. He was an observant Jew and prayed in the House of Study. He loved to say his family was the forefathers as his father was Avrom (Abraham), he was Yitzkhak (Isaac) and his son was Yakov (Jacob). This was a fine, respectable home, and he raised his children in the traditional spirit. His three daughters Hella, Tobke and Ruzha live in Israel, and his son Max lives in Poland.

[Page 339]

> **Raukh** Polik
> His wife: Aydl
> His son: Heniek
> His daughter: Manya

Polik Raukh, his wife Aydl and family lived in the same house. He was a chicken dealer. He was a quiet man. This was a traditional family, supporters of the Zionist movement. The children were members of the Mizrachi organization.

> **Krel** Shmuel Leyzer
> His wife: Golda
> Their sons: Yehuda Leyb, Notte, Elye
> Dovid.
> His daughters: Pessi, Khaya

Further down on Chodecz Street, which they called the highway, and just before the end of the restricted Jewish area where Jews were permitted to carry things on the Sabbath, lived Shmuel Leyzer Krel, a custom tailor. He mainly sewed long Jewish coats (malbushim) and barely supported his family. He was an observant Jew and among the first to arrive for prayers at the House of Study all year long. He was a quiet man. He had three sons and two daughters who helped him provide for the family, working all day until late at night. They were all quiet, honorable people. No one from this family survived.

[Page 340]

> **Zuker** Khaim from the village Rivne and his
> family.
> **Berman** Moishe from the village Rivne and
> his family.
> **Langnoz** Moishe from the village of Rivne
> and his family.

If you continue down the highway about three kilometers from town, you will arrive in the village Rivne, which was the only village where Jewish families lived. There was a large pine forest which belonged to the Jewish Langnoz brothers. They had a large sawmill to cut trees into beams and planks. The family of Khaim Zuker lived there too. He was the administrator of this undertaking. Reb Khaim Zuker of blessed memory was a learned Jew, observant with an imposing stature and a long brown beard. Even though they lived far from town, he and his son-in-law would come to town every Sabbath to pray in the House of Study. He would often be the representative to lead the morning prayer at the pulpit on the High Holidays. His son-in-law **Moishe Berman of blessed** memory was a cantor. He would often pray in the synagogue and in the House of Study and pleased the congregants with his beautiful voice. He would also bring his own cheese and butter to sell in town. We do not know exact details about what happened to this family as they left town at the beginning of the 1930s.

> **Librakh** Berish
> His wife: Alta
> 4 children

Berish Librakh was a tanner and leather merchant. He was born in Linshitz and moved to Przedecz. He ran a beautiful Jewish household. He was an observant Jew who was able to teach. He did not get involved in community affairs; however, he was admired in town due to his charity and welcoming of guests. He was a smart man and well informed in world issues. His wife Khaya was a woman of valor, helped her husband in business and ran a nice Jewish home. Their children received a religious education. No one survived from this family.

[Page 341]

> **Makovitsky** Yehoshua
> His wife: Ava
> His sons: Eliezer, Shliamek
> His daughter: Hella

Mrs. Ava Mokovitsky in her youth

We return to the same street in town to the home of Yehoshua Makovitsky, a passionate Zionist. He sat on the community council and was an activist. He was admired in town. He ran a grain business in partnership with Nosn Skarvansky. This was a nice, wealthy Jewish home. He gave a lot of charity, and his door was open for those suffering and in need. He raised his children in the same spirit. His sons and daughter were very intelligent people. His two sons, Eliezer and Shliamek, and his daughter Hella were killed in the camps. Mrs. Makovitsky was killed in Chełmno . Reb Yehoshua died just before the war. Their son Shaul lives in Israel.

[Page 342]

> **Raukh** Moishe
> His wife: …
> His son: Pinkhas
> His daughter: Manya

Raukh Manya

Moishe Raukh lived in the second half of the house. He was a wealthy man and sat on the community council and the board of directors. He had a large wholesale chicken business. He sent hundreds of slaughtered chickens, geese, and turkeys to Łódź and Warsaw and other large cities such as Wloclawek (Vlotslavek In Yiddish) and Taron. He employed many people. He ran a fine, Jewish, well-off home. He was a religious man, and he was given the privilege of leading Friday evening services in the synagogue every other Sabbath. He raised his children in this traditional national spirit. He was a member of the board of the bank. No one survived from this family.

[Page 343]

Engel Rokhl – a widow
Sons: Shloime Yisakhar, Asher, Efraim, Ruven.
Daughters: Tauba, Khana, Bryana

Chodecz Street, which we are describing here, was not inhabited by artisans or workers like most of the streets in town. This was a street of businessmen and merchants. It was really not a large street but was inhabited almost exclusively by Jews. We arrive at the lumber warehouse of the Engel family, the wife who was a widow with her sons Shloime Yisakhar, Efraim, Asher and Ruven and two daughters. They have a fine Jewish home and a coal and lumber business. They were all Zionists and one of the sons, Shloime Yisakhar, was a founder and leader of the Betar organization. No one from this family survived.

Ofenbakh Shabtai
His wife: Blema.
His sons: Yekhiel Moishe, Yitzkhak Leybush, Yisakhar, Shloime,
Aron Meir.
His daughters: Frimet, Brayne

Now we arrive at the new house on the corner of Chodecz and Tilna streets. This is where Shabtai Ofenbakh lived. He had a food store but was not a rich man. He barely earned enough to feed his large family. This was an intelligent Zionist family. He was an enlightened Jew and a passionate member of the Mizrachi organization. He was a councilor on the community council and a member of the board of directors of the bank. His middle son, Yitzkhak Leybush, was active in the Mizrachi organization. He was a student of Rabbi Zemelman and a member of the Religious Guard. He spent years with a group training to move to the Land of Israel. Unfortunately, his dream was never realized and, together with his large family, he was killed by the Nazi murderers. No one from this family survived. The eldest son Yekhiel Moishe was active in the Public Library. All the children received a religious Zionist education.

[Page 344]

Vasertzug Notte
His wife: Esther

Reb Notte Vasertzug, his wife: Esther

We now arrive at the home of one of the wealthiest men in town, Reb Notte Vasertzug, of blessed memory. He was a rich man, a grain merchant, good hearted and generous. He supported the Jewish religious learning institutions. He was a member of the board of directors of the bank and was an admired, well-respected personality in town. His house was open for the poor and the needy. In 1935, he and his wife Esther moved to the Land of Israel, but unfortunately, he returned to Poland to liquidate his business and collect debts from property owners. Meanwhile, the war broke out and he remained. He and his wife were killed by the Nazi murderers.

[Page 345]

> **Zikhlinsky** Leyzer
> His wife: Rivka Rokhl
> Their sons: Pinche, Bunim, Binyumin, Avrom

*Binyumin (Yomek)
Zikhlinsky*

Bunim Zikhlinsky

Reb Leyzer Zikhlinsky of blessed memory lived on the corner of the market. That is where he had his wholesale and retail food business. He was a religious Jew. He was wealthy, gave a lot of charity and welcomed guests. He was a member of the board of directors of the bank. He prayed in the House of Study. His wonderful sons Pinche and Bunim helped him run his business. Pinche was also the only Jewish fire fighter. In 1935, he went on a visit to the land of Israel. All his children were intelligent and well-read. They were active in the Public Library and were involved in cultural activities in town. His son Yomek was in the young Mizrachi movement. The only member of the family to survive was their daughter Baltche, who lives in Mexico.

[Page 346]

> **Zikhlinsky** Yehoshua
> His wife:... and his family

In the same house lived his brother, Yehoshua Zikhlinsky with his wife and children. He was a grain merchant and a wealthy man. He was good-hearted and supported those in need. He was a quiet, religious man and was not involved in community affairs.

> **Vayden** Moishe Aron
> His wife: Ava and his family

Moishe Aron Vayden lived in the same house with his wife and family. He was a hat maker. He had a large workshop and employed a few people. He was a religious man and sat on the Jewish community council. He was also involved in other institutions and was a member of the board of directors of the bank.

> **Frenkl** Binyumin
> His wife: Andzia
> His daughters: Mala, Rivtche, Esther

Binyumin Frenkl lived in the house next door. He had an iron business and was a wealthy man. He was one of the founders of the Public Library. He provided his children with a religious Zionist education. He and his wife were involved in cultural activities in town. His daughter Mala was a member of the Religious Guard organization and was actively involved in the Hebrew classes they offered. Unfortunately, no one from this family survived.

[Page 347]

> **Prokhovsky** Wolf
> His wife: Brayna
> His son: Yakov

Wolf Prokhovsky lived in the same house. He was a tailor and would sell his goods at the market. He had a large workshop and employed workers. He sat on the Jewish community council and supported Zionism. He donated to the Jewish National Fund. He was a religious man and educated his children in a national traditional spirit.

> **Buks** Yisroel
> His wife: Ruzhe

We now arrive at Warshavsky Street, or as we Jews called it, "the House of Study Street" (Bes Ha Midrash Street), because the House of Study was located on this street. This street was inhabited exclusively by Jews, merchants and artisans, market workers and laborers. The elderly butcher Yisroel **Buks** lived at the beginning of the street. He was advanced in age and, because of his age, ran his business on a small scale, slaughtering the occasional calf or goat. This is how he earned a living.

Vishnievsky Yosef – a widower
His son: Moishe Alter and his family
His daughter: Bluma

Yosef Vishnievsky, a widower, once had a paint and quicklime store, but in his old age he sold fruit. He was, like most Jews in town, religious. Between afternoon and evening prayers, he would study "Ein Yakov" with other men at Reb Leyb **Lentshitsky's**. He had a married son Moishe Alter who lived in Łódź. His daughter Bluma ran the household.

[Page 348]

Zielinsky Yeshayahu
His wife: Soreh
His son: Khaim Hersh. His married son Wolf and his family.
His daughters: Khana, Leah

Kupert Khana, the daughter of Yeshayahu Zielinsky

Yeshayahu Zielinsky was a tailor. He ran a workshop with the help of his children and sold their finished goods at the market. After the children married, Wolf lived in Chodecz and the eldest daughter Khana lived in Włocławek (Vlotslavek in Yiddish). The youngest daughter Genendl married Fishl **Topolsky**. All his children were members of the Public Library. Yeshayahu was a religious man who prayed in the synagogue. He was not involved in community affairs. He gave charity. His wife Soreh was also involved in helping the needy.

His son Khaim Hersh was an intellectual. He was a member of the board of the Public Library and one of the founders of the drama club of the library. In the 1920s, a Zionist training camp was founded in Przedecz, and he was one of the most active participants. In 1932, he opened an independent tailor workshop.

[Page 349]

> **Kladovsky** Khaim
> His wife: Rivka Hinda
> His sons: Moishe Aron, Elye Dovid, Levy

Khaim Kladovsky was a tailor. He ran his own workshop and employed two people. He lived in his own home with his wife and 4 children. He was one of the people that knew a lot and spoke little. Even though he worked until late at night, he found time to be involved in the communal life of the Psalm Society and the VolksBank. His wife Rivka Hinda worked hard to serve the family, and helped her husband at work, and managed to find time to help the needy. Their eldest daughter Ruzhe was saved from Hitler's hell, and, after being in many labor camps, had the good fortune to come to the Land of Israel. This was one of the most beautiful families in town.

> **Rafael** Wolf Levental
> His wife: Esther

Rafael Wold Levental of blessed memory was a learned Jew and a generous, wealthy man. He had a large grain business. When his wife died, he remarried and moved to Łódź.

> **Zikhlinsky** Dovid
> His wife: Manya
> Son: Shloime

Dovid Zikhlinsky was a grain merchant and chairman of the board of the Jewish community, as well as a member of the board of the bank. During the Nazi occupation, he was appointed the elder (Representative) of the Jews. He and his family were killed in Chełmno .

[Page 350]

> **Plotzker** Moishe
> His wife: Shayna Ita
> His son: Nakhman Abba
> His daughters: Feyge, Ruzhe

There were four children in the Plotzker family, two daughters and two sons. They had a butcher shop. This was an observant, traditional family. The mother Shayna Ita ran the shop. She was the butcher. Her husband Moishe travelled to the villages to buy cattle to slaughter and supply meat for their butcher shop. They were not wealthy people; however, she loved to do favors for others. No one from this family survived.

> **Polkovsky** Bezalel
> His wife: Blema

This family had a small food store, and, in addition, the husband dealt with chickens in the village. They did not have any children. They were good people and loved to help others. They were not involved in communal affairs. They lived a quiet, honest life. They were both killed in Chełmno.

> **Zikhlinsky** Shimshon
> His wife: Frimit

Shimshon Zikhlinsky and his wife Frimit comprised their whole family. They did not have any children. Their life was calm but also positive. They spent all their time working in the hat making workshop and travelled to markets to sell their wares. They were quiet, simple, honorable, observant people.

[Page 351]

> **Rivinsky** Moishe
> His wife: Rivka
> His sons: Dovid, Mikhal
> His daughters: Shayna, Gitl, Mindl

Moishe Rivinsky was a tailor with a large family. All his children helped him earn a living. They sold their sewn goods at the market. The daughters sewed underwear. They were cultured people. They all were well read. The parents were religious, pious, good-hearted people.

> **Zielinsky** Moishe
> His daughter: Kazer

Moishe Zielinsky was a widower. His daughter kept house. Like many Jews in town, he did not have a profession. He did a bit of village peddling, at times worked as a glazer, but barely earned a living. He was a religious, simple man and died in 1932. Shortly before he died, his youngest daughter Kazer married and moved to Włocławek (Vlotslavek in Yiddish).

> **Opas** Hersh
> His wife: Soreh Gitl
> His sons: Itche, Dovid, Shmuel Leyb, Avrom,
> Moishe.
> His daughters: Esther Dreze, Ruzhe

Hersh Opas – his wife Soreh Gitl and their seven children – five sons and two daughters. He was a tailor, a religious man who raised his children in a national religious spirit. He supported the Mizrachi movement. His children helped him earn a living. The family worked hard until late at night and barely managed to provide for this large family. No one from this family survived.

[Page 352]

A page in memory of our town's soldiers fallen in the battle against the Nazis

Translated by Marshall Grant

With the end of the list of our dear ones who perished in the Holocaust, we dedicate this page to the memory of the sons of our city who fought in the Polish military against the Nazi war machine and fell in battle.

The soldier	Neta, son of Shmuel Laizar, Karal	1916-1939
"	Azriel, son of Mania, Danialeski	1910-1939
"	Yitzhak, son of Reuven, Pranankanstein	1917-1939
"	Yitzhak (Itsche), son of Mania, Danialeski, fell in battle	1917-1939
"	Naftali, son of Lev, Klodawski	1910-1939
"	Hanan, son of Lev, Klodawski, his brother	1912-1939
"	Michael Hirsch, son of Yehiel Yosef, Goldman murdered by the Germans as prisoners of war	1915-1939
"	Hirsch, son of Moshe, Topolski Fell in battle against the Germans after taking part in the prisoner revolt and blowing up the crematoriums in the Birkenau death camp.	1912-1944

May these lines always preserve their memory

May their souls be bound in the bundle of life.

[Page 353]

Sons of our city who perished after the Holocaust
Of eternal memory

Yisrael Rusak, of blessed memory

Son of Moshe Aharon, of blessed memory

Died on 8th of Nisan, 5719

Survived by:

His wife, his daughters, and his sister

Yisrael Rusak, of blessed memory

[Page 354]

Yisrael Rusak, of blessed memory

Reuven Yamnik

I met him when he was young and still living with his parents in Przedecz. He studied to be a tailor; he was modest, simple and was satisfied with what he had, always with a smile on his face, the son of a large and respectable family in our city. His father, Moshe Aharon, of blessed memory, was the secretary of the Jewish community, a religious and wise Jewish man. He was knowledgeable in Judaism and world matters. He was a good speaker, intelligent, well read, and a supporter of the Zionist movement and a member of the Mizrahi movement. When Yisrael grew older, he left his parents' home and moved to Łódź. There he had a better chance of making his living as a tailor, which he did until the outbreak of World War II.

When Hitler's soldiers invaded Poland, he was able to escape in a difficult and roundabout way to Russia. He worked hard there to make a living, but always maintained his Jewish values – he prayed and kept Shabbes as was required. There he met his wife, Miriam. According to some accounts, when she saw first saw him, he was troubled and living a measly life, alone and lonely and barely making ends meet, but when it was time to pray mincha in the afternoon – he would make time and pray. That was when she decided that this is a man who was worthwhile making a life with, and they were married in Russia. They experienced all the horrors of the war, and when it was over, they left Russia and went to live in Łódź , which was just a stopping point for the young couple. After their first daughter, Zahava, and Rachael, their second, were born, they came to Israel, but there too, their lives were hard. They overcame all the hardships of immigration during those times, the early 1950s, the period of transient camps. They had the most modest life - no home, no livelihood, no work. The couple lived in the transient camp of Pardes Katz in a leaking tent, without any facilities, and raised two infants without even the most minimum of sanitary conditions – and it was terribly difficult. One day when Yisrael was at work, a snake that had snuck into the tent from the surrounding vegetation attacked Miriam. Her screams brought the neighbors to her aid and killed the snake. Sometime later, a long time later, they moved to Bnei Brak, to the *Hey* neighborhood, a religious neighborhood established by the *Hapoel* Mizrahi movement, and they received a two-room apartment there as they wanted to live in a religious community. Yisrael was a religious man, kept Shabbes, and regularly participated in the neighborhood's large synagogue. He gave his daughters a religious education. After a while, he received permanent work in the Bnei Brak municipality, but then, when his fortunes finally improved and he was more or less stable – he had a steady job, beautiful home and apartment, a terrible disaster hit the calm and quiet home like lightning on a clear day. While at work in the municipality, he felt poorly, knelt down and fell. He died on the 8th of Nisan, 5719 and was unable to enjoy the happiness of his daughters with whom he was very close. He was eulogized by the great local rabbi, Rabbi Friedman from the *Hey* neighborhood. He was buried in the cemetery for those keeping the Shabbes in *Zichron Meir* in Bnei Brak. May his memory be blessed and may he be bound in the bundle of life.

[Page 355]

Of eternal memory

Mrs. Rivka Danielless, of blessed memory
of the Kronburg family

Your nobility and beauty will always be with me.
Your memory is forever in my heart.
Died in the USA in 1969

Her husband: Moshe Hirsch Danielless

Mrs. Rivka Danielless, of blessed memory

[Page 356]

Of eternal memory

Golda, of blessed memory
The daughter of Michael Hirsch Neymark, of blessed memory

A modest woman who was active in the Jewish community.
Died in Brazil in 1972.

Her family and brother, Simcha.

Mrs. Golda Neymark, of blessed memory

[Page 357]

Of eternal memory
David, son of Katriel and Masha Yaakobovski, of blessed memory

Died in Boston, USA, on August 16, 1972, aged 70.

David Yaakobovski

[Yiddish text]

[Page 358]

Moshe Yechimovitch, of blessed memory, the father

Died on the 1st of Iyar, 5732
1902-1972

Meir Yechimovitch, of blessed memory, the son
Died on the 28th of Adar, 5733
1946-1973

Moshe Yechimovitch

Meir Yechimovitch

We called him Meir after his grandfather, Yaakov Meir, of blessed memory, one of Przedecz's most honorable men. He was born in Przedecz after the war. We tried to renew the lives we had before the war in our city, but the hostile environment that had assisted the Nazis in eradicating the Jews of Europe and Przedecz would not accept our return. In 1957, we moved to Israel. Meir finished elementary school and jr. high in Tel Aviv and continued to learn a profession. When he was conscripted into the IDF, he volunteered for the navy commando unit and was recognized for his excellent bravery. He played an active part in the Six Day War. Following his discharge, he was accepted to a military factory, and there too, he excelled in his work. He married and the couple had two children. Several months after his father's death he became ill, and after four months, succumbed to his sickness.

Born: April 10th, 1946
Died: April 2nd, 1973.

Survived by his mother, his wife, his two daughters and his brother.

****

[Page 359]

Conclusion

Translated by Jerrold Landau

We now come to the final resting places for the Jews in our town, the end of the journey.

No, not so. It isn't finished.

We wander through the alleyways of our hometown.

From time to time, our memories will wander through the places where the murderous miscreants violently ripped away the lives of people who had no ability to defend themselves.

Coming into contact with some 1,000 of our loved ones, we tried to listen to the frightful descriptions of their lives and deaths. We visited some 200 dwellings. We went from house to house. With minor exceptions, these were single-room dwellings. There were workshops in small living quarters, from which they extracted a hardscrabble living. Families of seven, eight or more people had one table and two beds, a kitchen, bedroom, dining room, as well as hygienic necessities [translator: possibly lavatory]. With one such family in such a room, we did not find any furniture. In a shadowy corner, an area was set apart with two boards where there was straw covered with coarse linen sewn together from sacks. This was the sleeping area for six people. This was the resting place and the sitting place for eating.

In many houses, there was nothing with which to cook or to heat in the kitchen. The people had little joy in their lives. Many toiled to support themselves in a meager fashion.

We met with the leaders and organizers of various legal and illegal political organizations, mostly youth. All were searching for a solution to the Jewish question in Poland. All were concerned with the same issues, even though they were not following the same paths.

Young voices resonated in the party locales. They would sing songs and anthems, including Yiddish folk songs, Hebrew songs, as well as Polish ones. The words of Hatikvah rang out. The melodies of the International and La Marseillaise reverberated. Everything was with seriousness and confidence, but we also heard laughter mixed with tears in the joyous songs.

We also talked with the leaders of volunteer and philanthropic institutions, such as the Gemilat Chesed fund, Bikur Cholim [Society for tending to the sick], Linat Tzedek [for providing lodging], Hachsnasat Kalah [tending to poor brides]. They told us that the need was great and that there were also many donors, but unfortunately, they all could not cover everything, because the financial situation of many Jewish families was very difficult.

[Page 360]

We talked with elderly people, with young people, with children, men, and women, at various hours of the day and night. Summer and winter, in the spring and the autumn, step by step, we traversed with alertness and care through the byways of the town, through the mud and rain, over sand and swamps. We slid over the wet stones with which the alleys were paved. Together with everyone, we survived the invasion of the murderous creatures, the torture of the Jews in the middle of the market, the cutting off of beards. We cried with great sorrow over the fire that consumed the synagogue. We were present during the collection of money for the Germans (contributions) to pay for the burning of our holy places. We stood at the fence of the cemetery when the others burnt and destroyed the graves, and heard the mocking words at the expense of those who had been reposing there for hundreds of years, and had had the merit of dying a natural death.

We saw the glances of people who were accusing us for being alive.

Young children who did not understand death talked like older ones on the way to Chełmno. They knew what crimes were taking place on that accursed ground and whispered tremblingly that they wanted to live. To this day, we still hear the weeping of the mothers suckling their young babies at the breast. These are memories that burn and sting, and do not grant us peace. One cannot blunt them.

Therefore, we survey the alleyways and seek and listen. We cannot uproot the path.

There is the place, this is the place.

All of our thoughts turn back to there.

[Page 361]

The Organization of Former Przedecz Residents

Translated from Hebrew by Marshall Grant

The organization was established when all the former residents of our city living in Israel gathered during the *Pesach* (Passover) holiday in 1961, at the initiative of Moshe Belivsky, Itzhak Levin, Reuven Yamnik, in Mr. Belivsky's home. It was proposed to memorialize our loved ones, victims of the Holocaust, by erecting a memorial plaque in the *Chamber of the Holocaust* Museum on Har Zion in Jerusalem. The members eagerly approved the proposal. A committee was established, and its members were Belivsky, Yamnik, Levin, Motkov, Schwitzer and Leah Pnini-Zemelman. Large sums of money were donated to achieve this goal by all our city's former residents: both those living in Israel and those the diaspora.

Former Przedecz resident in the Chamber of the Holocaust at the unveiling of the plaque dedicated to our city's victims

On Holocaust Memorial Day, on May 18, 1963, 6 Iyar, 5724, all the former residents of our city living in Israel gathered in Jerusalem. A memorial ceremony was held in the Yad Vashem Memorial Hall on *Har HaZicharon* (now Mount Herzl). A memorial candle was lit and we recited psalms and the *kaddish*; *El Maleh HaRachamim was* sung by a cantor for the souls of Przedecz.

We laid a wreath on the symbolic grave there. We later went to Har Zion, where the Chamber of the Holocaust was located, to unveil the memorial wall. Here too, a ceremony was held with the cantor, candles were lit for the memory of the victims, and eulogies were recited by those present. Afternoon prayers were recited, as was the *kaddish* for the memory of their souls. We then walked to the memorial dedicated to the heroism of fighters in the Warsaw Ghetto. When the event was over, we were all invited to the Brand family's home.

[Page 362]

There, members proposed to continue the memorial efforts by publishing a memorial book. On the spot, the first donations were made for this goal.

Every year, on Holocaust Memorial Day, we gather and hold a memorial evening in Tel Aviv, with all the former residents of our city and other former residents who reside abroad. A memorial ceremony, eulogies, *Yizkor* and *El Maleh HaRachamim* are recited by the cantor. The participants also recite psalms and a general *Kaddish* is held for all the victims.

With the book's publishing, we continued to discuss the memorial for our loved ones who perished in the Holocaust. May their souls be bound in the bundle of life.

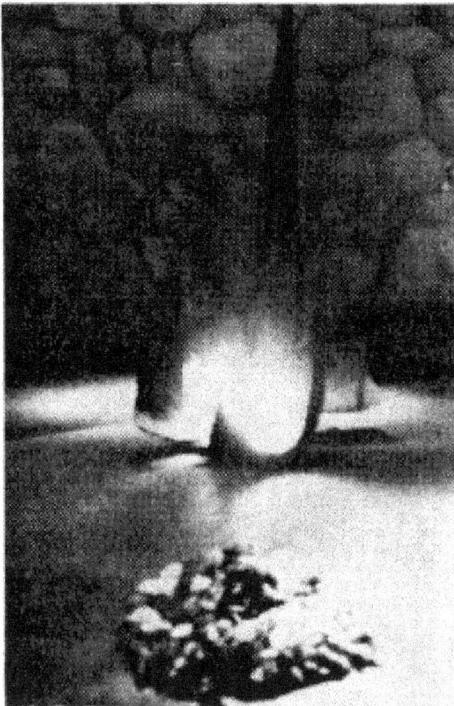

Memorial candle that was lit in the Yad Vashem Memorial Hall by Mr. Levin

Rozesha Mokotov lights a memorial candle next to the list of victims during the memorial evening held in the JNF Hall in Tel Aviv

[Page 363]

Bluma Zupkerman (Mokotov)
Chava Rauch and her children:
Moniek and Manya

[Page 364]

List of former Przedecz residents living in Israel

Transliterated by Judy Petersen

Surname	Given Name(s)	Residence	Remarks
BILEVSKY	Moshe	Ramat Gan	
BILEVSKY	Yosef	Ramat Yitzchak	
BILEVSKY	Avraham	Givataim	
LEVIN	Yitzchak	Bnei Brak	
MENDLINGER	Sarah	Bnei Brak	
POLMAN	Esther	Ramat Gan	
YECHIMOVITZ	Shoshana	Ramat Gan	
SCHWEITZER	Levi	Kiryat Motzkin	
GARBINSKY	Zahava	Kiryat Chaim	
YAMNIK	Yehoshua	Kiryat Yam A	
YAMNIK	Reuven	Bnei Brak	
DAVIDOVITZ	Yehoshua	Yad Eliahu	
MAKOVITZKI	Shaul	Tel Aviv	
MOKOTOV	Moshe	Tel Aviv	
MOKOTOV	Rozsa	Tel Aviv	Mrs.
YECHIMOVITZ	Bella	Tel Aviv	Mrs.
GOLDMAN	Fishel	Haifa	
RUSEK	Miriam	Bnei Brak	Mrs.
GREIF	Tzipora	Tel Aviv	Mrs.
ZYCHLINSKI	Chaim	Tel Aviv	
ZYCHLINSKI	Hersch	Yivne Hadromit	
HIMMEL	Manya	Kfar Mishar near Gadera	
ETTINGER	Chaya	Kiryat Tivon	
ETTINGER	Yona	Kiryat Tivon	
EIGLINSKI	Yisrael	Haifa	

FODER	Yische Kiryat	Shalom
BERNAD?/ BRAND?	Aharon and Mala	Jerusalem
BERG	Esther and Shimon	Afridar Ashkelon
PANINI	Yakov and Glilit	Jerusalem

[Page 365]

Former Przedecz residents living outside of Israel

Transliterated by Judy Petersen

Surname	Given Name(s)	Residence	Remarks
AFTERGUT	Irena	London, England	Yirke DANIELSKA
BRYM	Fajga	New York, NY, USA	Fajga PASHDETZKI
DANIEL	Morris	Chicago, IL, USA	Moshe Hersch DANIELSKI
DANIELS	Milton	Chicago, IL, USA	Mordechai Wolf DANIELSKI
DANIELS	Sol.	Chicago, IL, USA	Zalman DANIELSKI
DANIEL	Israel	Sao Paulo, Brazil	Yisrael DANIELSKI
DYSKIN	S.	Paris, France	Sala SOCHCHEVSKI
FISHER	Jacob	Cincinnati, OH, USA	Yakov Fisher son of Moshe
HERSHBERG	Hyman	Winchester, MA, USA	Chaim HERSHBERG
JAMNIK	Leo	Sao Paulo, Brazil	Leibush YAMNIK
JAKUBOWSKI	M.	Montreal, Canada	Moshe Aharon YAKUBOWSKI
MORGENSTERN	Saul	Bronx, NY, USA	Yissachar MORGENSTERN
MUSMAN	Eva	Brooklyn, NY, USA	Chavtshe ZIELINSKI
MOSS	David	Woodmere, Long Island, NY, USA	Kaila WISHNIVSKI
MOSS	Mark	Cleveland, OH, USA	Ronya GOLDMAN
NEUMARK	Simao	Sao Paulo, Brazil	Simcha NEUMARK

| PIZER | Morris | Brooklyn, NY, USA | Moshe Shaya PASHEDETZKI |

[Page 366]

Surname	Given Name(s)	Residence	Remarks
PEYSER	A.	Brooklyn, NY, USA	daughter of Zalman BUKS
RAPAPORT	Morris	Lincolnwood, IL, USA	Moshe RAPAPORT
SKOWRONSKY	Henry	Springfield, IL, USA	Chaim SKOWRONSKY
SKOWRONSKY	Jack	Chicago, IL, USA	Yakov SKOWRONSKY
TOPOLSKI	Jacob	Eastchester, NY, USA	Yakov TOPOLSKI
TORNER	Arje	Arlington, VA, USA	Arje TORNER
TORONCHIK	Jack	San Isidro, Argentina	Yakov TORONCHIK
WEIS	Jack	Moriston, NJ, USA	Yakov RAVSKI
WISHNEWSKY	Zelig	Brooklyn, NY, USA	Zelig WISHNIVSKI
WISHNIAK	Herman	St. Louis Park, MN, USA	Hershel WISHNIVSKI
ZYCHLINSKY	H.	Condesa, Mexico	Beltcha ZYCHLINSKY
ZIELINSKI	C.	Nebraska, USA	Chaim ZIELINSKI

[Pages 367, 368 Blank]

[Page 369]

History of Przedecz and its Jews

By Professor Dr. Aharon Brand-Urban

Organization of Natives of the City of Przedecz (Pshaytsh) in Israel

[Page 370 Blank]

[Page 371]

Przedecz – General Historical Review

Translated from Hebrew by Marshall Grant

The name of the city is Przedecz, and this is the way it appears in all historical Polish documents, and maybe even those written earlier.

In Yiddish, the city is called *Pshaytsh*, and during the period of autonomous rule of Polish Jews, 1580-1764, meaning during the period of the Council of Four Lands (the Council of Three Lands, the Council of Five Lands) the city was called *Pshaytsh* and belonged to Poland - it was governed by the Brzesc Kujowski voivode, often called Brezesc-Koya in rabbinical literature. In the period between the two world wars, the city was affiliated to the district of Wloclawek, and up to 1936, it was governed by the Warsaw voivode, then the Pomerania voivode, meaning the city of Torun. In the years preceding the second world war, large areas belonging to the Warsaw and Łódź regions were transferred to the Turan voivode [***Ed. Note***: Probably Torun] – Pomorze and Poznań, with the goal of leaving the division of Poland in the past and emphasizing their affiliation to genuine Polish areas – as opposed to those that were annexed when Poland was divided by Prussia. This would later be the real reason for transferring the area in which Przedecz was located to the Turan voivode.

From a geographical perspective, Przedecz is located not far from the Koło district on the Warta River, and Kutno and Wloclawek. It is 9 km from Kłodawa to the south, 9 km from Chodecz to the north, 27 km from Koło to the south, 24 km from Krosniewice to the east, and 10 km from the Izbica Kujawska, Brdow and Dabrowice forests. Chełmno , the Nazis' first death camp in which Jews from the area were murdered, including from Przedecz, was 30 km from the city.

The city of Przedecz is situated on a hill along the eastern bank of the Przedecz lake, which stretches into a semi-circle from south to north. It is 3 km long and 1 km wide. Due to the swamps located near Arkuszewo and a tributary near Zbijewo, a long strip of the lake reaches all the way to the village of Szczecin. The Zglowizczka tributary connects in the direction of the Vistula River. In addition, the lake's waters were also connected to the west by the Korzecznik and Modzerowskie lakes to the Goplo lake and the region known as Poland's historical cradle, located 35 km from the city – Gniezno. This is where the first eagles of Poland existed and the source of the connection to Germany, as was shown in the visit of Otto III in the year 1000.

It is worth focusing on the etymology of the word Przedecz, although I was unable to find any information in existing literature. It appears the source comes from Przedzic (today Wyprzedzac), meaning to be early to go, to pass. An analogy is the etymology of the adjacent forest Chodecz, which comes from *chodzic.* These terms show that these cities were used in the past by travelers. Other cities in the areas show that this kind of terminology was used, such as *Konin, Koło*, and *Kowal* whose meanings stem from travel by horses and *Izbica* and *Kłodawa*, whose meaning is affiliated to crossing a river.

[Page 372]

A straight line can be drawn between Kalisz, Koło, Przedecz and Czudec all the way to Wloclawek on the Wisla [Ed. Note: Vistula] River, and from there to Turan and Mazovia. It appears to me that this route was used during the period for transporting merchandise in general, and for amber specifically, toward the center of the southern shore of the Baltic Sea, which was rich with this material. In the beginning of organized settlement of this area, which began in the beginning of the 20th century, this was actually the area where the amber trade was concentrated. In the 12th century, the crusaders took control of the amber trade and Christian Czechs (Zucnfte) organized the purchase of amber from them. The amber trade was controlled by the Princes of Pomerellen – Little Pomerania, which was part of western Prussia stretching along the left bank of the Wisla River between Pomerania and the Poznań region, all the way to the Baltic Sea. From these princes, it was transferred to the crusaders, and at the outset of the 14th century, it was transferred to Danzig fishermen and the Oliwa monastery.

In any case, the geographical area of the Przedecz Lake and the city appear ideal for the transfer of merchandise, especially for amber merchants and due to the early presence of Jews there. These Jews came from the southwest – Kalisz, and from the west – Gniezno, and from the direction of Wloclawek. It should be noted that in these places, coins made by Jewish coin makers in the beginning of the second century were found with Hebrew inscriptions.

Przedecz's landscape is typical of the Kuyavia region of Poland. A land of broad expanses of flatlands, reaching up to the Goplo lake, and slowly declining towards the Wisla. It is covered with wetlands, sands, and small forested hills. The region is divided into an area rich with pastures, on which a few trees grow, and a more forested area, located beyond Brezesc and Kowal. This area is mostly dominated by white pine, with a small amount of oak. Many lakes have dried up, or were drained, and green grassy pastures have evolved there. Agriculture is developed and the farmers are rich. The dress of the local population in Kuyavia is well known in Poland, it is colorful, but dominated by shades of blue. The women's head coverings were red and flowery. The city of Przedecz, which grew from the west to the Przedecz Lake, has been in the heart of Poland since its inception, and its settlement began around the year 1000.

The adjacent city of Kłodawa, which is an excellent transfer point, is southwest of Przedecz, and has been historically recognized since the 11th century. King Boleslaw, "crooked mouth", was born in 1085. Kłodawa later served as the center for Polish Christian culture. Many prominent and well-known people lived there and established famous schools there. Kings of Poland in the 14th, 15th and 16th centuries would visit there often, making the city a respectful one. There is no doubt that this city influenced Przedecz.

A historical mention of Przedecz can be found as early as 1136 when Pope Innocent I, when approving the belongings of the archbishops in Gniezno, mentions the city's lake by the name Przedecz. Of course, the special importance of this place was well known due to it being a transfer point for merchandise and the fishing villages in the area. Przedecz was first officially recognized as a city before 1393.

[Page 373]

The Knights of the Cross (Krzyżacy) fought many wars with the Poles in this region and Przedecz became their military stronghold. They are the ones who built a castle there and named it Mossburg, a name used by the Nazis to name the city after it was captured. In 1360, Casimir the Great acquired lands there from the Archbishop Yaroslav Skotenitzki of Gniezno. He laid down a rampart that was specially made and was 100 meters long, 20 meters wide and 10 meters high – which made the fortress into a mighty castle that still stands today.

In 1383, Ziemowit the Prince of Mazovia gave the city and all its assets to the Bartosz Wezenburg duchy. The deed of sale mentions that the city is part of "terra nostra Cuyavie", our land of Kuyavia, with the castle geographically affiliated to "Super Kłodawa". In 1437, this protective fortress in Przedecz was under the control of Kasztelan Wiślica. He allowed the city's residents to live their lives according to German laws (Magdeburg Law) and awarded special rights. In 1459, the city was small and provided only two armed soldiers for the Malbork War *[Ed. Note: Possibly Marienburg].* The rights awarded by Kasztelan Wiślica were reaffirmed in 1562 by King Zygmunt the Old. [*Ed. Note:* These dates may be a bit confused. According to Wikipedia, Sigismund II Augustus, son of Sigismund I the Old, took the throne in 1548.]

During this period, the city was the district capital. In 1538, it was destroyed by fire and King Zigmont II, August, immediately upon ascending to the throne, awarded special rights to promote its development. He repealed the starosta rights and other rights of the city's residents in 1437. The noble Wojciech Korycinski, Minister of the Army (Chorazy) of Kalisz, who was supported by Bona, the king's wife, was appointed starosta and purchased forests and villages from the local Soltys and promised to rebuild the ancient castle that was slowly deteriorating. The castle was renovated in 1555 and August Zigmont tried to award more rights to the villagers. It is interesting that he also awarded them the important right to purchase alcoholic beverages without taxes. In 1564, a census was carried out and the findings showed that there were only 28 people of employment age. The starosta of Przedecz expands, and Kłodawa, which was the spiritual and economic center, was now affiliated to the growing city (possibly due to the fire that destroyed the city in 1523) – as did many other neighboring villages. The civilian rights of the city's residents, generously given by August II, were reaffirmed by future kings. In 1722, August II declared two main market days and six large market days (Jarmark). Stanisław August expanded civilian rights in 1774; in 1793-1806, after the division of Poland, the city was transferred to Prussia, and between 1806-1812 it was affiliated to the Warsaw duchy.

In 1815, following the Vienna Congress, it was part of the Kingdom of Poland (under the Russian Empire), meaning Congress Poland. Parts of the city are now allocated to the settlement of textile experts who came from Germany (Sukiennicy), which promised to forever pay their rental fees.

[Page 374]

Of the ancient buildings that once stood, now only the church from the 15th century remains. Of the evangelical church, built on the remains of the fortress that was again destroyed in 1789, only the round tower, which once housed the church's bell tower, remains. In 1862, the city had 1,864 residents, however, in 1867 it loses its municipal rights and again becomes a community with rural characteristics. Municipal rights were once again awarded to Przedecz in 1919.

In 1961, the city stretched over 7.7 square meters and had 330 households – many of which belonged to Jewish residents. When the World War II broke out, there were 2,112 residents in Przedecz.

****

[Page 375]

The History of the Jews of Przedecz
with Some Data about the Jews of the Area

Translated by Jerrold Landau

Przedecz is situated in the center of Greater Poland, the location of the oldest settlement of Jews in Poland. The earliest history of the Jews of Przedecz cannot be determined precisely, but general knowledge of the development of the city and its geographic area can be the basis for conjectures about the earliest times that Jews were there. Jewish settlement in Poland began in the west of the country and expanded toward the area in which the city of Przedecz is situated.

During the ninth century, the Slavic tribes dwelling in the area of Greater Poland united under the leadership of the earliest of them – the Polians who lived in the area of Gniezno. This alliance was established at the end of the tenth century, and formed the conditions for the advancement of the Polish kingdom.

As has already been explained above, the area was an easy route from east to west, rich in agriculture and ripe for economic development. As can be surmised, Jews were also attracted to the area; and the geographic-topographic situation, with easy routes of passage, provided an easy arena for business. It seems that the etymology of names (see earlier) of the old areas of settlement in the district perhaps confirm this matter. During the Roman era, when Jews were residing in Western Europe, the trade route passed through this district to the north-eastern Baltic Sea, from where valuable amber was brought to the empire. The geographer Ptolemy (Ptolomius) from the second century mentions Kalisz (Calissa) in our district. In any case, it is clear that the first Jews arrived in this area of western Poland during the 11th and 12th centuries and settled there. They came from the west and the southwest. Later, the influx increased during the era of the Crusaders and other tribulations of the 12th, 13th, and 14th centuries. Coins from the 12th century, imprinted with Hebrew inscriptions, note names of Polish rulers. It is interesting that the names and titles of the Jewish money imprinters have been found in the areas of Kalisz, Gniezno, and Włocławek. The geographic locations of these three cities form a triangle, with Przedecz at the center.

The Jewish settlement in Greater Poland continued to develop during those centuries. During the 11th century, Jewish commercial caravans travelled from Regensburg to the duchies in southern Russia (where the Khazars also lived), especially to Kyiv. They passed through southern Poland. However, we first hear of Jews passing through Krakow in 1304. On the other hand, we find permanent settlements in Poland before this time, especially in the western part of the country, particularly in Greater Poland and Polish Silesia. Jewish settlement in that district was commensurate with the settlement of Germans. Even the legal charter given to the Jews was based on those brought in from the cities of Germany, such as the Magdeburg Charter.

Duke Mieczyslaw Stary (Mieczyslaw the Elder) granted privileges to Jews during the middle of the 12th century, according to which a large monetary penalty would be inflicted for ignoring them. In 1264, the Jews were granted the Kalisz Charter (*status kaliski*) by Duke Bolesław V, the Pious. Principles of this charter were: the Jews were to pay the property of the prince They were obligated to pay taxes to him, but they were to benefit from his protection, freedom of commerce and dealing with money lending. Jews were given the rights of movement from place to place. They could travel from place to place and from state to state throughout the entire land of Poland with all sorts of merchandise, to do business to their hearts content, to sell, buy, and barter. There was a common law for Jews and gentiles in matters of taxes. A Jew hosted in a gentile home could dwell in security. Jews were permitted to perform ritual slaughter [*shechita*] in all places where they lived, and sell non-kosher meat[1] to gentiles. The Jews lived as *servi camerae regis*, servants of the king's chambers. They were worthy of this protection as they brought benefit as lenders and merchants.

[Page 376]

Despite the involvement of Pope Innocent III (1198-1216), who stated that Jews are not cheaters and do not engage in ritual murder, the clergy opposed rights for the Jews, and Jewish settlement in lands under rule of the clergy was forbidden. As noted above, during that period, Przedecz was a settlement belonging to the Archdiocese of Gniezno. As a place under church rule, we can assume that there was no permanent Jewish settlement, although it is perhaps possible that Jews involved in trade passed through the north and west trade routes that went through it – especially since there were Jewish money changers in nearby Gniezno. However, since the time that Kazimierz the Great took over Przedecz from Archbishop Jarosław of Gniezno, and from the time of the fortification of this entire area at his hands in the middle of the 14th century, including the fortified Crusader Castle in Przedecz, for the purposes of defending the area from the clerical strongmen on the one hand, and for the development of commerce on the other hand – we can surmise that Jews lived there, albeit their numbers were certainly small. Rights were given to the settlements in this area in accordance with the Magdeburg Charter. In any case, Jews are mentioned in Gniezno in 1267, in Posen [Poznań] in 1379, and in Pyzdry in 1382. Jews are mentioned in the city of Koło (in the notebooks of the district court in Konin) in 1429, in Łęczyca in 1468, in Kłodawa in 1487, in Kutno in 1513, in Brisk-Kwia [Brześć Kujawski] in 1538. There is no doubt that there were Jews in those places before those days.

During the 15th century, the number of Jews in all of Poland is estimated at twenty to thirty thousand. It is therefore clear that the settlement in those cities was small.

It is worthwhile to note here that in 1538, there were fifteen Jewish houses in Brześć Kujawski, which is close to Przedecz. One hundred Jewish families were killed in that city in 1656 by the Polish soldiers of Czarnecki, who were fighting against the Swedes, after they were advised to convert to Christianity to save their lives, but they refused to do so.

In the Lustracja, a population census and economic survey that took place in 1628-1632, that is before the Swedish wars, it is noted that the city of Przedecz was, to some extent, destroyed. Of the 88 houses that existed in 1612, only 40 remained, some of which had been damaged by the fire. The number of residents was small at that time. The census does not mention Jews.

King Zygmunt August (1548-1572) granted the Jews of Kłodawa the rights of settlement, but this privilege was interrupted during the period of King Władysław IV (1632-1648).

In the years 1720 and 1739, the fundamental rights of Zygmunt August were reconfirmed, and Jews were given the possibility of residency. There were already 164 Jews in the city in 1765.

Przedecz was notated as Pshaytsh by Y. Heilpern in the map of the Council of the Four Lands

[Page 377]

in 5427 -5524 (1667-1774) and noted as a community that was not independent (see the map). It is appropriate to note that throughout the entire Voivode [Ed. Note: Wojewoda in Polish, meaning warlord or an administrative district or County] of Brześć Kujawski, to which the city was affiliated, there was no city that was listed as a primary community or that was independent. Nearby independent cities were Kalisz, Krotoszyn, Leszno, and Poznań, which had hegemony in the Council of the Four Lands, to which they sent their representatives. There were no cities in the area of Przedecz in which Jews were forbidden from living, such as the city of Bydgoszcz, which was in the Leslau Wojewoda (Włocławek Wojewoda), north of the Brześć Kujawski Wojewoda.

Greater Poland from a map of the Council of the Four Lands, 5427-5524 – 1667-1764). Przedecz is notated as Pshaytsh. Independent cities are notated with a double circle.}

In the year 1774, the total sum of taxes paid in the city of Przedecz was 752 zloty and 15 groszy. Of this, the Jews of the city were obligated to pay 500 zloty. Jews were forced to pay relatively large sums. Half of this sum was transferred to the treasury of the crown, that is to the treasury of the Kingdom of Poland. The Jewish population of Poland was 430,000, and that of Lithuania was 157,649, not including infants less than one year old. We can surmise that the total number was larger – that is 750,000 individuals. 42% were listed as tradespeople, and only 6% as merchants. In accordance with the ledgers of

[Page 378]

the Four Lands, the number of Jews in the Brześć Kujawski Wojewoda, which included Przedecz, totaled 1,267 individuals; the Łęczyca Wojewoda – 2,903; the Kalisz Wojewoda including Gniezno – 12,995. The number of Jews in Przedecz does not appear. However, in the surrounding cities, for example Kalisz, there were 609 Jews, 133 in Konin, 256 in Koło, and 262 in Kleczew. The average of all the cities and towns in the district of Kalisz was 256. In the villages of that district, the average was 6.5 Jews. It should be noted here as well that the Jewish community was interested in hiding the total number of individuals to avoid the taxes that were set by population and were enforced with pressure and threats. In any case, it is clear that the number of Jews in Przedecz was not large.

After the partition of Poland, the Germans conducted a census in 1793/4 using a precise questionnaire. The city was not known as Przedecz at that time (the Crusader name Mossberg, used [later] by the Nazis, was not mentioned, even though a special question was asked about additional names of the places included the census). The city belonged to the General Directorium, Suedpreussen VI, and was "royal."

It is worthwhile to mention a few details from the plethora of data in that census: The streets were paved with stone. There were 78 houses, of which 72 were covered with straw roofs and 6 with wooden shingles. A synagogue is not mentioned; however, there is no doubt that a house of worship, a *mikva*, and a cemetery existed, based on the number of Jews enumerated there.

A magistrate building [city hall] existed. Heating was only with wood. There were no sources of peat or coal. There were 355 residents of the city, including 146 children below the age of ten. The population included 216 Catholics and 139 Jews. I estimate that the number of Jewish families was approximately 20-30. The division by source of livelihood was as follows

	Christians	**Jews**
Bakers	1	1
Butchers	0	3
Blacksmiths	2	--
Merchants	--	3
Weavers	1	--
Tanners	1	--
Smiths	--	1
Belt makers	1	--
Locksmiths	2	--
Tailors	--	10
Shoemakers	7	--
Pavers	1	--
Wagon builders	1	--

| Carpenters | 1 | -- |
| Wood engravers | 1 | -- |

In addition, in the city there were: a barber and surgeon –, a liquor distiller – 1, tavern owners

[Page 379]

– 2, a beer brewer – 1, a merchant of firewood – 1, a midwife – 1, an organ player – 1, an undertaker – 1. All were Christians. There were no organizations for professional guilds.

At that time, the census indicated that there was room for another baker, butcher, wagon builder, weaver, and tailor. The intention was that they could be brought to that place, and would be able earn their livelihoods there. In any case, another gentile tailor should be brought. According to that census, most of the Jews were working in tailoring, and only 3 of the 18 mentioned worked in commerce. On the other hand, there were no Christian merchants. The report specifies that the three Jewish merchants did not have a concession or monopoly for commerce.

The city council consisted of six individuals. The names mentioned were not Jews (and this makes sense, since Jews were not granted all the rights of civic citizenship at that time). None were fluent in the German language.

There was a four-room hospital in the city under the auspices of the priest. The city was permitted to conduct six annual fairs (*jarmarki*), but they did not actually take place. There was no pharmacy in the city. One had to travel to the pharmacy in Lubraniec to obtain medicine.

We can learn about the number of Jews in the following period from the various censuses that took place. They are summarized in the following table.

Year	General	Population Jews (percent)
1808	645	210 (32.6%)
1824	1,562	?
1827	1,935	346 (17.9%)
1857	1,955	606 (31.0&)
1921	3,040	840 (27.6%)
1940	?	769

From the numbers, we can see that the gentile population grew threefold between 1808 and 1827, whereas the Jewish population only grew by 65%. In 1832, there were 1,562 residents, living in 125 houses. This population included 109 weavers. This was the period when weavers (*sukiennjcy*) from Germany settled in the city, leading to its development, albeit not as hoped. One of the conditions made by the German settlers was the restriction of Jewish settlement in their places, something which was not fulfilled to its full extent. On the other hand, the number of Jews doubled by 1857, whereas the gentile population did not grow. This was because the village Jews were forced to leave their places since they lost their livelihoods based on the leasing of taverns and the selling of liquor. From that time, the percentage of Jews in the city remained at around 30% until the great Holocaust. Of the 3,040 residents in the city in the 1921 census, there were 2,149 Poles, 93 Germans, and 798 Jews. The total number of Jews was 840, since 42 Jews registered themselves as "Poles of the Mosaic persuasion," something that seemed strange in our region. According to that census, the percentage of Jews was 28%. This was one of the

[Page 380]

lower percentages relative to the situation in other cities. That census indicated that the population of Poland was 25,694,700 (aside from Silesia and Vilna), of whom 2,771, 949 were Jews – i.e., 10.8%. The areas with the largest concentration of Jews were Warsaw, at 33%, followed by Łódź at 14.5%.

Przedecz was part of the region of Warsaw. However, large parts of greater Poland were transferred to the regions of Poznań and Toruń (see further on) before the Second World War, and Przedecz was joined to the latter. In those Wojewodas, the census only shows a percentage of Jews of 0.3%-0.5%. The regions of Poznań and Toruń were relatively empty of Jews. Following the annulment of the restrictions of Jewish life in Prussia in the middle of the 19th century, the crowding in those areas was great, as was the aspiration to improve their economic life, and there was a mass migration of Jews to Germany. Przedecz and other cities at the border of this region had belonged to Russian-Congress Poland, and therefore, the proportion of Jews in the city itself did not change, despite the fact that at that time, and especially at the beginning of the 20th century, a significant Jewish immigration to America and the Land of Israel began. This relatively static situation also applied to the Jews of the region of Włocławek, where the proportion of Jews grew from 8.9% in 1897 to only 9.9% in 1921.

Chaim Hertzberg (Hyman Hershberg), in the United States,
a native of Przedecz, who volunteered with the Hebrew
Brigade of Jabotinsky, and served in the Land of Israel
when the country was conquered from the hands of the
Turks. He was named after Rabbi Chaim Auerbach of
blessed memory, the rabbi of city, who died before he was
born.

[Page 381]

Finally, we will note in this chapter that 769 Jews were listed in the city in the census of 1940, following the outbreak of the war.

Special articles published here will discuss the communal organization of the Jews of Przedecz. In our survey, we will include only the following words: At the beginning of the 20th century, an awaking of the communal organization of Przedecz began. Jewish Economic-cultural organizations and political movements of all stripes began, as was common in Poland. The community operated in a democratic fashion, and Jewish representatives operated within the rubric of the city council. In addition, an Orthodox Beis Yaakov School was started, albeit most of the Jewish children studied in the general public schools. There was a Jewish bank in the city, and a rich Jewish library. A portion of the youth studied in the high schools of the cities of the area. The townsfolk will describe all this, however.

I wish to bring here an interesting statistical fact that was found in the Zionist Archives in Jerusalem. The number of individuals who paid *shekels* [tokens of membership in the Zionist organization] in the city for the 20th Zionist Congress, according to the elections of July 11, 1937, was 70. 67 voted by cards, of whom 30 voted for the Working Land of Israel, 28 for Mizrachi, and 9 for the General Zionists. The Revisionists, whose numbers were large, did not vote at that time for the congress, which was after the founding of the new Zionist movement. The head of the community was a Zionist. The relations between the powers in the city can be estimated according to the composition of the community. The rabbis of the city were Hassidim of Gur, Kock, and Przysucha. The final rabbi, Rabbi A. Zemelman, may G-d avenge his blood, was chosen as a man of Aguda, which testifies that the power of that organization was great in the city.

Surnames were only established officially in the city during the years 1821-1824. The names were given in accordance with the former places of residence or were chosen according to the will of the people. Sometimes, a derogatory name was given to a Jew. There were families that had traditions brought in from afar. This was the case with two rabbis who are mentioned in the chapter dedicated to the history of the rabbis of Przedecz: the name Horowic came from a large family of rabbis and great ones who originated in Hořovice, Bohemia in the 15th century, and the name Auerbach has its source from the end of the 15th century from the city of Auerbach [Auerbach in der Oberpfalz] near Regensburg in southern Germany. Many names testify to the roots of families in nearby cities such as Klodawski, Lencicski, Sochaczewski, Zichlinski, Pozner, etc.

At the beginning of the German occupation, Przedecz belonged to Warteland (the land of the Warta River), which encompassed the oldest area of the Polish land. The situation of the Jews in those regions was very difficult. There, the Nazis operated quickly to annihilate the Jewish population. Harsh steps had already been taken in the regions of Poznań and Toruń, to which Przedecz belonged, during the first months. The desire was to render the region Judenrein. The racist Nurnberg laws immediately applied to this region, which was home to 400,000 Jews. The first death camp, Chełmno , began to operate not far from Przedecz on December 8, 1941. The labor camps in that area operated under particularly harsh conditions, and they quickly turned into death camps.

In Włocławek – the Powiat [*Ed. Note*: a Polish subdivision similar to a County] city of Przedecz, the Commissar Kramer was the first during the Holocaust period, on October 24, 1939, to issue the order for the Jews to wear the yellow triangle. Around the same time, the order was given to wear the yellow armband on sleeves. Forced labor was also imposed on the Jews and gypsies in that month.

[Page 382]

The decision to annihilate the entire Jewish population was taken no later than October 1941. At that time, all the processes in Chełmno were ready. On January 2, 1942, Greizer issued the command to annihilate the Jews of Wartegau. Thus, all the Jews of Koło (2,300 individuals) were sent to Chełmno between December 7-11, 1941. The Jews of Dębia (1,000 individuals) were sent between December 14-17. The Jews of Kłodawa (1,500 individuals) were sent between January 9-12, 1942. The Jews of Izbica Kujawska (1,000 individuals), and the Jews of Bugaj (600 individuals) were sent between January 12-14, 1942[2]. The first group from Łódź arrived on January 16. On January 24, the Jews of Piotrków Kujawski were sent; on February 2, the Jews of Sompolno (1,500 individuals) were sent; on February 2, the Krośniewice, Żychlin, and Kutno ghetto was liquidated; the Jews of Łęczyca (1,200 individuals) were sent on March 29. The Jews of Przedecz were sent for annihilation between April 21-24, 1942. After that time, the annihilation of tens of additional towns continued. The process was to gather all the Jews into the church or synagogue, where they were crowded with terrible density, without water. Many died of suffocation. Human excrement filled the place. Some of the people, especially the elderly and children, were shot during the roundup. This is what also occurred in Przedecz, where the local Commissar ordered the Jews to pay for the windowpanes that were broken by those locked in the church so that they would not suffocate from crowding and lack of air.

A large number of youths from Przedecz perished in the labor camps of Poznań, which were infamous for their cruelty and complete isolation from the outside world. The first camps were set up there in 1940. In 1943, there were 100 such camps. During the first period, the laborers were allotted 320 grams of bread, 14 grams of fat, and 35 grams of horsemeat per day. Sometimes, some sugar or jam were added. However, in 1943, terrible hunger prevailed, and the prisoners were forced to work from 7:00 a.m. to 7:00 p.m. These camps turned into death camps, for the people worked outside in all types of weather without significant clothing. Diseases spread, especially skin diseases, infestations, and most prevalently, diseases due to malnutrition.

When the writer of these lines visited Przedecz in 1966, he found two Jewish families: one about to immigrate to Australia, and the second a Jew who married a gentile woman. The place, with all houses standing on their ruins as previously, looked like a ghost town. The synagogue was destroyed, the cemetery was devoid of gravestones, and fear pervaded in the streets.

Translator's footnotes:

  1. This refers to ritually slaughtered kosher animals which were later found to have defects, or in which a mishap occurred in the slaughtering process itself, rendering the animal non-fit for kosher consumption. Rather than losing the investment, such slaughtered meat would be sold to gentiles.

  2. The text indicates 1941, but I suspect this is a typo, and 1942 was intended. [Ed. Note: Considerable detail about Chełmno and the populations from each town sent to Chełmno can be found in Patrick Montague's excellent book Chełmno and the Holocaust: A History of Hitler's First Death Camp © May 2020.]

[Page 383]

The Rabbis of Pshaytsh

Translated from Hebrew by Marshall Grant

  The important rabbis who lived and worked in the city of Pshaytsh over recent generations. We present the names of four important rabbis who served in the city up to Rabbi Alexander Zemelman, may God revenge his soul. I remember rabbi Zemelman as having a wonderful personality; he was witty, sharp, and diverse in his endeavors. His two daughters live in Israel, as do several other of his students who will share their memories of his life and of his death as a courageous soldier in the Warsaw Ghetto. The first rabbi of Pshaytsh for whom we were able to find relevant material was Rabbi Yaakov Ori Shraga Horowicz.

Rabbi Yaakov Ori Shraga Horowitz

  Rabbi Yaakov Ori Shraga Horowicz, son of Yitzchak Itzik and Reina Michla, was a recognized and rare scholar. Every Friday night he would light many candles. In his childhood he traveled to the great rabbi of Ciechanów, who told of how he would dip in a ritual bath before lighting the Chanukah candles.

  He filled in for his father, Rabbi Yitzchak Itzik from Rypin, in the local rabbinate, but he decided to forgo this institution and settled in Przedecz. He left many new Torah interpretations and a commentary of the Passover *Hagada*, "Hagadat Yaakov" (see picture). His father, Rabbi Yitzchak Itzik was the student of Rabbi Moshe Leib from Sassov. He refrained from all of life's luxuries, and in his last will and testament wrote that he never benefited, "even in the smallest amount from this world, except what he earned by his own hands to feed his soul." His friend, Rabbi Natka Makover, said he had righteousness in every bone and fiber in his body. Rabbi Bonam, the respected rabbi from Peshischa, would visit his home when he passed through the city, even though he lived in a small room. He left many innovative ideas regarding oral Torah, the five books of the Torah and many kabbalah scriptures. When on his deathbed, on the evening of Sukkot in 1823, he asked that he be brought to the *sukkah* in his bed. When he arrived in the sukkah, he was very moved and kissed the sides of the structure. After saying the kiddush and prayers blessing the sitting in the sukkah, he was returned to his home. He passed away on during the Sukkot holiday, 1823, the 18th of Tishrei 5583. In his city of Rypin he was called "Mr. Righteous". The father of Rabbi Yitzchak Itzik, Rabbi Meir, was the head of the Rabbinate court in Zaloshin and later a judge in Leszno. His book, *Meir Hashachar* (Dawn's Light) was printed in 1746 in Frankfurt, and he shared his writings during morning prayers and when receiving the Shabbes.

The family provided commentaries for the Ba'al Halevushim (Mordecai ben Avraham Yoffe), *Shelah HaKaddosh* (Yeshayahu Ha-Levi Horowitz), *Tosfot Yom-Tov* (Yom-Tov Lipmann Heller) - some family members called themselves *Gutantag* - the translation for Yom Tov (good day), and there was also commentary for Rashi's volume 75.

Rabbi Yaakov Ori Shraga from Pshaytsh had two sons, one was Rabbi Meir Pshytshaar who settled in Łódź, and the second, Rabbi Itzik who settled in Kwawel. The entire family lived in the cities near Pshaytsh.

[Page 384]

***The cover of the Passover hagada with commentary by the honorable Rabbi
Yitzchak Itzik Horowicz, Mitaamei Yitzhak, and commentary by his son, the
honorable Rabbi Yaakov Ori Shraga Pshaytsh Hagadat Yaakov/BILGORAJ, 1929***

The commentary for the Hagada by the renowned late Rabbi Yaakov Ori Shraga is commentary full of the spirit of *kabbalah*, full of Gematria and longing for redemption and the return to Zion. He notes that the joy from the miracles that God made for our forefathers in Egypt is nothing more than the yearning for miracles to happen to us for our redemption from the "bitter and bustling" diaspora. He was gifted in *piyyut* (poetry), and at the beginning of *Hagadat Yaakov* is a poem that he recommends reading before the *seder*. The poem is arranged in alphabetical order and uses the first letters of his name as the first letters of each verse. This poetic work has concentrated content and boasts a sophisticated rhythm. It has pictures that testify to his fertile and original imagination that is entirely

[Page 385]

steeped in the *Zohar*. The Hebrew is rich mixed with Aramaic from the Talmud and kabala:

> Your hands have created and guided me, I call you to help me,
> See our terrible state, our souls have been given to strangers
> The voice of Jacob calls to you like a dove in the depths of the sea

He makes being joyous difficult for all Jews in the diaspora, "and we are still his servants" [based on Talmudic quote] and "we are now in a tragic diaspora due to our many transgressions." But we are happy because we know that we, with G-d's help, are committed to holiness, and it is known that no messiah will come until the entire generation is completely deserving, or God forbid, completely undeserving. Then Israel must be redeemed, lest they sink into the 49 gates of impurity… and the Gomorrah hints that even before the redemption, the messiah will come."

The goal of holding a Passover seder means to become holy and free from all spiritual impurity, then the spirit of God will reside among Israel.

He passed away in Pshaytsh on Adar 16, 1839; March 2, 1839.

[Page 386]

Rabbi Haim Auerbach,
of Blessed Memory and Source of His Wisdom

Translated from Hebrew by Marshall Grant

In memory of my father-in-law, the late Rabbi Avraham Shlomo Auerbach, the community elder of the Jewish community of Pshaytsh, the son of Rabbi Aharon and grandson of the great Rabbi Haim, of blessed memory. In the memory of his wife, Sarah, the daughter of the late great rabbi Shmuel Lemel Aiman, may God revenge him, and in the memory of the soul of my brother-in-law Rabbi Haim Aharon Auerbach, who died a martyr's death in the camps of Poznań, may God revenge him.

Rabbi Haim Auerbach, the Rabbi of Pshaytsh
5627-5660 (1867-1900)

Rabbi Haim Aurback, the esteemed rabbi of Pshaytsh served as the community rabbi and judge in the rabbinical court during 5627-5660 (1867-1900). He is a member of one of the most renowned rabbinical families in Poland, and his roots come from the well-known Kara family. According to the Jewish community's genealogy records in Liegnitz, the family comes from the great Jewish sage from Prague, Rabbi Yosef Karo.

[Page 387]

Memory of our Fathers!

From the book, Memory of our Fathers, by the great rabbi, Rabbi Menachem Natan Neta Auerbach, and the great rabbi, Rabbi Meir, Jerusalem, 5653 (1893)

In that genealogy document, it is told that the family's source of wisdom comes from a Jew who was exiled from Spain and lived in Amsterdam. He brought Torah to the city and its Jews - Szlomo Zalman Lipszyc of Poznań. He studied in the school led by the brilliant Rabbi Naphtali Katz, who was considered a present-day sage, where he discovered the writing of commentaries and Hasidic Judaism. The wise Rabbi Eliyahu Getz from the Pozan rabbinical court married his daughter. The brilliant young man forged his reputation following his commentaries of the Prophet Eliyahu. As written in the book *Divrai Mishpat*(Legal Issues) by Rabbi Haim Auerbach, the grandfather of the rabbi from Pshaytsh, he wrote many articles, although few were ever printed. His commentaries of *Kohelet* (Ecclesiastes) were printed in 1837 in Breslau (Wrocław). His son, Rabbi Shlomo Zalman was the head of the rabbinical court and head of Poznań's yeshiva and grandson of Rabbi Yitzhak Itzik, a judge from Leszno , the son-in-law of the wise Rabbi Haim Kara, the head of the rabbinical court of Liegnitz and Leszno. Rabbi Yitzhak Itzik was born and named Haim after his grandfather Rabbi Haim Kara, the brilliant Rabbi Haim Auerbach, a legal expert. He

[Page 388]

was educated in Leszno and served in the rabbinical court of Liegnitz. Rabbi Akiva Eigor, a contemporary, deemed him the "Great Wise Rabbi from Liegnitz". His brilliant son, Rabbi Yitzhak Itzik replaced him in Liegnitz following a term in Płock. The son of Rabbi Haim was Rabbi Menachem, the head of the Ostrava rabbinical court, Rabbi Yitzhak Itzik, the head of the Dobra rabbinical court, and Rabbi Eliezer, who wrote respected commentaries.

The grandsons of Rabbi Haim, a son of Rabbi Menachem, were Rabbi Zvi Hirsch, of the Leszno rabbinical court and head of the Konin rabbinical court and author of *Divrei Torah*; Rabbi Yaakov, head of the Yarutshin rabbinical court in Prussia; Rabbi Meir from Kepno and Rabbi Eliezer from Ostrava. His grandsons from Rabbi Itzik were Rabbi Meir, considered to be very wise and head of the Kovel, Dobra, Koło and Kalisz rabbinical courts and the first Ashkenazi rabbi in Jerusalem; Rabbi Yehoshua Faulk from Kleczew; Rabbi Avraham Moshe from Turek; and Rabbi Sholom Zalman from Łódź.

Amongst the grandchildren of Rabbi Haim, a legal scholar, ("*divrai mishpat*") was Rabbi Haim Auerbach in Pshaytsh, a widely accepted sage. As I heard from his granddaughter, he was generous and devout, and always fasted on Mondays and Thursdays. He was involved in Torah day and night, and was known to fall asleep on hard benches, and not always his bed. The residents of Pshaytsh who survived remember his headstone in the local cemetery.

Pshaytsh

The great revered rabbi and teacher, Haim Auerbach, of eternal memory

Rabbi Coppal Zumar
His son, Rabbi Nachman Zumar
His son-in-law, our teacher, Rabbi Yitzchak Pearlmutter
Yitzhak Rosen
Leiv Pozner
Eli Sachtshevisky
The late David Zachlonesky,
Nachman Roich
His son, Avraham
Avraham Yosef Hamburger
Avraham Morgenstern
Yechiel Bialagalsky
Michael Sachtshevisky

A list of Pshaytsh residents, led by the great rabbi and teacher, Rabbi Haim Auerbach, from list of pre-subscribers for the book, *Be'er Yehuda, Part I – the Rambam*, by the great rabbi, Rabbi Avaraham Be'er Yehuda, head of the rabbinical court, Warsaw, 1885.

[Page 389]

He had a son who lived in Pshaytsh, the late Aharon; another who lived in Łódź, Yisaschar; the son of Aharon was Avraham Shlomo Auerbach, who supported the community of Pshaytsh from 5643-5683 (1883-1923). The children of Avraham Shlomo are Aharon Haim, 5670-5701 (1910-1941) who died a martyr's death in the Poznań workcamp, and his daughter, Esther Malka Brand-Auerbach, who currently resides in Jerusalem.

The origins of the Auerbach family begins in Germany. A document on the large family relates to Moshe Auerbach, the court Jew of the Bishop of Regensburg until 1497. According to the document I hold (see photo), in 1499 Moshe received the right to settle and trade in the city of Auerbach, located in the German state of Pfalz, not far from Regensburg, where the Hitlerist movement began. One of his daughters settled in Krakow, and became the mother of Moshe Ben Yisrael Isserles, 5280-5332 (1520-1572), an expert in Jewish law.

The entire Auerbach family of Poland died in the Holocaust, may God revenge their souls.

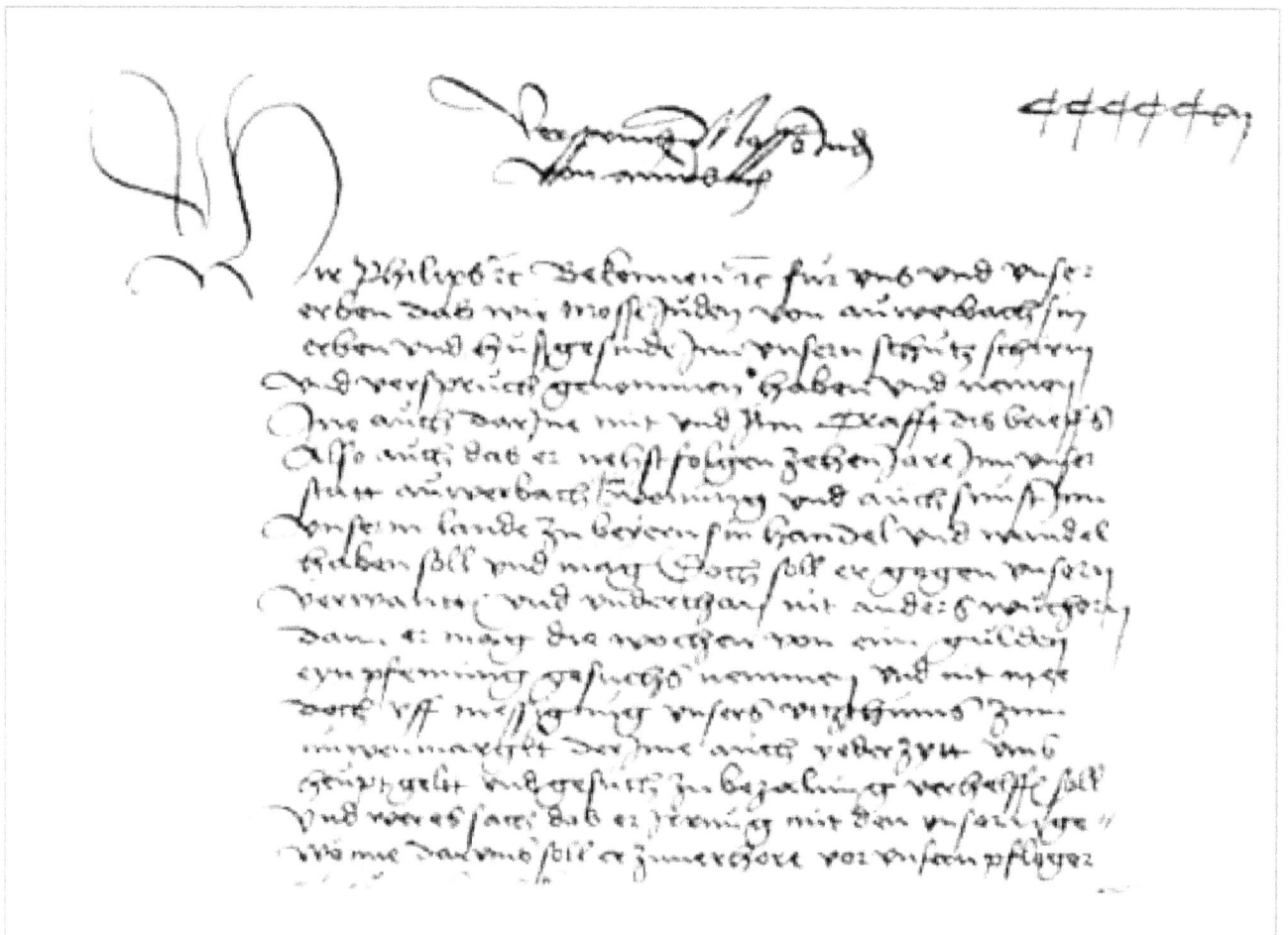

The writ of sponsorship for Moshe the Jew from Auerbach

Translated from the German version (above)
We, Philip et al, hereby declare to us and our descendants that Moshe the Jew from Auerbach and his descendants and his family members have been taken under our protection and provided sponsorship by virtue of this document, and he can, for the next 10 years, live in our city of Auerbach and in our country of Bayern. He is allowed to trade. He should be treated as if he was a member of this family. He is allowed to lend with interest and is allowed, under oath, to charge one pfennig for one golden, etc. Issued on September 2, 1499, by Prince Philip of the Palatinate (1476-1508)

[Page 390]

R'Moshe Chaim Blum z"l

Translated from Hebrew by Marshall Grant

For the eternal memory of my father and teacher, Natan, son of my rabbi, Rabbi Yosef Zeev Brand and his wife Sarah Rivka, and my mother and teacher, Esther Chaya, daughter of the late Rabbi Mordechai Blum (son of the great and respected community leader, the late Aharon Blum), and his wife, Yenta, the daughter of Rabbi Eliezer Shapira. For the eternal memory of my brothers, the young Mordechai and Meir, and for the eternal memory of Shmuel Zvi, son of Rabbi Yosef Zeev.

Rabbi Moshe Haim Blum, son of the great Rabbi Avraham Binyumin, the head of the Vayaroshov rabbinical court, was born in 5332 (1875) and, at the age of 45, he was appointed as the rabbi and head of the rabbinical court of Pshaytsh in 5660 (1900) and served in the rabbinate for five years, and was recognized for his fairness and deep knowledge of all aspects of the Torah. He was later chosen by the community of Padamitch to be their rabbi and head of the rabbinical court. He served his people for 24 years.

פשייטש

ידידי הרב המאה"ג מו"ה משה חיים בלום
הנגיד ר' נחמן זומוטר נ"י
חתנו מו"ה רפאל זאב
ובנו הכהן חיים זומוטר
ר' יצחק בהר"א ז"ל פערלמוטער
ר' אברהם יוסף זאחלינסקי
ר' נעע ליב וויטבאהרליג
ר' שלמה סאחאילשאהסקי
ר' חיים געלער
ר' משה אברהם מהרשעק
ר' גוטמאן זאחלינסקי
ר' יעקב זאחלינסקי
ר' שמעון לאגדה
ר' שמשון דאגעלאסקי עבור בהמו"ד
ר' משה מיכאל שערלהר

Pshaytsh

A list of Pshaytsh residents the great rabbi, our teacher Moshe Haim Blum.
From signatories of the book, Be'er Yehuda, Part II – the Rambam, laws of
Tefillin, etc., by the great rabbi, Rabbi Avraham Shultzhower, head of the
rabbinical court of Piotrków, 5665 – 1905.

[Page 391]

At the age of 55, he was honored with his appointment of rabbi for the city of Zamość in the Lublin Voivodeship, known for its rich Jewish history and esteemed rabbis.

He was known throughout Poland and many prominent scholars and rabbis often referred inquiries to him. Some of his responses were published in *Sha'arai Torah*, a religious magazine published by the great Rabbi Yitzchak Hakohen Feigenbaum of Warsaw. These commentaries revealed his immense knowledge, even at a young age while a member of the Pshaytsh rabbinate. He was dedicated in his writings and addressed various *halacha* issues. He also was a known author having written about the order of *masechot* (Talmudic tractates), one part of which, *Tiferet Moshe*, was even sent for printing.

When the second world war broke out, he escaped to Russia, and there made his way to the depths of the Siberian taiga. His writings were left with Rabbi Zvi Rimlat, the head of the rabbinical court, for safekeeping.

Rabbi Zvi died a martyr's death, all the Jewish homes in his city were destroyed, among them the great rabbi's. All the writings of Rabbi Moshe Haim were also lost, while news of the destruction of European Jewry reached Siberia. Rabbi Moshe Haim was already old and exhausted from suffering for so long without any of his holy books or even paper to write his Torah-related thoughts. However, his spirit was strong, similar to an ever-growing spring. Then he learned of the loss of his writings, which caused him sorrow that even he could hardly contain – the entire collection of his life's work concerning the Torah and Talmud were gone.

Conversations with every visitor he met always focused on future redemption and consoled them with the redemption of the Jewish people. Some of his thoughts were written on snippets of paper, in pencil, and only titles, so he could return later and fill in the details. However, this task was never completed.

On the morning of the 9th of Kislev, 1943, while singing "*Shir Hamaalot Mimaamakim*" (From the depths I have called You, O Lord), he passed away in the city of Achinsk in Siberia and was buried there in the Jewish cemetery.

Some of his original commentaries and sermons published in *Sha'arei Torah* were also published with writings of his son-in-law, Rabbi Haim Moshe Gostinski from Zamość, in his book, *Nachlas Chamisha*, in New York, 5709 (1948). Here, the thoughts and ideas written on scraps of paper during his time in Siberia, which could now be photographed, were included. Since the writings were very difficult to read, Rabbi Gostinski completed sections that were incomplete. The name given to this collection, *Tiferet Moshe*, is for his novel commentaries of *Shisha Sedarim* - the Six Orders of Mishnah, which had been prepared for print, but had yet to be published.

The scriptures of the great wise rabbi, Rabbi Haim Moshe Blum are clearly written as he delves into the depths of the Talmud and expresses both traditional and contemporary opinions. However, he also quotes the great sages from the area of greater Poland, mainly Rabbi Simcha Bonim from Peshischa, Rabbi Menachem Mendal of Kotzk and Rabbi Haim Larman from Płock. There were times when he would argue with the *Admor* of Peshischa, but he would do so in a soft and respectful manner, such as, "I was unable to understand his revered writings," or, "in my humble opinion….it is not so severe." However, in his sermons and commentaries concerning the weekly Torah portion, some of which were published in *Tiferet Moshe*, he would also use external sources from the *Zohar*, mainly in gematria (as can be seen from the last section of the book concerning *Shabbes Nachamu* (the Sabbath of Comforting) in *Tifert Moshe*). Most interest focused on the challenges of redemption and the answers that will bring it to be.

[Page 392]

תפארת משה

מובחר

יבּעים אחדים מחידושי וחדושי הגאון והצדיק

חסיד ועניו חיים ובני

מוהר״ר משה חיים בלום זצ״ל

אבד״ק פשיטש, פאריסבורג, ואמשטין

בסריית פולין

ניו יארק

שנת תשי״ם לפ״ק

יצא ר׳ יצחק מוינעסטער
חורעסטער פאבלישינג קאמפ
ניו יארק

The cover of the book, Tiferet Moshe, containing the collection of Nachlas Moshem, written by the great and esteemed Rabbi Moshe Haim Blum, New York, Moinester Publishing Co.

I was unable to uncover more details about his family. His wife was from a family of rabbis and one of their sons was the late great Rabbi Shlomo Yechiel Mekalish, while the other was the late Rabbi Mordecai Zvi of Kagine. Another son was mentioned, Shmuel and Yehuda Arje Meir.

The life of the righteous Rabbi Moshe Haim Blum symbolizes a life of Torah and the sanctity of Poland's Jewry.

[Page 393]

Rabbi Yehoshua Heschel David Goldshlag

Translated from Hebrew by Marshall Grant

סימן נד .

ב"ה חיים טובים . ושלושים רבים כטלים ורביבים אל בני
יקירי וחביבי מו"ה יהושע העשיל דוד שיחי'
(כעת ... פשיטטש) וידין יהושע בעמקה של
הלכה . ויהי דוך לבל דרכיו משכיל ונוחה עכ"ב וזוה
שיחיו אחת היא לכם חברכה חיים ושלום ומנוחה שטירה
בכל וערוכה :

יקרתך בני הנועי כנירוק הקונטרס מחותנך הנ"ל שלים"א
והוח לתמיד גק... ומגמתי עד כה להשיב
בסבת טרדותי ותלחותי אשר לא יתנו הפוגות לפטות כדברי
למח . גם מכיר אני מקומי וממשמוש את כלי ולוגי מילוך ח"ע
בכלל הכמי חרב"ים יהושפי מחשבות בחשבונו של עולם לטמיד
בפרליה לגדור . בכ"ו חללה לי מתטוך . מלהקם אחזרותיו
הטהורים וכידוע מזוה"ק (בסלח דמ"ו ע"ב) ותם' הס"ל (ככר"ק
נהך ס"א) ופ"ע בס' לקוטים מרב האי נאון ז"ל וח"ל זמן הידוע
לחכמים כי כל דיבורים היוצאים מספתי החדם בחיתוך לכבן
הם נכתבים בלזיך ונרשמים בו והם מרקבלים בעלמם כחית
עליונית דקרת רוהגיות נעצלמות המתפסטית בלויך . ויש מומגים
לטובה ויש לרעה כו' והלחמת לטעלה מזטה מרוכבת . כי דברי
הבחי הין בהם כח לכמום בפתח סער רקוע כי יש מוגעים הרבה
עכלה"ק . אבל תפוג לבי מהלמין חם יבנו כל העם אחריו קול
אחד אם לא בהתחשך רחשי עס יהד במכתביהם להחזיק במצוו
הענין ולהכות בכפתיר עד כי יגוטי לויות הספיס מקולם אבר
כמתם ילך ובהיל יכזאי . אי או הולי יבנע לבב כולם לבן קבה
מהך בטיני העבודה אשר העניים על שכמי כי מי יודע ריח
כל הדכנים והרחשים בעתים הללו . ויש אכר לבנם שלם
להתגיל מרזח ספתם לרחן ע"פ הלבבות לפתח הרלובות וזון
העם . ויתהפוכותיו . אבל נחספים וגהבחים . הלו מצפלות ידיהם
ורפיון כחס . ולו מירחתם יעגורם מסביב להתחרות בעושי
פילה . פן יתגרו לעומתם לאריב לרעתם ומחויבים לדוגם לזכות
מל' המאכרי"ו המוכח כתגבות רמ"א ז"ל . (יו"ד ס" של"ד
בסופו) יכ"כ וכ"כ גאבגדה כלוגבחל דח :

*From VeYechye Ya'akov, questions and answers concerning the four parts
of Shulhan Aruch, by Rabbi Ya'akov Zelig Goldshlag, Warsaw 5669 (1909)*

[Page 394]

Rabbi Yehoshua Heschel Goldshlad, son of Rabbi Haim Zelig, the rabbi of Przedecz, served on the Pshaytsh rabbinate from the 15th of Av 5664 (1904) until 5684 (1924). In the past he served on the rabbinate in the city of Sierpc, where his father, Rabbi Yechiel Michal, preceded him. His father, Rabbi Ya'akov Haim, belonged to the Gur Hassidic movement and frequently travelled to see the Rebbe. He left the rabbinate and settled in Warsaw. There he published a book, *Questions and Answers*, including new evocative commentaries of the Talmud and the four parts of the *Shulchan Aroch* – Warsaw, *Everything Written for a Good Life* 5669 (1909). He also wrote the book, *Marom Harim*, containing new Torah interpretations by the great rabbi, Rabbi Yechiel Meir Megastinin that included commentaries from the rabbis from Kajac, Gur, Tschachenau and Radzymin. In the book, *Bechi Harim* (Cries of the Mountains), he laments the loss of great *Admor* from Gur. This collection contains commentaries from Rabbi Zelig Sharanyzker. Rabbi Ya'akov Haim Zelig also compiled a collection of philosophy and new interpretations of book by the late Yonatan Eybeschütz.

His grandfather was Rabbi Yechiel Michal Goldshlag, the head of the Sierpc rabbinical court. He was born on the 12th of Tevet, 5591 (1830) in the village of Sharanzak from the Shach family, and his mother was from the family of the late Rabbi Yechiel Michal Manamrov. He studied under the tutorship of Rabbi Yehoshula Cotner and the Gur rabbis. At the age of just 17, he was accepted to the rabbinate of Kikkel, Sharanzak, Padamvitch and Australanka. In the year 5625 (1865), he was appointed to head the rabbinate court of Sierpc. His brother, Rabbi Avraham Mordechai Goldshlag was the rabbi of Plonsk. The rabbi from Pshaytsh, Rabbi Yehoshua Heschel David was the son-in-law of the great rabbi Haim Lerman, who came from the family of Rabbi Yoel Sorkish (*Habayit Hadash* – the New Home) and the family of Rabbi David Ben Shmuel Halevi (*Hatori Zahav* – the Golden Lines). He was a generous and a generous person, a student of Kazek and Peshischa, was known as *The Admor from Płock, Dovrin and Krashnovitch* and wrote many books. He passed away on the 1st of Tevet, 5679 (1911). (Ed. Note: There is a date discrepancy. 5679 corresponds to 1919, whereas 5671 corresponds to 1911)

An old Hasidic Jew, a disciple of Rabbi Haim Lerman, once told me that the rabbi from Pshaytsh would meet with his son-in-law for long hours and discuss life's hidden wisdoms. He was tall with a welcoming personality. The chief rabbi of Tel Aviv, Rabbi Yitzhak Yedidia Frankel, told me that he knew Rabbi Yehoshua Heschel personally and described him as having an impressive personality; he was tall and everything about him radiated splendor - and he was a Torah scholar. The father of Rabbi Yitzhak Yedidia went to Pshaytsh to study Torah from the rabbi. He stayed with the city's families and was impressed with how generous they were toward Torah students. Pshaytsh, which was a small town, had no renowned yeshivas, but due to its great rabbis, it became a place where the students learned important things. This was its contribution to the students and the studies in Poland.

Words of the last rabbi or Pshaytsh, Rabbi Alexander Zemelman, will be written separately.

[Page 395]

Yiddish and Hebrew Reading in Przedecz

Translated by Jerrold Landau

The first Jewish settlers in Poland used the Polish language for hundreds of years. Jewish settlement took place simultaneously with German settlement in the area of Greater Poland. The German language was a common spoken language in the cities of Poland, as can be learnt from the many German words that also penetrated into Poland. However, it is possible to establish, with Dr. Y. Ben-Nun, that at the end of the 15th century or beginning of the 16th century, Yiddish overtook the Slavic spoken language. In that language, German of the ostmitteldeutsch form [Ed. Note: East Central German or Middle High German] dominated, but it also included Hebrew and Slavic roots, and later, even a few Russian expressions, including in our area. According to the divisions of the aforementioned research, Yiddish can be divided into the western form of Alsace, Burgland, Slovakia, and Hungary, and the eastern Yiddish of Eastern Europe. Lithuanian Yiddish is north-eastern. Central-eastern Yiddish is that of southern Eastern Europe, including Eastern Galicia. Central Yiddish is the Yiddish of western Galicia and of Greater Poland. Central Yiddish in its restricted meaning is that of Greater Poland, that is of our region. However, the Yiddish of Greater Poland differs from area to area, and even from city to city.

It is possible to establish that there was a great similarity in the Yiddish spoken in western Greater Poland from Kalisz to Włocławek. One can especially note the phonological similarity of the use of the demonstrative suffix similar to the German *chen* pronounced as *che*, which is soft, like the German demonstrative suffix. In Yiddish the suffix is written כיע.

We will present here a transcription in Latin letters of words and typical pronunciations as was spoken in Przedecz. It seems that this has not yet been done and is worthwhile to record. The transcription is based on the book by Y. Bin-Nun with modifications based on Polish phonetics and will be easier to understand by those not expert with the phonetics of that language, which influenced the Yiddish expressions in Przedecz.

Therefore, all the letters are written here with capital Latin letters. A significant shortening of the vowels, especially at the end of the words, as well as in the pronunciation of two or more words from one word (something common in the Yiddish of Przedecz), will be noted by a small letter. For example, מאכען (to do) MACHN will be listed as MACHyN. On the other hand, at times, the vowels are elongated and pronounced as diphthongs. Thus, for example the aleph with a *kometz* is written as Uu. However, at times there is an addition of a short e or y. When the word וואס [what] stands alone as a sentence, as the question "וואס?", it is notated as WUyS, but when it is found as part of a sentence, it is pronounced in a shorter form, for example וואס ווילסט דו (what do you want) (וואס ווילסטו) – WUSWyLSTy. Vowels with a dagesh [a diacritic dot] are noted with a line on top. In the word "וואס?" as a question, the WUyS is pronounced as a diphthong Uy, but diphthongs are also found with other vowels, such as גייען – געהען (to go) is pronounced GAJN. On the other hand, וויין (wine) is pronounced as WAaN. Similarly, the vowel א is the same as ע (that is an *aleph* with a *segol*), is pronounced as it is expressed in German, and is expressed as a diphthong – for example געלער – GEJLyR. On the other hand, with the ה that is equal to ע

[Page 396]

(that is, like an *aleph* with a *segol*), such as מענש MENS), the S is notated in Polish with a comma on top).

The ל is notated in Poland as a hard l with a line through it[1], or as a UAMyD, that is as a U with a vowel following. Apparently, there is a principle that this is the sound of the ל in all places, just as the name of the principal city of the general geographic area is notated with a l with a line through I – for example, in the areas of: Suwałki, Koło, and Włocławek.

The spoken language in the homes was almost exclusively Yiddish. However, in the latter period, between the two world wars, some of the youth spoke Polish amongst themselves. This was especially the case amongst girls. The Yiddish of the young generation was regular, and the Polish was good. Writing was primarily in Polish. The older generation spoke poor Polish from a grammatical and phonetic perspective, with the cz, sz, and rz being expressed in a soft fashion, like the שׁ in Yiddish. The youth spoke Polish even in the Zionist organizations. On the other hand, the Bund and left-leaning Poalei Zion were more particular about Yiddish. Even Aguda families spoke Polish at times.

The newspapers that were read were primarily *Heint, Moment, Hentige Nies*, and *Der Veltshpigel* from Warsaw. They also read the Jewish-Polish *Nasz Przeglad*.

In day-to-day life, the writing in Yiddish was according to the orthography appropriate to German – Deutschmerish. The knowledge of German was good enough, for many Germans lived in the area, and they naturally spoke German with the Jews. The knowledge of Polish among the Germans was often poor. Few in the city wrote Yiddish in the form used in the newspapers. In official speeches, they attempted to use the journalistic literary style. The Jews of Przedecz in Israel and the world speak Yiddish, Hebrew, or Polish amongst themselves. Many attempt to accustom themselves to the phonetics that is close to the north-eastern – i.e., Lithuanian – Yiddish, but they are not usually successful with this.

It would be worthwhile for the appropriate scholarly institutions collect the Yiddish expressions of the city of Przedecz and the surrounding area, for the memory of future generations, as well as for academic reasons – and study them in in a scientific fashion.

The reading of Hebrew was similar phonetically to Yiddish. We will suffice ourselves with brief examples in transcription to Latin characters, as per the following:

BU'RIyCH A'TUu ADONOJ' ELOJHA'JNI MEJ'LECH HOOJ'LOM HAMOJCI LEJCHEM MyN HUUu'REC.[2]

Here is a section from *Ashrei Yoshvei Beitecha*[3]

AS'RAJ JOJ'S'WAJ BAJSEJ'CHu
OJD JEHALeLI'CHU SEJ'LU,
AS'RAJ HOOM' SEKU'CHU LOJ

The ל is hard in Polish, a l with a line above, pronounced as a u followed by an appropriate vowel. The ש is noted as an S and s notated in Polish as an S with a comma above. The *kometz* is notated as a

[Page 397]

U but is expressed as a closed O followed by a silent *shva*. For the most part, the stress is penultimate syllable, and expressed with a comma following the notation.

The reading of the Torah, Haftarah, and Megillot was in accordance with the cantillation used throughout the Ashkenazic communities, and the prayer melodies were almost equivalent in those communities.

At the conclusion of this article for "The History of Przedecz and its Jews" I express my thanks to Dr. Yosef Kormish and Mrs. D. Dombrowska from Yad Vashem, and to Dr. Yaakov Goldberg from the Hebrew University for their assistance in collecting historical material; to Dr. Y. Bin-Nun for his advice that he gave me for the chapter in Yiddish. My special expression is extended to Mr. A. Wein from Yad Vashem for reviewing the manuscript. He stood at my side with advice and knowledge.

May they all be blessed.

[Page 398]

{***Translator's note:*** This page gives examples of Yiddish words and expressions, with the transliteration into Latin characters, as per the protocols outlined in the above article. The page is included in this translation in its original. The structure, with the headings, is as follows:

Examples of the Phonetics of Yiddish in Przedecz

[Words included (in a simpler transliteration) are: *mir viln (m'vil), men dertzeilt (m'dertzeilt), saychel, A feig, tzvei, drei, finef, nein, tate, shein, shteiner, shener, ich, du, es zenen da (s'zenen da), es shteit geshriben (s'shteit geshriben), kelbenen lung un leber, eiyer, a hun, heiner, hihner, kalb, kelber*.]

Text from the book of Dr. Y. Ben-Nun. A phonetic transcription of Przedecz.

Yidn Gein in mikvaos arein, un das vasser is kalt, vi iz chlomish men in yeden shtetl tzo koyfn an oyvin. (Translation: Jews go to mikvas, and the water is cold, so in every shtetl they dream of purchasing an oven.)

The transcription also demonstrates the phonetical connection of words. A line above the letter indicates the stress.

y is read in the shortest possible fashion, and at times is pronounced as a very short e.

Ś is as in Polish

The excerpt was chosen as it is possible to compare the phonetics described above with the various phonetics of Yiddish brought by Bin-Nun.}

מיר ווילן (מ'וויל)‎-   M'WYŁ   ;מען דערצײלט (מ'דערצײלט)

‏-   ■'DyRCAJŁT   ‏שכל-; SAJCHŁ   ‏א פײנ-; AFĀ&G ;

‏צוויי -   CWAJ ;‏דריי-   DRĀa ‏;פינעף-FYNyF ‏;ניין(9)-

‏,- ; MĀMy   ‏,-מאמע; MĀaN,DĀaN - ‏;מײן,דײן NĀaN,

‏מאמע-   TĀTy ; ‏שײן -; SAJN ‏;שײנער- STĀJNyR ;‏סענער- ŚÉNyR

‏איר-   IiyCH ‏;דו- DĪi ‏;ער- EJyR ‏;עס זענען דא , S'ZENyNDŪu

(‏ס'זענען דא)-(‏ס'שטײט SZĒNyNDŪu;‏עס שטײט געשריבען)

‏געשריבן)   S'STĀJTGySRÝBŃ ;‏קעלבערנע לונג און לעבער-

KĒLBRNyLyNGyŁEJByR

‏אײער-   AaR = ‏ÆNKyR ‏האהן-; AHŪuYN ‏;א הוהן- AHĪiN;

‏הײנער-   HEJNyR ‏;היהנער- HĪiNyR ‏;קאלב- KĀŁyB ;

‏קעלבער-   KĒLByR

★ טעקסט מספרו של ר"ר י. בן-נון

‏עם טרנסקריפציה פונטית של פשײטש

‏יידן - JiDN ‏ייעו- GAJiN ‏אין מקווה ארײן -   yNMYKFyARAa

(‏און דאס וואסער- yNSWĀSyRySKĀŁT ‏איז קאלט (מחובר לקידם)

‏ווי איין - WIĀaZ ‏, חלומם מען- CHŪŁyMTMy

‏אין יעדו - YNJĒJDN ‏שטעטל- STEJTL ‏צו קריפו - C'KŌJFN

‏אן אוייוון - ANQJWN

‏הטרנסקריפציה מראה גם את חיבורי המילים הפונטיים.קו מעל הקל
‏מצײן הדגשה.
‏ע נקרא בצורה קצרה ביותר ולפעמים מצלצל כ- e קצר מאוד.
‏ś - כמו רפולית.

★הקטע נבחר מפני שאפשר להדגיש את הפוניטיקה הנחונה
‏לעיל עם פוניטיקותשונות של ייידש המובאות ע"י בן-נון.

Translator's footnotes:

1.   Ł or ł -- see https://en.wikipedia.org/wiki/%C5%81
2.   The *Hamotzi* blessing on bread.
3.   A prayer recited three times a day.

****

[Page 399]

Bibliography

{***Translator's note:*** This bibliography contains sources in Polish, German, and Hebrew}

[Polish and German Sources]

Encyklopedia Orgelbranda ; Tom 21, Warszawa 1865.
Balinski-Lipinski Starozytna Polska, Wydanie drugie, Warszawa 1885.
Słownik geograficzny krolestwa polskiego, Warszawa 1887.
Wielka Encyklopedia Powszechna, Tom 9, str. 509. Warszawa 1905.
Rawita Witanowski, Michał ; Wielkopolskie miasto Koło, Piotrkow 1912.
Majerski Stanislaw, Opis Ziemi, Wieden 1914.
Jewrejskaja Encyklopedja ; T. 12, Str. 911 "Przedecz". Dombrowska Daniuta; Zagłada skupisk Zydowskich w "kraju Warty" w okresie okupacji hitlerowskiej. Bjul. zyd. instyt. histor. Nr. 13-4, 1955.
Wasiutynski Bohdan. Ludnosc Zydowska w Polsce. Warszawa, 1930.
Wasicki Jan ; Opisy miast polskich z lat 1793-1794, Cz. 1, Poznam 1962.
Miasta polskie w tysiacleciu. Zaklad narodowy im. Osolinskich, 1965.
Guldon Zenon ; Lustracja wojewodztw wielkopolskich i ku-jawskich 1628-1632, Cz. 3, Bydgoszcz, 1967.
Encyclopedia Judafca, Jerusalem, 1971.

* * *

Lawin L.; Deutsche Einwanderung in polnische Ghetti. Jahrb. jued. liter. Gesellsch. Bd 5, 1907.
Lawin Izak; Udzial Zydow w wyborach sejmowych w dawnej Polsce, Menorah, Warszawa 1932.

[Hebrew sources]

Mahler, Rafael; A Bundle of Information about the Jews of Koło. Sefer Koło, Tel Aviv, 1958.
Brand-Orban, Aharon: The rabbis of Koło From the End of the 18th Century. Sefer Koło, pp. 212-221, Tel Aviv, 1958.
Heilpern, Yisrael: The House of Israel in Poland, The Division for Youth Issues of the Zionist Histadrut, page 231, Jerusalem, 5704 [1944].
Heilpern, Yisrael: The Ledgers of the Council of the Four Lands, Mossad Bialik, 5705 [1945].
Zionist Archives, Elections for the 20th Zionist Congress, June 11, 1937, Jerusalem.

* * *

[Page 400]

Blum, Rabbi Moshe Chaim, Nachalat Moshe (Responsa, Exegesis) in the book Tiferet Moshe, New York, Moigeshter Ferlag, 5709 [1949].
Goldshalg, Rabbi Yaakov Chaim Zelig, Vayechi Yaakov, Responsa on the Four Sections of the Code of Jewish Law, Warsaw, 5669 [1909].
Horowitz, Rabbi Uri Shraga, Passover Haggadah, Explanations – the Haggadah of Yaakov Bilgoraya, 1929.
Sochaczewer, Rabbi Avraham, Avnei Nezer, Responsa, Piotrków, 5672 [1912].
Feigenbaum, Rabbi Yitzchak HaKohen, Shaarei Torah, Torah Manuscripts, Grossman, New York, Photocopies from the years 5663-64 [1903-04].
Kutner, Rabbi Yisrael Yehoshua, Yeshuot Malko, Responsa, Piotrków, 5687 [1927].
Sulzower, Rabbi Avraham, Beer Yehuda on Maimonides, Section I, Warsaw 5645 (1885); Section II, Piotrków, 5665 (1905).

* * *

Sefer Zamość
Sefer Lenchich [łęczyca], by Rabbi Yedidya Frankel, Tel Aviv. [Translator's note: Rabbi Frankel was the father-in-law of Former Chief Rabbi of Israel, Rabbi Yisrael Meir Lau].
Beit Halevi, Yisrael David, History of the Jews of Kalish, Publushed by the author, Tel-Aviv, 5721 [1921].

Sefer Kalisz
Sefer Koło, Edited by Mordechai Halter, Tel Aviv, 1958.
Sefer Ripin

* * *

Bin-Nun Jechiel, Jidisch und die deutschen Mundarien, Niemeyer Verlag, 1973.

Map of the city of Przedecz

Key:

1. Synagogue
2. Cemetery
3. Chevra Tehillim
4. Mikva
5. Bank
6. Beitar
7. House of the rabbi
8. Beis Midrash
9. Slaughterhouse
10. Young Mizrachi
11. The pump
12. Firefighters
13. Butcher shops
14. City Hall
15. School
16. Police Station
17. Library
18. Post office

NAME INDEX

A

Abramovitch, 61, 129, 184, 191
Aftergut, 271
Ajchenbaum, 149
Akerman, 145
Albert, 102
Angel, 100, 123
Anielewicz, 143, 144, 145, 149
Aniliewicz, 149
Appel–Rozneka, 121
Archbishop Yaroslav Skotenitzki, 274
Asch, 168
Ash, 75, 151, 220, 221
Auerbach, 183, 245, 246, 280, 281, 285, 286, 287, 288
Aurback, 286
Aurbakh, 72, 245, 246, 247, 248
Avigdor, 197, 198
Avrmovitch, 179
Ayman, 245

B

Bambrovitz, 71
Banashek, 117
Bartosz Wezenburg, 274
Bednarz, 47, 52
Belevsky, 114, 115, 116
Belinski, 100
Belivsky, 267
Ben Itzhak, 29
Ben Shalom, 161
Ben-Nun, 293, 295
Berg, 271
Berkenfeld, 77
Berman, 143, 181, 251
Bernstein, 173
Bialagalsky, 287
Bialaglovsky, 109, 223
Bialogluvsky, 191
Bielańska, 146
Bilavsky, 1, 221, 222, 223, 234, 238, 248
Bilbasky, 131, 183, 192
Bilbosky, 176
Bilevski, 159, 160, 172
Bilevsky, 174, 179
Bilevsky, 270
Bilewski, 167, 169, 171, 172
Bilski, 168
Bin-Nun, 294, 295, 298
Birenbaum, 149
Blum, 102, 183, 289, 290, 291, 297

Books, 1, 8, 42, 43, 60, 65, 69, 71, 75, 79, 83, 85, 87, 90, 92, 107, 109, 110, 127, 129, 131, 153, 161, 175
Borenshteyn, 229
Bornshteyn, 76, 201
Bothmann, 50, 51
Brand, 48, 121, 154, 185, 268, 272, 288, 289, 297
Brand-Urban, 272
Braude, 145
Brostovesky, 114
Brym, 271
Buf, 90
Buks, 3, 4, 6, 69, 76, 78, 126, 192, 200, 206, 208, 256, 257, 272
Bur'nshteyn, 89
Burg, 11, 19, 20, 22, 95
Burmeister, 50
Burnshteyn, 44, 74

C

Casimir The Great, 274
Chanskovsky, 219
Chanstkovsky, 219
Chanstovskys, 221
Chodecz, 71, 181, 182, 186, 251, 253, 254, 257, 273
Chodotzki, 100
Chotcher, 209
Claudevsky, 179
Czanskowski, 168
Czerniak, 156

D

Danialeski, 100, 260
Daniel, 271
Danielless, 262
Daniels, 271
Danielska, 271
Danielsky, 69, 72, 89, 90, 130, 208, 209, 214, 223, 224, 228, 231, 232, 238, 246, 248
Danilska, 168
Danilski, 168
Darin, 147
Davidovitch, 235, 247
Davidovitz, 75
Davidovitz, 270
Davinsky, 196
Dawidowicz, 77, 78
Dayan, 22, 39
Dezalna, 142
Diament, 90, 184, 217
Dielsky, 238

Dombrowska, 295, 297
Drakhman, 181, 238, 239
Duke Bolesław V, 275
Duke Mieczyslaw Stary, 275
Dyskin, 271
Dzerzhinsky, 145, 146
Dzhike, 151

E

Edelman, 151
Eiglinski, 270
Ekert, 76, 168, 195, 233
Engel, 72, 75, 78, 81, 82, 89, 90, 184, 253
Erlich, 149
Ettinger, 270
Eybeschütz, 293

F

Fajka, 64
Faulk, 287
Feigenbaum, 290, 297
Feyntukh, 250
Finklshteyn, 112
Fisher, 76, 82, 134, 194, 216, 235, 271
Fisher, 271
Fiszer, 77, 168
Flatzker, 90
Foder, 271
Fondiminsky, 145
Francisca, 128, 151
Frank, 89, 221
Frankel, 63, 142, 144, 147, 293, 297
Frankenshteyn, 45, 69, 74, 76, 198, 209, 210, 212, 215
Frenkel, 75, 168, 185
Frenkl, 256
Fried, 102
Friedman, 157, 174, 262
Fuchrer, 145
Fuder, 191

G

Ganesha-Dazika, 142
Garbinsky, 270
Gensha, 151
German, 162
Getz, 287
Geyzler, 66
Glassman, 204
Goebbels, 67
Goldberg, 148, 295
Goldman, 60, 62, 63, 64, 65, 69, 72, 74, 89, 90, 126, 127, 130, 168, 185, 205, 206, 207, 237, 241, 242, 244, 247, 260
Goldman, 270, 271

Goldschlak, 102
Goldshlad, 293
Goldshlag, 89, 292, 293
Goldshlag, 293
Goldshlag, 183
Goldszlag, 149
Goldszland, 149
Gostinski, 290
Graydans, 233, 234
Greenblat, 45, 198
Greif, 270
Grinblat, 168, 198
Grizlatz, 145
Grushtzinska, 155
Grushtzinsky, 184

H

Haber, 243, 244
Hadetch, 66
Haflaks–Deutsch, 65
Halevi, 102, 104, 293, 297
Haltrikht, 89, 90, 130, 229, 230
Hamburger, 287
Hamelch, 118
Hayman, 107, 114, 219
Heilpern, 276, 297
Heller, 283
Heltreich, 179
Henebauer, 129, 248
Henebower, 61
Henkel, 61
Henkl, 129, 191
Hershberg, 280
Hershberg, 271
Hertzberg, 3, 213, 280
Herzberg, 3
Heschel, 102, 147, 292, 293
Himmel, 270
Hirschberg, 96
Hitler, 11, 61, 65, 66, 67, 68, 70, 73, 74, 99, 156, 183, 222, 258, 261, 282
Horowic, 148, 149, 281
Horowicz, 282, 284
Horowitz, 282, 283, 297

I

Iglinsky, 89, 213, 214
Inglinsky, 215
Izakobanna, 106
Izbicka, 168
Izralubanna, 106

J

Jabotinsky, 122, 280

Jaczinsky, 96
Jakubowicz, 168
Jakubowski, 271
Jamnik, 271
Janner, 147

K

Kaminer, 149
Karal, 260
Karmelitzka, 151
Kashirskiy, 3
Kaszinski, 50
Katz, 147, 261, 287
Kazhimirsky, 212
Kazimiersky, 72
Kazipszinski, 51
Kenigsberg, 149
Kennigsburg, 139
Khadetsher, 75
Khadetsky, 212
Khatch, 162, 250
Khatcher, 72, 74
Khodetsky, 206, 218
Khotch, 185
Khudtsky, 89
King Boleslaw, 274
King Kazimierz, 180
King Władysław Iv, 276
King Zigmont Ii,, 274
King Zygmunt August, 276
Kirszenbaum, 149
Kladovsky, 69, 79, 81, 82, 197, 207, 209, 212, 225, 231,
    258
Klar, 70, 179, 190, 196, 197, 211, 212, 243, 244
Klein, 32
Klepfish, 152
Klinski, 230
Klodawski, 126, 260
Klodovsky, 202, 207, 208
Klodowsky, 92
Kocznica, 50
Komiskovsky, 116
Kopieca, 148, 149
Kora, 44
Korczak, 139, 147
Kormish, 295
Korycinski, 274
Kotek, 104, 195
Kovalsky, 104, 131, 133, 134, 195
Krashinsky, 151
Krauskopf, 204, 205
Krel, 44, 69, 81, 90, 251
Kroll, 50
Kroshinsky, 157
Kubyiak, 45

Kulmhof, 47, 49, 50, 51
Kutek, 228
Kviat, 82, 241, 244

L

Landau, 4, 5, 52, 148, 149, 266, 275, 293
Lange, 47, 50
Langnoz, 88, 251
Lantzitzki, 126
Lapatkevitch, 197
Larman, 290
Leibish, 173
Lenchitzki, 160
Lentshitsky, 44, 257
Lentsitsky, 76
Lenz, 50, 52
Lerman, 293
Levental, 258
Levin, 12, 23, 29, 31, 89, 90, 106, 107, 108, 110, 111,
    114, 219, 267, 268
Levin, 270
Levine, 61
Levkovitch, 200
Levkowitz, 179
Librakh, 251, 252
Liek, 192, 193, 213
Linchitsky, 199
Lipman, 90, 109, 110, 116, 174, 192, 200, 222, 223, 247,
    248
Lipszyc, 287
Litman, 174
Lntzitzka, 82
Lodviski, 51
Lorentz, 67
Lovinska, 121
Loyn, 88
Lundy, 147
Lvkovitz, 89

M

Majdan, 78
Makover, 282
Makovitsky, 82, 119, 252
Makovitzki, 33, 100
Makovitzki, 270
Makovitzky, 33, 34, 39, 40
Malkovsky, 45
Manamrov, 293
Mandlboim, 102, 105
Mandlboym, 236
Mandlinger, 60, 62
Manik, 164
Marchak, 231, 233
Markovitch, 199, 210
Martshok, 207

Megastinin, 293
Mekalish, 291
Mekovitzia, 12
Mendal, 179, 290
Mendlinger, 270
Menkhe, 181, 238, 239
Mila, 144, 148, 149, 151
Milanvach, 64, 65
Mile, 32
Miller, 201, 209
Miszczak, 47, 52
Mitaamei, 284
Mokatov, 88, 239
Mokotov, 1, 11, 89, 90, 116, 117, 119, 120, 122, 241,
   243, 268, 269
Mokotov, 270
Mokovitsky, 252
Molotov, 148, 149
Morgenstern, 287
Morgenstern, 271
Morgensztern, 78
Morgnshtern, 226, 227
Moss, 271
Motkov, 267
Muranov, 151
Musman, 58
Musman, 271

N

Nalevky, 151
Nalewki, 142
Navalipiye, 151
Naymark, 97, 98, 112, 133, 164, 201, 203, 209
Neklin, 199, 200
Neumark, 161
Neumark, 271
Neymark, 263
Nimchovka, 206
Novek, 157
Novkovsky, 117
Noyman, 73
Noymark, 46, 124, 162, 163, 201, 202, 203

O

Ofas, 168
Ofenbach, 173, 174, 175
Ofenbachs, 174
Ofenbakh, 89, 254
Offenbach, 168
Ofnbakh, 82
Opas, 259
Oppenbach, 179
Orbach, 48, 78, 121, 168
Orbienski, 161
Orlian, 150

Ostrovsky, 52
Ostrushke, 61
Oyfek, 60

P

Padro, 111
Panini, 271
Pardansky, 225
Pashdetzki, 271
Pashedetzki, 272
Pat, 151
Pavashinsky, 96
Pavyie, 151
Pawia, 142
Pe'er-Danski, 100
Pearlmuter, 11
Pearlmutter, 17, 175, 287
Perele, 90
Perl, 247
Perla, 77, 168
Perle, 228, 229
Perlmuter, 220, 231
Perlmutter, 17
Petrikoz, 113
Peyser, 272
Piaskowsky, 157
Pizer, 272
Placker, 78
Plotsker, 76
Plotzker, 110, 211, 258
Plotzki, 156
Pnini, 123, 267
Polkovsky, 259
Polman, 270
Pope Innocent I, 274
Pope Innocent Iii, 275
Poyzner, 184, 239
Pozner, 40, 76, 239, 281, 287
Pradanski, 168, 170
Prakhovsky, 76, 202, 219
Pranankanstein, 260
Pretzol, 242
Prochovesky, 179
Prokhovsky, 219, 256
Prost, 114
Przdecki, 3
Pshaytcher, 175
Pshaytsher, 8, 9, 10, 56, 57, 71, 73, 74, 76, 82, 92, 129,
   132, 135, 178, 181, 183, 246
Pshedetsky, 201, 213, 216, 221
Pshedetzky, 221
Pshytshaar, 283
Pullman, 179

R

Rabeski, 100
Rabski, 77, 78, 168
Radzievsky, 238
Rapaport, 231
Rapaport, 272
Rappaport, 81, 244, 245
Ratze, 238
Ratzoynzer, 110
Rauch, 78, 100, 123, 168, 179, 269
Raukh, 44, 66, 76, 82, 207, 208, 230, 231, 239, 251, 252, 253
Ravski, 129
Ravski, 272
Ravsky, 70, 76, 89, 248
Rembo, 149
Resel, 157
Reuven, 17, 52, 102, 104, 105, 148, 149, 156, 164, 260, 261, 267, 270
Ribinsky, 179
Rimlat, 290
Rivinsky, 200, 224, 259
Rivnitsky, 74, 215
Rizuv, 113
Rodal, 149
Roich, 287
Romer, 76, 239, 240
Rommel, 11
Rosen, 158, 287
Rosenberg, 67
Rotblat, 145
Rozen, 123, 192, 235, 236, 240, 241
Rozenberg, 228
Rozenkrantz, 244
Roznekrantz, 100
Rufsky, 61
Rukhshteyn, 206
Rumek, 168
Rumer, 82
Rumkowski, 49
Rusak, 229, 260, 261
Rusek, 270
Rusk, 11, 13, 14, 15, 16, 172, 173, 174, 175, 179

S

Sachatchavesky, 179
Sachtshevisky, 287
Saika, 179
Saike, 208, 210
Sayka, 44, 90, 100
Schweitzer, 270
Schwitzer, 267
Seidman, 96, 124, 135, 139, 148, 149, 150, 151
Shach, 293
Shapiro, 89, 90, 200

Sharanyzker, 293
Shashkas, 147
Shenirer, 183
Sherptser, 110
Shikorsky, 73
Shimonovitch, 197
Shlibitsky, 71
Shlifkovitz, 100
Shlipkovitch, 248
Shlomi, 42, 79, 109, 153
Shmul, 231
Shnerer, 96
Shperke, 197, 198, 200
Shpringer, 203
Shraga, 282, 283, 284, 297
Shtrauch, 118
Shultzhower, 289
Shveitzer, 65, 71, 90, 128, 196
Shvientoyorske, 151
Skabransky, 74
Skavransky, 89, 217
Skierniewice, 115, 116, 125
Skobronski, 77, 78
Skobronsky, 179, 249, 250
Skovorondkin, 64
Skovronski, 100
Skowronsky, 272
Skubronsky, 73
Smotche, 151
Sochachevsky, 64, 179
Sochchevski, 271
Sokhachevsky, 235
Sokhchevsky, 204
Srebrnik, 52, 60
Stanisław August, 274
Stelmanshtsik, 73
Stramsky, 203
Streicher, 67
Stupengel, 157
Szcrabti, 149
Sziper, 149
Szpancer, 145
Szwajczer, 78
Szyc, 71

T

Tajlblum, 149
Talmid, 135
Tapalaski, 101
Tapalski, 100, 260
Tapalsky, 179
Tapinsky, 224
Tapolsky, 136
Taranchik, 190, 191
Targuva, 114

Tarner, 92, 94, 180
Tatralani Platz, 146
Taub, 106, 111, 114
Tchanskovsky, 203
Tchenaskowski, 100
Tekovsky, 16
Tkorsh, 173
Topolesky, 117
Topolski, 168
Topolski, 272
Topolsky, 74, 88, 89, 90, 130, 176, 233, 234, 235, 257
Torner, 207, 238
Torner, 272
Toronchek, 179
Toronchik, 179, 193, 203, 208, 248, 249
Toronchik, 272
Toronczyk, 78
Tsanskovsky, 89
Tsaytunger, 114
Tshanskavesky, 173
Tsun, 71
Twarda, 145, 146
Tyusia, 149

U

Ulezniko, 204
Urbakh, 89
Urbansky, 80
Urnbakh, 244

V

Valter, 195
Vart, 156
Vasertzug, 239, 243, 254, 255
Vayden, 61, 89, 127, 169, 176, 190, 197, 256
Vaydman, 176, 177, 178, 184, 197
Vaydn, 76
Velder, 70
Vengrovsky, 215
Vishinsky, 104, 179
Vishnievsky, 76, 82, 127, 213, 257
Vishnivksy, 213, 214
Vishnivska, 82
Vishnivsky, 127, 195, 196, 197, 208, 213, 214, 227, 228

W

Walter, 132, 134
Warshavsky, 112, 217, 257
Wasertzog, 172
Wasserzog, 122, 179
Wayden, 118
Weidan, 100
Weiden, 160, 179
Wein, 295

Weis, 272
Wiclinski, 77
Wilner, 145
Wishnewsky, 272
Wishniak, 272
Wishnivski, 271, 272
Wlter, 161
Wolborska, 103
Wysniewski, 78

Y

Yaakobovski, 264
Yacoboveski, 100
Yakhimovitch, 74, 79, 81, 90, 129, 153, 192, 216, 243
Yakobovitch, 130
Yakubovitch, 66, 79, 80, 82, 83, 84, 250
Yakubovitz, 44
Yakubovsky, 74, 197
Yakubowski, 271
Yamnick, 102
Yamnik, 17, 52, 67, 76, 102, 103, 105, 124, 161, 169, 170, 174, 175, 180, 184, 195, 228, 236, 237, 261, 267
Yamnik, 270, 271
Yamnil, 236
Yechimovitch, 265
Yechimovitz, 160
Yechimovitz, 270
Yedidia, 142, 144, 293
Yemenik, 156
Yoffe, 283

Z

Zachlonesky, 287
Żagiel, 145
Zalisher, 111
Zamenhhof, 148
Zamer, 91, 184
Zanderman, 144
Zayde, 113
Zaydman, 152
Zechlinski, 64
Zeliensky, 249
Zemba, 149
Zemelman, 11, 13, 19, 66, 70, 75, 76, 77, 78, 85, 89, 95, 96, 97, 102, 115, 118, 123, 135, 136, 137, 140, 141, 142, 148, 149, 150, 151, 152, 167, 169, 173, 175, 183, 185, 186, 190, 204, 217, 229, 235, 247, 248, 254, 267, 281, 282, 293
Ziabe, 216
Zichlinski, 78, 168, 281
Zichlinsky, 179
Ziecik, 4
Zielienska, 63
Zielinski, 78, 82, 168
Zielinski, 271, 272

Zielinsky, 58, 76, 82, 89, 134, 193, 194, 199, 200, 208, 209, 210, 214, 218, 225, 226, 234, 235, 249, 257, 259
Ziemba, 149
Ziemowit, 274
Zikhlinsky, 67, 68, 71, 75, 76, 79, 89, 90, 127, 182, 185, 196, 211, 218, 224, 232, 255, 256, 258, 259
Zingarman, 100
Zingerman, 44, 76, 168, 194, 206, 207
Zomer, 104

Zuker, 251
Zukerman, 119, 122, 241, 243
Zumar, 287
Zumer, 89, 216, 217, 218
Zurawski, 52, 60
Zychlinski, 270
Zychliński, 3
Zychlinsky, 272

www.ingramcontent.com/pod-product-compliance
Lightning Source LLC
Chambersburg PA
CBHW050409110426
42812CB00006BA/1840